D1518404

SIBLINGS OF SOIL

*Joe R. and Teresa Lozano Long Series in
Latin American and Latino Art and Culture*

SIBLINGS OF SOIL

Dominicans and Haitians in the Age of Revolutions

CHARLTON W. YINGLING

UNIVERSITY OF TEXAS PRESS
Austin

Copyright © 2022 by the University of Texas Press
All rights reserved
Printed in the United States of America
First edition, 2022

Requests for permission to reproduce material
from this work should be sent to:
Permissions
University of Texas Press
P.O. Box 7819
Austin, TX 78713-7819
utpress.utexas.edu/rp-form

⊗ The paper used in this book meets the minimum requirements of
ANSI/NISO Z39.48-1992 (R1997) (Permanence of Paper).

Library of Congress Cataloging-in-Publication Data

Names: Yingling, Charlton Wesley, author.
Title: Siblings of soil : Dominicans and Haitians in the Age of
Revolutions / Charlton W. Yingling.
Description: First edition. | Austin : University of Texas Press, 2022. |
Includes bibliographical references and index.
Identifiers
LCCN 2022008345
ISBN 978-1-4773-2609-1 (cloth)
ISBN 978-1-4773-2610-7 (PDF)
ISBN 978-1-4773-2611-4 (ePub)
Subjects: LCSH: Dominican Republic—Relations—Haiti—History. |
Haiti—Relations—Dominican Republic—History. | Hispaniola—
Ethnic relations—Political aspects—History. | Dominican Republic—
Politics and government. | Haiti—Politics and government.
Classification: LCC F1938.25.H2 Y56 2022 |
DDC 327.729307294—dc23/eng/20220223
LC record available at https://lccn.loc.gov/2022008345

doi:10.7560/326091

for
Marissa & Mariemma
I love you

CONTENTS

ACKNOWLEDGMENTS

I owe a great debt of thanks to many people. I am forever grateful for having been the doctoral student of Matt Childs. Thank you, Matt, for your advice, generosity, and support from the start of this project as a dissertation several years ago to this day. Choosing to work with you was one of the best decisions I have ever made. Thanks to the faculty during my time in the Department of History at the University of South Carolina, in particular Gabi Kuenzli, Dan Littlefield, and Martine Jean. Special thanks to Chris White, Montserrat Miller, Dan Holbrook, Chuck Gruber, Cicero Fain, Frank Robinson, Jane Landers, and Marshall Eakin for thoughtful courses and conversations along my way.

I would also like to thank my colleagues in the Department of History and beyond at the University of Louisville. Chris Ehrick, our recent department chair, provided excellent general advice, including on the book publication process. Tracy K'Meyer added helpful thoughts about that process, and Blake Beattie served as department chair for most of my junior faculty years. I am especially grateful to Tyler Fleming for feedback, support, and camaraderie. Thanks also to Kate Adelstein and my PhD-student-turned-professor Nick McLeod for great conversations and for welcoming us to Louisville.

Thanks as well to colleagues from my PhD years and beyond, including Andrew Kettler and Antony Keane-Dawes for their feedback on significant portions of the manuscript as it neared completion, and to the following for sharing works in progress, coursework, and conversation: Tyler Parry, Neal Polhemus, Mark VanDriel, Erin Holmes, Lewis Eliot, David Prior, Caleb Wittum, Caroline Peyton, Michael Woods, Randy Owens, Jennifer Gunter, Mitch Oxford, Robert Greene, Kate McFadden, Kate Crosby, Sadegh Foghani, Itamar Friedman, Evan Kutzler, Jake Mach, Meg Bennett, Brian Robinson, David Dangerfield, Gary Sellick, DJ Polite, and Maurice Robinson.

Across the academic profession, many scholars have offered a range of support, from engaging in provocative discussions to answering research queries to providing friendship. Anne Eller deserves special thanks for taking an early interest in my work, commenting on previous iterations of this project, and sharing archival insights. Very special thanks to Julia Gaffield and Rob Taber for taking part in debates and panels and sharing sources. Thanks to Manuel Barcia, Anne Eller, Kevin Dawson, David Geggus, Kate Ramsey, John Garrigus, Carolyn Fick, John Thornton, Philippe Girard, Linda Rupert, Robert Smale, Bill Van Norman, Tom Rogers, Sarah Franklin, Tam Spike, Celso Castilho, Angela Sutton, Erin Zavitz, Erica Johnson, Caree Banton, Alec Dun, Cristina Soriano, Andrew Walker, Theron Corse, and John Marks. Commentators Sue Peabody, Ada Ferrer, Michele Reid-Vazquez, Daniel Domingues, Terry Rey, Manuel Barcia, João Vasconcelos, and Alexandre Dubé deserve thanks as well. For feedback on papers that formed this book, I thank participants at various meetings of the American Historical Association, Southern Historical Association, and Consortium on the Revolutionary Era and smaller conferences at Duke University, the Instituto de Ciências Sociais da Universidade de Lisboa, Rice University, the University of Utah, and Washington University of St. Louis.

I am fortunate to have conducted months of archival work across the Dominican Republic, Haiti, Spain, the United Kingdom, the Vatican, and several other locales. Thanks to the hardworking archivists who manage the records upon which my research relies. I have valued greatly the support of several national and international competitive grants. Thank you to the Ministerio de Educación y Cultura of Spain for the Programa Hispanex Grant, the Conference on Latin American History for the James R. Scobie Award, the Academy of American Franciscan History for the Dissertation Research Fellowship, Harvard University for the Research Grant in Atlantic History, and, though not specifically for this book, support from the John Carter Brown Library at Brown University. I am also grateful to generous competitive funding from the University of South Carolina, including the Presidential Fellowship and the Bilinski Fellowship, and support from the Institute for African American Research, the Walker Center for International Studies, and the Office of the Vice President for Research. I appreciate as well conference and final research funding from the College of Arts and Sciences and the Department of History at the University of Louisville. Thanks to my friend Ulisse for sharing many aspects of Haiti and the Dominican Republic during my stays.

I am honored to place my book with the University of Texas Press, which for decades has earned a reputation for publishing excellent scholarship on

Latin America. I thank Kerry Webb for her professionalism, responsiveness, clarity, timeliness, support, and confidence in my work. I am grateful to the two peer reviewers, who exemplified attention to detail, expertise, and goodwill toward enhancing the final product. Thanks to the editors of *History Workshop Journal* and Oxford University Press for the permissions to include reconfigured segments from my 2015 article.

Very warm thanks to my parents, Kevin and Mary Alice, for their love and encouragement. Thanks also to the Nash and Yingling sides of my family, including my grandparents, aunts, uncles, cousins, nieces, and nephews, and to my life sojourners: my sisters, Hannah and Kathryn; my brother, Luke, and sister-in-law, Kaity; and friends Jonathan, Drew, and Eric.

My greatest affection, appreciation, and admiration is for Marissa, a beautiful thinker and beautiful person who has been my closest friend for approaching two decades. We have made and traveled our own path together. No words can capture the solace in your understanding eyes. As the years of work on this book neared an end, we welcomed a new companion with whom we love learning more about life. I cannot wait to finish these final words so that I can play with Mariemma, whose curiosity and smile daily pull at her daddy's heart. I love you both beyond measure and dedicate this book you, Marissa and Mariemma. Now we can enjoy life a bit more together.

SIBLINGS OF SOIL

INTRODUCTION

The Entire Island Has One Family

From November 1821 through the early weeks of 1822, a cry of "Long live the Haitian Republic!" rang out from several Dominican towns as the residents welcomed the unification of Spanish Santo Domingo with Haiti. Dominican invitations for unity had followed revolutionary decades, growing disdain for Spanish rule, and years of expanding relationships with Haitians. When the locals of Neiba asked Haiti to accept them "among its children," their parental figurehead passed peacefully from the king of Spain to the president of Haiti, Jean-Pierre Boyer, who Samaná inhabitants said would "embrace us like a tender father." Boyer was a present leader of color, not a distant white king. This seemed rather natural to the residents of San Juan de la Maguana, who asserted that the "entire island has only one family."[1]

In February 1822, Boyer unified Hispaniola, to acclaim from many new co-citizens across social classes and geographies. The event was the culmination of a distinctly Dominican anti-imperialism that had followed circuitous paths opened in 1791 and before. By popular request, these two populations of majority African descent became one. Most dramatically, enslaved or oppressed Dominicans, whose families faced systemic disruption, gained new rights in the first universally emancipated state in the Americas, as well as a new sense of belonging among fictive kin as Haitians. In fact, Haitian officials embraced all Dominicans as "siblings of soil," people born of similarly vexed colonial pasts.[2] Their pluralist experiment believed in an inevitably shared future built upon common interests. However, harmony in their shared home proved brief.

Perhaps today this egalitarian, liberatory, multiethnic, even radical familial past seems counterintuitive. Dominicans and Haitians have since endured one of the most fraught relationships in the Americas. For example, ideas of irreconcilable differences honed by a Dominican elite of planters, merchants, officials, and sometimes clergy in the three turbulent decades preceding 1822 reemerged during unification. Building upon these narratives, a prominent and sometimes dominant form of Dominican nationalism has since depicted 1822 as a depraved invasion rather than an invitation for unification. In recent times, anti-Haitian discourses, many with racist overtones bolstered by selective memories of the Age of Revolutions, have assailed Haitian immigrants as the most recent supposed invaders in an alleged generational succession of Haitian aggressors.

Underestimating and even obscuring one of the most consequential and unique cases of Latin American independence, Black Atlantic solidarity, and emancipation in the Americas has scholarly and contemporary social consequences.[3] Among many exceptional influences in the Atlantic, adjacent Dominican society absorbed by far the greatest impact of revolutionary Haiti. The immediacy and practicality of a Haitian future countervailed imperial control and ineffective alignment with mainland Latin American independence movements. Arguably, because of Haitian options Dominicans witnessed less violence at their imperial end in the 1820s than many of their hemispheric neighbors.

This book explains two major, entwined processes with original interpretive focuses built from new archival research. First, it shows that Dominican and Haitian differences, overdetermined today, seemed surmountable in the Age of Revolutions. Often overlooked anti-colonial cooperation by Dominicans and Haitians defied imperialism and racist restrictions. Decisive events emerging from this collaboration challenged elite traditions and hierarchies. Alongside Dominican actors, this book adds new insights and new archival findings about Haiti's revolutionary generation, its independence, early national era, and realpolitik. It reveals novel understandings of the tactical calculus and cultural politics of major leaders, including Toussaint Louverture, Jean-François, Georges Biassou, Alexandre Pétion, Henry Christophe, Jean-Pierre Boyer, and other, less famous figures. Their cross-island lives influenced Haiti's eventual welcome of multiethnic citizens on an integrated, liberated island, a vision that many Dominicans embraced.

Second, this book clarifies the origins of Dominican anti-Haitian sentiment and action, which developed and solidified in response to revolution. Unfortunately, the dominant narratives deriving from the Age of Revolutions have persistently misrepresented cross-island collaboration and accentuated ideas about why Dominicans later grew apart from Haiti. These narratives often depict Santo Domingo as a victim of the Age of Revolutions—the watershed era from the 1770s through the 1820s in the Atlantic world that challenged monarchies, empires, social exclusions, and in some places slavery, in the Caribbean, South America, Europe, and North America. Rather, this book shows Dominicans of all backgrounds as extremely active and adaptive amid the dynamic changes of this era. Further, as the content that follows shows, the underestimated and ubiquitous role of belief tied meaning to action and swayed processes across the revolutionary era.

Comprehending the tensions and hostilities of the past two hundred years requires rigorous, detailed attention to what transpired in the four revolutionary decades preceding 1822. More than many Dominican nationalists prefer to admit, momentous convergences starting in the 1780s built toward the ambitious experiment of Haitian unification. For example, Dominicans were deeply involved in Haitian independence. Unique sources herein show that these ties formed before and at the outset of the Haitian Revolution, far earlier than consensus analysis recognizes. Support from Santo Domingo in the early 1790s enabled leading insurgents of the Haitian Revolution to persevere and successfully pressure the French to abolish slavery. Some of these once-allies later founded Haiti.

Dominican separation from Spain and unification with Haiti emerged adaptively from two societies that grew up together. Today, many residents of Hispaniola are unaware of this mutually beneficial revolutionary collaboration, the two societies' shared historical defiance of empires, and their development of social, political, and economic ties. Also, many are unfamiliar with the origins of Dominicans' anti-Haitian tropes.

Rather than cooperation, most citizens, observers, and scholars know far more about Dominicans' grievances and confrontations with Haiti. Ideas about Haitian contamination have persisted since at least the early nineteenth century. In these discourses, Dominicans embody moderation, urbanity, Catholicism, and Iberian heritage and language, all supposedly antithetical to alleged Haitian incivility, poverty, Vodou, Kreyol, and African racial and cultural legacies. Rhetoric about idle, hostile, or backward Haitians impeding Dominican society has legitimated injustices. The tones of cultural racism and the scales of its impact have been wide ranging. Perhaps most notoriously, it primed the vicious dictatorship of Rafael Trujillo from 1930 to 1961, and the 1937 massacre of twenty thousand ethnic Haitians and Dominicans of Haitian descent by the Dominican army. More recently, it resurfaced in the 2013 revocation of Dominican citizenship from tens of thousands of people of Haitian ancestry, followed by their deportation.[4]

Anti-Haitianism reinforced with distorted historical memories has filled Dominican cultural politics and policy. Readers must not conflate more recent contentions with all actors. Rather, revealing these historical distortions and recalling a shared past of kinship that defeated empires perhaps has the potential to influence a more empathetic and cooperative future. Most contemporary Dominican discourses of irreconcilable difference emerged not from national-era strife, but amid real and imagined challenges to Iberian colonial norms from racial rights, secularism, and Vodou, among other factors, during the Age of Revolutions. Perceiving threats to their truth claims and privileged places in their known universe, elite Dominicans retreated to *hispanismo* (idealized Spanish cultural heritage). They momentously rewrote negative connotations of heresy, radicalism, and violence, drawn partly from anti-French tropes from the 1790s, and conflated them with older ideas of anti-Blackness to develop a modern anti-Haitianism. This also further excoriated already marginalized and less pervasive African diasporic beliefs among Dominicans.[5] Contemporary echoes of racially tinged nationalism build from these historical foundations, sometimes without knowing these inaccuracies. Dominican identities developed alongside, and even within, the founding of Haiti. Furthermore, the significance and change over time in historical racial concepts and terms carried specific cultural connotations that this book considers throughout.[6]

Persistent notions that Haiti uniquely disturbed Dominican history forecloses reflection on crucial past convergences and complex reasons for divergences. Emotive misrepresentations about supposed recurrent and wanton Haitian impositions on Dominican society today are revisions of tropes from the past two centuries. Much of Dominican intellectual and political tradition, even that which is not explicitly anti-Haitian, has shown disinterest in effectively critiquing or empirically invalidating these axioms. It has instead built upon selective narratives of national belonging, influencing the very production of knowledge and perception of reality.[7]

Rendering serious coverage of unification in 1822 unpatriotic censored the momentous cross-island solidarities that made this era revolutionary and imposed presuppositions of an inevitably separate Dominican state upon the past. The esteemed Haitian anthropologist Michel-Rolph Trouillot once argued that the Haitian Revolution "entered history with the peculiar characteristic of being unthinkable even as it happened." To many, Dominicans unifying as citizens of the resulting innovative state represented another unthinkable event as it happened. Eventually, world histories wrote around Haiti, because Haitian history shamed hypocritically restrictive Western enactments of "universal rights." By association, Dominican unification suffered a similar fate.[8] Writing on Haiti that did proliferate after independence negatively racialized the new state and diminished its liberatory inception compared to the supposedly normative French or American Revolutions.[9] In some ways Dominican elites began this trend with tropes of Haitian anti-modern Black aggression, a theme they continued to emphasize in order

4

to excuse later persecutions. Nevertheless, hidden Haitian historical legacies have resounded, whether in revolutionary generations who embraced Haitians as family or among those Dominicans whose daily cooperation with Haitians defied prevailing discourses of difference.

Whitewashing revolutionary events and their memories has had damaging results over subsequent generations. The problem demands a critical rewriting from the archive of profound Dominican and Haitian interdependence in achieving independence. Indeed, a rigorous reappraisal of this era requires purposeful reevaluation of presuppositions that brought about two centuries of strife. Historicizing archaic yet pervasive Dominican xenophobia, cultural exclusions, and pious pretenses weakens rationales for anti-Haitianism. Representations of often overlooked historical actors in the chapters that follow thus matter to ongoing cultural politics, as the epilogue will show.

This book demonstrates how across the Age of Revolutions Dominicans and Haitians consistently expanded their cooperation and camaraderie, including in antislavery and anti-imperial revolts. Together they accomplished a liberatory, inclusive, multiethnic, cross-island nation-building project through unification in 1822. This was one of the most unique and peaceful episodes of Latin American independence.

By explaining the colonial ends and early national beginnings that Dominicans and Haitians shared from the 1780s to 1822, this book answers several critical questions. How did these two populations of majority African descent collaborate in antislavery, anti-colonialism, and nation-building projects to shape Dominican society and its relationship with Haiti? How did racial, revolutionary, and religious entanglements generate social changes? Why did some Dominicans believe they were irreconcilably different from Haitians and later deny their shared past?

This book refutes selective memories and assertions of immutable Haitian incompatibility by demonstrating myriad collaborations during the Age of Revolutions. Contextualizing later strife requires a nuanced reconsideration of Hispaniola during the period. During the Age of Revolutions, rather than seeing Haitians as unmodern or debased, many Dominicans came to desire the citizenship rights, markets, and values of Haiti, the first universally free nation in the Americas, founded by the largest and most successful revolt of enslaved people in world history.

Whether in intermittent cooperation from the 1790s up to unification in the 1820s, or across the two contentious centuries since, the need for Dominican and Haitian coexistence has proven inescapable. Considering critical contexts of group formation through familial appeals, belief, and social belonging demonstrates how the people once cooperated to alter empires that had divided their island. While addressing scholarly questions, recalling past kinship and community offers to demystify contemporary divisions and, perhaps, to invite cooperation or empathy anew.

BELIEVING AND BELONGING

In the Age of Revolutions, together Dominicans and Haitians navigated emancipation and slavery, republicanism and royalism, and the public role of Catholicism, secularism, and African diasporic values. Sometimes historical analysis retrospectively places actors within one of these categories at the expense of considering the multifaceted motivations and personal connections that influence humans. This book shows how and why people developed their consequential affiliations and affinities. It attempts to avoid anachronistically overdetermined labels for figures who confronted the layered, complex, transformative schisms that defined this era.

Subjects viewed themselves at generative intersections of not only racial modes or political tenets but also revolutionary or restrictive familial metaphors, spiritual lenses, and common pasts. These discourses were extremely influential two centuries ago, yet perhaps do not correspond with assumptions today about seismic social shifts. Closed elite concepts of kinship drawn from Iberian culture and reactions to revolution survived to influence the national era. Yet the liberatory, cross-island, radical, and multiethnic family of Dominicans and Haitians who challenged old exclusivity and realized anti-imperial and anti-racist objectives together has suffered disregard.

In their shared home, Dominican society was born into modernity as a fraternal twin to Haiti. Haiti (or *Ayti, Hayti, Ayiti, Hayty*) was the name that Spanish colonizers in the 1490s inherited from Taínos overcome by European disease and violence in early colonial decades. Spain dissipated Taíno memories by renaming it "Spanish island": La Isla Española, or Hispaniola.[10] Yet as this book shows, Dominicans colloquially called themselves "Haitian" well into the national era. The island they share is today the most populous in the Caribbean, with some twenty-two million residents.

Santo Domingo, founded on the island in 1496 as the first permanent European colony in the Americas, was a model and hub for the expanding Spanish Empire. The colony witnessed the Americas' first gold rush, sugar boom and bust, and indigenous decimation. By the mid-1500s, Santo Domingo's centrality had diminished in Spanish plans with the rise of Mexican and Peruvian silver. Because of locals' trade with smugglers and

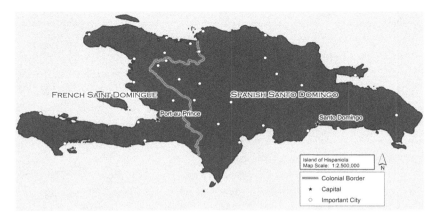

FIGURE O.1

Map of Hispaniola, 1791. French Saint-Domingue was territorially smaller than independent Haiti, which later absorbed the westward-arcing border. Map courtesy of Matthew H. Ruther.

boucaniers, Spanish officials depopulated western Hispaniola in 1606. Spain's overreaction allowed rivals to settle that land, which became French by treaty in 1697. For the next century, the French in Saint-Domingue profited from a brutal slavery regime that sowed seeds of liberatory motivations. Eventually, revolutionary Haiti shredded the imperial fabric. Dominicans unraveled the stitches of colonialism binding Hispaniola to Europe more gradually.[11]

Appeals to literal and figurative family ties that proliferated in the Age of Revolutions developed from the many decades of commonalities, exceeding geography, that fused these two societies together. Dominicans and Haitians endured variations of colonial co-parentage under Bourbon dynasties, racial stratification, Catholic institutions, agricultural export economies, and shared military and political events. Their relationship cycled from kinship, at best, to sibling rivalry or outright renunciation, at worst. Whether in admiration or admonishment, their conversations were essential to new self-definitions in the revolutionary era.

Aside from recovering nuance on racial formation and resistance, the examples detailed in this book show a cultural prevalence of familial and supernatural meaning often absent in studies of liberatory projects in the region. Revolutionaries and elites alike reconciled their lives within key continuities of relationships and values amid the rapid changes that dominate scholarly attention. Such human complexity demands nuanced

7

appraisal, whether regarding the roles of African ethnicity, the development of racial ideas, or themes of religious cultural politics.

This point requires further explanation. This book explores the words and actions of the actors themselves to examine how they tied their momentous lives with the two braided threads of believing and belonging. In the fall of empires and the rise of independence and emancipation on Hispaniola, people made and experienced intricate choices in communities of mutual meaning. We should consider how historical figures saw themselves and their choices within the universe as they understood it.

First, whether famous or forgotten, these were humans who were aware of their own mortality and who learned meaning from their progenitors, made meaning with sojourning siblings who lived alongside them, and taught meaning to the youths who would outlive them. People mark the passage of life within these biological, kin, and metaphorical relationships. As families broadly defined raised the next generation, the allegorical family—whether national, spiritual, political, or ethnic—raised ideas. Though exclusivist definitions persisted, during the revolutionary era these foundational groups, however fractured, fictive, and flawed, became critical sites for the construction of belonging and belief and for solidarities around newly shared values.[12]

Analogies to family were used by elites, whose limited kinship groups predominated politically and stood in diametric opposition to actual family-making among the enslaved, whose lives were fraught by difficulty and constrained by a condition they were typically forced to pass down to descendants. Before the Age of Revolutions, hierarchical family imagery often described the enslaved as juveniles needing paternal order. It was then doubly revolutionary that oppressed people eventually achieved kinship affiliation and political commonality with whomever they wished, an enactment of personal rights and collective futures. As the disruption of exploited families declined in the era of abolition, the metaphor of revolutionary solidarity shifted to that of siblings. Built upon commonality and equality, this ethos eventually yielded Dominican and Haitian citizens a more familial *égalité* and radical *fraternité* than those realized by the French Revolution or by other Latin American independence movements.[13]

Second, a key debate of the Age of Revolutions revolved around whether societies would reject or retain extant ethics. Among political and social vernaculars that built and broke group belongings on Hispaniola, perhaps the most religiously diverse venue in this era, evidence clearly shows faith expressions as salient. At best, shared beliefs could facilitate trust in liberatory, fictive families. At worst, religious divisions exacerbated cultural and political divides.

Alongside its many other implications, the Haitian Revolution was also a cosmological upheaval. It rapidly and fundamentally challenged prevailing explanations for the meanings of life itself. Novel social and political forms forced people to reassess natural notions of what it meant to be human and supernatural suppositions of where they fit in the universe. Inescapable reminders of mortality from constant warfare over imperial aims and extractive slavery amplified these emotional contemplations. The angst of new unknowns and conundrums also animated imperfect ontologies of justice, hope, and freedom. These were not simply subplots to well-known revolutionary events.

As the ensuing chapters show, in practice, believing mediated networks, proxied politics, influenced the founding of Haiti, and shaped Dominican identities. African diasporic cultural communities famously worked to start the Haitian Revolution. Adherents to French Deist forms made fervent, if divisive, political change. Dominican elites felt intense concern for their tangible lives and intangible afterlives when revolution defied their hierarchies, traditions, and beliefs, exacerbating racist descriptors and mistrust toward confluences of Black power, secularism, and visible Vodou. Beyond restrictive Catholicism, which is most associated with Dominican elite religiosity, later Haitian leaders who achieved emancipation and autonomy often also observed Catholicism and attempted to express their beliefs to Dominicans in the interest of building a unified, cross-island state.

In these contexts, belief—as sets of ideas and ways of group belonging—was central to the project of sifting new concepts and situations and adaptably apprising worldviews. By these mechanisms, lived religion influenced the material world. Observable believing often premised belonging, even if personal intent ranged from sincere to cynical. How it changed over time to influence networks, ideas, and outcomes is far more discernible than in individuals' interior motives. Interweaving personal life and social views, belief echoed *religare*, meaning "to bind," a likely Latin root word for religion. Belief operated as a visible, significant force, even if participants attributed positive outcomes and punishment to both providence and principle and were not fully aware of how their outward rituals, behaviors, and vernaculars generated trust that mutually reinforced network cohesion. In sum, this book considers how belief was publicly causative while avoiding narrow concerns of how staunchly individuals presumed certain truth claims or asserted sacred or metaphysical moments.[14]

While reconstructing salient events of the revolutionary era, each chapter explores critical cases of familial and spiritual cultural politics and community making. Beyond simply relating strains among Vodou, Deism, secularism, Catholicism, and even Islam and Protestantism, this analysis of belief exposes decisive social and political junctures. Assessing familial rhetoric and kin-making offers the same. Both aspects are necessary to better understanding motives and meanings.

AN OVERVIEW

Chapter 1 outlines African ethnicities, evangelization, and political economy on both sides of the island. It contextualizes Dominican racial formation as a Spanish colony on an interconnected Hispaniola. Before the Age of Revolutions, Dominican elites, such as planters, merchants, and professionals, and even the prominent priest Antonio Sánchez Valverde, resentfully admired efficient French exploitation of their much smaller side of Hispaniola, where hundreds of thousands of enslaved laborers built the most valuable plantation landscape in the Americas. In 1785, Sánchez Valverde lamented that "distinguished families" of Santo Domingo, whom he called the "*criollos* of Hayti," a narrowly defined belonging and kinship built upon cultural, racial, and religious exclusivity, were struggling financially on "fertile soil" equal to that in French Saint-Domingue. As later chapters show, his reference to Santo Domingo as "Hayti" reflected a concept common across the island until Dominican nationalists rejected the term in the 1840s.

With an envious eye on Saint-Domingue, Sánchez Valverde and Dominican elites in the 1780s appealed to the Spanish crown for help in reviving a supposedly glorious Hispanic past in Santo Domingo by emulating French slavery. Mere years before the Haitian Revolution erupted in 1791 because of ruthless French exploitation, Dominican elites attempted to enforce racial order by punishing or confining the enslaved, free people of color, and maroons with new codes that influenced major legal debates across the Spanish Empire. Also, Sánchez Valverde foreshadowed later contentions within Dominican national identity when he bristled at observations regarding African culture or ancestry among Dominicans and instead postulated indigenous heritage. He and others felt similar cultural or racial precarity and made such claims perhaps in part because their own partial African ancestry jeopardized personal privileges in the Spanish Atlantic.[15] Rather than profit, reinforced racial strata produced heightened social unrest and eventually primed oppressed Dominicans to engage the revolutionary stimuli of the three decades that followed.

Dominican elites' enforcements of aggressive evangelization to mediate social strife and instill compliance enhanced only their own conceits of cultural whiteness and racial or Hispanic superiority. Their agenda asserted that fellowship in the Dominican family required acceptance of Spanish cultural heritage, Catholicism, and a corporatist social structure curated by paternalist elites, themes that sometimes later recurred in some nationalist forms.[16] They also critiqued perceived French hedonism, brutality, and lack of evangelization toward the enslaved. Such anti-Black and anti-French ideas in this prerevolutionary era related directly to the development of anti-Haitian sentiments. Dominican elites later disparaged the egalitarianism and anticlericalism of the French Revolution, racial rights in the Haitian Revolution, and eventually the alleged heresy, violence, and radicalism of Haitians, whom they often saw as prodigal children.

Chapter 2 focuses on the disproportionate importance of Hispaniola's colonial border during early revolutionary tensions on the island from 1789 to 1791. Following paths into Santo Domingo well traveled by maroons, merchants, cattle herders, exiles, and families, eventually insurgents from Saint-Domingue made unexpected alliances with some Dominicans and even the Spanish crown. In November 1790, dissidents led by Vincent Ogé also sought Dominican safety following their failed uprising for equal rights for free people of color.

In March 1791, the French governor crossed this same border, seeking refuge in Santo Domingo from white mobs in Port-au-Prince influenced by the French Revolution. Finally, in August 1791, a more radical tree of liberty than the French Revolution envisioned grew from the same soils upon which the enslaved toiled. After commencing the largest revolt of enslaved people in history, insurgents leading what became the Haitian Revolution immediately looked eastward, into Santo Domingo, for resources to support their resistance. Structural and cultural factors enhanced potentials for successful revolt of the enslaved in Saint-Domingue.

In September 1791, enslaved insurgents from Saint-Domingue cited "God, and King" to build common spiritual and material cause with potential allies who might listen in Santo Domingo. Importantly, among the revolutionary leadership, many with Catholic familiarity from missions in Atlantic Africa or uneven French evangelization made faith professions that corresponded with, and at times deliberately flattered, Spain's supernatural idiom. Nevertheless, thousands in their ranks observed nascent Vodou.

Eventually, blessings of guns and cash rewarded their expressions of belief. Elites in Santo Domingo first saw the upheaval as a chance to capture fertile French lands, and thus ignored white French officials in favor of appeals from Black rebels. They received the insurgents' Catholic, royalist, and anti-French professions with cautiously optimistic incredulity, judging them a possible sign of divine providence in counterpoint to the ongoing French Revolution.

Chapter 3 explains how these most formidable self-liberated insurgents from Saint-Domingue became the "Black Auxiliaries of King Carlos IV" of Spain with legally freed status, whose performances of piety bound them into a family of "true Spaniards." For a time, Spain offered racially inclusive upward mobility to adherents who sought liberty from their former French enslavers. Officials in Santo Domingo made this gamble to extinguish French revolutionary values, evangelize, and capture Saint-Domingue's plantation economy. With support from Madrid and the papacy, they championed popular religion and royalism as an alternative to republicanism.

The Black Auxiliaries' mutually affirming professions of faith and monarchism included ornate weddings, priests riding alongside them into battle, and blessings for their capture of half of Saint-Domingue. Chapter 3 also shows new details of how three major figures, Jean-François, Georges Biassou, and Toussaint Louverture, affirmed their Spanish ties. They did this by, among other things, rewriting the history of the legendary planner of the original revolt in 1791, Dutty Boukman, as having been enlivened also by Catholic righteousness, not only Vodou. Their influence in Santo Domingo was enormous. Competitive pieties also reinforced Dominican ideas of difference from their neighbors, which promoted a Catholic redemption narrative and heightened spiritual expectations for Dominicans of color, ensconcing a litmus test of professions required for Dominican belonging.

Their victories pressured the French Republic, which never intended to fully extend its values to people of African descent, to abolish slavery in hopes of attracting support and avoiding destruction on Hispaniola. Ultimately, officials in Santo Domingo had unwittingly furthered Black power they could not control. Infiltration of French anticlericalism, secularism, and permissiveness toward African spirituality in Santo Domingo compounded this division. Dominicans of color, tied to and inspired by nearby Black power, also increasingly pursued their own social aspirations through revolt. With social unrest growing in Santo Domingo and loss of Black allies, most importantly Toussaint Louverture, Dominican elites retreated to conflations of Blackness with suspicion, heresy, and duplicity, with additional associations of egalitarianism, violence, and, eventually, being Haitian.

Chapter 4 analyzes the fallout of the unexpected Treaty of Basel in 1795, which abruptly ended Spain's hostilities, exiled the Black Auxiliaries' generals, and ceded Santo Domingo to France. Spain's outward-looking mission of conquest and Catholicism promptly pivoted to protect Dominican territory and Iberian traditions and belief. Santo Domingo remained under weakened Spanish governance for six years as the French cession lagged. Arriving French envoys included a racially *tricolore* French delegation that unsuccessfully attempted to abolish Dominican slavery. During this time, French officials recruited their "Dominican siblings" to embrace a new revolutionary family, and they asked the archbishop of Santo Domingo to become "bishop of Ayti" for a French-unified island. Dominican elites demurred. Their definitions of Dominican belonging as Catholic and Iberian hardened in differentiation against Black revolutionaries to their west and, eventually, within Santo Domingo. Despite elite resistance, exuberant French rights discourses swayed new Dominican supporters to celebrate Bastille Day in 1796, to read revolutionary texts, and to use churches for republican meetings. Dominican popular unrest increased.

Kin-making analogies for shared synergies or sufferings again appeared in new struggles over revolutionary *fraternité* versus Catholic brotherhoods, partisan divorces versus socially binding weddings, and symbolic siblinghood versus exclusive Hispanic genealogy. Very personal familial and spiritual fights mediated macro-revolutionary processes as a priest denounced the king, renounced his vows, married an enslaved girl in a secular ceremony, and declared himself a French *citoyen*. A French envoy goaded the archbishop by requesting a divorce from his politically moderate wife in order to wed a revolutionary woman of color. When the enslaved at the Boca Nigua sugar plantation near Santo Domingo revolted in 1796, an investigation revealed that the rebels were Kongolese kin responding to the death of a beloved friend. British agents recognized elite disgust and covertly attracted prominent capital residents with pledges to protect Catholics despite their state Protestantism, to provide stable and moderate constitutional monarchy, and to open prosperous forms of commerce.[17] Though little known, a few Dominican towns even raised the Union Jack. And though these efforts were largely unsuccessful, as were British attempts to control Saint-Domingue, their interventions further hardened Dominican elite distinctions against the Black revolutionary citizens to their west.

Chapter 5 recounts the increase in French influence in Santo Domingo that grew after 1799 toward direct French rule from 1802 to 1809, which more fully enveloped Dominicans in ongoing Haitian revolutionary struggles next door. This era further engrained religious ire among Dominican elites. New findings show that in 1799, secular French officials briefly revived the Cult of the Supreme Being, a state-sponsored Deism that had faded in Paris five years prior, despite repeated promises to respect Catholicism. The Hispaniola iteration of the Supreme Being accepted Vodou, Freemasonry, and Christianity as coequal predecessors and named Toussaint Louverture in prominence alongside Mohammed and Jesus. Further, during direct French rule from 1802 to 1809, officials closed churches, imposed pliant Catholic officials, sold church property, and emblematically converted a monastery's belfry into a cannon turret, alienating many locals. This attempt to galvanize popular support confirmed the worst elite Dominican assumptions about the French and their new Black co-citizens.

Santo Domingo soon became a proxy site for the power struggle between Toussaint and André Rigaud raging in Saint-Domingue. When Louverture prevailed, he strategically chose to control Santo Domingo in 1801, yet left the terms of Black liberty unresolved. After Napoleonic officials arrived in 1802, Dominicans of color witnessed French attempts to revive slavery and retract rights. Meanwhile, the independence of Haiti in 1804 and recuperation of this Taíno name by Jean-Jacques Dessalines began the most inclusive and radical idea of kinship yet. Adjacent Santo Domingo was of course the society most related to and influenced by Haiti. Dominicans also proved most receptive and reactionary to Haitian inspiration across the Black Atlantic. This "Haiti," unlike exclusive earlier uses by Dominican elites, represented the previously unthinkable transformation of exploitative French Saint-Domingue into the first antislavery, anti-imperial nation. As slavery expanded in North America and neighboring Spanish colonies into the nineteenth century, the self-determination by Haiti appeared even more unique and profound for hemispheric liberty. Compared to expansive experience with Haiti, momentary British, French, and eventually Latin American independence influences in Santo Domingo were meek.[18]

At Haitian independence, Santo Domingo also unexpectedly became the last bastion of French power on Hispaniola. French presence attracted immediate and constant efforts from Haitian leaders to finally end imperialism on the island, including Dessalines's failed 1805 campaign in Santo Domingo. For these very reasons, in ensuing years elite Dominicans increasingly self-defined against Haiti with negative tropes that had emerged during the revolutionary era. Subsequent Haitian leaders used far more effective soft power to attract cooperation from a Dominican majority that had grown weary of Napoleonic rule and, eventually, they explored independence sentiments together.

Chapter 6 examines the deluge of the anti-imperial, cross-island coop-eration and conspiracies that commenced in 1808 and increased throughout the 1810s. Dominicans and Haitians cooperated to initiate major geopolitical change. This era, marked by small and large plots of varied ideological asso-ciation, solidified demand in Santo Domingo for emancipation, citizenship, and independence. Anti-French revolts erupted after Napoléon Bonaparte invaded Spain in 1808. Haitian leaders eagerly bankrolled a Dominican *Reconquista*, or reconquest, of Santo Domingo from France and for Span-ish recolonization, led by Juan Sánchez Ramírez. Though Dominican leaders collaborated with Henry Christophe and Alexandre Pétion, who respectively ruled northern and southern Haiti at this time, their interests most aligned with Christophe, who strategically supplied ample guns and funds. Together they toppled the last French stronghold on Hispaniola and increased routine contact between Dominicans and Haitians. With its con-tinuance of slavery, aggressive re-evangelization, and restoration of property to elites, the Spanish recolonization that began in 1809 only allowed unre-solved tensions for the Dominican majority of color to simmer.

Eventually, Dominican elites contented with restored Catholicism and Iberian culture became discontented with subservience to a restrictive, negligent, and distant monarchy for other reasons. Royalists remained, but, increasingly, the younger, mostly white professionals in the capital feared Haitian unification while admiring the comparatively moderate independ-ence projects in South America. Popular demand threatened the continu-ance of generational privileges for elite Dominicans. The last thing many elites wanted was to become equal with people of color from Haiti in a new civic family.[19]

Gradually, commonplace symbioses between the two populations of majority African descent expanded. Though Haiti inspired revolts across the Americas, Dominicans had Haitian texts available, including items transcribed into Spanish.[20] More importantly, they had access to Haitian operatives. Constant arrests uncovered agents of Pétion conspiring with Dominican collaborators and stockpiling weapons. Even a spy from Cara-cas explored popular support for Simón Bolívar. Society stretched among affinities for Haiti, Gran Colombia, and Spain. However, more than in pre-vious eras, abounding plots in the 1810s were clearly not only anti-racist but anti-colonial, and even pro-Haitian. Exceeding Enlightenment abstractions or distant independence leaders, Haiti posed a tangible, sturdy example of liberty and citizenship. Dominicans who engaged these promises challenged elites' narrow constructs of belief and belonging, causing some Dominican nationalists to write such anti-colonial agitation out of their own family history.

Chapter 7 uses new archival evidence to show how two Dominican groups moved toward independence, one aligned with Haiti and another with mainland Latin American movements. Following decades of growing popular collaboration, it shows how the new Haitian president, Jean-Pierre Boyer, who succeeded in reunifying the west under a republican government from 1818 to 1820, began sending emissaries to explore Dominican independence sentiments. Specifically, Boyer measured interest in "the whole island of Hayti" unifying as one citizenry under one government.[21] Invoking Taíno legacies, he said, in both proclamations and letters, that Dominicans should reject the European extractions that had afflicted the entire island. His proposals for unification founded upon these commonalities and envisioning a future of prosperity, equal rights, and security gained support. Dominican elites in the capital chafed at Spanish inability to stop Haitian persuasions and pondered news from Caracas and Cartagena about Bolívar's independence efforts. Boyer reminded Dominicans that Bolívar himself had relied upon Haitian aid to survive, and that Haiti, not Gran Colombia, represented the vanguard of independence. For many, compared to the familiar example of ambitious emancipation and racial inclusion in Haiti, the separatism sweeping mainland Latin America was more distant and less thorough.

President Boyer of Haiti began calling Dominicans siblings, displaying his own belief and trustworthiness while offering new appeals for a radically different community of kinship belonging. Critical cross-island commerce also appeared in conversations about unification. Some interior Dominican towns welcomed unification and raised the Haitian flag in late 1821. In response, a second, moderate, elite-led independence project commenced in the capital. José Núñez de Cáceres declared a "Spanish Part of Hayti" and requested annexation to Gran Colombia. Bolívar never responded. Boyer, who held more Dominican support, then arrived in Santo Domingo by invitation. On his way, towns accepted the Haitian army—some in support and others in concern for retribution. Anticipating support from enslaved Dominicans, Boyer averted tropes of a "race war" and instead attempted to use persuasion with the larger free populations of color and Iberian descent. With growing Dominican support, Boyer also promised to incorporate local elites and offer Spanish-language governmental representation.

Pablo Alí was among the few who supported Núñez de Cáceres. Alongside many other relatively unheeded figures, this book adds extensive detail to Alí's fascinating life. Alí spent decades struggling to build his own families in every sense of the word, often in tension with exclusive, elite ideas of belonging. Born a Muslim in Atlantic Africa, Alí had been captured and sent to Saint-Domingue. He eventually converted to Catholicism, escaped slavery, and fought in the Haitian Revolution with the Black Auxiliaries for Spain. His closest colleagues became some of the most important figures in the history of Hispaniola. Unlike many of his famous contemporaries, Alí made Santo Domingo his permanent home. There he earned a reputation for his exceptional ability and uncanny importance to crucial events.[22] Spain had rewarded his exemplary decades of service with repeated denials of petitions for rights and pay. Though he had protected Santo Domingo, raised a Dominican family, and participated in beliefs endorsed by the elite, he remained underappreciated and under constant scrutiny. His break with Spain, and soon with Núñez de Cáceres, was indicative of the failures of both Spain and the moderate Dominican independence leaders to end racial exclusions and offer equal citizenship. Eventually, Alí joined Boyer as an esteemed official. Symbolically, he was a member of a unified Haitian family in Santo Domingo that had taken his lifetime to build.

Many thousands of Dominicans equated liberty not with Enlightenment ideals espoused far away, but with the immediate example of Haitian citizenship. Before 1791, people with talent equal to revered Enlightenment pedants lived and died in the plantation fields of Hispaniola. In 1804, survivors of this cruelty founded Haiti. In February 1822, thousands of Dominicans embraced Boyer as their president and Haitians as their fictive kin and fellow citizens.[23] Without popular support, Núñez de Cáceres chose to personally hand Boyer the actual city keys. Instead of old, privileged Hispanic links across oceans, Boyer cultivated Dominican collaboration for multiethnic, multilingual nation-building across a unified island once again called Haiti. As opposed to often-corrosive Dominican nationalist memories, the Dominican variant of independence was the culmination of decades of collaboration amid complex contingencies.

Newly emancipated Dominicans and old Spanish families alike became Haitian citizens and siblings of soil in an abolitionist, multiethnic state. Thus began twenty-two years of a unification that was mostly peaceful and, at first, popular. Individual cross-island families followed, temporarily eclipsing exclusive Dominican identities fashioned upon a nostalgic Hispanic heritage. Unification followed four decades of familial appeals and intricate spiritual interactions and produced a new, and previously unthinkable, governmental state. This era also initiated a remarkably ambitious state of being, believing, and belonging. Dominican independence from Spain by joining Haiti represented one of the most peaceful, innovative, and liberatory nation-building projects in the Age of Revolutions. Perhaps the most immediate victory for popular rights and independence in the Americas came as a "Black republic" achieved one of the most astonishing revolutions in history, offering all Dominicans freedom, rights, and equality as Haitian citizens. Unfortunately, over the ensuing generations, some prominent Dominican voices either deliberately overlooked or distorted these essential events.

The epilogue considers the recurrence of anti-Haitian themes in Dominican culture, including the return of many tropes developed by elites during the Age of Revolutions, from unification onward. Unresolved tensions of race and nation lingered. Dominican elites revived an exclusivist hispanismo cultural repertoire to differentiate themselves from Haitians, whom they continued to depict as immoderate, African, and socially aberrant, resorting to selective, historicized memories that miscast the 1822 invitation as an invasion of depraved Black aggression.[24] Such stereotypes worsened Haiti's challenging diplomatic and commercial status in a hemisphere of expanding slavery in the United States, Cuba, and Brazil.

Eventually, in 1844, the Dominican Republic broke away from Haiti. Dominican national historical memory frequently excludes the aspirations of those for whom membership in the Haitian state was the epitome of citizenship, solidarity, and future. Rather, it often wistfully heralds the defeated elites who tried to ally with the more moderate projects of Bolívar and Gran Colombia, depicting the decisively anti-colonial actions of Dominican and Haitian collaborators as a menace that impeded Dominican modernity. This legacy distorts the long-standing political prominence of Dominicans of color and justifies attacks on ethnic Haitians to the present.[25]

As a litany of historical events and trends in the Dominican Republic show—from the conflicts in the nineteenth century through the Trujillo dictatorship of 1930 to 1961 and the authoritarian presidencies of Joaquín Balaguer from the 1960s to the 1990s, and from the ongoing mistreatment of Haitian workers to revocations of citizenship from ethnic Haitians in the 2010s—anti-Haitian actions have built on selective memories that still resound. And yet prevalent renunciations have not prevented some Dominicans from cooperation, family life, empathy, and working-class solidarities with Haitians. Ties of antagonism and amicability, hostility and harmony, conflict and cooperation have long entangled Dominicans and Haitians. Understanding the turbulent Age of Revolutions is essential to understanding the events and memories that shaped the sibling rivalry between these two nations of majority African descent. At the bicentenary of unification, this past still carries enormous contemporary consequences.

SCHOLARSHIP AND APPROACHES

This book derives from underexplored records on underrepresented peoples found in over twenty archives across the world, with the majority of cited primary sources held in the Dominican Republic, Haiti, Spain, the United Kingdom, and the Vatican. This book features accounts of those who remade Dominican society at the epicenter of the Age of Revolutions while engaging their cases with scholarly canons that often overlook them. These microcosmic episodes shaped macro processes as Dominican cultural politics engaged antislavery revolts, the French Revolution, Spanish imperial responses, the formation of Haiti, and Latin American independence.[26]

Understanding marginalized actors entails using extant collections often composed by state, ecclesiastical, military, and commercial institutions made up of elite men whom people of color may have avoided, appeased, or attacked. Such sources necessitate critical discursive analyses to cut against textual intentions and reconstruct the ambitions of the disempowered majority whose actions sometimes perplexed these same institutions. By accessing the archival depths on Hispaniola and attending to the languages of this Atlantic moment, this book avoids telling a tale of any single state, ideological vantage point, or structural mechanism.

Certain venues of the Age of Revolutions garner wide recognition. Despite its undeniably decisive connections, contests in Santo Domingo remain less conspicuous in scholarship on Latin American independence, the French and Haitian Revolutions, the African diaspora, the Hispanic Caribbean, and race and religion in the Americas. Rather, many extant narrations rationalize national-era outcomes as continuities from colonial contexts, concealing Dominicans who initiated a peaceful emancipation and imperial end by joining a multiethnic, multilingual Haiti.

Recent scholarship has examined Colombian, Venezuelan, and Cuban ties to revolutionary Haiti.[27] However, Dominicans, the people who actually shared the same island, have been somewhat less prominent in this wave of excellent work on the Spanish Caribbean. Rather than fitting exogenous timelines of emancipations and independence, the complex cultural configurations and contingencies of Santo Domingo produced unique motives, semiotics, and actions by Dominicans and Haitians that complicate its place in regional and national narratives.[28]

Historiographical expansions have yet to provide a thorough explanation of the influence of Dominicans upon early Haiti, of Haitians upon Dominican anti-colonialism, and of the decades-long developments preceding unification on Dominican identity. This book responds by developing these themes while engaging Dominican and Haitian historiography with broader Latin American, Caribbean, and Atlantic scholarship. To avoid shoehorning Dominican events into exogenous French or Haitian chronologies that elide local specificities, it grounds analysis of Santo Domingo in the three-hundred-year legacy of Spanish institutions, Catholic presence, royalist ideas, and particular demographics among the free and enslaved.

This book also attends to factors that preoccupied the actors themselves and to other themes dominating recent historiography. For example, the cultural politics of religiosity in the Spanish Caribbean during the Age of Revolutions remains underappreciated despite its obvious importance across the Hispanic Atlantic. Aside from exploring Vodou in the initial revolts of 1791, certain leaders' spiritual compasses, and some philanthropic thinking, Haitian revolutionary studies are still catching up to the consequences of competing, ubiquitous belief.[29]

Studies on the Haitian Revolution have recently proliferated, though they often overlook important Dominican influences. While Haitian scholars never forgot the importance of this topic, it faced generations of intellectual neglect in the English language. In the past decades, scholars have added archival nuance to explain influences emanating from Haiti throughout the Atlantic, including prerevolutionary colonial combustibility, the organization and motivations of self-liberated insurgents, the significance of African political culture among insurgents, the impact of French rights discourses, and the white French colonial politics that preceded emancipation.[30] Recent studies have examined the strains for a new Haitian state seeking stability in a hostile Atlantic, French plantations, Haitian peasants, Toussaint Louverture, French demise in Saint-Domingue, and Vodou.[31] New dissertations have revealed more on Kongolese culture, maroons, royalism, memorials, property, and *gens de couleur* families.[32]

This book contributes to understanding how Dominicans and Haitians saw themselves as negotiating debates over the sacred and profane. These views materially influenced their reactions to rights discourses, abolitions, citizenships, or nationalisms that prevail in historiography. As much as any society in the revolutionary era, Santo Domingo traversed quandaries about religion in the public sphere, monarchical sanctity, and the balancing of secular states with protections for faith. The eventual sense of Spanish abandonment and Dominican criticism of empire eventually left among many a Catholic cultural core tied to an idealized Hispanic past rather than a shared Iberian imperial future.

Earlier work by Dominican scholars outlined the politics and major events of this era. Contemporary researchers on Santo Domingo have focused on questions of abolition, though the enslaved just exceeded 10 percent of Dominican society. Additional analysis has detailed the significance of brief French rule from 1802 to 1809, early nineteenth-century Dominican ties to Haiti, and later cooperation and strife during unification.[33]

Some scholars of Dominican society have also noticed the intermittent appearance of cross-island solidarities that occasionally emerged as some Dominicans and Haitians continued to "sibling themselves," or use other familial language, in spite of later revived reactionary hispanismo. Haitian aid resumed for Dominican anti-imperial fights versus Spanish recolonization in the 1860s. At times in the twentieth century, kinship concepts reemerged.[34] Analysis of belonging and familial metaphors in this book shows not only that there has been more profuse and profound use of kinship idioms by actors themselves, but that these appeals began early in the revolutionary era and were foundational both to that era and to subsequent relations on the island.

This book also attempts to examine race in context as part of explaining unique cases in the history of Blackness. This includes how racial ideas influenced actions and changed over time in relation to events and associations. Such analysis requires attention to certain details. Terms familiar in the Caribbean two centuries ago, and in some cases still familiar today, may seem unfamiliar or awkward to some audiences. These terms typically appear italicized at first mention. They are mostly in Spanish or French, and, where necessary, are accompanied by definitions and discussions of usage. These introductions consider the interchange of these terms both locally and transnationally. The book also uncovers specific African cultural backgrounds, both in an effort to dignify overlooked details of these actors' lives and because ethnicity and race were crucial to society and events.

Racial descriptors in Dominican culture developed from a Spanish colonial schema that tied into other cultural markers, including traits of supposed respectability, ideas of religious racial redemption, language and dialects, and notions of political and ideological affiliation, genealogy, appearance, and social status. Though in a way that was less binary than in North America, Spanish and French Caribbean colonial societies construed Blackness as inferior. In the revolutionary era, radicalism, heresy, and violence joined extant conflations of Blackness with suspicion and criminality.

When considering the many people who historically experienced discrimination under Eurocentric conceits, even if dissimilar in extent, this book also uses the terms "of African descent" or "people of color" as conventional scholarly nomenclature to speak to broader racial and social groups. This usage follows primary sources that might inscribe people as *de color* or *gens de couleur*, terms typically applied to people of European and African descent, including many who were born free. To connect with analytical interests spanning the Americas, this book engages Blackness and "Black" descriptors as a transcription following terms such as *moreno* or *negro*, although the latter typically also meant "enslaved," or, eventually in this specific site, Haitian. As these meanings mattered, Spanish files on French *mulatos* appear here as *gens de couleur* or *mulâtres*. *Mulato* or *mulâtresse* were Spanish and French terms for a man and woman usually of both African and European descent, respectively. Often, actors used these terms laden with additional cultural dynamics, and sometimes in context they were deliberately pejorative. As pertinent, this book also looks at what being "white" meant regarding local or European figures of Spanish, French, and British backgrounds.

As the epilogue details, from the late nineteenth century and intermittently since, Dominican public figures have developed and disseminated the identity of a majority mixed-race nation (*mulataje*). Some who do downplay African ancestry assert indigenous heritage (*indio*), or at least use this term to describe skin tone. Some social groups still adhere to *hispanidad*. Amid current racial descriptors such as *trigueño* (wheat) or *prieto* (brown), darker-complected Dominicans, who could be identified as Haitians, fit uneasily along this spectrum. Today, Dominican racial ideas are akin to those of other Hispanic American societies, where self-descriptors of brownness often prevail. Blackness appears on this spectrum of identifiers, yet it is not a common reference point for identities or injustices among Dominicans, partly because of unwanted links to slavery and Haiti. However, this does not simply mean a denial of African ancestry, as many North American observers have mistakenly believed. Racist schemas then and now appear on a spectrum from subtle to overt and, though not always, anti-Blackness and anti-Haitianism often intersect. Accordingly, many Dominicans perceive Haitians as the actual Black residents of the island, even if Haitians use other self-descriptors. This book shows how ideas about Blackness in relation to Haitians and Dominicans have changed over time, and how some old racist resonances remain.[35]

Finally, the cases discussed in this book stand out among Latin American independence movements. Constant uncertainty, fragile sovereignty, and three decades of existential turmoil ended without a culminating independence war. Dominican anti-colonialism was rife with labyrinthine contingencies rather than being based on a consistent strategy driven by coherent principles formulated in the interest of working toward a clearly defined objective. Thousands of Dominicans explored a variety of sovereignties before settling on a conclusion. The limited literati in the capital, unlike some of their mainland Latin American peers, failed to run a functional state or to present an idea of nation that won popularity. Juxtaposed to neighboring struggles against the Spanish Empire and their questions of how independent citizenries would relate to Spain after independence, Dominicans experienced a more radical outcome. Independence, partly a consequence of imperial insolvency, was in the Dominican case also uniquely caused by the readily apparent example and transferable political structure of revolutionary Haiti, an easily available solution to anti-imperial, abolitionist, and commercial needs. While Dominican events were tied to major themes of the Iberian Atlantic in this era, the Dominican case remains largely unintegrated in Latin American independence historiography.[36]

Rather than conceptual fixation, Dominicans of color and their Haitian interlocutors often sought benefit and security wherever opportunity and conviction coincided amid the tumults of revolution and reaction. This book attempts to add clarity and nuance to this complexity, yet declines teleologies that celebrate, mourn, or mythologize.[37] The frequently idiosyncratic choices of Dominicans and Haitians exuded creativity and situational practicality that sometimes confounded analytical abstractions of Enlightenment ideals or assumptions of racial solidarities. Ultimately, this peaceful, practical union, based on myriad common interests, was a revolutionary result that was more impressive than reliance upon reductionist categories.[38] Dominicans and Haitians rethought their island's future from first principles. Their independence outcomes were never inevitable. Intricate decades of revolution and reaction that defined race and nation on Hispaniola demand reconsideration. As the epilogue explains, misrepresentations of the unique and innovative 1822 independence project on the island have had repercussions to the present day. The many faces of independence, including many Dominicans and Haitians of color, deserve their place in scholarship.

ONE

RACE AND PLACE IN
EIGHTEENTH-CENTURY HISPANIOLA

Before revolutionary unrest crossed old paths connecting the island, Saint-Domingue's sugar, coffee, and indigo profits cultivated extensive jealousy among Dominican elites. In the 1780s, the prominent priest and writer Antonio Sánchez Valverde judged that weak Dominican slavery law and lax racial enforcement were "paramount cause[s] of the difference between the wealth of Saint-Domingue and Spanish poverty" on Hispaniola. These and other complaints featured prominently in his treatise about the unrealized value of Santo Domingo, which he published in Madrid to broadcast elite lamentations to a metropolitan audience. Alongside acerbic allegations that faulted Dominicans of color for various types of social malaise, he demanded increased importation of enslaved captives and a reinforced racial hierarchy to emulate the brutality of Santo Domingo's French neighbors.[1]

With an envious eye on Saint-Domingue, elites in Santo Domingo thus attempted to emulate French exploitation. Their major reformulation of racial laws in the 1780s, mere years before the island erupted in revolution as a result of this very brutality, prompted a new "Código Negro" for the entire Spanish Empire. In this decade, Dominicans of color endured harsher punishments than before, more restrictions, forced resettlements that disrupted families, and enhanced scrutiny of their beliefs. However, elite Dominicans' reinforcement of local racial hierarchies only undermined their domestic control. Rather than profit for planters, the ultimately ineffectual laws amplified racial tensions that further divided Dominican society. The policies antagonized maroons, free laborers, peasants, and the enslaved, who all experienced forms of alienation that were increasingly similar to that of the oppressed majority in Saint-Domingue. Dominicans of color, both free and enslaved, became prime audiences for radical movements to their west starting in the 1790s. Long-standing cross-island connections, including precedents of resistance, were thus essential components of the revolutionary complexities that followed.

SANTO DOMINGO AND SAINT-DOMINGUE TO THE 1780S

Three centuries before the first so-called "Black Republic" came into being, the Taíno island Ayiti, renamed Hispaniola, witnessed many other consequential firsts. Perhaps most notably, it was the site of the first European fort in the Americas, established by Christopher Columbus and thirty-nine of his crewmembers in 1492. Four years later, it hosted the founding of the city of Santo Domingo, the first permanent European settlement in the Americas. Generations of privileged Dominicans celebrated such distinctions. The colony became a hub for Spanish colonization. The indigenous Taínos resisted the violent Columbus family, which Spain punished for misconduct. From a population of at least 400,000 Taínos in 1492, only 3,000 remained in 1519, because of atrocities, disease, and forced labor and resettlements. Dire demographic collapse inspired one of the most significant figures of the sixteenth century, Bartolomé de las Casas, a priest who championed indigenous protection. His influential writings also encouraged the nascent African slavery trade, and some captives of this trade soon joined other imperial resisters in the island's interior.[2]

The depletion of limited gold supplies shifted export enterprises toward sugar and livestock, including horses to support regional colonization efforts. Cattle escaped into the newly depopulated interior of Hispaniola, constantly reproducing and consuming vegetation. African slavery rapidly expanded, and by the mid-1560s only a few thousand Spaniards lived in a colony that enslaved tens of thousands of people. At least a few thousand maroons fled to form small, autonomous communities that would resell goods to smugglers along unguarded coastlines. Many Dominicans similarly engaged in contraband commerce, which dominated the north and west of the island by the 1570s and rivaled legal trade. Dozens of *ingenios* (sugar mills) pocked the landscape near the capital, the only population center with requisite funds for investment. Sugar output in the sixteenth century exceeded even eighteenth-century levels. Eventually, new sources of sugar (namely Brazil) captured market share and outperformed Spanish production on Hispaniola.[3] Santo Domingo hosted the first gold boom, the first sugar boom, and the first economic bust in the colonial Americas.[4]

Alongside Spanish officials' loathing for contraband was their related fear of foreign spiritual ideas and political affiliations that might infiltrate a Dominican society already afflicted with hunger, hurricanes, and epidemics. Therefore, in 1605, Governor Antonio de Osorio evicted colonists from the western and northern coasts. These "devastations" hindered Santo Domingo's economy: the enslaved fled, crops rotted, livestock escaped, and profitable contraband connections crumbled.[5] Spanish officials effectively emptied fertile lands on which pirates and rivals encroached. The Dutch, English, and French jockeyed to settle this space over the course of the seventeenth century. By the 1670s, the French controlled several small, prosperous ports across western Hispaniola. France formally acquired this territory in the Treaty of Ryswick of 1697. Saint-Domingue became the most profitable acreage in the Americas, while Santo Domingo sputtered.[6]

Over the ensuing century, a symbiotic rhythm of trans-imperial, cross-island connection developed. As the French dedicated little fertile land to livestock or to subsistence crops, by the eighteenth century they were using profits from their coveted commodity exports to purchase cattle, hides, and staple foods from Santo Domingo, opening a negative trade balance with Spanish domains. Dominican elites owned massive herds tended by thousands of freed people or the enslaved. As draught animals or food, Dominican cattle accompanied Saint-Domingue's brutal expansions of slavery.

This dynamic exchange transformed the interior of Santo Domingo. Dominican traders constantly strained against regulation and taxation by Spain and sometimes France in a culturally fluid region where the permeable border remained in dispute despite demarcation treaties. By the 1760s and 1770s, the importance of livestock to both colonies necessitated imperial-level negotiations to secure prices, property rights, and the annual export of nearly 10,000 head of cattle. In 1787, the French deregulated cattle ordinances and allowed free purchase at market rates. Thereafter, Saint-Domingue annually imported perhaps 33,000 bovines, which crossed the border and sea via Monte Cristi, Puerto Plata, or Samaná, as most Dominican regions participated.[7]

However, Dominican elites remained painfully aware of their dependence upon French markets. They knew, too, that livestock yielded inferior profits compared to Saint-Domingue's sugar and coffee. This was the state of affairs that motivated Antonio Sánchez Valverde's appeal in the mid-1780s and the new racial codes based on planters' critiques. Elites in Santo

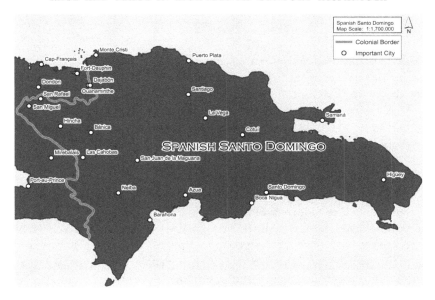

FIGURE I.I

Map of Colonial Spanish Santo Domingo. Map courtesy of Matthew H. Ruther.

Domingo desired to curtail the mobility of Dominican peasants, ranchers of color, maroon communities, and urban enslaved wage earners, who lived more autonomously than their counterparts in the sugar and coffee economies of Saint-Domingue.

In contrast, the meteoric, one-century rise of Saint-Domingue flourished atop a vicious, ruinous agricultural regime. Between 1785 and 1790, Saint-Domingue imported about 31,400 African captives a year, creating a population of about 500,000 enslaved people out of nearly 600,000 residents.[8] Santo Domingo, three times the territorial size of Saint-Domingue, had less than 14,000 enslaved people, 125,000 total residents, and fewer than 50 ingenios.[9] Saint-Domingue's approximately 8,000 plantations (800 sugar and cotton plantations each, and 3,000 coffee and indigo plantations each) tied into at least 40 percent of France's overseas economic activity. Perhaps jobs for 1 million of France's 25 million people tied into Saint-Domingue. This relatively small territory exported commodities greater in value than the those exported by the United States and more total exports than the whole British Caribbean. In the year 1790 alone, Saint-Domingue produced 60,000 metric tons of sugar, four times more than Cuba. It yielded 40 percent of the world's sugar and half of its coffee.[10]

ELITE EXCORIATIONS

Elite Dominicans coveted their neighbors' ruthless prosperity. In the 1760s, imperial inertia stifled their attempts to strengthen the racial hierarchy. In the 1780s, Dominican elites again schemed toward economic resurgence. Their complaints about Black autonomies, such as freedom of movement, small-scale commerce, and perceived rowdiness, convinced a key Enlightenment-influenced adviser, José de Gálvez, as well as the Consejo de Indias (Council of Indies) and eventually King Carlos III, of the need for new "Black" laws in Santo Domingo and beyond, similar to the Code Noir in the French Caribbean.[11] Thus, just prior to the Haitian Revolution, Dominican elites endeavored to emulate Saint-Domingue's precarious success. It mattered not that in the century since its implementation in 1685 the Code Noir had been heavily revised, that provisions for evangelization had been upheld, though only unevenly, and that planters often ignored French attempts to restrict beatings, tortures, and mutilations in 1784 and 1785.[12]

Dominican elites began to pursue legal and structural change. The resultant Código Negro Dominicano, provisionally adopted in 1785, influenced the less severe imperial Código Negro Carolino of 1789. This latter code technically opened the slavery trade, but most planters declined to seriously implement laws that seemed more lenient than previous practices.[13] The Hispaniola contexts that influenced one of the most ambitious but least effective Bourbon Reforms remain obscured. Elite testimony that guided this experiment reveals friction points in prerevolutionary Dominican society. These tensions and the haphazard local enactment of the preliminary 1785 statutes have been forgotten as critical precursors to resistance by Dominicans of color in the 1790s.

In March 1784, then governor Isidoro Peralta reviewed prevailing laws and planters' criticisms.[14] Participating *hacendados* (owners of *haciendas*, or plantations), other local notables, and military officers all aimed to stimulate productivity by further restricting both the enslaved and free people of color.[15] Nearly all deponents wanted to reduce the perceived abuse of the roughly ninety Catholic holidays by the enslaved. Supposedly, their "excessive *fiestas*" were costly, unruly, and a waste of time.[16] Many enslaved Dominicans slowed their productivity until the owners would financially support their Festivals of Two Crosses, a massive annual celebration that excused them from work.[17]

Debates balanced "Christian care" against alleged indulgence in *aguardiente* (strong alcoholic beverages) and acts of disorderly conduct.[18] Religious holidays had a reputation for being raucous across Latin America.

All people rested and heard Mass on Sundays and could attend an evening vesper, by the instruction of Pope Paul III nearly three centuries earlier.[19] Additionally, around Christmas many enslaved and freed people could travel extensively without oversight.[20] The enslaved in Saint-Domingue endured harsher exploitation, but less ecclesiastical oversight, which provided a space for African cultural recreations. The more creolized Dominicans, whatever their spirituality, savvily extracted time and space from Iberian beliefs.[21]

The influence of some Dominicans of color who observed African diasporic beliefs was far more modest than that of their counterparts in Saint-Domingue.[22] Some practices parallel to emergent Vodou appeared throughout the revolutionary era among a minority in Santo Domingo. However, this does not seem to have been a primary catalyst for later cross-island cooperation.

Dominican elites also attacked self-purchase by the enslaved, sometimes called *coartación*, a practice scrutinized across the empire.[23] Owners, who often undermined this process, advocated prohibition.[24] Elites asserted that freed people availed themselves of arcane protections or lax laws like the "Incas of Peru."[25] They speculated that free people of color helped the enslaved raise money and accused the formerly enslaved of criminality and poverty, or of becoming "bad women" or vagrants.[26] Sánchez Valverde's widely circulated treatise repeated these concerns and promoted restrictive French limitations on self-purchase.[27] Per capita, Santo Domingo's free population of color was possibly larger than Saint-Domingue's, as self-purchase in the latter was infrequent.

Differences in the Spanish and French practices derived from the *Siete Partidas*, a thirteenth-century statutory code created by King Alfonso X of Castile. Though it posited enslavement as unnatural and opened paths to manumission, it was also the precedent for forms of Spanish royal patronage that managed coexistent slavery and Catholicism.[28] Against this standard, many elites endorsed the more restrictive French practices. Officers familiar with Saint-Domingue even submitted their favorite French laws for consideration.[29]

Planters also attacked the mobility of *jornaleros* (day laborers) and suggested that even free Black travelers in the countryside without passes should be jailed. They requested segregated free Black settlements governed with strict moral, political, and labor laws. They also suggested prohibiting planters from renting them land. Elites also sought to dissuade people of color from carrying weapons. Furthermore, to cut their own costs, planters planned to force the enslaved to cultivate their own food by producing plantains, potatoes, rice, maize, beans, millet, and other crops, as the French

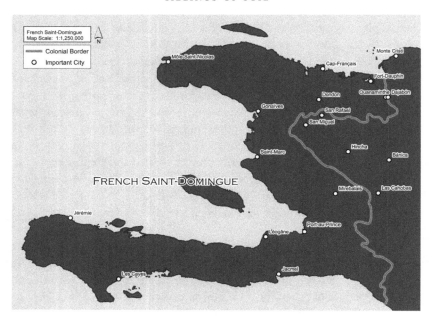

FIGURE I.2
Map of Colonial French Saint-Domingue.

did. Elites proposed scrutinizing illnesses among the enslaved and aiding slavecatchers in their pursuit of runaways. To enforce changes, planters also sought greater scrutiny in court over conduct by the enslaved, including allowing planters to co-judge cases in order to enforce subordination.[30]

Perhaps the most in-depth testimony came from the experienced officer Joaquín García, who later served as a pivotal governor. Born in 1731, García arrived in Santo Domingo from Puerto Rico in the late 1760s. To aid the "wise and pious decision" of crafting a "Código Dominicano" or "Código Americano," García relayed his experience of owning a "few domestic slaves that God has given me." He argued that planters knew best how to arrange the various "distinct classes of Blacks and their descendants" and recommended that, aside from the Code Noir, they consult the widely used *Traité sur le gouvernement des esclaves* (Treatise on the government of slaves) used in the French Caribbean. García prejudicially alleged that Dominicans of color persisted with "lethal idleness" and were driven by a "propensity to theft" and other momentary impulses. He alleged they had only the patrimony that "their ancestors brought from Guinea" and that they were "content . . . only because they are free." To stop runaways, who supposedly had support from freed people, and who were said to steal Spanish mules, horses, or cattle for resale to French buyers or coastal smugglers, García suggested that all slaveholders contribute annually to a fund to pay for patrols that would more robustly enforce slavery and find maroons. García's biases soon weighed heavily on his influential actions during the revolutionary era.[31] However, untethered from governmental and property relations and interspersed across the expanses of under-occupied Santo Domingo, Dominicans of color strained simplistic racial controls borrowed from Saint-Domingue.

Distilling these complaints, Sánchez Valverde's polemical treatise appeared almost simultaneously in Spain with a direct appeal to King Carlos III. It underscored lobbying efforts to pass the ambitious, newly drafted Código Negro of 1785. Though Dominican elites began restricting Dominicans of color, they failed to replicate Saint-Domingue's success. The crackdowns only primed Dominicans of color to welcome, and eventually contribute to, a rising Atlantic radicalism. Eventually, this development changed Santo Domingo more than restrictive race laws ever could.

CONFINING DOMINICANS OF COLOR

As the laws approved by the Audiencia de Santo Domingo in March 1785 lingered in imperial de jure limbo, and before the empire disseminated a diluted version to limited impact in 1789, Dominican momentum precipitated de facto attacks against the autonomy of Dominicans of color in travel, property, and upward mobility. These changes included harsh new ordinances that regulated the access of people of color to silk, lace, gold, swords, and education. Free Dominicans of color could face fines for simply verbally contradicting whites. Physically hitting a white person could yield a hundred lashes, two years in prison, and fetters. Enslaved people convicted of such a crime could suffer execution.[32]

Beyond coercion, officials endeavored to make all Dominicans of color self-censoring royal subjects through faith and service. In Santo Domingo, as across the Spanish Americas, officials relied upon free people of color to staff local militias and defend the colonies. Soldiers could accrue social prestige and pay for brave or loyal service. Foremost to encouraging compliance through cultural soft power, intensified religious initiatives attempted to supplant "superstitions" with faith and loyalty to Spain. The *cofradías* (confraternities), sanctioned Catholic religious groups that had once prominently represented distinct African ethnicities, and which had been spaces in which it was possible to re-create African belief and belonging, accordingly declined in importance in Santo Domingo.

Other efforts targeted visible dissenters against colonial order whom the oppressed might admire. Prominently, bureaucrats confronted the *negros ganadores* (Black earners) of San Lorenzo de los Mina near the capital and the famed Maniel maroons, who were sometimes defamed as *bárbaros* (barbarians) of an incorrigible African culture. Elites thought that assimilating them could stabilize the fringes of imperial control. Broadly, the relocation attempts mirrored the long-running Spanish practices of using centralization into missions, often called *reducciónes*, to expedite subjugation and acculturation.[33]

By the 1780s, the town of San Lorenzo de los Mina, which had formed in the 1670s when Spanish officials agreed to allow it as a sanctuary for formerly French-enslaved maroons, had several hundred residents. The "Mina" designation likely corresponded to Akan ethnicity on the Gold Coast of West Africa.[34] Exemplifying redoubled repression, in 1786 the Cabildo of Santo Domingo accused free Dominicans of color around the capital of neglecting their civic duties and forced San Lorenzo to absorb alleged thieves, late-night dancers and singers, and apostates.

This coerced, abrupt resettlement to San Lorenzo deliberately whitened nearby *barrios*. The policy tore farmers, vendors, and artisans from their livelihoods and heavily restricted their economic and social opportunities. A new priest at San Lorenzo, whom officials forced residents to pay, gave mandatory lessons in church doctrine to children and sermons to all. A new magistrate adjudicated their every action. Severe regulations governed their travel, use of horses, and livestock breeding and restricted their sales of goods to one central marketplace. If legally free San Lorenzo residents attempted to relocate, they could receive fifty lashes and be forced to wear shackles for six months. Third-time offenders could suffer two hundred lashes, six years in public works, and rental as plantation labor.

Dominican elites wrenched commercial viability and physical mobility from workers who had already experienced limited autonomy, adding to their rightful grievances. Enslaved wage earners, the jornaleros, also faced new restrictions. These mobile, skilled day laborers sometimes earned enough to purchase their own freedom. Their influence over others' aspirations attracted attention from officials, however, who threatened fines against those who failed to procure work licenses, did not report payments, or accepted pay above fixed rates. The officials encouraged owners to send

all the enslaved into fieldwork, and those who ventured from their owners' properties after evening prayers could receive dozens of lashes or be
pilloried.[35]

Subduing maroons also became paramount to elites' implementation
of new racial codes. Annually, the number of maroons arriving in Santo
Domingo from Saint-Domingue likely exceeded the number of African
captives directly imported into the colony. Dominican society featured
quite a heterogeneous mix of creole and African cultures. At most, the direct
trade from Africa was only around 2,000 captives in the entire eighteenth
century.[36] Runaways from Saint-Domingue regularly appeared in Santo
Domingo. For example, a *bozal* (an enslaved person who was unacclimated
to local culture and likely recently arrived from Africa) whose body bore
the marks of both ritual scarification and French branding walked into
Azua, seventy miles east of the Saint-Domingue border.[37] Many others may
have been "Congo," or "Nâgo" (that is, Yoruba, generally).[38] Dominican
maroons joined them in the interior, where maroon communities successfully defied colonial racial hierarchies.

The most visible, consistent fixture of Black autonomy on Hispaniola
before the revolution was Maniel, a formidable maroon community in
the mountains and dense forests of southwestern Santo Domingo. Indeed,
the name of this community defined the colloquial sobriquet for other
maroon communities—*manieles*.[39] Spanish lore about Maniel noted that the
Neiba mountains had been "inhabited by some [three hundred] entrenched
Blacks" for "over a hundred years," and that they were known for raiding
nearby plantations.[40] Lax Spanish policies toward such refugees from rival
empires worsened Spain's tenuous ties with France.[41]

This region, along the southern coast, called Baoruco, had harbored
anti-colonial defiance since the time of the sixteenth-century Taíno uprisings, such as the pivotal Enriquillo revolt. It was an ungovernable periphery
between the Spanish and French colonies nearly 125 miles west of the
capital. Maniel's residents exploited their location to draw metropolitan-
facing officials inward for several failed expeditions.[42] By removing themselves from slavery's modes of production, maroons destroyed the capital
valuations of their commodified bodies. Their raids, illicit trade with peasants and smugglers, and military victories all worked to deplete imperial
resources.[43]

Thus, unlike many other targets of the new race laws in Santo Domingo,
the residents of Maniel wielded negotiating power. Coinciding with the
curtailment of Black autonomy, in the mid-1780s the maroons pragmatically
chose to make peace and rejoin colonial society on their own terms. This

decision was partly due to lingering illnesses and food scarcity and partly due to fear of French recapture. The town sent three envoys—Santiago, a fifty-year-old Dominican maroon; a freeborn maroon named Philippe; and a bozal, LaFortune—to work on trading their fugitive autonomy for agricultural land and legally sanctioned freedom as Spanish subjects. Amid this détente, Juan Bobadilla, a creole priest in nearby Neiba, visited Maniel to build rapport, and a few dozen maroons reciprocated by agreeing to baptism.[44]

Santiago led 137 maroons, lower than rumored totals, and ultimately 133 maroons were listed in the treaty. Most had fled Saint-Domingue, though a few were Dominican.[45] Roughly half of the earlier African arrivals in Saint-Domingue were from Angola and the Kongo, so, unsurprisingly, many maroons from Maniel reflected these regions.[46] Names on the roster included "Pemba," possibly referring to the Mpemba region of the Kingdom of Kongo, along with "Masunga," "Macuba," and "Sesa," which broadly correspond to Bantu languages. Other names, such as "Quamina" and "Ybie," indicated possible Akan and Edo origins, respectively. Many maroons were born free and raised at Maniel.[47] The names on the roster represented African ethnic diversity.[48]

After lengthy delays, in 1785 Bobadilla mediated a final deal with the well-armed maroons, who received pardons and resettlement under supposedly "civilizing" Catholic tutelage. From the outset, though, some refused to acquiesce, remaining unsettled and welcoming new runaways. To the chagrin of officials, these two groups of Maniel maroons never ceased collaborating with one another.[49] Maroon submission was partly performative, as counterintuitive alignment with Spain bought temporary defense against more invasive legal and property claims. By demanding additional concessions and consorting with enemies, they savvily navigated cultural and material constraints to augment their quality of life. Their evasive strategies perplexed Spanish officials, who sought to make them new subjects through religious and royalist rituals, a scheme reflecting a pragmatic multivalence that later reappeared to thwart Spanish efforts to manage people of color elsewhere.[50]

As with the confinement of San Lorenzo, officials prioritized instructing the Maniel children in hopes of raising cooperative new subjects. So salient was conciliation with the maroons that King Carlos III personally authorized Spain's treaty with Maniel in 1787.[51] This familial strategy resounded in Spanish domains and echoed across rival empires.[52]

Remarkably, within a few years the maroons' leaders had met personally with the highest European officials on Hispaniola, a testament to their importance.[53] In this era, the assertive officer Joaquín García, who had testified about race codes, became governor, and the firebrand and activist priest Fernando Portillo became archbishop.[54] However, the Consejo de Indias accused the maroons of "capriciousness and absolute resistance," racist aspersions that obscured how their tactics rivaled those of European diplomats in extracting concessions.[55]

Some maroons who decided to cooperate resettled at Naranjo in 1790, suspending mistrust for temporary stability.[56] This new stage incarnated Spain's dream of ex-maroons supposedly purified by a Christian lifestyle and rescued from "the cruel bondage of heathenism."[57] The church constructed a hospital to treat the maroons' ailments, and the archbishop praised initial progress.[58] The residents received land, and eventually they served in administration and formed a militia, though Spanish administrators still worried that the maroons would eventually flee or become "useful instruments" of French power.[59] In Naranjo, near both the coast and Maniel, the residents lived in small *bohíos* (small, thatched homes) and would meet nightly with Bobadilla to learn about doctrine and the sacraments under a state surveilling its new ostensible subjects.[60]

By 1791, the piety of some maroons had assuaged officials who craved control.[61] García bitterly whined about many of the others, however, complaining of their "treachery, fickleness, and infidelity" and calling them a "body of outlaws" who "mock[ed]" the government and the laws. Some maroons, with their proximity to the coast, had illicitly traded with trespassing foreign smugglers. Although García said some maroons accepted the "gentility and fairness" of the Spanish, he postulated that most had manipulated their "candor and sincerity." "Perhaps nothing will ever accommodate them but their existence in libertinage," he said, adding that he feared "cruel offences" if the maroons returned to their "native character."[62] García's racist assumptions of the 1780s reappeared. Cleverly, one maroon leader, LaFortune, suggested that if they could only hear their pardons directly from the king of Spain, then they might become more cooperative.[63] Contrary to European protestations faulting their fickleness, they had, as much as possible, protected their own interests. Awaiting new opportunities, tactful Maniel maroons again ensnared imperial politics.[64]

The centrality of Maniel maroons to racial and territorial control portended Spanish plans during the epochal geopolitical turmoil that soon arose, as did Hispanic racist recursions when Black agency confounded their interests. After metropolitan bureaucrats considered new laws at length, the long-awaited 1789 Carolino Código Negro arrived from Spain, but with more protections for the enslaved than the statutes that had been crafted in Santo Domingo. Elites saw directives on food, clothing, and punishment as worsening the status quo. Few complied, and the code became ineffective and was forgotten.[65] Regardless, frictions in the 1780s clarified limits regarding civility, inclusion, and hierarchies. Constant scrutiny and pressure caused social tensions to simmer, and in ensuing years they came to a boil.

CONCLUSION

Elite Dominicans' nearly decade-long effort to emulate Saint-Domingue's profitable practices failed, and the attempts to revitalize slavery in Santo Domingo instead only succeeded in causing domestic racial strife to fester. Saint-Domingue soon erupted as a result of these very legal structures and social strictures. Soon, exiles and self-liberated revolutionaries tried to build much-needed alliances with Dominicans. They followed paths connecting the colonies that maroons, cattle traders, and families had created. Early, opportunistic Spanish responses to the Haitian Revolution eventually led them into unlikely common cause with enslaved insurgents who espoused Catholicism and royalism.[66] Later, in the turbulent 1790s, as France embraced emancipation and Spain lost Black allies, Dominicans of color embraced popular revolutionary-era demands as remedies to redress the heightened oppression of the 1780s and the legacies of colonialism that preceded it.

TWO

FOLLOWING A REVOLUTIONARY
FUSE, 1789–1791

In September 1791, troops in Santo Domingo watched self-liberated insurgents defeat French troops by day. By night, burning plantations illuminated their skies. Over the preceding month, in a massive liberatory uprising, tens of thousands of the enslaved across Nord in Saint-Domingue had overwhelmed French rule. By then, the dead and captured Black insurgents numbered roughly twenty-five thousand. This astonishing figure represented only a fraction of the rebels encircling Cap-Français. To the French, their bravery in gaining more humane lives mostly signified millions of lost livres in investments. The rebels, who were resisting their status as a form of legally commodified capital, eliminated the coveted wealth of real estate and crops in a world they had been forced to build.[1]

A garrison on the Dominican side of the border near Saltadero anxiously monitored the approach of eight heavily armed Black insurgents. Rather than overwhelming the vulnerable Dominicans, the insurgents explained that they would only burn French property and intercept white French residents, who were so frightened that "if only the Blacks would yell," they would flee their homes, "leaving them in desertion to the rebels." Surprisingly, considering their fight against France, these rebels had greeted the Dominicans with a shout of "Peace with Spain." Elsewhere, troops in Santo Domingo met "thirty-six insurgent Blacks close to the border saying in an elevated voice *God, and King*." The camaraderie and affability they offered was not isolated, and certainly not arbitrary.[2]

Only one month into what became the largest and most successful revolt by the enslaved in history, officials in Santo Domingo were motivated to keep peace along their weakly defended border. To do so, they bypassed racist assumptions to listen to Black rebels with cautiously optimistic incredulity. And, before the insurgents' creative destruction challenged Atlantic logics of slavery, race, empire, citizenship, and Enlightenment universalism, their immediate survival against a powerful French state was precarious. Insurgents from Saint-Domingue, and residents and officials in Santo Domingo, existentially benefited from rapport.

Understanding how self-liberated Black rebels in Saint-Domingue and white officials in Santo Domingo arrived at this juncture requires stepping back chronologically. To fully comprehend their temporary need for each other, it is imperative to recognize that this was only the most recent instance of interchange in a seemingly unstoppable history of interdependence that had lasted for generations and that had involved people from many walks of life, families, maroons, and merchants, traveling well-worn paths across the island. After the start of the French Revolution in 1789, cross-border entanglements intensified in 1790 and 1791, connecting the island with a new revolutionary fuse. Black insurgents in need of support followed these ties into Santo Domingo by late 1791.

Elites in Santo Domingo blamed old French plantocratic brutality and new French radicalism for the growing instability in Saint-Domingue after 1789. Portents of irrevocable change for all of Hispaniola had increased. Already in 1790, surges in political strife had caused Spanish officials to predict that "you can consider [Saint-Domingue] lost." They blamed the instability of the French, who they said regularly "profaned the Catholic religion and offended our creator." They feared that waves of exiles and evacuees would infect Dominicans with similar dissenting attitudes.[3]

The French colony had already spiraled into unrest by 1790. For example, ten months before the insurrection by the enslaved, Vincent Ogé, a wealthy *mulâtre* planter from Nord, had demanded political rights for his caste of propertied free people of color. In November 1790, after spending time in revolutionary Paris, he led failed armed protests in Saint-Domingue. Thereafter, he and his numerous followers fled into Santo Domingo, exposing Dominicans to political and social critiques. By extraditing Ogé the Spanish intended to dissipate dissent and assuage French tensions, but this move proved a poor deterrent to Dominican involvement in Saint-Domingue's civil strife.[4]

Rather ironically, only days after Governor Philibert-François Rouxel de Blanchelande of Saint-Domingue approved the execution of Vincent Ogé, he, too, took refuge in Santo Domingo.[5] In March 1791, six months before the major social revolution began, Blanchelande begged to be permitted to hide in the Dominican border town of Las Cahobas. As Governor Joaquín García of Santo Domingo learned, French republicans had "ignited a new fire" in Port-au-Prince when a white mob forced Blanchelande to abandon a government building in a disheveled panic. He arrived without even a change of clothes, along with some family members and aides.[6]

Blanchelande said that "malicious" white radicals had enticed newly arrived French troops to join in with spontaneous anti-royalist discord, creating "deplorable circumstances" that required Spanish support to guard against "revolutions" that had "cut off the head of Monsieur Mauduit."[7] Colonel Thomas-Antoine de Mauduit du Plessis had bought Blanchelande time to escape by confronting the crowd. After decapitating Mauduit, white radicals, who had commandeered churches for raucous political meetings, paraded his body to a priest, whom they forced to perform a Te Deum blessing.[8] Such sacrilege shocked elite Dominicans, yet, despite fearing dissent, they myopically viewed strife in Saint-Domingue as a geopolitical opening. García withheld resources, partly in self-preservation, commencing a pattern of opportunistic neglect.[9]

These three new, tumultuous connections in 1790 and 1791—to white radical ideology, *gens de couleur* demands, and antislavery insurrection— presaged three revolutionary decades shared by Dominicans and Haitians. Before the major revolts of August 1791 began, the patterns of officials in Santo Domingo rebuffing white French officials and gens de couleur partisans were set. Their extraditions of gens de couleur activists to near certain death and their reluctance to support royalist French politicians more actively furthered the ongoing fracturing of the ruling classes in Saint-Domingue that had managed the exploitative status quo.

Dominican non-intervention against early French Revolution influences, and later, liaisons between insurgents, formed two of the many waves to crash upon Saint-Domingue. These waves eventually became a riptide that submerged the French ruling class. Elites in 1791 Santo Domingo did not simply retreat into royalism and faith as they anxiously watched the French elites drown in the very currents they had created.[10] Although Saint-Domingue became the exemplar of greed gone awry, those in Santo Domingo who had attempted to emulate French profit-making strategies during the 1780s also saw unrest as a new opportunity that might enable them to reroute neighboring prosperity into Spanish domains. They gradually adjusted their stance to seek temporary strategic benefits in territory squandered a century before.

In this context, interfacing with Black insurgents who claimed monarchism and faith made cultural and geopolitical sense to officials in Santo Domingo. Amid growing French anticlericalism and rights discourses from 1789 to 1791, insurgents espousing royalism and religiosity seemed like a gift of divine providence. By the end of 1791, the timing was right to consider previously unthinkable alliances. With time, officials' decisions that seemed appropriately defensive and opportunistic in 1791 correlated to even greater circulation of unrest into Dominican society.

FRENCH REVOLUTION, HISPANIOLA FALLOUT

In 1789, sparks of political ferment from the French Revolution lit a fuse leading to explosive inequities and demographics in Saint-Domingue. There, debates soon abounded over popular sovereignty and the Declaration of the Rights of Man and of the Citizen, the new French universalist decree. Exacerbating Caribbean racial tensions, in France abolitionists in the Société des Amis des Noirs (Society of the Friends of the Blacks) and the prominent priest Henri Grégoire, known as Abbé Grégoire, advocated ending the slave trade and extending citizenship rights to gens de couleur. Following the protests of working-class white sans-culottes across France, and the establishment of the French National Assembly in 1789, white residents of Saint-Domingue elected their own new assemblies, where local elites quibbled bitterly over rights and representation in Paris.

By 1790, the new assemblies and the militias had undermined the power of Governor Blanchelande, a royalist appointee. For example, the audacious Colonial Assembly of Saint-Marc drafted a constitution that rebuffed metropolitan oversight and entertained independence. The pompons rouges (radicals known by their red tassels or cockades) had already pushed Blanchelande into an uneasy dependence upon conservative planters in Nord. In Port-au-Prince, petit blancs (little whites) confronted Blanchelande with revolutionary demands echoing those of the metropolitan sans-culottes in France. Politics and ideological debates among free people, an extreme minority in Saint-Domingue, fractured the ruling class. However, French liberté, égalité, and fraternité still mostly ignored racism.[11] By the end of 1790, racial tensions had begun to preoccupy key towns near the Dominican border, such as Dondon, Ouanaminthe, Fort Dauphin, and Grande-Rivière.[12] Careening turmoil shocked elite observers in Santo Domingo and reaffirmed their sense of moral superiority over their French neighbors.

The gens de couleur formed influential militias.[13] When Ogé, an affluent planter of color, a slaveholder, and a merchant, returned to Saint-Domingue from Paris in October 1790, he carried citizenship demands rooted in the French Revolution that melded with the ongoing petitions from his acquaintances in his home region. However, Ogé envisioned political inclusion only for gens de couleur, not a social revolution. The second-class status of the gens de couleur had worsened since the 1770s, when reclassification as *affranchis* (a term for freed people) had diminished their status and ability to engage in civic life. Ogé and hundreds of other gens de couleur demanded equal rights and representation while ignoring the thousands of people without rights whom they enslaved. The wealth and privilege they derived from their economic status obscured more severe injustices.

Ogé collaborated with Jean-Baptiste Chavanne, an ambitious free man of color from a coffee-planting family. The two of them plotted at Ogé's properties near Dondon, a mountainous region south of Cap-Français and near the Dominican border. Unlike Ogé, Chavanne had actual military experience. Alongside the later notables Henry Christophe, Jean-Baptiste Villate, Louis-Jacques Bauvais, and André Rigaud, Chavanne had fought with French forces in Savannah, Georgia, during the United States' War for Independence. He had participated in illicit gens de couleur conventions in early 1790, and after French persecution temporarily sheltered in Santo Domingo.

In November 1790, Ogé and Chavanne sent provocative letters to French officials asserting their citizenship rights. Meanwhile, they had amassed roughly three hundred supporters, mostly gens de couleur, to give weight to their claims. After French forces crushed their uprising, Chavanne, Ogé, and many of their supporters fled into Santo Domingo, including some who attempted to hide with Maniel maroons. Officials in Santo Domingo scrambled to quarantine the revolutionary contagion from an unprepared Dominican society with an even higher percentage of free people of color.[14]

Ogé and Chavanne spent months imprisoned in Santo Domingo pleading to avoid extradition. To French satisfaction, after extensive debate Spanish officials extradited Ogé, Chavanne, and their associates to Saint-Domingue.[15] Ogé and Chavanne both unsuccessfully used religious rhetoric to request reprieves from King Carlos IV. Spanish officials feared Ogé's claims that gens de couleur were "men, citizens, and French" who once enjoyed treatment like their white neighbors. To them, he embodied the incendiary words on his self-portrait, "Vivit, et Ardet" (He lives, and he burns), a firebrand precedent they feared.[16] News arrived in Santo Domingo that just before Ogé's scheduled execution, in February 1791, armed sympathizers came in his support. However, they failed to ambush the prison guards, leaving the prisoners to face gruesome forms of public execution designed as deterrence for anyone considering following their example.[17] As "true anarchy" engulfed Saint-Domingue, officials in Santo Domingo chose caution and neutrality to keep the "sparks of that volcano" away from Dominicans.[18] They hoped Santo Domingo would be a firewall to forestall wider Caribbean revolutionary conflagrations.

FRACTURED FRENCH ELITES

To avoid the "confused and bellicose" conditions of Saint-Domingue, for the time being officials tried to "conserve the best harmony with the French." Nevertheless, Dominicans regularly encountered rumors of revolution from docking ships or cross-island travelers.[19] Also, the churning press in Saint-Domingue circulated fractious texts to Dominicans, repeating gossip about war, Parisian decrees, speculation of independence, an effort to seek British support, and debates over "incontestable rights" and slaveholders' property claims.

Governor Blanchelande desperately called for domestic stability and patriotism in January 1791. To disperse radical white mobs, he needed military escorts around the colony, which Colonel Mauduit offered to provide. He even sent a delegation to Santo Domingo requesting "civic virtue" and cooperative support from Dominicans and from "Joachim de Guarcia [sic]," the governor, whose name he did not bother to spell correctly but whose aid he expected.[20]

As social maladies continued to afflict Saint-Domingue, including brazen violence and fissures in white rule, Catholicism seemed to present an appealing, familiar cultural antiseptic for officials seeking to cleanse the Dominican body politic from the spread of "false liberty."[21] Their French counterparts, most of them still Bourbon royalists, faced inundation.[22] As both Spain and Santo Domingo shared land crossings with French domains, the Consejo de Indias said that French "anarchy" had "beheaded their government at our borders." French revolutionary churn incited "total division and [was] heading for ruin," owing to "differences between whites, Blacks, mulâtres, slaves, and freed."[23]

Heightening tensions, in February 1791 two French ships docked in Port-au-Prince with battalions from Normandy and Artois, along with a notorious radical, Jean-Baptiste de Caradeux, whom Colonel Mauduit had expelled months before. Caradeux claimed to have orders from the National Assembly and said that thousands of more troops were en route. The three thousand soldiers who had arrived to keep peace for Blanchelande ignored their officers and instead joined the local revolutionaries. Refusing to support Blanchelande, they supported Caradeux's militia, the dissident assemblies, and the demands of the petit blancs. Emboldened, Caradeux called for a political rally in the church on 4 March 1791. Mauduit, wearing a white royalist cockade, confronted Caradeux, who demanded that the colonel remove his hat. Mauduit retorted that he had "sworn to that emblem" and that "nobody would take off the cockade without his head." Thus, a Caradeux follower "removed both with a strike of a sword."

White radicals then dragged Mauduit's body through the streets, following his head atop a pike. After the assassination, Caradeux wrote to towns across Ouest claiming command and freeing prisoners, while Blanchelande fled to Santo Domingo.[24] Spanish troops helped the governor, his son, his nephew, and others in his fleeing group wash their clothes, as they had brought no extra sets. Meanwhile, Caradeux's men theatrically paraded Mauduit's head to the church and forced the priest to perform a Te Deum blessing over their actions. Spanish officials doubted Caradeux's claims of having orders from the National Assembly, but he flew an unknown white flag with purple and black stripes, and García took this as a sign that Caradeux would declare Saint-Domingue independent.

From this chaos, officials in Santo Domingo deduced that Saint-Domingue would soon be lost in a conflict that might engulf the whole island.[25] White-on-white violence signaled republican ascendance alongside metropolitan shifts. Crucially, the ruling class fractured in Saint-Domingue, increasing the odds that future uprisings by the enslaved could find success. Checks against revolution were eroding.[26]

A momentary calm befell Saint-Domingue in June 1791 as the French National Assembly sent new commissioners to pacify the colony. Nevertheless, their free press still circulated papers in the Dominican public sphere disseminating ideas judged to be "diabolical and insulting" to Spanish imperial values. These publications included eloquent appeals to "*Glory*" and "*French Liberty*" that might inspire mobilization.[27] The lull proved fleeting. In July 1791, conflict erupted anew in Saint-Domingue over a May decree from the National Assembly that granted mulâtre men of free fathers citizenship and admission to assemblies.[28] One of the "noisy voices" offended by the notion of égalité suggested that "planters would take arms" against people of color. Some opponents even hanged the Abbé Grégoire, the well-known French abolitionist—who they supposed had influenced this decree of equality—in effigy. García predicted that the law would "ignite a war among the troops[,] . . . the white locals, and the free people of color."[29]

To prepare for war, ill-defended Santo Domingo welcomed the Cantabria regiment and funding from the viceroy of New Spain (Mexico).[30] Heavy dependence upon wealthier Spanish colonies to cover what eventually became exorbitant expenses in Santo Domingo began to develop. This cycle angered elites in neighboring colonies, who saw no benefit to the military endeavors they funded, a leading indicator of an eroding Spanish Empire.[31]

Newspapers reported the secret flight of King Louis XVI from his court in Paris, his failed attempt to disguise himself as a butler, and his detention at Varennes, where a postmaster had recognized him. In August 1791, García was also disturbed to learn that a British ship had appeared at Cap-Français from Jamaica with an offer of troops and warships to bolster French royalists against the National Assembly and decree. Expectations of civil war in Saint-Domingue soared.

The sudden preposterousness of French affairs flummoxed officials in Santo Domingo who might have mocked their rival's demise had the potential consequences been less dire.[32] While twenty-five British ships anchored nearby, officials in Santo Domingo debated how to pursue their own economic and political interests. As Dominicans pondered the past two tumultuous years, a massive revolt by the enslaved in Saint-Domingue that would change their world was only days old.[33]

"A MOUNTAIN OF ASHES"

On 22 August 1791, the enslaved who cultivated the wealth that allowed a French leisure class to debate rights chose to destroy this world that they had been forced to build. Across the Plaine-du-Nord, they set the most valuable sugar acreage ablaze, and the plantations burned as funeral pyres to the greed of the white managers and owners whose bodies the flames often consumed. Planned by Dutty Boukman and other enslaved coconspirators, one covert meeting in the days preceding their revolt purportedly featured a binding ritual of nascent Vodou that blended a Kongolese *Petro* tradition with Aja-Fon *Rada* blood oaths. Participants avowed amelioration for their brutal conditions and retribution against their exploiters. Boukman supposedly prophesied that three trusted peers, Jean-François, Georges Biassou, and Jeannot Bullet, would be the generals to lead the revolution. This ceremony, called Bois-Caïman for the "alligator wood" in which it reputedly occurred, has become an origin story for the Haitian Revolution. Whatever meeting transpired, even during the insurgents' lives French myths projected anti-Christian and even diabolical dimensions upon their motivations.[34]

Elites blamed the supposedly "mistaken philanthropy" rising in France for the revolt, but that critique missed the important fact that Boukman and the other rebels had consciously organized to change their world. Their interior culture and lives had survived the severest insults and harshest physical pains. Leaving his past as the Clément plantation's coachman, Boukman gained legendary status as the revolt spread for myriad personal reasons that influenced the antislavery, anti-French whole. Together the rebels held owners to justice and burned "canes and buildings of upwards of two hundred sugar and coffee plantations."[35]

Ineptitude abounded among the colonists, including the underestimation of Black talent. An inability to fully acknowledge Black agency suffused early reports, including a rumor from the border that "130 men from Europe" had "put the Blacks in movement," a convenient critique of white French radicalism.[36] Also, after royalist commander Marquis de Rouvray's French forces near Rocou defeated 800 insurgents, they claimed that "one of the Blacks after examined and washed was found to be white."[37] One Black captive even stated that Monsieur Vincent, apparently a reputable local, was involved in the uprising. French commanders doubted this, and the prisoner may have simply been trying to confuse or perplex fractured elites.[38] A free Black prisoner in Cap-Français repeated that, within the territory, some six hundred whites were part of the conspiracy.[39] More stories circulated about a white man in a blue uniform leading rebels.[40] Rouvray even claimed that "a multitude of whites" had "put our slaves to revolt by the principle of the Declaration of the Rights of Man." They "deserved hanging," he added. As of September, the insurgents had not asserted the Declaration as their motivation.[41]

Miscalculations of the insurgents' bravery and ingenuity did nothing to stop the eastward spread of the revolt toward the Dominican border. Within days of the opening revolts, and within miles of Santo Domingo at Dondon, Spanish officials monitored casualties, arsons, and plantation insurrections nearby. The rebels obliterated symbols of French oppression, including planters and towns, while impressively defeating French troops with mostly swords and makeshift weapons. They spared many women and priests, using the latter for spiritual support, correspondence, translation, or prisoner exchanges. Rather than considering the exploitative cruelties that motivated the resistance, Hispaniola elites corresponded about the idea that the Black insurgents had rebelled because of a rumor that the French National Assembly had abolished slavery. Perhaps rumors of a suppressed royal emancipation decree had also circulated, rekindling royalist nostalgia about monarchs protecting their subjects. Other reports alleged, errone-ously, that gens de couleur were stoking the rebellion.[42]

Dominicans were awash with news of the alleged "depraved intention" of the Black rebels in Nord and pondered their own stability, given the near inescapability of their own involvement. Stories about Petit-Anse and Limbé paled in comparison to those of the residents of Ouanaminthe—a town forty miles east of the initial revolts, on the Saint-Domingue side of a key river crossing to the Dominican border town of Dajabón—who were fleeing into Santo Domingo by the dozens.[43]

Immediately after the major revolts began, Spanish officers on the border frantically transmitted intelligence to García about the total war ringing Cap-Français. For the next decade and beyond, nearly every vying faction in Saint-Domingue would seek refuge, resources, and support from poten-tial partners in Santo Domingo. Avenues for mutually beneficial coopera-tion with Black rebels eventually opened up, temporarily expanding Span-ish power while irreversibly exacerbating Dominican social strife.[44]

Dominicans consumed many more panicked reports about the insur-gents before this convergence took place. As the revolution annihilated Saint-Domingue, Governor Blanchelande and Rouvray informed border-ing Dajabón of French military failures and begged for Dominican assis-tance as imperial allies. To save resources, Spanish officials prevaricated.[45] In the ensuing weeks, the Assembly of Saint-Domingue also futilely requested Spanish assistance. The important port Fort Dauphin witnessed significant militant activity as combat steadily approached the Dominican border. By the end of September, one hundred thousand insurgents had made Nord "a mountain of ashes."[46]

White evacuees streaming into Santo Domingo emphasized to officials that an expanding social revolution was well underway. New uprisings rocked the previously quiet Cul-de-Sac region of Ouest, over one hun-dred miles south of the initial revolts. There, gens de couleur partisans, enraged at their exclusion from rights, armed themselves and the enslaved before routing French forces. Enslaved people in the Cul-de-Sac were far more involved than those in Nord with mulâtre and white political com-petitions. Some white French residents proposed peace with the gens de couleur to reunify the ruling class. More importantly, the enslaved in Ouest retained their weapons, making this idea tenuous and a general insurrection possible.[47]

At the prospect of a second general uprising, more evacuees followed kin and commercial networks eastward, introducing more Dominicans to revolutionary strife. For example, the informant, a Monsieur Coustard, found shelter with Gregorio Recio, a Dominican resident who had married a "natural daughter" of Coustard's uncle (perhaps a woman of color). While there, Coustard collected daily updates for Spanish officials on developments in the Cul-de-Sac, often within hours of events transpiring. A mantra that French royalist evacuees repeated to attentive Dominicans blamed French revolutionary politics. A loss of the "principles of their parents, their customs, and their religion" had supposedly preceded Saint-Domingue running "inevitably . . . to its total ruin." This analysis reduced two social revolutions to threats against family and faith.[48]

"In two years' time Spain will have no more colonies," said the French commander Marquis de Rouvray. His appeal for Spanish support recognized that "this is a disorder for the world." He also played upon white and royalist solidarity, saying that "under the eyes of Europe" officials in Santo Domingo were obligated to unite against Black insubordination.[49] Rouvray requested permission for his own family to hide in Dominican territory.[50] The insurgents had already destroyed border towns "with torch in hand," he claimed, leaving the French to beg for aid "in the name of the House of Bourbon" to also prevent the revolts from spreading to enslaved Dominicans.[51] In desperation, Rouvray assailed Spanish officers' honor for idly watching Saint-Domingue burn and warned that the enslaved were wielding a "great conspiracy that threatens the whole globe with total subversion." Even appeals to protect a shared "Roman Religion" failed to persuade the Spanish officials to abandon their commitment to self-preservation and their concerns about leaving Dominican territory undefended.[52]

Counterproductively, when the beleaguered French troops, who had been incapable of defeating the insurgents or dissuading the revolts, discovered caches of purified sugar and French clothing in the living quarters of the enslaved at the Paruese plantation near Limonade, they massacred two hundred Black men and women, supposedly to set an example against theft and subversion. When a handful of insurgents surrendered and requested mercy, they were disarmed, taken to Rouvray, and likely executed.[53] Recalcitrant French repression, however, only redoubled revolutionary resolve.

The "horrors that . . . fermented" Saint-Domingue eventually permeated the French stronghold of Cap-Français.[54] From the earliest weeks of the insurrection, the insurgent army relentlessly pressed the city edge. When Boukman, Biassou, and Jeannot approached, they were said to have enjoyed support from a dissident nun of some African descent named Améthyste, who supposedly practiced Vodou at night, away from Catholic control. Her convent on Cap-Français's outskirts, which had long accepted women of color, supposedly housed other Vodouizan who sympathized with the insurgents.[55] The insurgents captured a French commander, decapitated him, and placed his head on a pike at the same place where Vincent Ogé's head had been displayed outside the city. This homage signified the conscious reversal of French repression.

To preempt swelling sympathies among the enslaved in Cap-Français, owners forced many onto ships in the harbor.[56] One prisoner confessed that a certain Black resident in Cap-Français had relayed information about the revolts to people of color in the city and provided updates on French actions toward the insurgents. French officials immediately decapitated him.[57] Furthermore, an enslaved baker in the city made two fresh batches of bread. They were presumably intended for French customers, but from nonverbal cues, the bakery owner became suspicious. He pulled a pistol to force the enslaved baker to eat a loaf, which made him nauseated. He fell at the proprietor's feet, victim of the very poison he had intended for others.[58]

Insurgents attempted to burn Cap-Français in late September to expel the French. Merchants shuttered their shops and protected their goods. Families barricaded their doors. French soldiers roamed the streets with loaded guns, and on the rue Espagnole encountered a mulâtre recently in from the countryside. When he understandably tensed under interrogation, a French officer drew his sword and killed him. This was not an isolated incident. As French suspicions of all people of color near the revolts increased, so did summary executions.[59] Brazen retributive violence only deepened the widening racial chasm.

DECISIVE DISENGAGEMENT

Eventually, elites in Santo Domingo accepted that the revolts were profoundly distinct from the political unrest of recent years. Predicting outcomes was more daunting. Officials in Santo Domingo, aware of their own fragility and French failures, sustained decisive disengagement.

In mid-September, Saint-Domingue's General Assembly pleaded for help from a distracted French National Assembly, reporting that about 100,000 rebels had secured most of the mountains and burned hundreds of plantations.[60] In desperation, Blanchelande sent new falsehoods into Santo Domingo. Realizing that Spanish officials were withholding support because of French failures, he claimed that the "white race, the class of the people of color, and the free Blacks are reunited," and said he needed aid to stop "60,000 souls from being slaughtered" and to suppress the "400–

48

500,000 enemies within" who might overrun Santo Domingo.[61] Emissaries from Saint-Domingue's assemblies also begged for cooperation.[62] Spanish officials, who knew that the esteemed French forces were perishing en masse, again refused to expend resources.

Stories of intimately interpersonal violence seeded new paranoias about the reach of racial strife and revolution among elites in Santo Domingo. Furthermore, García factually rebutted Blanchelande's depictions of unity and deduced that French factions were unstable allies incapable of dispersing revolts.[63] Instead, García halted most Dominican exports to stockpile resources. Given the inured factionalism and disorder across Saint-Domingue, he increasingly scrutinized French evacuees entering Santo Domingo. The "bordering towns of Ouanaminthe and Dondon" were restricted to sending children, women, the ill, and the elderly. In Ouanaminthe that September, French authorities hanged one free mulâtre and two enslaved people from the Pitober plantation for alleged sedition. When the unrest there dissipated, officials sent the evacuees home to uncertain fates. Isolation, to stop "infection" among Dominicans, typified early responses to revolts that could spread into Santo Domingo.[64]

Without Spanish support for the French elites, combat accelerated, including directly adjacent to the Dominican border. There were perhaps 15,000 rebels near Fort Dauphin and the border who were affiliated with Jean-François and Georges Biassou.[65] Their ascendant leadership gradually galvanized fragmented insurgent groups. Although similar personal experiences motivated the insurgents, their adherence to different African ethnic groups or local personalities initially superseded collective action. Those in "fermentation" across Saint-Domingue had grown up within various cosmologies, had re-created African cultures, and had endured painful experiences that influenced their worldviews more than the European rights discourses emanating from the unstable French state that enslaved them.

Their demands became clearer as the talented generals Jean-François, Georges Biassou, and Jeannot consolidated an army over the course of several months.[66] Among their coalescing officers was Pablo Alí. African born, just over thirty years old, and likely raised a Muslim, Alí had adopted the separate Abrahamanic tradition of Christianity under slavery in Saint-Domingue. He grew up in Grande-Rivière, also the hometown of Jean-Jacques Dessalines and Jean-Baptiste Chavanne, only miles from what was then the border with Santo Domingo at San Rafael. This area witnessed some of the most intense early fighting of the revolution. Nearby Dondon became the stronghold of Biassou, under whom Alí served. He may have even known of the Bois-Caïman meeting. Though some of his peers garnered more fame, Alí outlasted them all. After surviving various hardships, Alí had defined himself in adulthood by tact and bravery, and he made an uncanny appearance in major events over the next decades.[67] Alí and his colleagues, who aligned with each other based on their common interests across Hispaniola, also opened a new era of Dominican history.

As they had yet to interact with the insurgents, officials in Santo Domingo were poorly positioned to comprehend revolutionary motives. Only gradually did they realize that the rebels were not interested in simply replicating French political squabbles. Alongside causal factors such as brutality and limited evangelization, they contextually faulted "the seditious in Paris" and their acolytes, who they believed had seduced the enslaved "with the philanthropic doctrine, of liberty of man, assuring them that all would enjoy it since slavery was contrary to the rights of man." Thus the French revolutionaries had supposedly "deceived these rude and innocent wretches with [a] flattering hope." The French revolutionaries had transgressed religious norms, and rights discourses certainly had fractured Saint-Domingue's ruling class.[68]

More complexly, combinations of opportunity and cultural continuity aided the insurgents, who themselves later cited French cruelties as a salient motive, horrors that predated 1789.[69] With time and exposure to the insurgents, Dominican observers honed an explanatory framework imbued with rhetoric about inevitable destruction due to divine providence for the impious, hedonistic French, a righteous leveling of ill-gotten wealth for an increasingly apostate nation.[70] Blaming France also left space for the insurgents to justify themselves.

CAUTIOUS CONTACT

Amid self-preservation and some schadenfreude, Dominicans encountered a new shock: Black insurgents who decimated Saint-Domingue yet amicably approached their border with peaceful intentions, contradicting French predictions that they would overrun Santo Domingo. Tentative, informal meetings between Spanish troops, which had been sent to prevent incursions, and ascendant Black leaders, particularly Jean-François and Georges Biassou, eventually yielded mutually beneficial relationships.[71] More so than the historiography represents, ties were early, substantial, and pivotal.

Personal conversations between insurgent and Spanish generals began within the first month of the revolution and quickly expanded. Jeannot had captured territory near Dondon in September, providing insurgents direct access to Santo Domingo. Following contact with General Joaquín Cabrera, a leader at Dondon sent a letter to the nearby border town of San Rafael. In this remarkable overture, an "Ethiopian General" promised cooperation on important shared interests with the king of Spain.

"After a lengthy reasoning of fine . . . political expressions in favor of the Spanish nation," the Black general offered "sugar . . . asking in recompense powder and balls to continue the war made in the name of God and of his King against the [French], rebels to both majesties," said Cabrera. "After . . . these relations, so distant from that which I had conceived," Cabrera politely declined, instead expressing "gratitude for his reverent offers."[72] The Black officer departed in his "blue [uniform], adorned with a cross," with an "entourage adorned with epaulettes." They numbered "about 200 men of his color, and some *mulatos*, all on horse, well-armed with shotguns, pistols, and swords." Cabrera sensed no hostility, and rather perceived "in these people of color much pride, much disposition to combat against the [French]."

This insurgent general assiduously impressed his counterparts in Santo Domingo with compatible politics and religion, discipline and organization, and anti-French, not broadly anti-white, sentiments. The Spanish officers' trepidations diminished. The precision and tact of the insurgents, who had ambushed and captured lax French officers as the latter casually sipped their coffee, thoroughly impressed them.[73] These initial interactions incrementally led to trust, trade, and military and political ties between the insurgents and the Spanish officers that covertly undermined their mutual adversary—France.

The insurgent general that Cabrera met may have been Georges Biassou. Clearly, this interaction reduced the Spanish officials' fears, influenced their decision to withhold aid from the French, and marked the beginning of a cautious collaboration, which eventually caused officials to speculate about reclaiming territory ceded in 1697. In a context of French rights discourses, irreligion, gens de couleur empowerment, and publications insulting Spanish norms, the Black insurgents unexpectedly and uniquely affirmed cultural conceits and social mores that many Dominicans felt were under threat.[74]

Among this network of insurgent officers who proposed strategic connections with Santo Domingo were individuals who had known each other personally or by reputation for many years before the revolution. Revolutionary leaders emerged from the outlying regions of the Plaine-du-Nord, near Cap-Français, where the revolts began. Many of the formerly enslaved generals who rose to prominence had worked in positions requiring more geographic mobility across plantations. Dutty Boukman, Jeannot, Toussaint Bréda (later Louverture), and Jean-François had all been coachmen. Prisoners confessed that a network of coachmen had led the revolt. Jean-François and his partner, Charlotte, frequently fled the Papillon plantation, and likely knew other regular resisters. Provable or probable ties long existed among Biassou, Toussaint, Toussaint's adopted nephew Moïse, Jean-Jacques Dessalines, Charles Belair, and Henry Christophe.

Though Saint-Domingue's Catholic cultural predominance lagged behind that of Santo Domingo, some among the enslaved practiced Catholicism, and the Black leadership network notably arose from a small area where Capuchin priests, known for their relative racial inclusion, held significant influence. In part, local priests influenced the leaders' disproportionately Catholic public professions and cultural politics, as poignantly enunciated by Jean-François, Biassou, and Toussaint. Such faith professions did not automatically exclude African diasporic beliefs, however, which proliferated among the insurgents' ranks. Indeed, there had been surges of recent arrivals from north of the Congo Basin, where Catholic mission activity had been less prominent than in the more southerly Kongo or Angolan regions of West Central Africa, the main source of earlier arrivals. In any case, an important portion of insurgents engaged their new Iberian interlocutors by drawing from deep Afro-Catholic wells of knowledge, and this was possible in part because so many of them were the descendants of people who had experienced Portuguese and other Catholic evangelical contact. African diasporic specificities have proven crucial to understanding the Haitian Revolution beyond often essentialist imperial records. These religious aspects, along with African-derived monarchism, help to explain how many insurgents saw themselves and chose to approach the Spanish crown.[75]

Together these factors shed light on how, amid a significant degree of African ethnic diversity, the insurgent leadership formed a network around long-standing reputations and trust. At least publicly, they shared Catholic or Afro-Catholic vernaculars for suffering and ambition among themselves and many of their troops. This belief and sense of belonging appeared disproportionately in their cultural politics during the Haitian Revolution. Insurgents created trust with Spain through this commonality. Whatever their interior spirituality was, belief offered them a network-building social practice at the convergence of utility, sincerity, and partisanship. Beyond rhetoric, belief thus offers a window into power relations, cultural politics, and group cohesion. However, scholarship yet reveals little about how the insurgents connected with Spanish subjects through later shared rituals, such as prayer and marriage, and less about the long legacies this left in Dominican society.

Through this worldview the insurgents approached the time-consuming and improbable task of cultivating favor in Santo Domingo to overcome their resource scarcities. A simmering tension revolved around Spanish assistance for white French royalist evacuees, including many who asserted ownership of the insurgents.[76] Nevertheless, covert cooperation between the insurgents and officials in Santo Domingo gradually developed over the next two years.

Insurgent leaders made their plight intelligible to officials in Santo Domingo by, for example, explaining French brutality and prevention of access to Christianity. When dealing with Spanish subjects, Jean-François and Biassou regularly occupied this reductionist category and flattened the many internal ethnic and spiritual distinctions among their ranks. The insurgents thus positioned themselves to receive the blessings of guns and money from Spain to become frontline proxies for the Christian deity in a holy war against the increasingly sacrilegious French. However, their presentations inadvertently legitimated potentially burdensome narratives of racial redemption through religiosity, a trope that would become more corrosive in ensuing years.

CREATING CONFIDENCE

In the days surrounding the Black general's initial conversations with officials in Santo Domingo, rebels advanced to the Dominican border near the Jatiel summit. There, an insurgent, "with his machete, spear, and holster with pistols," realized that he was about to enter Santo Domingo and pre-emptively explained to nearby Spanish guards that he and the others had no quarrel with Spain. Trying to allay the tensions, he implied that he did not want to kill all white people, only all the French.

Insurgents sometimes provoked the French with taunts of "Long live Liberty," flaunting their self-liberation while deriding the French discourse on freedom that was en vogue. As the rebels expanded their territory, Saint-Domingue's roads became impassable because of the large number of French women and children fleeing for Santo Domingo, particularly at San Miguel and Hincha. Soon, fighting erupted adjacent to the Dominican town of San Rafael. Residents there suspected that the rebels were launching attacks from Dominican territory and using it as a base from which to capture horses and weapons.

To allay Dominican fears, the insurgents further explained that they only hoped to burn select French properties, as they did with the nearby Flaman plantation. They claimed to want only friendship with Dominicans, as their general had ordered. Despite their revolutionary incineration of Saint-Domingue's brutal society and their reputation for supposedly celebrating "well provisioned with bottles," they did keep their promise to protect Dominicans.[77]

Furthermore, elsewhere on the border Spanish troops encountered the "thirty-six insurgent Blacks" who exclaimed "*God, and King*" and offered to share food and camaraderie with them. They requested only to prohibit any white French travelers from entering Santo Domingo unless they had been given permission. They reported that the French were so afraid of the insurgents that they would flee and abandon their homes if they heard the rebels shouting. Evacuees who were permitted to escape into Santo Domingo were issued passports. Spanish officials nevertheless continued to accept many white evacuees, which caused a constant strain to exist between them and the Black insurgents.

In early October 1791, some insurgents traveled along the border at Villarubia to the home of a Spanish subject married to a French woman of color and captured several French women hiding there. In response, insurgent officers at Dondon punished these soldiers for lacking discipline and entering Santo Domingo. Elsewhere along the border, boisterous insurgents shouted insults, perhaps playfully, at Spanish border guards. In response, those Black soldiers received exemplary punishment. In these instances, Black generals warned their troops to be on their best behavior in their conduct toward Spanish subjects and attempted to appease the Spanish officials who had complained about the incidents. Both the request and the response implied recognition, reciprocity, and developing respect.[78]

Jean-François, Biassou, and Jeannot—the same commanders that Boukman purportedly prophesied would lead the revolution—directed these policies. In the earliest weeks of the insurrection, of the three, Jeannot had been closest to the famed Boukman. He was also the supposed "judge" of the revolution, overseeing the torture and gruesome executions of white prisoners. In early October 1791, a Black rebel general based at Grande-Rivière who identified himself as Médecin Général, because of his Vodou healing abilities, debated how to best entreat with Spanish officials. This was likely Jeannot.[79]

In his missives to other generals the general considered the opinions of "Bouqueman" (Boukman) and Jean-François and pondered how to attract Spanish connections. (In one of these letters, apparently to Biassou, he also sarcastically referenced Boukman's and Jean-François's retinue of young women.) Jeannot hoped to negotiate from a position of strength with new military successes. This included plans to destroy more properties around Cap-Français, a priority, because without this "their people" would suffer "butchery" from the French.[80] However, Jean-François soon delegated the task of nurturing Spanish amity to his less prominent officers Fayette and Bouce.[81]

This reassignment was likely due to the fear that Jeannot's reputation might stymy the increasingly important Spanish outreach campaign. However, though historians have thoroughly documented Jeannot's violence, the fact that his downfall was partly tied to the project of creating confidence in Santo Domingo is hitherto unknown.[82] In one story, Jeannot and Biassou approached Cap-Français and captured the convent of the supposed Vodouizan nun Améthyste with chants of "Glory to the Almighty, eternal hatred to France." Allegedly, Jeannot approached the convent with a white child atop a pike and commenced attacking all the women he thought were French. To avoid the bayonet, or worse, nuns who claimed they were creoles had to pass a simple shibboleth pronunciation test. Jeannot had some victims' eyes gouged, appendages amputated, and torsos sawed in half. He may have even collected their blood in a receptacle mixed with rum and gunpowder to consume later.[83] Deaths of defenseless nuns, many of whom had treated the Black population with dignity, scandalized his peers and new Spanish contacts.

Devastating the insurgents, only weeks later, in November 1791, French troops killed Boukman, severed his head from his body, and placed it on public display. His death prompted profound mourning, spiritual ceremonies, and a three-day commemorative celebration. Jean-François assumed dealings with their neighbors in Santo Domingo and engaged the French on tentative peace queries. With the stakes rising, Jean-François rejected general impressions of excessive violence, personally granting clemency to French prisoners. Jeannot, who was known for committing acts of violence, exemplified the problem. Jean-François ordered his colleague's execution.[84] Jeannot, like many of his peers, had employed Vodouizan consultants. Realizing his demise was near, he desperately clung to the priest from Marmelade who advised Jean-François. His pleas were to no avail. The more judicious revolutionaries Jean-François and Biassou consolidated command of the insurgents.[85]

The prominence of priestly connections only increased. To continue building trust with Spanish subjects they had to allay other concerns. For example, weeks before, officials in Santo Domingo had been baffled by reports that, as the French retook the Gallifet plantation, an epicenter of the initial revolt of the enslaved, they found that the "Capuchin father" had married a couple, "and that after the nuptial prayer the two were proclaimed King and Queen." One source indicates that this "king" was Jean-François and the "queen" his partner, Charlotte, who may have been Fulani and an enslaved domestic worker. The Spanish source identified the new queen as the "daughter of a sugar planter." It is possible that the Spanish conflated two concurrent events as the priest, known as "Cachetan," had also been accused of arranging relationships between captured French women and insurgents. In any case, after the ceremony, the "Queen of the Brigands" was arrested, along with the "priest of Petit-Anse." To see if she might divulge information, as the priest had, the French delayed her execution. Whether or not this was Charlotte, she indeed was at some point captured, an event that played into Jean-François's peace negotiations.[86] If the case of the king and queen involved Jean-François, his prominent wedding two years later becomes even more intriguing, as it displayed his royalist and religious dispositions.

More broadly, in the range of religious practices among the ethnically diverse African population of Saint-Domingue, often colloquially grouped together as *le vaudou* (Vodou), the designation of a king and queen in a community could signify spiritual leadership as much as political power.[87] Compared to what were considered the "sacrilegious revolutions of the French," which had exhibited "restlessness leading to the removal of governments . . . , and the execution of leaders," the words and actions of the insurgents were considered a viable alternative.[88] The insurgents embraced priestly oversight and monarchism. Their use of the sacraments and conferral of royal titles, however, seemed racially insubordinate to some Spanish officials, a usurpation of power. For the Spanish, comfort with their self-liberated allies came to revolve around their acceptance of more orthodox clerical advice.[89]

Insurgent officers sometimes made counterintuitive choices to build trust, including the decision to attempt to assuage Dominican planters' protests. For example, when rebels attacked a French coffee plantation adjacent to Santo Domingo, about twenty enslaved Dominicans from the nearby Aponte plantation joined their offensive. Apparently, this property in Santo Domingo was temporarily in Black control. However, a priest intervened for Aponte by crossing the border and complaining. There he met an officer named "Bautista" (perhaps Jean-Baptiste Marc), who promised to return forty-four enslaved Dominicans to their plantations. Bautista insinuated that the insurgents' policy was to prevent enslaved Dominicans from participating and to discourage Dominican revolts.[90] Such strategic choices helped to reinforce the notion that France was the intended enemy, and concerned officials in Santo Domingo again took this as a sign of divine providence.

Meanwhile, the insurgents had competition. As Dominicans watched fires approach Dajabón, other nearby militants, both gens de couleur and enslaved people, placed the white cockade in their hats and carried signs reading "Long live the King." Such acts marked a rejection of French revolutionary imperatives.[91] Appealing to royalism and righteousness toward officials in Santo Domingo, they declared, "We, the citizens of color of . . . Ouanaminthe and Fort Dauphin, together have taken the resolution of living and dying as good Christians and faithful to our King." They also complained that Catholicism was languishing in Saint-Domingue.[92] More royalist voices, including white evacuees, piqued Spanish interest in forming a coalition for an opportunistic intervention. The risk of entertaining multiple groups was that it might alienate more powerful Black rebels already in their goodwill.

Regarding possible insurgent allies, Governor García learned, near the end of 1791, that amicable insurgent leaders had engaged the French in peace talks. The eighty-year-old priest of Ouanaminthe, a "dandy" Capuchin who had fled to the Dominican side, reported these developments. Led by Jean-François, Biassou, and the rising Toussaint Bréda, negotiations transpired amid a political transition. New commissioners were arriving from the National Assembly in Paris, carrying news of the radical limitations recently imposed upon the French monarchy. The new commissioners hinted that insurgents could earn pardons if they put down their arms. One insurgent peace demand requested three days off per week. The French planters balked, and the negotiations faltered.[93]

BORDERING BLACK POWER AND THE CRITICAL CASE OF GÉRARD

In late January 1792, despite earlier conversations with the insurgents, officials in Santo Domingo entertained collaboration offers from white and gens de couleur leaders with extant Dominican ties. Jean-François and his colleagues learned of these covert overtures as their own peace talks with France failed. In need of resources, they astutely outmaneuvered new local competitors for regional dominance, control of essential Dominican border crossings, and access to impressed officials in Santo Domingo, who accepted the insurgents' proposals and tipped the balance of power toward their secret partners. Such tact, exemplified in the case that follows, made Jean-François and Biassou arguably the most potent figures in either Saint-Domingue or Santo Domingo for the next two years.

That January, a little-known trial began in Santo Domingo that, in its surprising course, revealed exactly how insurgents under Jean-François had co-opted prerevolutionary cross-island networks to forge their improbable cooperation with Spain. The defendant on trial was Charles Gérard, a thirty-one-year-old planter from Marseille living in Maribaroux near Ouanaminthe.[94] Days before, as he fled from Jean-François, Gérard had been arrested in Santo Domingo to "prevent ills . . . in our towns." Court records show that Spanish officers knew him unusually well and seemed uneasy about revealing his connections and intents.

Gérard had been a "firebrand and accomplice" leading gens de couleur militants near the border and mediating peace negotiations between Black insurgents and French officials.[95] Local gens de couleur trusted his advice, as he had lived amicably alongside them for eighteen years. In the preceding weeks, Gérard had convinced them that he represented a high-ranking French officer who might offer amnesty. Strategically, the insurgents disrupted this deal.

Like many figures from Saint-Domingue, before the revolution Gérard had spent several months in Dajabón and Santiago to avoid arrest. The allegations against him included falsifying ownership of a sugar plantation and then trying to burn the property to the ground.[96] His connections into Santo Domingo also involved trafficking captives across the border, including to the property of François Espaillat, an émigré tobacco merchant in the Cibao whose son Santiago and grandson Ulises were later selected as Dominican presidents.[97] Gérard finally returned to Saint-Domingue in February 1790, spared by political upheavals that left the charges against him unresolved.[98]

Gérard revived his old ties to officers in Santo Domingo and in November and December 1791 passed them intelligence on affairs in Saint-Domingue.[99] He also informed Spanish officials about the rebels' negotiations with French officials.[100] He told them that "the chiefs . . . have repeatedly sent deputations toward the end of pursuing pardons," and that they had apparently amassed their white prisoners, perhaps in preparation for an exchange.[101] As they recruited informants, Spanish officers continued quietly vetting potential allies.[102]

Gérard's connections with Dominicans, gens de couleur militants, Black insurgents, and French officers uniquely positioned him as an intermediary. Spanish officers were perplexed to learn of rumors in Saint-Domingue that Spanish forces would soon intervene.[103] However, their development of ties to Gérard and other militants belied discreet planning toward their own direct involvement.

Officials in Santo Domingo were wary of Gérard's ties to seemingly all the warring factions, though Gérard prevaricated about his well-known role and blamed Jean-Baptiste Marc for nearby revolts.[104] Marc, a free Black man, had led insurgents near Dondon while feigning submission to General Anne-Louis de Tousard, the French officer for whom Gérard claimed to work. Tousard supplied Marc with weapons that helped him occupy the Ouanaminthe area. With calculated duplicity, Marc and his troops had tricked Gérard and gens de couleur militants into cooperation. Soon thereafter, they simply handed Ouanaminthe to the army of Jean-François.[105] While Gérard admitted to helping the gens de couleur rebels take the town from white French personnel on 2 November 1791, he denied blame for the ineptitude that allowed insurgents access to the Dominican border. In fact, Gérard hid in January 1792 when Jean-François's army, derided as "maleficents" and "incendiaries" by the French, took the town.[106] Though Gérard had met Jean-François, he claimed it was under duress.[107]

Jean-François's interest likely revolved around Gérard's territorial hold, his role in arranging a détente for the gens de couleur with the French, and his connections to officials in Santo Domingo. At minimum, Jean-François was annoyed at the harsher negotiations he endured, and the fact that officials in Santo Domingo had yet to take his entreaties seriously enough. To remedy these constraints, he had first briefly occupied Ouanaminthe in November 1791, after his troops encouraged uprisings nearby. Following a few days of occupation by a gens de couleur militia, very early on 9 November, "eight Blacks from Santa Susana [Sainte-Suzanne] . . . incorporated themselves with the *mulâtres*." Soon thereafter, six hundred more insurgents arrived and "took over the town of Ouanaminthe." This occurred as parties needed options amid precarious peace talks.

Fearing invasion, Spanish troops in Dajabón hurriedly mobilized when, "at four in the afternoon[,] four Blacks on horseback arrived at the mouth of the river." They said they wanted to present a "message from their general," who would have "the honor of visiting" the next day. As Spanish officers watched Ouanaminthe burn while white French evacuees fled into Santo Domingo, a rumor preceded the "General of the Brigands": it was said that his insurgents might force white residents to declare all of the enslaved free. On the morning of 10 November, Black troops approached the river on horseback escorting their general, who was "decorated with the Cross of St. Louis that the king had given him." Spanish officers described him as "very dark Black with two crosses on his chest, one of Saint-Louis and the other which was unknown," and said that "he spoke little" compared to the others. Though Spanish officers apparently knew his name, the court took the unusual precaution of anonymizing the general as "Monsieur :::::::::::" in the records. In possible misunderstandings, they said the general was a "free Black" (though many leading generals had self-liberated) who may have visited France. Perhaps they thought this because of his medals, his resolute royalism, and the supposed orders he carried from the king.[108]

Given the description, this general could have been Jean-François, who sometimes wore the Cross of Saint Louis. Those who saw Jean-François, the "supreme chief of the African army," said he "was always well dressed" in a "coat of superb gray cloth," and that he wore "the Cross of St. Louis and the red cord." Jean-François's and his officers' passports were all worded to say they were the king's army and conducting his business. As Jean-François haltingly negotiated his own peace terms with the French, he benefited from the involvement of the capable officer Toussaint Bréda, who also moderated the less predictable Biassou.[109] He would master the art of keeping his options open and enticing empires to outbid each other. In this case, a direct connection to Dominican resources at Dajabón offered an alternative to appeasing the French with a peace deal that their ranks disdained.

Toward this end, Gérard presented another path. Depending on the audience, he had cynically instructed his gens de couleur militia "to put in their hats [cockades] that said long live King Louis XVI," and later that month, during negotiations for a pardon from Tousard, to use the "national cockade," likely the new revolutionary French *tricolore*. Despite his denials, Gérard had actually disarmed *blancs* during the first occupation of Ouaminthe. He had seized their armory, executed dissenters against his risky plans, and even cooperated with Jean-François's troops. However, when Gérard settled a separate peace with French officials and surrendered Ouaminthe, he alienated Black insurgents, whose own negotiations with France faded.[110]

Gérard thus unwittingly necessitated the insurgents' decisive January 1792 takeover of Ouaminthe when their talks failed. His equivocation also jeopardized his position as a trusted powerbroker. However, insurgent generals such as Jean-François, whom he bypassed, had already duped Gérard into meeting and facilitating new ties to officials in Santo Domingo to complement the rapport they had already built in Dajabón and elsewhere along the Dominican border.

In failed negotiations with France, Jean-François had patiently requested pardons, four hundred manumissions, and improved treatment of the enslaved, including those three days of free time a week. French elites had no interest in compromise, however, and refused even to offer sixty manumissions or any improved living conditions, instead insisting that the insurgents' crimes against France deserved unconditional surrender and punishment. A white planter slapped Jean-François during one meeting. By January 1792, the negotiations had disintegrated.[111]

Jean-François quickly moved to capture important towns, to further his friendly contacts in Santo Domingo, and to secure much-needed resources to continue combat against the hated French. Fearing that Gérard, Tousard, and the gens de couleur of Ouanaminthe would solidify French control of the critical border region, Jean-François had already planted allies in Ouanaminthe. Desperate to secure these positions, Jean-François's army reentered Ouanaminthe in January 1792.

Gérard immediately hid in the home of free mulâtre Jean Tamplier. As Black insurgents encircled the house, Tamplier hid Gérard in a box, and then he had an enslaved mulâtre carry the packaged Gérard toward the river and the Dominican border beyond it. On the morning of 15 January, Spanish troops intercepted Gérard on the Dajabón riverbank, yet permitted him to house there with Martine, who is described, perhaps pejoratively, as "a French *mulâtresse*." Gérard faced arrest the next morning.[112] He carried hidden papers that demonstrated his connections and duplicities.[113]

With their other potential allies outmaneuvered, and worried about revolutionary spillover into Dominican society, Spanish officials realized they had only one viable ally—the insurgents. As peace talks failed, Dominicans watched to see if Saint-Domingue would career to total ruin. García knew that he could satisfy the insurgents' terms.[114] The officer who just years before had testified about how to remake Dominican slavery in the image of Saint-Domingue slavery eventually offered better terms than those Jean-François had requested from the French, culminating months of friendly contact from the most powerful insurgents. Ouanaminthe, the town in which Jean-François would choose to live, offered the critical border crossing to procure support.

At this nexus of Black power and Spanish ambitions, Jean-François's faith professions to Spanish subjects acquainted him with a particular priest from Dajabón, José Vázquez. This priest would help pull Santo Domingo into the Haitian Revolution. Despite having witnessed firsthand the shrewd tactics of insurgent generals, in ensuing years officials in Santo Domingo would regularly underestimate their counterparts' complex motives and tact.[115] In 1792, this unique cooperation from unexpected contingencies, between those formerly enslaved by the French and officials in Santo Domingo, would change the course of Caribbean history and inspire domestic Dominican ideas that would influence lasting cross-island tensions.

CONCLUSION

In 1791, Dominican observers watched Saint-Domingue become a volcano building toward eruption. The eventual watershed revolution opened unanticipated avenues for the self-liberating insurgents and for the officials in Santo Domingo. As Spanish officials reflected upon their own weaknesses and geopolitical interests vis-à-vis the revolution in Saint-Domingue, the unexpected calls to cooperation, religion, and royalism by astute Black insurgent leaders gained understandable appeal amid years of French revolutionary rights discourses, republicanism, and anticlericalism. Envious of taking lucrative French lands, Dominican elites ignored the existential risk of exposing Dominicans of color to revolutionary influences.

This cautious contact developed into a formidable force built on shared beliefs that would shape the Haitian Revolution, race and slavery in the Americas, and future strife on Hispaniola. Unexpectedly, this cooperation supported talented Black officers who became Haitian leaders, pushed the French Revolution to extend triumphalist Enlightenment universalisms far beyond original French intents, affirmed elite Dominican notions of piety and superiority, and provided an example of upward mobility and resistance to Dominicans of color. The island, becoming more entwined than ever, would never be the same again.

THREE

BELIEF, BLASPHEMY, AND THE BLACK AUXILIARIES, 1792–1794

In June 1793, mere months after the most powerful, best organized, and largest self-liberating insurgent group formally became the "Black Auxiliaries" of King Carlos IV of Spain, their brilliant general Jean-François received yet another French recruitment offer. This was an abrupt reversal for the French, and they had recently rebuffed negotiations. The new French commissioners Léger-Félicité Sonthonax and Étienne Polverel had just selectively recognized the freedom of Black rebels who were willing to defend them from their rivals near Cap-Français. José Vázquez, a *mulato* priest from Santo Domingo who had become Jean-François's close adviser and intercessor with Spanish officials, learned that the Black general's loyalty might be jeopardized. Vázquez immediately galloped on horseback to confront a surprised Jean-François, who then "put himself on his knees and pledged [obedience] before God and the sacred name of the King of Spain." Jean-François handed his unopened recruitment letter to a satisfied Vázquez. The general then showed the priest his newest plans to expand Spanish conquests in Saint-Domingue.[1]

The hitherto exclusivist, utopian, and mostly white French project of *égalité* was in retreat on Hispaniola. However, pressed by the Black Auxiliaries and their white rivals, in August 1793 Sonthonax and Polverel emancipated Nord and later all Saint-Domingue. General abolition has sometimes been presented as an inevitable extension of magnanimous universalism.[2] In the moment, however, it was an emergency measure to attract the Black troops who had revealed the fragility of French rule. Revolutionary virtue was secondary to survival. Although Sonthonax and Polverel attracted *gens de couleur* support by extending citizenship, into 1794 they grew more desperate to entice the formidable generals Jean-François, Georges Biassou, and Toussaint, who had recently taken up the iconic surname Louverture.[3] The enduring legacy of this Haitian revolutionary leadership on both sides of Hispaniola derives in part from the salience of belief demonstrations and blasphemy accusations that went beyond the undoubted influences of royalist African culture, especially as the Black Auxiliaries partnered with Spain to become the most formidable forces in the Haitian Revolution from 1792 to 1794.[4]

Clearly, to arrive at these pivotal alignments, the first amiable contact by Black insurgents at the Dominican border in 1791 had advanced rapidly and substantially, developments that require explanation. By early 1792, the armies of Jean-François and Biassou had outfought their rivals to gain access to coveted Dominican borders and indispensable Spanish resources. Two years later they held three-quarters of Nord and half of Ouest—nearly half of Saint-Domingue—momentarily restoring to Spain fertile lands lost a century before. At their peak, their fourteen thousand legally freed troops represented the liberatory vanguard of the Haitian Revolution. The Black Auxiliaries likely outnumbered all enslaved Dominicans, a population they greatly influenced as examples of racial resistance. The formal freedom that Spain granted to them and their families, coupled with their robust espousal of royalism and religiosity, pressured the French to move toward a pragmatic abolition.

Publicly, the Black Auxiliaries avoided supporting African diasporic beliefs such as Vodou. They even recast the revered Vodouizan Dutty Boukman as a martyr for Catholicism, and the epochal August 1791 revolts he planned as a defense of monarchy.[5] Records of their rituals, including the ornate Catholic weddings of Jean-François and Biassou at the frontlines, show how they utilized belief as a social practice to bind their ambition to new networks with Spain.[6] The Black Auxiliaries' acts of loyalty so impressed their allies in Santo Domingo that Governor Joaquín García called Jean-François "a true Spaniard." He welcomed their public piety as a racial redemption that overrode his racist assumptions tied to "the stain covering" their bodies—at least for the time being. Sonthonax scolded the Black generals for their affiliations, warning that they would die for a losing cause. Such condescension failed, in part on account of the seemingly providential connection to guns, money, and geopolitical cooperation that Vázquez could facilitate. Vázquez thus became "the principal spring of Jean-François and [his people]."

At this convergence of sincerity and practicality, the revolutionaries gained a spiritual network that materially blessed them with weapons and cash. Though Vodou absolutely was influential among the metaphysically flexible Black Auxiliaries, limited exposure to Catholicism in Saint-Domingue and a lengthier history of evangelization in West Central Africa among their forebears influenced their beliefs. Priests escorted them into battle, they saluted the sacraments, and the archbishop supported their spirituality. In these acts, they affirmed Spanish initiatives to *españolizar* (Hispanicize) them as new subjects in occupied Saint-Domingue and to challenge French revolutionary secularism.

The Black soldiers engaging Iberians in belief and related ideas of monarchism built formidable Black power. A side effect of their public piety was that it further defined notions of racial improvement, civility, and trustworthiness, in conjunction with royalism and religiosity. In the long term, these rhetorics exacerbated elite Dominicans' notions of distinction alongside anti-French ideas, hardened notions of racial redemption against supposedly radical egalitarian republicanism, and inadvertently led to heightened standards of popular piety that restricted Dominicans of color.[7] Elites in Santo Domingo came to believe that Catholicism had refined the Black Auxiliaries from their natal race, and that the Black pro-French troops in Saint-Domingue, whom they judged as embodying African heresies and protecting secularism, were their opposites.[8] Conflations of heresy and violence with Blackness and republicanism also developed in Santo Domingo. These concepts of the sacred and profane influenced lasting, exclusive Dominican ideas of irreconcilable difference with their neighbors to the west. A makeshift family spanning the island, and even the Atlantic, thus came into being, and yet the same expressions simultaneously amplified political divides and created strains at the intersections of politics and belief.

Despite these accomplishments, the rationale, methods, and, most importantly, long-term consequences of this moment remain obscured in scholarship, which generally overlooks religious themes and shoehorns Dominican cultural politics into teleological narratives tied to French and Haitian chronologies, events, and themes. Archival findings on Jean-François, Biassou, and Toussaint and their complex ties to Santo Domingo nevertheless show how, amid the spiritual upheaval of the Haitian Revolution, a mutual supernatural idiom helped to forge an alliance between the insurgents and Spain against a France that had abused and attempted to destroy the insurgents.

However, the war's course reversed when the talented Toussaint, formerly subordinate to Biassou, defected to France in mid-1794. In the elite cultural registers of Santo Domingo, he and his troops regressed into depravity, duplicity, and Blackness, categories imbricated with being radical, secular, and French. The Black Auxiliaries' collaboration with Spain eventually strained internal amity and abetted defections as the Spanish retained a supposedly more moderate slavery in annexed Saint-Domingue, traded of prisoners of war, and aided exiled French planters who hoped to revive a society that had been heaven for the plantocracy and hell for the enslaved. The war increasingly entangled Dominicans as combatants, readers of reports and revolutionary texts, and, eventually, refugees.

Though they fade in most narratives, the Black Auxiliaries' appearance in some elite Dominican ideas of Hispanic refinement resonated in Santo Domingo long after this era. However, many Dominicans of color admired their examples of upward mobility, rather than complying with exaggerated spiritual standards. By late 1794, French revolutionary ideals and newfound Black empowerment had infiltrated Santo Domingo. Dominican society then became an Atlantic battleground between the conservation of prevalent assumptions about the divine right of monarchy, human nature, and social hierarchies and surging discourses of anticlericalism, egalitarianism, and social reordering. Judged unfit for Hispanic inclusion, Dominicans of color who explored revolutionary themes regressed in elite eyes, just as Toussaint had. Spanish observers saw those who rebelled as more heretical or evil than before, or equated them more thoroughly with being Black or African, traits that elite Dominicans later conflated with being "Haitian." Exploring these contingencies further clarifies the diasporic divergences between two populations of majority African descent that sometimes complicated their cooperation.

DIVINE OPPORTUNISM, 1792

After peace talks with France collapsed, having developed contacts across the northern Dominican border, by January 1792 Jean-François, Biassou, and Toussaint had begun to rely on regular engagement with officials in Santo Domingo.[9] Years later, Spanish officials casually transcribed court records suggesting that some Black insurgents had affiliations with Spain dating to that year.[10] This accidental admission reveals some sort of early covert cooperation. Findings here reveal previously obscured details of this cooperation. Black soldiers had clearly allied with the Spanish by 1793, and from that time Spain was engaged in warfare against France.

All collaboration with the insurgents remained clandestine and ad hoc, lest French forces attack Santo Domingo. Subtly, the "Black chiefs" demonstrated "extraordinary attention and utmost respect," and showed "that they [were] addicts" to the same cause as Spain. However, given the insurgents' desperate state, their dire need for resources, and the difficulties they encountered trying to sustain their impressive successes, some in Santo Domingo doubted their religiosity and royalism. Also, in March 1792, "Biasiu [sic], having brought himself up to our frontier . . . complained that we were assisting the whites, and denying the Blacks," one man wrote. Although French royalist planters receiving Spanish aid still claimed insurgents as property, some officials perceived these requests and lingering tensions as haughty.

Endlessly, the Black soldiers had to allay doubts. For various reasons, officials in Santo Domingo typically preferred interacting with Jean-François, who expressed "the greatest affection and respect to the Spanish at all times," as one Dominican reported. In one incident, a Dominican of color was helping some of Jean-François's soldiers drink from the Río Masacre at the border as a distracted Spanish sentinel bathed nearby. When one of the soldiers took two horses from the Dominican of color, the Spanish officers immediately complained, and Jean-François investigated. He arrested a suspect, and even sent the prisoner to the Spanish, then issued threats of harsh punishment, including execution, against any soldiers who might be considering committing such "insults" against Dominicans.[11] When the new French commissioner, Philippe-Rose Roume de Saint-Laurent, requested that Spain apprehend and return insurgents as if they were runaways, the Spanish did not comply. Indeed, Jean-François regularly engaged with officers in Dajabón, who enjoyed his insights on French political *mentalités*.[12] Roume, who participated in rigid French peace talks with insurgents and who reappeared in significant ways over the next decade, had arrived in Cap-Français in November 1791 alongside commissioners Frédéric Ignace de Mirbeck and Edmond de Saint-Léger.

With the French unable to stop the escalation of hostilities in Nord, and antagonism toward the French growing throughout the colony, revolution spread. By spring 1792, Ouest had witnessed its first large revolts. Romaine la Prophétesse, who was originally from Santo Domingo, and tens of thousands of his enslaved supporters captured Léogâne and Jacmel. In his brief and stunning rise, Romaine, who had children and had likely presented as male, took up the feminine title of prophetess, wore women's clothing, held a "mass" in a church with an upside-down crucifix, and claimed the Virgin Mary as a godmother who communicated directly in writing. This presentation may have drawn upon Kongolese traditions recognizable to Romaine's followers. As Romaine's movement collapsed, the prophetess's troops pondered fleeing to Santo Domingo.[13]

Ouest began to resemble Nord.[14] To restore order, in June 1792 French officials again attempted to unify *blancs* and *gens de couleur* against the insurgents, which Jean-François correctly predicted would cause Black support to wane. Governor García recognized that the enslaved would never resubmit to the demeaning French yoke, observing that "since the day in which they took up arms against their owners," the men had enjoyed a previously "imponderable liberty."[15]

Thus, when a new insurgent leader, known as Hyacinthe, began dominating Ouest, García extended Spanish connections to influence the critical region. Hyacinthe, whose brief and bold career is shrouded in ambiguity, proved unpredictable compared to Jean-François.[16] All along the border, including in Hyacinthe's new territory, insurgents encamped "a gunshot away" from Dominican towns. Reinvigorated by access to Dominican resources, Jean-François's army burned more properties near Fort Dauphin. They celebrated with a splendid banquet for Jean-François in Maribaroux, just over a mile from Santo Domingo.[17] Success for the insurgents and for the officials in Santo Domingo had become symbiotically intextricable.

Relatedly, Spanish officials scrambled to forestall French dissent from disrupting Dominican society domestically.[18] The corrosive content of "arrogant" and "satirical" French pamphlets roused cultural ferment.[19] Other publications told the stories of evacuees and of how they had been displaced from their homes and regions by the revolution.[20] "This is the much-vaunted French liberty," one official in Santo Domingo retorted. It had only destroyed laborers and lands, causing the sugar, coffee, and subsistence economies to crash amid the "obstinacy and tenacity" of "dissensions." The economically languid Santo Domingo thus siphoned hundreds of thousands of pesos from México and other Spanish colonies to pay for defensive measures, in part by depicting their efforts as a bulwark against the influence of the "new philosophers," whose ideas were spilling across the Atlantic in the aftermath of Bastille Day in Paris to cause daily turmoil on Hispaniola.[21] The religious and royalist offensive in Saint-Domingue kept the upheaval out of Santo Domingo.

Eventually, Dominicans' dealings with insurgents became widely assumed. In June 1792, the French general Rouvray briefly recaptured Ouanaminthe to disrupt insurgent ties to Santo Domingo. Rouvray sent officers into Dajabón to gripe, complained to García about Dominicans consorting with insurgents, and asked Dominicans to print copies of a decree for distribution to white French evacuees.[22] Soon, the insurgents killed fifty French partisans in retaking Ouanaminthe and pursued those who fled to "make them feel the lack of obedience to their General Jean-François." The event accentuated the growing power of his strategic abilities, supported by his Dominican resources.[23]

Any remaining reticence among officials in Santo Domingo about providing support dissipated as Jean-François demonstrated his accomplishments. Jean-Jacques Desparbès, a new interim governor, had arrived at Cap-

Français in October 1792 accompanied by three new civil commissioners and six thousand additional soldiers. By then, a total of eleven thousand new French troops had arrived, and French forces nearly equaled the main insurgent army. Anticipating further attacks on Ouanaminthe and other strongholds, Jean-François recruited geographically dispersed and politically disparate rebels to join in a common defense.

Jean-François also had his forces burn terrain in the plains between Ouanaminthe and Cap-Français to more easily view and interrupt French maneuvers. He deliberately exposed French troops to the "strength of the sun" and the "excessive humidity of the night," to which the insurgents were more accustomed. This "intelligence in the art of war" impressed officials in Santo Domingo, though they nevertheless disrespectfully described it as a "skill uncommon to Black rusticity."[24]

Half of the new French troops would die within a year from combat and conditions. Soon, only two of the newest commissioners, Sonthonax and Polverel, remained. However, the strategic successes of Jean-François's insurgent army over the next year impelled them to unexpectedly oversee defining decisions for the revolution.[25]

Before then, Ouanaminthe remained strategically prominent. On 7 November 1792, French forces returned there directed by General Donatien-Marie-Joseph Rochambeau and raised the *tricolore* over the town's church. As insurgents fled, Rochambeau visited Dajabón, personally begging for officials to return any Black rebels who had entered Santo Domingo.[26] García recounted that Jean-François's troops hid in Santo Domingo, and that providing this sanctuary represented an escalation of direct Dominican involvement. French recovery attempts included incorporating gens de couleur militants, who re-enslaved captured rebels. Black soldiers, "vigilant and attentive of conserving their liberty," made "most *mulâtres* pay with their lives for the treason." Extending the conflict into Santo Domingo, hundreds of gens de couleur also fled into Santo Domingo, "asking for asylum in our lands to free themselves from the fury of the Black rebels."[27] Though the evacuees followed the same path as Ogé, the fact that the Spanish had deported this exile and his cohort did not help their odds of allying with gens de couleur in Saint-Domingue.[28]

As 1792 progressed, the insurgents, supported by Dominican resources, responded to the ongoing French commitment to slavery by pressing more clearly explained revolutionary goals. A powerful letter, attributed to Jean-François, Biassou, and Belair (likely Gabriel Belair), excoriated the French for their hypocritical fixations on metropolitan liberties while under their "barbaric whips we were accumulating the treasures . . . in this colony."

They argued, "If nature likes to diversify colors in the human species, it is not a crime to be born Black, nor an advantage to be white." In their own egalitarian rhetoric, the Black generals demanded amnesty for the rebels and general liberty for those whom France had enslaved.

Scholars have debated the provenance of this widely printed message. An overlooked textual hint that an insurgent leader had contributed to its composition is that their peace demands hinged on the "guarantee of these articles by the Spanish government." Covert coordination from Santo Domingo gave them crucial aid to "live free or die."[29] This document partly confirmed rumors of insurgent coordination with Santo Domingo. Furthermore, the insurgents probably reasoned that if France did not acquiesce, Spain would still back their fight.

Nevertheless, French re-enslavement efforts persisted, proving to be perhaps most effective near their key border crossings with Santo Domingo. In a remarkable arc, García, the highest-ranking Spanish official on Hispaniola, simultaneously became more invested in the Black generals.[30] Together they walked a path toward realignments in direct Spanish military engagement and toward Black affiliations that produced desperation among French republican commissioners.

PROVIDENTIAL INSURGENTS, 1793

In January 1793, Dominican audiences reeled from reports about the formation of the French Republic and cessation of royal privileges the preceding September. García noticed similar "perfidious ideas" in discourse in Saint-Domingue that took "in one hand the wick, and in the other the revolution for this new world." He recognized that pragmatic expansions of French universalist rights to the enslaved could reverse French fortunes in Saint-Domingue.[31] Spanish officials' choices at this juncture changed the course of history in the Americas.

These concerns coincided with news that France had declared war on Spain and other states. That month, French troops undertook military offensives along the southern border near Neiba. They also recaptured Dondon, driving Jean-François's armies to the border mountaintop of Jatiel. French ideologies and military maneuvers were poised to overrun vulnerable Santo Domingo. Countering French attacks on their territory and traditions, elites in Santo Domingo redoubled their defense of Hispanic beliefs and belonging and formalized their long-standing, covert ties to Black insurgents who avowed royalism and religiosity.[32]

In early 1793, as revolutionary war captivated Dominican society, Spanish officials rushed to legally incorporate collaborative Black rebels. Their ambitious partnership aimed to retake all of Saint-Domingue for Spain. Armies of the formerly enslaved, led by Jean-François, Biassou, and Toussaint in Nord, and Hyacinthe in Ouest, became the new Black Auxiliaries of King Carlos IV.[33] While militias and veterans of color across the Spanish Empire held social capital, on Hispaniola the Black Auxiliaries carried even greater military importance and cultural weight.[34]

As these events transpired, across the Atlantic French revolutionaries beheaded King Louis XVI of France by means of the guillotine. The new French body politic had thus purged itself of its royalist parental figurehead. By March, the "disgraced death" of Louis XVI convulsed Hispaniola.[35] Santo Domingo tensed with "the greatest dread, horror, and emotion" in expectation of an overwhelming French revolutionary "scourge."

Jolted by the Black Auxiliaries, Sonthonax and Polverel issued "a pardon decree for all the Blacks who surrender their arms and deliver themselves to the nation," García recounted. These were far more generous terms than those that French officials had rejected only a year before. Also, "the civil commissioners dispatched three deputies—a *mulâtre* and two whites—to General Biasou [*sic*] with advantageous propositions for . . . passing to the party of the Republic." In response, Biassou "manifested his love for the Spanish nation." They still feared French imprisonment or re-enslavement. Throughout 1793, Sonthonax and Polverel expanded their pleas to Black insurgents. The volatile new French Republic faced a long path to establishing trust. Rationally, Black generals perceived the French offers as belated expressions of their desperation.[36]

Meanwhile, the Black Auxiliaries and officials in Santo Domingo developed a truly unique project. To solidify their relationship, the archbishop, Fernando Portillo, sent "his vicar at Dajabón," the priest José Vázquez, who some identified as mulato, to advise Jean-François. Generally, he entreated clergy working among the Black Auxiliaries to proselytize about the freedom, stability, and joy of serving Spain. Revealing his own racism, he said that the new Black allies would otherwise contentedly "sit under a tree to eat, drink whatever is closest . . . and kill a man to get a plantain." In earlier insults, around December 1791, Portillo had condescendingly proposed that a show of mercy could curb alleged African heresies and insolence among the "five hundred or six hundred thousand" Black people on Hispaniola and work to "achieve greater progress" in security and assimilation.[37]

Broad diatribes, however, faded into affection and admiration for Jean-François, in particular. He and his colleagues increasingly occupied categories intelligible to Spanish officials, such as being victims of French excess and abuse, or as Black people seeking Christianity. Their religious repertoire, partly derived from limited French evangelization, Afro-Catholicism from Kongo and Angola, and even familiarity with their Dominican neighbors and their "Catholic Majesty," informed appeals comprehensible to Hispanic spirituality.[38]

The insurgents' engagements with Spain show both their African cultural influences and the social conditions of Saint-Domingue as causative contexts. To elites in Santo Domingo, their professions of Catholicism and royalism ameliorated their Blackness and essentialized internal African ethnic divisions. Their ranks featured a multiplicity of personal beliefs. Rather than hewing to a mutually exclusive orthodoxy, they held a cultural diversity that was adaptive to social instability in the revolutionary Caribbean. From those who sincerely held Catholic convictions to those who practiced Catholicism alongside African observances, or those who simply performed faith professions in an opportunistic way, the result was to create and solidify trust networks with their allies in Santo Domingo.

As a social practice, belief amalgamated and animated this political, cultural, and military project. This strategy inarguably yielded the Black Auxiliaries benefits. However, in the longer term, their exhibitions of Catholicism reinforced presumptions of civilizing piety within elite Dominican discourses of difference. Away from Iberian eyes, many Black Auxiliaries likely incorporated Christian ideas alongside other extant spiritualities. Similarly, many insurgents also already had experience from African contexts with combat and royalist institutions. For example, their officer known as Macaya famously proclaimed that he was the subject of the kings of Kongo, France, and Spain, perhaps also making a veiled biblical reference to the three magi.[39] When Biassou declared himself the "chief of the counterrevolution" against hated France, and promised to serve heaven and religion, he also endorsed centuries of durable African and European monarchist tradition as a stable option compared to the regicide of a seemingly self-immolating republic.[40]

Alongside Catholicism, Biassou and many other Black Auxiliaries also reportedly enlisted Vodou practitioners and African talismans. Haitian historian Thomas Madiou, who knew many of their veterans, said that Biassou and Jean-François led groups of "Congos, Mandingos, Ibos, and Senegalese, etc., as much by the superiority of their intelligence as by superstition." Though perhaps overdramatized, one account of Biassou's camps said that "great fires were burning," around which people danced vigorously, "singing words that are understood only in the deserts of Africa." Under additional spiritual advisement to Catholic clergy, Biassou even supposedly told African soldiers that if they succumbed in fighting, they would rejoin their natal communities in Africa in spirit.[41]

The Black Auxiliaries struck a skillful balance of exclusive public Catholic belief and private pluralist complementarity. Rather than scrutiny, García accepted that the "Lord touches them" to be "instructed in the Christian doctrine and employed with utility."[42] This interpretation conflated contextual confluences with the idea that the insurgents were part of a providential plan.

A more complex collaborator, Hyacinthe, professed muted Catholicism. He was a Vodouizan known for waving a talisman in front of his forces to divert bullets. Many of his troops bravely fought with knives, slingshots, and farm tools, emboldened by desire for liberation and the idea that if they perished they might rejoin an African spiritual family. Despite their bravery, Hyacinthe's forces in Ouest retreated into the border mountains that March. Hyacinthe's sometime collaborator Hanus de Jumécourt, a claimed clairvoyant, an ex-planter, and former colonial official, requested and received more assistance from Spanish officials, who increasingly doubted their loyalties. Only under pressure did Hyacinthe, who, according to priests, dealt with their French enemies, reiterate his Spanish affiliation.[43]

Like Hyacinthe and Biassou, Jean-François received personalized offers from the transitory French governor François-Thomas Galbaud du Fort that summer. His public, "fierce" rejection of this offer confirmed his "most solid" loyalty to Spain. Thereafter, he proudly wore an impressive new Spanish general's uniform. His troops drilled with new Spanish guns, while priests from Santo Domingo preached against French wiles.[44] Spain also gave Jean-François 4,000 pesos to distribute among his troops.[45] In particular, Vázquez, the "zealous ecclesiastic" who was "full of love," earned the king's praise for having become the "principal spring of Jean-François," likely a reference to his spiritual support and the resources he could help provide. Jean-François gave Vázquez the unopened French recruitment letters and reaffirmed his affection for Spain.

To bolster this relationship, Jean-François sent one of his closest aides to visit Santo Domingo with a letter of respect and appreciation. On the morning of 1 July 1793, two Black officers, "Bernardino" and the interpreter "Pedro" (Bernardin and Pierre), met García. García said Pierre was "insightful," with "liveliness of mind," and that Bernardin had a "great presence[,] . . . with a pleasant and good mode of expression that contradicts the stain covering his body." García called these allies reliable and clever, distinct from unaligned, hostile Black combatants, especially those allied to France. However, he also assumed that the Black Auxiliaries had progressed into a trusted status that transcended negative assumptions about their race.[46] With Vázquez developing their trust and tying the Black Auxiliaries to Spain, by mid-1793 Jean-François had relentlessly recruited new supporters to fight France.[47]

Countering him were relentless offers of significant pay increases from Sonthonax for Black Auxiliaries to join the French Republic. Spanish officials, though, never worried that the "valorous and loyal . . . Toutsaunt [sic]" would defect. In fact, they hoped that Toussaint Bréda, as he was then known, would command the entire army if Biassou or Jean-François defected.[48] Following his rapid ascent as an officer, Toussaint mediated the sometimes tempestuous relationships among the Black Auxiliaries' leaders. Early compliments of Toussaint in Spanish records referred to him as an officer under Biassou who was free long before the revolution.

Perhaps as early as August 1793, Toussaint chose a new surname, Louverture. *Toussaint* meant "all saints," and *l'ouverture* meant "the opening."[49] A French official who knew both Toussaint and Étienne Laveaux, a general who also served as governor from June 1793 to May 1796, later recounted that the latter had first called Toussaint "an opening" in hopes that he might disengage from García and Spain and build Black support for France.[50] Others suggested that Laveaux noticed Toussaint creating "an opening" wherever he ventured. Regardless, in adopting a possibly offhanded compliment in this way, Toussaint crafted one of the most iconic names in the history of the Americas.[51] However, he continued relentlessly fighting with Spain well after changing his name.

Toussaint Louverture became known as a "famous Black supporter" to Spanish officers.[52] His expansive abilities provided optimism to officials mired in letters from Vázquez and Jean-François complaining of bad pay, bad conditions, and a lack of supplies that hampered their progress.[53] Louverture earned Spanish trust with his professions of Catholic piety and support for evangelization, contrasting with the generally indulgent and unreliable white French royalist partisans.[54]

These white émigrés depleted Spanish finances, damaged morale, and disparaged the Black Auxiliaries. The Black Auxiliaries warned their allies in Santo Domingo that the former planters would eventually betray Spain.[55] Despite the grievances against them, Louverture protected the white émigrés from "despotism" in Saint-Domingue. He and the Black Auxiliaries continued their military successes, unlike the Spanish soldiers who were routed at San Miguel, a key border town, in August 1793. The valiant "Spanish Blacks from Dondon" rescued their besieged allies at Grand-Boucan. Despite this valor, Spanish officials still worried over constant French attempts to recruit the Black allies.[56]

Partisans of the republic, "brave French citizens of all colors without distinction," for example, attempted to persuade their "brother" Louverture that "the good father Sonthonax" would implement abolition as an extension of revolutionary benefits from the "motherland." Apparently, it had required two years of total war for all people in Saint-Domingue to become "her children" who could struggle together to "live free or die."[57] Despite Louverture's rejections of their offers, by October 1793 Jean-François had grown wary of his familiarity with the French and warned "the good father" Vázquez about the situation.[58]

Allaying Spanish concerns, through ingenuity Louverture soon recovered border positions. His troops ambushed dozens of French troops who were foraging for food. One captured French soldier carried a letter detailing the dire needs of his army. On this intelligence, Louverture rerouted his troops to overrun the weakened enemy by surprise, preventing bloodshed by taking six hundred prisoners. As a gesture of gratitude, García sent him 400 pesos and considered commending him with a gold medal, like those that Jean-François, Biassou, and Hyacinthe had received.[59] Louverture eventually did receive a gold medal while encamped with Biassou at San Rafael. In response, he joined in with chants of "Long live the King of Spain." Spanish officials said that God had shown them favor "by handing us our enemies without costing us a drop of blood."[60] It was Louverture, though, who was with them.

Salutes to the sacraments confirmed the Black Auxiliaries' morality to their Spanish allies. That summer, Jean-François "asked permission . . . to live in the security of his conscience," meaning, in the Catholic parlance of the era, that he wanted to marry his fiancée, Charlotte, in conformity with Catholic cultural expectations. Archbishop Portillo and Governor García both asked Vázquez to officiate the wedding and to treat Charlotte, who was staying in Dajabón, with lavish distinction, to solidify the couple's loyalty. At quite a cost, officials in Santo Domingo sent silk and stockings for the bride and provided new blue cloth and golden braids for Jean-François and his officers.[61] Along with these gifts, which in fact would have broken sumptuary laws imposed a decade earlier, the marriage partners and their families enjoyed a unique degree of social prestige, honorifics, civic exemptions, due process in military courts, and pensions (transferable to widows).[62] Their wedding enhanced vows of alliance between the Black Auxiliaries and their allies in Santo Domingo.

INTERNECINE TENSIONS

To interrupt this momentum, Sonthonax and Polverel attracted some Black soldiers and even Dominicans with "many proclamation papers." They even pondered "uniting sea and land forces . . . to have a landing in Ocoa" and sack Santo Domingo in July 1793. In response, Spanish officials sent competing proclamations to Saint-Domingue, which yielded supporters with a "lively [desire] to fight against . . . [the] enemies of human society and religion." García began distinguishing Black soldiers who accepted French invitations as being of "indefensible character," charging that from birth they had been set apart "from all men of rational principles," and that this dubious distinction had allowed them to commit "villainies" for the French Republic.[63] Such statements manifested the gradual entwinement of negative ideas about Blackness, heresy, egalitarianism, and even violence with extant fears of French radicalism.[64]

To quarantine Dominican society from the French contagion of revolution, in mid-1793 Governor García warned against interactions between Dominicans and people from Saint-Domingue, in order to preempt "treacherous domestic enemies." Those caught consorting with republicans could be labeled traitors and "suffer *the penalty of death by the gallows, without distinction.*"[65] Simultaneously, numerous Black prisoners of war arrived in Santo Domingo, overburdening the one thousand or so Spanish troops in the capital.[66] García began selling Black prisoners of war, unclaimed runaways, and eventually random noncombatants from Saint-Domingue to buyers on and off the island. He rationalized this decision with the excuse that he was evangelizing the unassimilated, expelling radical influences, and defending Santo Domingo.[67] Such crass revenue streams delayed insolvency.

Theft, graft, and disorder plagued Spanish supply chains, particularly on routes to border positions.[68] Soldiers defending Santo Domingo lacked basic supplies.[69] The sale of fourteen prisoners netted 2,149 pesos for the Spanish treasury, roughly equivalent to two-thirds of one day of Spain's wartime operations on the frontier of Hispaniola.[70] Despite their personal convictions about emancipation, Jean-François and Biassou participated by exchanging captives in Santo Domingo for supplies, inciting tension among their ranks.[71] Officials in Santo Domingo off-loaded thousands of captives to neighboring Spanish colonies through San Juan, Caracas, and Havana.[72] With the callous justification of supposedly "strengthen[ing] . . . interior security," Spanish officials sold hundreds more "Black slave prisoners of war" in the ensuing months.[73] Spain, though supporting the most

76

successful revolutionaries from Saint-Domingue, damaged their appeal by seeking craven incentives.

Defeated by the Black Auxiliaries and challenged politically by white rivals, Sonthonax and Polverel proclaimed abolition in August 1793. In the near term, French officials met with ambivalence from major generals of the Black Auxiliaries, who mostly loathed their former French owners. Moreover, the generals of the Black Auxiliaries were still rather cynical toward governmental arguments deriving from the Enlightenment, and they distrusted an unstable French state that had tried to crush them for two years. It would take time for universal emancipation to entice them to defect from the Black Auxiliaries. Spain had steadfastly offered the insurgents better avenues of upward mobility and material support than the French. Even if a weakened France promised greater liberties, not all people of color were automatically ready to trade supposed supernatural security for de jure distinctions. France still had to prove its stability and credibility, and it had to compellingly counter pro-Spanish views and offer preferable resources.[74]

The insurgents' peers held more sway than the French commissioners. Pierrot, a prominent Black general who had already joined France, invited Jean-François and Louverture to unite under the French "banner of liberty." He told them that few white French residents remained in Nord, where people of color were enforcing the start of a new, racially egalitarian era. Pierrot and Macaya, both of them former Black Auxiliaries, had answered the first panicked local emancipation offers from Sonthonax and Polverel and rescued these commissioners from French conspirators in June 1793. Even then, some preliminary defectors preferred Spain and still held thinly veiled contempt for the French. Macaya even returned to the Black Auxiliaries, whose salient generals—including Louverture, who arrested French envoys sent to entreat with him—repeatedly ignored French abolitions and offers.[75]

Despite unity in rejecting French offers, by September 1793 competition and outright acrimony had beset the Black Auxiliaries' generals as a result of the worsening rivalry between Jean-François and Biassou. Furthermore, Louverture increasingly disregarded both grandiose personalities and defied their orders. García had no choice but to accept Louverture's likely contrived claims of contrition. Friction between Jean-François and Biassou stemmed partly from competing claims of superiority in rank and success. The rifts expanded after Spanish officials chose to favor Jean-François, whom García placed first in command, infuriating Biassou. Subsequently, each general requested the arrest of the other. To little avail, Biassou even sent close aides to the governor to argue his merits.[76]

Preoccupations with prestige and power, and exorbitant expenditures, distracted Jean-François and Biassou from effectively leveraging their disparate forces against a revived French Republic. All the while, French opponents busily circulated offers and details of emancipation. Amid rancor between the two generals, officials in Santo Domingo grew even more impressed with Toussaint Louverture's honor and professionalism.[77]

With the Black Auxiliaries' top generals still refusing their offers, France pursued gradual, debilitating attritions from the lower ranks, issuing invitations to Black officers who were overshadowed by their superiors and who might defect, whether for survival, for an ego boost, for advancement, or because they could be persuaded by ideology. Just as the eastward flow of revolutionaries toward Spanish Santo Domingo became nearly inevitable, the ebb of influence began to sweep back to French Saint-Domingue, with abolition, personality conflicts, and resource scarcity all playing a role. When pro-French gens de couleur envoys arranged a meeting with "Colonel Candi, Black subaltern of Jean-François," about defecting, Jean-François marched with Vázquez to visit Candi, who reassured them of his loyalty.[78] Yet no general could control Candi as well as his late superior Jeannot, whose retributive violence toward France Candi had allegedly emulated by removing prisoners' eyes with a corkscrew.[79] Candi defected with his troops and received a key garrison at Terrier-Rouge.[80] French officials remained skeptical of his sincerity, however, and so they held his troops' families as collateral. These droves of sickly women and children convinced French officers that Candi's defection came in part due to hunger. Spanish material deficiencies and the Black Auxiliaries' strife as much as French promises motivated some defections.[81]

Hyacinthe added to losses for the Black Auxiliaries and Spanish influence in Ouest. After Spanish allies found that he had been dealing with pro-French gens de couleur while still ostensibly fighting for Spain, six Spanish officers invited him to breakfast, arrested him, and tortured him until he confessed and named accomplices. In mid-August, he "paid with his head" for this betrayal.[82] In comparison to Biassou, Jean-François, or Louverture, Hyacinthe had been on the fringes of power, given his central rather than northerly regional presence, his comparative youth, his more open practice of Vodou, and his enigmatic ties with various partisans.[83]

Rather than reorganizing to guard against further defections, the Black Auxiliaries continued their infighting. When Jean-François captured La Tannerie, he entrusted the position with "Miso" (Michaud), Biassou's officer and nephew. However, the French quickly retook the position. Given Candi's recent defection, Jean-François was infuriated at the prospect of treason. He quarreled with Michaud and then had him executed. The execution exacerbated the animosity between Jean-François and Biassou. Despite his fury, however, Biassou again rejected new French offers.[84]

Convincing officials in Santo Domingo that their "conquest should continue," Louverture yet again distinguished himself by quickly capturing Marmelade, "Pilvoro" (likely Morne Puilboreau), and Ennery. His allies, who still optimistically perceived the French as weak, desperate, and reliant on divided partisans, planned to forcibly remove French patriots, gens de couleur, and soldiers from Saint-Domingue in order to prepare it for Spanish rule. New, unacclimated European troops often fell ill in the countryside, making local allies even more crucial. Aside from French-held cities and unallied rebels in the hills, Spain was able to hold much of Saint-Domingue. Dominican officials thought that, "purged from that type," the colony would again prosper, hinting at the renewal of slavery for unallied Black residents in occupied lands.[85]

NEW FRONTS

Meanwhile, 1793 also witnessed the addition of two influential fronts. First, in response to the restrictive racial policies of the 1780s, the need for hypervigilance in the war in Saint-Domingue, and the eventual spread of French dissent into Santo Domingo, Dominicans of color began to more frequently subvert imperial prerogatives. Second, with opportunistic hopes of seizing Saint-Domingue, the British invaded.

Enslaved Dominicans began fleeing confinement more regularly. Even if claims of their ventures were exaggerated, their raids on properties took a financial toll and diverted military resources from external engagements. Allegedly, one notorious maroon, named Come Gente (People Eater), had a fabled appetite for white people. With piqued local anxiety, scores of Spanish troops were diverted to seek this fugitive. They spent weeks combing the Dominican countryside without success, but ultimately they did subdue a group of twenty-four maroons.[86]

Similarly, in a moment of heightened white fear of revenge from those whom they had oppressed, other mythologies of a "Negro Antropophago" (Black Cannibal) frightened Macorís, as the separate maroon Mate Gente (People Killer) had before him.[87] Only weeks before Dominicans had been terrified by "murders, fires, and injuries" committed by an "unknown Black vulgarly called *el Inconnito* [the Unknown]." Notices circulated to officials across Santo Domingo advising about the presence of supposed "Blacks and vagabonds," as "the neighboring French colony every day is found with more darkness and confusion."[88] The names and panics surrounding these scares revealed that vulnerable elite Dominicans were fearful about their fate, which they worried could be similar to that of their counterparts in Saint-Domingue.

Maroons and resisters took advantage of distracted Dominican elites more than claiming revolutionary aims. Runaways remained undeterred by the arrests.[89] Ignoring local discontents, officials told each other that the more "faithful" Dominicans had chosen to ignore the "echoes" of Paris's "grand and celebrated modern philosophers."[90] By blaming external influences, Dominican elites ignored the fact that their own repression could cause local resistance.

Yet another variable appeared in August 1793, when a British naval escort with twenty-five notable exiles from Saint-Domingue docked in Santo Domingo. They presented García with sealed letters from Jamaica, where they had recently fled. With British support, these envoys promoted the "legitimate authority" of the exiled French heir, Louis XVII, and sought a strategic partnership with Spanish Bourbon royalists. They even offered crucial British naval protection of Santo Domingo against the "criminal, bloodthirsty, and sacrilegious" republic. García received this contingent as a disingenuous British ploy, assuming, correctly, that it was a façade to quell Spanish angst about a British invasion of Saint-Domingue. He rejected their appeals, endorsed restoring Louis XVII, and increased his support for allied white French royalists.[91] Such expedient actions irritated the Black Auxiliaries.

British invasions began when a force from Jamaica captured the fort at Môle Saint-Nicolas. Nicknamed the "Gibraltar of Hispaniola," an irony for Spain, it was perhaps the most defensible harbor in the Americas, with portage for one hundred ships protected by one hundred cannons. British agents further interrupted Spanish operations by recruiting white French residents of Ouest under the pretext of common cause.[92]

As combat approached the southwest border, the priest Juan Bobadilla advised the Dominicans to prepare for incursions by retreating French soldiers or advancing British ones. He feared the arrival of agents inciting domestic dissent in Santo Domingo, including among the maroons of Maniel and Naranjo. Soon, Bobadilla reported the British siege and capture of Port-au-Prince, which pushed asylum-seekers into Santo Domingo. As the mulâtre republican Louis-Jacques Bauvais relocated his "Legion of Equality" away from British advances and to Mirebalais, Spanish forces prepared for hostilities in Dominican territory.[93] The British operations only compounded the desperation among the French. It also portended later British infiltration of Santo Domingo.[94]

The first overt French republican attempts to attract Dominicans began.[95] These new internal and external stressors irritated Jean-François and the Black Auxiliaries, who grew impatient with risking their lives only to face impediments from Santo Domingo, particularly officials' haphazard management of the situation and their leisurely pace. These faults put some of the Black officers' loyalties in jeopardy.[96] Disregarding the Black Auxiliaries' territorial and spiritual gains for Spain and their rejection of French "fanatics," certain Spanish officials wondered if only "a powerful hand" could control Blacks after the abolition decrees took effect, accusing them of "vile condition, rude education, and infamous conduct."[97] Though Dominican elites had momentarily suspended suspicion toward certain Black groups, their return to old critiques portended broader diatribes of racial regression directed against Black defectors.

In these moments of duress, priests proved to be decisive foot soldiers of pro-Hispanic cultural politics. Beyond advising the Black Auxiliaries, they preempted French influences among Dominicans. To neutralize French threats, Bobadilla even suggested to Archbishop Portillo that they offer trusted maroons a reward for sneaking into Saint-Domingue, finding Sonthonax and Polverel, and kidnapping them.[98]

Despite the strategic stressors, Portillo was thrilled with the spiritual successes taking place.[99] Jean-François helped Vázquez install a mendicant priest, named Quesada, in Valliere, a troubled parish under Spanish control.[100] Porta, the previous priest, had gone to Santo Domingo for interrogation for defaming Spain. Vázquez selected Quesada, who lived in Dajabón and spoke French, when Jean-François requested a more loyal Spanish priest. These actions actively expanded pro-Spanish religiosity in Jean-François's spheres of influence, but they also pleased officials.[101]

Strategies included sending Francophone priests, including royalist refractory French priests exiled in Spain, to minister among residents in occupied Saint-Domingue.[102] Jean-François received yet another letter from Sonthonax saying that unless he defected, he would meet an end similar to that of Ogé. Vázquez called the commissioner a "Pene" to Archbishop Portillo, almost certainly an unholy reference to male anatomy.[103] Against constant French recruitments, Spanish officials issued proclamations condemning Sonthonax and Polverel as "two monsters who unbound all divine and human links and . . . increase the horrors of fire and blood." The steadfast Jean-François and Biassou concluded 1793 in a personal truce as Spain invited unallied rebels to join the Black Auxiliaries, not France.[104]

Archbishop Portillo, aware of geopolitical opportunities—and that the church accounts held only 414 pesos—petitioned for more support for evangelization in parishes that bore the brunt of cultural combat.[105] However, despite the dire funding situation, he concerned himself with dedicating 1,000 pesos for his own holy garb, including a "precious miter," a liturgical headdress. Such personal pretensions were unlikely to win republican converts and interfered with geopolitical priorities.

Portillo celebrated intelligence reports from informant priests in Dajabón and Monte Cristi about Spanish forces nearing the critical Fort Dauphin. He ambitiously speculated that Spain would soon become the owner "of the whole colony, without leaving a piece for the British." Belief, binding together Black Auxiliaries and Spanish power, was still working.[106]

In 1793, the Black Auxiliaries had conquered substantial territory in Nord and Ouest, gains that continued into 1794 despite French abolition and British invasion.[107] However, lucrative offers from French officials began to attract the talents of those who were becoming increasingly alienated by myopic infighting, ostentatious behavior, and the continuance of slavery under Spanish flags. Most consequentially, Louverture soon found upward mobility and surpassed Biassou, Portillo, García, and Jean-François in status.

PIOUS PERFORMANCES

The publicly pious Black Auxiliaries retained the faith of the fictive family they had built with Spain, and officials in Santo Domingo still feared that the French Republic's familial "spirit of rebellion" would pass from "fathers to children" while "accustoming them to licentiousness and no religion." This "French genius" did continue to attract adherents on Hispaniola.[108] In Spanish-occupied Saint-Domingue, Portillo feared the "atheists, libertines, apostates, [and] schismatics." Factions had formed in favor of "the British, Spanish, royalists, and assemblyists."[109] To solidify Hispanic social and military successes, Governor García began 1794 by personally visiting the front lines.[110]

There he finally met Jean-François on 31 January 1794 in Dajabón. Jean-François's displays of hospitality and gratitude made a very strong first impression. In a backhanded compliment, García said the general was supposedly "adorned with some uncommon qualities among those of his color." The ever-present Vázquez, whom he noted that Black officers such as Jean-François Benjamin [Dubison], Vatable, Bernadino, and others "revered like an oracle," also impressed him.[111] Unquestionably, Vázquez's daily spiritual counsel with the Black Auxiliaries solidified this alliance. He regaled Spanish officials with anecdotes of their bravery. However, whether Vázquez was serving more as an irreplaceable propagandist for Spanish conquests in cultural politics or as a spokesperson for Jean-François's geopolitical initiatives among bureaucrats is debatable.

The Black Auxiliaries clearly knew how valuable they were to Spain and sought to capitalize on that importance. That January, Portillo received a long letter signed by Biassou's trusted officer "Bellair"—likely Gabriel Belair, and not the younger nephew of Louverture, Charles Belair.[112] This impassioned message seized upon their indispensability in Hispaniola's cosmological conundrum. To counter recent Spanish favor toward Jean-François, Belair wrote forcefully about Biassou's character. He even wrote about the influences of Vodou on their initial, pivotal revolts, making this letter a unique and insightful source on the Black Auxiliaries' self-styling to their Spanish allies.

With his "badly cut plume," Belair clarified their motives for their pivotal August 1791 uprising while correcting what he cast as deliberate distortions or myths propagated by their enemies. Reemphasizing French brutality, he said, "The protesting, sad, and sweet cries of the lamb are at least as touching as the howls of the wolf that devours us." This predation, "the most remarkable [barbarity] seen in the world," had preconditioned their liberatory war against "the shackles to which some dastardly men had reduced them."

These haunting memories dissuaded many Black Auxiliaries from defecting to a nation that had abused them in exchange for superficially more attractive offers. Belair also accused France of abandoning its Catholic convictions long before 1791. He argued that "our holy religion" was a catalyst making them "take up arms against these ferocious people," people who had converted "churches . . . into places of common assemblies . . . where they profess[ed] the most indecent words." Perhaps as a subtext of his accusations of religious persecution, he was alluding to French policing against African spiritualities, and yet he couched it in terms of anticlericalism intelligible to Spain. In fact, Belair echoed many of the Spanish officials' own critiques of French cruelty, hedonism, and impiety.

In describing the early core leadership, Belair named "General Biassou, the deceased Bouequeman [*sic*], as well as Jean-François" as the "three first chiefs of this revolution." Belair claimed to have worked extremely closely with his beloved leader Dutty Boukman, whose untimely death devastated him. Boukman, unable to realize the "sweetness" of his plots, became "the first victim of the perfidious maneuvers . . . to extinguish the holy religion," giving "his last breath fighting for God and our King."[113]

Belair's depiction of the legendary Boukman tactically recast his popular memory from being a Vodouizan to implying Christian martyrdom. Belair inverted the now-famous "pact with the devil" narrative that pervades Western misconceptions about the Haitian Revolution and concealed any Vodou connections in a possible Bois-Caïman meeting behind Catholic and royalist connotations. To advance their rights, resources, and desire for retribution, these earliest cadres of liberatory leaders relied on affirming Spanish perceptions of French irreligion and slaveholding excesses, their notions of piety as a social mediator and means of racial improvement, and the advantages of making common cause for the purpose of defeating French republicanism.[114]

This curated recounting might appear as a cynical revision to garner support. However, Vodou and Catholicism cohabited a spectrum of spirituality for many among the insurgents who had become Black Auxiliaries. Perhaps to them, in their struggle against the profane French, transcribing the acts of Boukman as sacred transcended demarcations of orthodoxy.

Belair dramatically asserted that the Black Auxiliaries "preferred . . . to die than to lose our Holy Religion . . . the only base of our existence." The letter cleverly recast Biassou's biography, explaining that after Boukman's death Belair and Biassou had become extremely dedicated to Spain despite every French seduction. Biassou intended to give his last drop of blood for faith and the king of Spain, a desire proven by his exhaustive fighting over two years in the worst of conditions. The French, despite ephemeral egalitarian niceties, were still their former masters, who until recently had tried to crush their revolt. Defying the seemingly self-immolating Republic, the Black Auxiliaries lamented "the loss of our monarch," King Louis XVI, a sentimentality more understandable when one considers the centuries-old durabilities of African and European royal institutions.

Returning to familial metaphors, here with royalism, Belair praised "all the benefits of a generous father for his children" that they enjoyed from "the most pious" King Carlos IV. His words intentionally appealed to the Spanish sense of paternal benevolence, a sentiment piqued by requests for more priests for the insurgents, to help their ranks withstand "satanic temptations." Incredibly, Belair recast the early years of the Haitian Revolution, identified by contemporaries and scholars as entwined with African spirituality, as a righteous restoration of Christianity and monarchism against French reprobates.[115]

Throughout this letter, Belair expertly crafted interpretations of their situation that affirmed Spanish theistic explanatory recursions away from the unquestionable influence of nascent Vodou and toward accruing needed material support. Beyond situational cynicism, their astute public piety also indicates the Black Auxiliaries' metaphysical malleability, with a Catholicism complementary to extant African-derived spiritualties. As such, between the armies of the formerly enslaved and their allies in Santo Domingo, belief offered binding social practices, mutually intelligible meanings, a geopolitical vernacular, and a common theistic punisher who would regulate ethical actions.

Racial and radical "others" intensified ingroup confidence tests and confirmed the French Republic as an enemy on a supernatural scale. Many sincere devotees were unaware of this profound trust-building and cooperative functionality, and those who were cognizant of it were loath to make their utilitarian intentions known. The Black Auxiliaries participated in setting expectations that, if violated, would elicit emotional distress and extreme distrust from their allies in Santo Domingo. Their pious performances preconditioned elevated expectations for Hispanic social inclusion among Dominicans of color, a litmus test for civility for Black people in western Hispaniola, and a precursor for Spanish rage against those who later challenged these norms and defected to France.

REVERSALS

Signs of decline emerged despite spiritual and territorial gains. On his northward trip in early 1794, García spent time in the Black Auxiliaries' muddy camps around the newly besieged Fort Dauphin, a key port near the northern border. When seven gens de couleur surrendered, they notified García of several notable deaths in the city, hinting that the Spanish strategies to diminish French resolve were working.[116] With heavy naval artillery aimed at their adversaries, Spanish officers drove a hard bargain. The French residents who surrendered Fort Dauphin asked for protection of their ranks and weapons, for "the political rights of the gens de couleur, our brothers," and for deserters in their camp. The Spanish officials demurred, but ultimately they did promise to protect their property and, notably, to prevent the Black Auxiliaries from entering the city.[117]

In a significant victory, by February 1794 the Spanish flag flew over Fort Dauphin, though at great financial cost in pay to the Black Auxiliaries and to the sumptuous French royalist evacuees, who despised each other.[118] Gains in Nord were short-lived. As Pierrot again circulated offers throughout the Black Auxiliaries' ranks, García had gallows erected at main roads to discourage contact.[119] Undeterred, the Black officers Petit Tomás, Barthélemy, and Louis defected to France and attacked Spanish camps.[120] Not only were they close to Jean-François, but Barthélemy had actually been one of Boukman's coconspirators at the outset of the revolution.[121] As symbolically significant defections mounted, French agents seeded rumors that Spain might re-enslave them.[122]

Meanwhile, morale was declining among the Black Auxiliaries. By April 1794 most of their troops were barely clothed, partly because of their generals' lavish expenditures. Jean-François's diminished force had recently spent an astonishing 16,000 pesos. The Spanish forces, though undersupplied, prepared to take Cap-Français at last.[123]

Opportunely for France, a ship arrived in Jacmel with news of the French Republic's confirmation of emancipation, which greatly enhanced French credibility. It finally showed more ideological consistency and commitment to Black liberty. Portillo rightly speculated that the news would "influence the increase in desertions." Fearing an "internal uprising," officials awaited "further disasters" and assumed that unrest would spread to Santo Domingo.[124] That spring, Spanish troops arrested five French republicans— one white, one mulâtre, and three Black *citoyens*—for inciting sedition at the border. Revolutionary encroachments into Dominican society became routine.[125] The tides turned for the French Republic.

Among the consequences of this proclamation was the shift in direction for Louverture, one of the most fascinating and consequential figures in the history of the Americas (and about whom new biographical details follow), who then began a protracted drift from the Black Auxiliaries and Spain. His decision to join France, a momentous move in hemispheric history, has invited much scholarly conjecture. The new evidence surrounding the decision presented here illuminates more about his deliberately opaque activities starting in early 1794, demonstrating a protracted, calculated break motivated by complex personal, principled, and political considerations.[126]

Louverture's relations with Biassou began to deteriorate when he received the same gold medal as Biassou, yet "resented" having to still answer to his mercurial, sometimes overbearing peer. For example, that spring Biassou had traveled past Louverture's quarters at Marmelade and commandeered some of his troops' cattle. A more infuriating affront occurred when an officer under Biassou asserted command at Dondon over Louverture's adopted nephew Moïse. This led to an argument, which escalated, and Moïse lost three fingers when Biassou's officer drew his sword.

Louverture, still described by Spanish officers as "noble in his actions," wrote a pointed letter demanding an explanation from Biassou, who was allegedly "without religion [and] given to drink." Unsatisfied, Louverture unexpectedly raided Biassou's camp in Dondon, perhaps on the night of 24 March 1794, "killing a few, and tying up his concubines," partners who may have been symbols of prestige in the Atlantic African cultural context. Projecting cowardice, Biassou fled into the mountains. After this measured reprisal, Louverture attracted many of Biassou's own troops. Jean-François, who was also furious with Biassou, for having executed his aide, Adan, for perceived insubordination, allowed the Spanish generals to broker a truce.

Spanish officials recognized Louverture as "very reflective in his business" but thought he was perhaps "not of a Spanish heart as surely as [Biassou]," and that he would be "fearsome" as an enemy. Although Louverture marched again under Spanish flags a week later, his curious conduct continued.[127] He and some of his officers, including Henry Christophe, protested Spanish trading of the enslaved and coddling of French émigrés.[128] Quietly, Jean-Jacques Dessalines, Louverture's closest aide, may have orchestrated covert dissent.[129]

Soon thereafter, Louverture met with an anti-Spanish republican identified as a mulâtre. Then, in late April, "Blacks under the command of [General Toussaint], so favored by Spain, attacked Gonaïves," which Spain had taken only months before in a major strategic accomplishment. Although Louverture kept his distance, likely to maintain plausible deniability, his troops had identified themselves as allies when they approached Spanish lines, but had then burned properties and killed certain residents around the city. Biassou, with diminished forces, could not intervene. After this, on the night of 2 May, a Black man approached Spanish sentinels at San Miguel, posing as an affiliate of Biassou. Upon questioning, he confessed to spying for those at Marmelade, where Louverture and his troops had gathered to prepare for combat.

On 5 May, two Black messengers arrived to explain away Louverture's unusual deeds in Gonaïves. These communications continued into 7 May. In his letters, Louverture indicated that his troops were angry at seeing émigrés they personally knew, prompting retributions. However, his depictions did not fully explain his army's other coordinated, cagey maneuvers. A factor likely influencing Louverture's protracted positioning was that his wife, and perhaps other family members, were still under Spanish protection at San Rafael.[130]

Shortly thereafter, at San Rafael, in a supposed gesture of peace, he perhaps met with Spanish officials, or even went to Mass with them. With the Spanish perhaps at ease, he then issued a surprise attack on Spanish troops from within the town.[131] Throughout the spring of 1794, Louverture's goals likely pivoted to attracting more troops, impeding rivals, safely reuniting with his family, continuing to access Spanish resources, and bloodlessly gaining strategic positions without overly alarming Spanish officers. Meeting these objectives was essential if he was to optimize a successful defection to France. Thus, though those who were still officially his allies saw his behavior as erratic or even suspect, and though he still professed loyalty to Spain and dismissed news of his alliance with France as rumors, his tactics were likely quite calculated.

Intriguingly, Louverture had been in no ideological rush to accede to new French promises of *liberté*, *égalité*, and *fraternité* for Black people. The practical Louverture, who certainly held his own convictions about Black liberty regardless of vacillating European opinions, watched and waited for eight months after the decree by Sonthonax and Polverel, and several weeks after news arrived of the French assembly's proclamation of abolition. Later, he claimed to have raised the tricolore because of emancipation. However, the always cautious, deliberate Louverture prudently waited to see if the decrees would hold and if popular support would follow. He was also irreversibly annoyed with Biassou, with his momentary professional ceiling, and with Spanish views on slavery.[132]

Louverture was unenthralled with his new French allies. He scolded Sonthonax for not abolishing slavery immediately upon his arrival, thus delaying trust for French policies. Louverture shamed his hesitancy about doing so "in the face of the Supreme Being," perhaps a reference to ongoing Deist experiments in metropolitan France. Sonthonax had criticized Louverture for aiding a "Vendée" on Hispaniola, comparing the Spanish campaigns to the enduring, horrifically bloody Catholic counterrevolution against the French Republic in northwestern France. Many others compared Santo Domingo to the Vendée. These ruptures were only two of many that would beset Louverture and Sonthonax.[133] With time, he would deftly ascend to shaping all of Hispaniola.

Born into slavery as the first son of an Arada prince, Louverture had once managed enslaved laborers, likely including Jean-Jacques Dessalines. Freed about two decades before the revolution, he had also bided his time before joining the insurgency against France. He was unequivocally brilliant in military, political, and strategic calculations, and he was able to maximize the major fractures of the era to grasp autonomy for his communities.

In the early revolution this meant aligning with Spain. Louverture likely had formally joined France by early May 1794, though he concealed it by continuing to communicate with Spanish officials for at least several more weeks, likely to buy himself space. He defected with three thousand troops along with his trusted officers Dessalines and Henry Christophe, who would also later change the course of Caribbean history.

By June, in a precipitous regression from his hero status, Louverture had become a traitor to his former allies in Santo Domingo. He publicly continued to champion Catholic virtues, and, for tactical reasons, despite having grown up around Vodou, began repressing it.[134] His unchanging faith professions mattered less than his duplicity against Spain's Catholic majesty, his abandonment of evangelism, and his alignment with an anticlerical and secular French Republic, however. He thus contributed to a template that would come to define elite Dominican suspicions of their neighbors to the west. Louverture and his adherents fell from grace and were irreversibly relegated into a Blackness tied to heresy, violence, and a radicalism associated with the quest for rights and emancipation.

Louverture therefore embraced the French Revolution's belated promotion of racial rights, and his perceived betrayal severely demoralized the Spanish ranks and damaged their increasingly beleaguered campaigns. García's near death from a mosquito-borne fever at around the same time exacerbated the fallout from Louverture's departure.[135] Officials in Santo Domingo, emotionally frayed by the disintegration of their once-shared religious ingroup, reacted with paranoia toward the Black Auxiliaries, which was counterproductive.

They also increasingly feared deceit among Dominicans of color. As the revolutionary tide rose and unrest seeped into the Dominican border towns, the Spanish Empire, unsurprisingly, responded with religious conciliation. A trusted priest intervened in "calming the Blacks" to stop locals from emulating Louverture.[136] To support stability and acculturation in Spanish-held territories, in mid-1794 the cardinal archbishop of Toledo sent six experienced French refractory priests exiled in Spain to assimilate ostensibly reprobate francophones in occupied Saint-Domingue.[137] The pope soon absolved several French ecclesiastics of "censures and irregularities" from having taken "the oath and adopted the maxims" of the French Republic, thus permitting them to serve Spanish projects.[138] Many priests in Saint-Domingue abandoned their churches.[139] The "vestiges of religion" that the "French erased" included some steadfast priests who had been sentenced to death by the commissioners before fleeing to Jamaica and Santo Domingo.[140]

Retrenching in cultural combat, officials in Santo Domingo still hoped to soothe conflicts through Catholic mediation. Portillo, like many elites in Santo Domingo, saw Hispaniola as a battlefront for defending eternal souls and nearly 1,800 years of Christian tradition. Portillo celebrated new believers, whose "submission," he said, had "filled us with joy." The archbishop stated that on the other side of the Atlantic, "the French nation offered . . . the mere terms for the political and temporal," while for Spain, "our principality is not of this world." France neglected the divine and threatened the "intimate connection to the spiritual." This was an impressive juxtaposition to the seemingly ephemeral novelty of the new French "project of governing kingdoms" that had elevated itself "against the science of God" to "extinguish the most flourishing monarchy of Europe [and] Christianity." The French, he said, were "ridiculing [Catholic] beliefs" and enraging "the whole Catholic world."[141]

Holy war rhetoric emanated more loudly from Santo Domingo, Spain, and Rome as French republicanism spread and attracted new Black co-citizens. The pope himself was aware of the Black Auxiliaries, who with other "true Christian soldiers" supposedly resembled the legendary Jewish warrior Judah Maccabee.[142] For them, spiritual assimilation had become essential to quelling social upheaval and key to españolizar (Hispanicizing) diverse Francophone subjects.[143]

In June, despite poor health, advanced age, and a grueling horseback journey, Archbishop Portillo visited the southern border to assess church initiatives, including among the Maniel maroons resettled at Naranjo. Amid nearby racial revolution, the maroons learned sacraments and tended their homes. Portillo, whose expensive miter hat and clerical attire amused the maroons, absolved them, inspected their homes and crops, and performed baptisms. He demanded more Spanish language instruction, as many maroons still spoke *guineo* (a general reference to African languages); the imposition of Spanish surnames; and cessation of their "superstitious" observances.

These maroons, who bid Portillo farewell with gunfire and log drums, soon bid the Spanish farewell altogether. Distracted by French and British actions, Spain failed to deter buccaneers from terrorizing locals. Portillo recorded that attackers bound several captives together by their throats, pulled them away, then sold them to smugglers roving the coast with impunity. As Spanish rule weakened, many maroons returned to Maniel rather than face re-enslavement or conscription as imperial instruments.[144] Their precarities caused Portillo to wonder if "kings on the coast of Africa" could have better protected them.[145] By 1797, Maniel maroons had even ambushed Spanish troops, showing that as conditions worsened, self-preservation prevailed.[146]

While some maroons sincerely embraced Catholicism and Spain, collectively they had expediently bided their time until they could regain autonomy amid state incursions and imperial conflict.[147] They were hardly alone. When Spain could neither contain domestic discontent, nor protect its newly absorbed subjects, nor offer the best terms to its Black allies, the groups reasoned through how to accomplish their own ambitions. Elites in Santo Domingo responded to this reversal with reductionist, racially accusatory explanations.

REGRESSIONS

Jean-François, perhaps the most trusted leader among the remaining Black Auxiliaries, compounded the contextual negativity for his allies through his "horrendous conduct" toward his white French counterparts.[148] The massacre his army committed at Fort Dauphin is very well-known among scholars as a turning point in the Haitian Revolution.[149] However, new analytical and archival findings herein shed more light on what happened, including details showing Spanish complicity. Afterward, the Black Auxiliaries explained their motives. Saliently, as they had complained to Spanish officials since late 1791, they said they had watched their former owners, who had brutalized them, gain resources and refuge from Spain. The French royalists regularly insulted them and taunted them about re-enslavement. With their recent defeats and the defection of Louverture, their frustration, ire, and paranoia were intense. All these events signified Spanish regression.

At seven o'clock in the morning on 7 July 1794, Spanish forces apparently received intelligence that Jean-Baptiste Villate, a mulâtre and top French general, planned to attack their new position at Fort Dauphin with a considerable force. Jean-François and his officer Benjamin Dubison helped them situate their defenses and doubled the Spanish forces on the outskirts of town. As recounted by a Spanish officer, "Between ten and eleven that same morning [General] Jean-François appeared in the land gate at the front of his cavalry." However, the terms of French surrender barred the Black Auxiliaries from entering the town. Perhaps the Spanish guards ignored these terms. Or, possibly due to the city walls, Spanish troops could not see that Jean-François led more than a thousand troops, and, thinking it was only the general and some officers, they welcomed him through the gates.

In any case, as his many troops packed the plaza, Jean-François, pistols in hand, spoke with Vázquez and some other Spaniards. Jean-François asked to speak personally with officer Fermín Montaño, who welcomed the general to his quarters by the square. Sword in hand, Jean-François explained that despite working tirelessly on the frontier, conditions were worsening. Noticeably agitated, "raising his voice, and with a decided tone, and uncomposed," he demanded that all the white French occupants leave Fort Dauphin within the hour. Montaño tried to dissuade him, explaining that evacuating them was impossible. Jean-François, frustrated, arose and said, "All will perish." As he stepped from the entryway toward the plaza, Jean-François gave a hand signal to his troops, who began moving into the streets.[150]

Vázquez, who had arrived at the center of Fort Dauphin at eleven that morning with a small entourage, busily assured residents of their safety. Witnesses recounted that "the priest Vasques [sic], a mulato, had a great influence" on Jean-François, for "Jean-François humbly kissed his hand when he came near." The Spanish officers begged Vázquez to prevent bloodshed by mediating with Jean-François and Benjamin. Vázquez's intercession failed, and Spanish officers promised to protect the disarmed, frightened white French people, who retreated into their homes to flee the Black Auxiliaries, many of whom they had previously enslaved. Some witnesses claimed that Jean-François whistled to his troops, signaling them to start the executions, which began sporadically roughly half an hour after their arrival. Some Black residents of Fort Dauphin may have even joined the Black Auxiliaries in attacking the French elites, shouting, "Long live the king of Spain: let us kill the French people and spare the Spaniards." Their acts were clearly against their recent oppressors, not all white people.

Most of the eight hundred Spanish troops present watched. Some leveled bayonets at the French to prevent their escape, while others exclaimed that the French deserved it. The Spanish officers did collect a few prominent residents into a defensible park, and they dressed others in Spanish clothing to disguise them. The massacre ended that evening, and the bodies of many of the French who had run toward ships in the harbor in hope of escape remained on the wharves for days. Jean-François counted 771 dead, while his secretary, Dupinous, estimated 742.[151] During the attack, Jean-François's troops wore mismatched and tattered men's and women's dress clothes, so lacking were they in supplies from their Spanish allies. Jean-François wore silver, jewels, and rosaries.[152] Myriad military frustrations and insults from their former French masters had risen to the surface to momentarily break his typical restraint toward civilians. Such extreme behavior was highly uncharacteristic of him.

Under scrutiny, and realizing his error, Jean-François tried to explain his actions. He claimed to have learned of Louverture's upsetting treachery just days before, in part after arresting several Black couriers who, suspiciously, were carrying correspondence between Louverture's camp and white French partisans at Fort Dauphin. Jean-François had also discovered a French plan to assassinate him, to send Louverture a gold medal from the French Republic to cement his services, and to counterattack Fort Dauphin to force Spain "to return all their Black slaves." These letters showed that the French were trying to convince Black Auxiliaries that Spain, with Jean-François's help, was still selling Black captives from Saint-Domingue, and that the French were offering more expansive liberties.

The day after he intercepted the couriers, Jean-François claimed that Louverture had approached his camp with his troops and a number of white French associates. Louverture's group had attacked with such fury that as his army scattered Jean-François lost the letters that had so upset him. His officers reported hearing rumors that white French residents around Fort Dauphin were inquiring about his whereabouts, that they had captured some of his officers, and that Vázquez had boarded a ship and abandoned him. All of this, he said, had left him worried about potential republican plots. He said he had intended to enter the town, arrest the bad actors who had corresponded with Louverture, and turn them over to the Spanish for punishment. However, far more French people were present than he had expected, and, he said, "many of my soldiers and some of my chiefs . . . put fire to all the French whites against my orders."[153]

As the sources developed in preceding paragraphs show, Jean-François was more involved than he ever admitted. The Black Auxiliaries present that day had felt insulted and were infuriated by seeing the familiar faces of former enslavers. These *grand blancs*, who were perhaps responsible for their most painful memories under slavery, had siphoned off much-needed Spanish resources. The Black Auxiliaries were understandably indignant that Spain had assured their French royalist collaborators that they could keep their property and continue the practice of enslavement.[154] Apparently, some of the dead grand blancs had recently sent messages to Jean-François's troops threatening punishment and hinting that they would soon return to plantation labor. This filled the Black Auxiliaries with "irreconcilable rancor against all white French for the atrocious punishments they [had] previously experienced." This is what had motivated the "sin committed 7 July."[155] Reasonably, the Black Auxiliaries feared re-enslavement.

The Fort Dauphin massacre did not have just a single cause. Once the encounter had begun, tensions had quickly escalated. Contextually, pro-republic forces had frayed the Black Auxiliaries' nerves with urban ambushes. Jean-François, specifically, suspected a plot among the residents of Fort Dauphin.[156] García had retreated from the area, due to illness, and could not intervene. Jean-François's wife had also departed, excluding her from possible reprisals.[157]

Officials in Santo Domingo lamented the impact of this "catastrophe" of "bloody furor" for Spanish trustworthiness in Saint-Domingue, and they soured on the Black Auxiliaries, feeling they were unreliable and lacking in ethics.[158] They were further perplexed by a rumor from Silvén, a Black Auxiliary who said that some among his ranks wanted to eliminate all Spaniards, too.[159] The rumor was possibly exaggerated, yet it showed that the break in trust was mutual. Soon thereafter, Jean-François's officer Noël Artó abandoned his post at Ouanaminthe, secured French support, and nearly captured Dajabón. Throughout the summer of 1794, officials in Santo Domingo despaired at their recent turn of fortunes.[160]

As Spanish efforts stumbled, José Urízar, regent of the Audiencia, warned commanders to watch their Black allies with suspicion to avoid more damaging defections or mistakes. He blamed "the Black general Tuzaint [sic] and his army" for the "bastard offenses" against Spain in Nord, where their forces had strategically retreated after also confronting an "epidemic of fevers." Realizing their sudden general weakness, Spanish officials rushed to maintain "domestic peace" by commissioning a new border militia, hoping to protect a Dominican society that had yet to face social revolution.[161]

Gaining territory that Spain never could, their former ally, Toussaint Louverture, with an "excess multitude" of Black support, defeated the British at Port-au-Prince and Saint-Marc in September 1794. Portillo lamented the new state of affairs: that Saint-Domingue was "today in the possession of the British or [Black] brigands, without the Spanish possessing more than Fort Dauphin and Mirebalais." Beyond the combat of Nord, his "poor priests of the South," so recently confident about their evangelism, now met with intimidation from British interference.[162] British forces crept ever closer to the Dominican border, and despite losses to Louverture attracted new inland supporters.[163] As expansive Spanish plans to rebuild Saint-Domingue's economy failed, many priests simply fled.[164] Spanish projects retreated.

Elites in Santo Domingo began to more directly link radical principles, Frenchness, and Blackness. They asserted that the French had "learned that their force is superior, and after all the Blacks have declared for the republicans, fanaticism has been made general." Reverting from their comparatively racially inclusive vision for Hispanic expansion, they concluded that "we should consider all of them our enemies." Expanding suspicions connected Blackness to the republic and doubts to the once esteemed Black Auxiliaries.

Furthermore, estimates suggested that continuation of the Spanish military campaign would consume millions of additional pesos beyond the millions already spent. Exacerbating the situation, in late November 1794, the *fiscal* (royal attorney) of Santo Domingo investigated the disappearance of about 48,000 pesos from Spanish accounts in Nord. Those in charge of the budget conveniently faulted the Black Auxiliaries under Jean-François who had been in Fort Dauphin. Although no direct evidence was found to implicate them, the mystery further burdened their reputation with their Spanish allies.

The near death of Governor García also hampered Spanish efforts. Urízar argued, perhaps in a power grab, that Santo Domingo needed an experienced substitute to calm the colony. Surprisingly, in October García finally reappeared in the capital after his entourage carried him there when he fell too ill to ride a horse. To recover his own health after visiting the borderlands, Archbishop Portillo also vacated the capital, to bathe in Baní.[165] Ineptitude and illness hastened the pace of Spanish decline.

In another brilliant maneuver by Louverture, Spanish defenses collapsed at key the border towns San Miguel and San Rafael.[166] Despite their enemy's lack of artillery, the seven hundred Spanish troops in San Rafael panicked when a supposed "mob" confronted them. They abandoned their own artillery and supplies in a disorderly retreat. The Spanish commander, Juan Lleonart, then also abandoned San Miguel and Hincha, prematurely surrendering the towns without actual combat. This development sent a stream of panicked Dominicans fleeing from the border to the ports. The peculiar, panicked decisions of Lleonart and his colleague Matias Armona eventually consumed two years of investigations and trials. The brilliance of Louverture, with his larger, more motivated forces under the French Republic, flummoxed Spanish forces.[167]

To guard and honor the "lives of their children and women," their "ancestors," and their "altars," dedicated Spanish subjects on the Dominican border fought against duress from Louverture and ideas of the French Revolution. In defense, these particular Dominicans invoked symbols of

Hispanic belonging, "to imprint upon the hearts of the French that every Spaniard was a Lion." Such defensive rhetoric defined Dominicans against the radicalism, irreverence, and Blackness they increasingly assigned to their neighbors.[168]

This Hispanic traditionalism and religious nationalism had taken hold among Dominicans resisting dire situations caused by the "General of the Party of Blacks named Tusen [sic]." In Azua, at least seventy-five miles from the border, locals watched the multitudes of families migrating from San Rafael, San Miguel, and Hincha and feared that further losses, perhaps of Bánica, Las Cahobas, and Neiba, would bring the war to them and eventually to the capital. Some Dominican residents resigned themselves to the "defense of the religion and our monarch and country."[169] San Juan de la Maguana voiced similar resolve.[170] The Audiencia praised them for being "worthy to occupy an honorable place in history."[171]

With the retreat of the outward-looking Spanish projects, in the mid-1790s some Dominicans turned to preserving Hispanic values at home against encroaching debates over republican principles. At first, this seemed an easy battle. Dominican elites increasingly redefined their supposed superiorities to their western neighbors, a trend that would only increase as Dominicans of color entertained similar revolutionary ideals. In Paris, the recently removed Sonthonax and Polverel insisted that their proclamations for the "genius of liberty and equality" had stifled this "little Vendée" of royalism on Hispaniola.[172] The tide had started to turn.

CONCLUSION

While Spanish military momentum stalled, Hispanic monarchism and religiosity continued to compete for adherents, including for those Dominicans who could be influenced by appeals to public piety in the face of social revolution, and for Black Auxiliaries still seeking material and spiritual benefits in their war against the French. In an elaborate Catholic ceremony, Georges Biassou wed his fiancée, Romana, on 1 September 1794 in the town of Bánica. Their marriage marked an apex for Hispanic Catholic cultural capital in the Haitian Revolution. The mayor and the priest, Juan Sánchez Valverde, who was related to Antonio Sánchez Valverde, served as witnesses for the couple, who resided in Hincha.[173]

The wedding took place after Portillo met Biassou during his border trip. "Biassou came here with a great escort to visit me," Portillo wrote.

"I strained my poverty to make him a decent gift . . . [and] he swore his loyalty to me . . . with the most solemn expressions." After exchanging pleasantries, the archbishop told Biassou he appreciated his request for edification, forging much-needed personal rapport. When Biassou then asked him for the "sacraments of confirmation and matrimony," Portillo said, "I changed tone." Portillo chastised Biassou, who allegedly "cohabited with seven women," for his lifestyle, and told him he would have to withhold the sacraments "until he [had] satisfied God, and me, with a noticeable correction." Biassou then "retired to his home without responding to me, nor speaking a word," wrote the archbishop. "He closed himself morosely in a chamber." With Biassou sulking, Portillo realized that in taking advantage of what he had seen as a teachable moment he had insulted the indispensable general, and to prevent geopolitical fallout he sent Juan Sánchez Valverde to Biassou to "console and encourage him." Biassou "received him[,] saying that he would like to save himself," and said he recognized that the archbishop "was an ambassador from God who had shown him a glimpse of the Gates of Hell."

Biassou may have experienced genuine remorse. On the other hand, his confession and outwardly visible lifestyle changes may have also been aimed at maintaining Spanish goodwill and gaining material blessings from their spiritual world. His affirmation of Spanish norms temporarily reinvigorated a shaky cultural and military project that was reeling from high-level defections, a path Biassou himself could have easily taken. Biassou agreed to change his amorous ways, and "for love of his fiancé . . . had separated from the other women, whom he confessed had been scandalous loves." Soon thereafter, Portillo officiated the ceremony, later recording that it was "a great gathering of all the principal people of the town." One of the likely attendees was Pablo Alí, a devoted aid to Biassou, who, over the many years of his career on the island, proved to be a remarkably adept operative within the cultural politics of Hispaniola. The local attendees amplified the royalist aspect of the festivities by bringing to the ceremony "the portrait of their King, which the groom took on his chest," Portillo wrote. In any case, Biassou's use of the image of the king of Spain displayed a spiritual aspect of the alliance that spanned the Atlantic yet divided the island.

After the ceremony, Portillo excused himself from the party "to leave the couple a decent liberty in the marriage bed." The raucous festivities that followed lasted until one in the morning, with Biassou, the "Black Titan," always the center of attention. "The table was large and abundant . . . nor did they lack their dance," wrote an attendant. The priest José Nolasco Mañon helped pay for the whole event. Like the marriage of Jean-François a year prior, by participating, Portillo deliberately ingratiated himself with the Black Auxiliaries and a key Dominican border town.[174] The Black Auxiliaries wielded both martial and marital savvy.

Such weddings bound a core of talented and ambitious Black leaders even more deeply into a marriage with Spanish Catholic culture, with social practices at the convergence of utility, sincerity, and partisanship. Their sentiments may have been sincere, and yet their actions also had a material function, as they helped them win weapons and cash. They also demonstrated a spiritual flexibility and an ability to mask extant African observances or blend them with Catholic beliefs and practices. Such rituals revealed power relations, partisanship, and social network affirmations. Vodou was unquestionably influential among their ranks, yet Catholicism was the supernatural idiom of their allies in Santo Domingo, who saw the Black Auxiliaries' success and upward mobility as blessings for their faithful service.

Through new connections forged early in 1792, public performances of devotion contrasted with perceptions of irreverence and mediated inclusion for people of color to distinguish loyal Spanish subjects from revolutionaries. The Black Auxiliaries' appropriation of Spanish spiritual vocabularies to explain their geopolitical motivations, most dramatically in their wholesale rewriting of their August 1791 revolts away from Vodou and toward Catholicism, bolstered elite Dominicans' conceits of difference from their neighbors in Saint-Domingue and established a litmus test for Black piety and Hispanic inclusion. This development unwittingly contributed to an embryonic Dominican religious exceptionalism, atavisms of which later bolstered the anti-Haitian nationalism tied to the 1790s. By the end of 1794, Santo Domingo was anticipating attacks by Louverture as well as French republican infiltration. As the Spanish campaigns collapsed into a defense of Santo Domingo, so, too, did their attempts to assimilate the Black majority of Saint-Domingue.

Black soldiers once seen as pious converts and collaborators who had avenged French brutality rapidly became supposedly heretical, untrustworthy, duplicitous, violent, and republican. These traits first correlated with anti-French views, yet with time, the negative connotations of Blackness and Africanness increased. Over ensuing years, when Dominicans of color explored similar radical ideals, in elites' eyes they fell into these same categories, and, after 1804, into being "Haitian." In this era, and amid a Dominican majority of color, sufficient spiritual signs mattered even more to Hispanic inclusion. Similar discourses of difference born in the 1790s have regularly reemerged to inform exclusionary Dominican policies. However, only months later, Juan Sánchez Valverde fled Louverture's forces at the border.[175] Rumors of a treaty with France portended a tidal rise in the revolution that began on the Dominican borders and inundated Santo Domingo in 1795, immersing Dominicans in the identity crises of the revolutionary era.[176]

FOUR

MANY ENEMIES WITHIN,
1795–1798

In October 1795, news arrived that Spain had ceded Santo Domingo to France in the Treaty of Basel. Sentiments of peril, outrage, and betrayal coursed through the streets of the capital, where one woman who read the treaty reportedly screamed, "My island, my homeland!" before dying. This story extolled an archetype of virtuous Hispanic femininity imperiled by, yet resisting, French sacrilege.

Elites feared how oppressed Dominicans of color would react to the end of Spanish rule amid surging rights discourses and growing Black power. Most could not believe the reversal of fortunes. Devout Catholics in the population watched as supernatural imperatives withered. A year after the Dominicans had nearly routed France, Spain had readily relinquished Santo Domingo.[1]

Exacerbating the situation, Paris instructed French officials to "conquer [their] new siblings."[2] This did not necessarily mean more violence. Rather, they intended to cultivate love and respect for France to "completely Frenchify" the Dominicans while simultaneously convincing them that the republic would tolerate Catholicism. Convincing devout Dominicans of this, given what they had read about revolutionary anticlericalism, heard from French priests, and witnessed in the Haitian Revolution, became a Sisyphean task for French officials.[3]

French efforts included sending a *tricolore* commission comprised of one Black, one *mulâtre*, and one white envoy to tell enslaved Dominicans— incorrectly, as the treaty timeline and terms remained incomplete—that they were free. This announcement briefly caused *infinitos cimarrones* (innumerable runaways). France also gave Archbishop Fernando Portillo the option of staying on as the "Bishop of Ayti." He declined and fixated his angst on the continuing French anticlerical persecutions. Convinced that pro-French Black operatives were surveilling his movements, Portillo embraced ideas of his own martyrdom. He warned Dominicans of retributive violence from the French, who he said were "equal . . . [to] a Mohammedan or idolater." These were "glorious circumstances," he added, "to sacrifice life in honor of the religion and the monarchy."[4]

This terminology exacerbated suspicions that the French posed an existential threat of supernatural significance to their culture. Many elite Dominicans started adhering even more vehemently to their Hispanic heritage, became more viscerally anti-French, and intensified their anti-Black responses toward assimilation attempts.[5] Papal officials recoiled at the secular and revolutionary purges France might perpetrate.[6] One priest, however, dramatically denounced Spain, married an enslaved woman, and pursued citizenship in the French Republic. He was not alone. Indeed, these cosmological conflicts reflected deep divisions among the population.

Imperial churn and racial mobility enveloped the colony, producing many new enemies within Dominican society. Some challenged Iberian traditions, while others challenged French occupation. Though they had been deeply connected to the Haitian Revolution, Dominicans had witnessed comparatively little domestic rebellion. From 1795 to 1798, Dominican society was finally consumed by the fundamental antagonisms of the Age of Revolutions.

Revolutionary conspiracies within Santo Domingo multiplied in this era, though only partly as a result of French revolutionary exposure. Many discontented Dominicans welcomed French influence, with hopes of realizing greater liberties.[7] Some elites briefly embraced the idea of British intervention. As Spanish protections weakened and internal dissent increased, a riptide of white flight swept hundreds of elite families from Santo Domingo, further cementing a Dominican majority of African descent.[8] These migrations and demographic reconfigurations accelerated the trend of people of color entering politics. Echoing familial metaphors, discourses on cultural descent and on who would control Dominican belief and belonging escalated.

This inward pivot amid the cessation of three consecutive centuries of Spanish colonialism precipitated a rethinking of Dominican identities and shared futures. As popular solidarities crossed the island, elite Dominicans felt attacked and abandoned. People of African descent across Hispaniola began to connect around common experiences and ambitions. Concomitantly, elite discourses wrote supposed racial regression onto many who embraced revolutionary ideals. These domestic power disputes sharply defined a virulent strain of Iberian distinction and Catholicism against perceived threats of entwined radical egalitarianism and impiety as a colonial antecedent to later elite Dominican national identity. This era opened foundational debates over ideas of Dominican nation-building and lasting discourses over differences and commonalities with the Dominicans' neighbors to the west.[9]

As the Black Auxiliaries declined and broke up, the French Republic became the salient promoter of Black mobilization in this era. However, their legacy continued long after their disbandment, disproportionately influencing Dominican society where many of their veterans settled. Some of them reappeared in major events over the next three decades. Their legendary civility and piety also became a benchmark against which Dominicans of color had to measure their actions. Dominican elites defined those who they thought fell short as more socially aberrant, as heretical, as more French, and sometimes as more Black, as they had with Toussaint Louverture and many others.

Another very different enemy to the status quo in Santo Domingo also emerged at this time. Some Dominicans, frightened at the prospect of losing their cultural and political power, sought British affiliation against the empowered Black partisans to their west. Archbishop Portillo said, "Every day the risk of sedition grows, dividing the people into two factions, one for the British, and the other the French." These divisions somewhat tracked racial divides.[10]

British promises of Catholic protections (despite state Anglicanism), of a robust commerce, and of moderate constitutional monarchy briefly surged in popularity. In 1796, many elites felt so thoroughly abandoned by the major powers of Spain and France that through "concealed maneuvers of stealthy spies and agents" a "positive foundation" formed in favor of British rule.[11] Capitalizing on this sense of abandonment, British officials leveraged "flattering promises and alluring cash" to attract Dominican support.[12] Merchants, clergy, bureaucrats, soldiers, and whole towns in Santo Domingo were "seduced" into supporting British rule, which was pictured as being more moderate than French rule.[13] This fervent and sometimes unsolicited Dominican support for the United Kingdom even often surprised British officials, who reacted quickly to prevent French rule from taking hold. Secret plots to put Santo Domingo into the British sphere occupied the colony for months.

The Spanish management of Santo Domingo lingered for nearly seven years after the treaty was signed. French provisional agent Philippe Roume, who wielded limited influence, resided in the capital to ease the cession. However, his actions to cultivate republican fervor often exacerbated cultural panic. This included panic over claims that the emancipation of the enslaved applied to Santo Domingo. Amid the tension, Spanish officials continued to manage slavery transactions, responses to revolts, and court cases.[14] By 1798, with Spanish and British interests in decline, and the French state increasingly in his sway, Toussaint Louverture began to plan how to integrate Santo Domingo into a cross-island political project. Though during this era lasting Dominican elite cultural identities solidified in opposition to France and Santo Domingo's Black neighbors, in the short term nascent, cross-island cooperation by people of color started bringing the island together.

INCURSIONS, SUBVERSIONS, REACTIONS

In the weeks and months before the Treaty of Basel legally punctuated three centuries of Spanish rule in Santo Domingo, popular unrest spilled over into Dominican society from the neighboring revolution. By mid-1795, Joaquín García had dramatically stated that constant vigilance had made him an "Argos," a reference to the hundred-eyed monster of Greek mythology. That May in Samaná—a coveted strategic port in the northeast on a large, protected bay far beyond the border—officials apprehended several local Blacks (some enslaved), three French republican agents, and the large stash of weapons they had smuggled onto the remote coast. The arrest followed a similar failed plot that had been discovered in Hincha. Governor García rushed troops to Samaná and sent the prisoners to Santo Domingo to make "an exemplary lesson" of them to intimidate other revolutionary Dominicans.[15] Pessimistic officials looked inward to defend Dominican society, insisting that Blacks were now "in the majority" and that "exhaustive surveillance alone outmatches them."[16]

Archbishop Portillo compared this new wave of anti-Spanish subversion to "a sponge," remarking on how it would absorb resources. He asked parishes under duress to send "sacred vessels, vestments, and jewelry" to the capital to prevent them from being stolen. Many priests near the battlefront had ceased their correspondence. Some had fled, but others were likely dead. Many free Dominicans of color in the borderlands acquiesced to French *gens de couleur* officers, who enticed them with promises to respect their property in return for compliance. As Archbishop Portillo cynically put it, the "French contagion of debauchery" had finally infected Dominicans. He suspected that "the perfidious Tousen [*sic*]" wanted to rule all of Hispaniola.[17]

Louverture stymied Spanish campaigns in 1795 after joining France the year before.[18] His perceived duplicity had caused elite Dominicans to pivot toward defending their traditions from encroaching tempests of revolution and growing suspicions of Dominicans of color.[19] At the border, Louverture's army appropriated Dominican cattle, further displeasing Dominicans, especially those invested in the livestock industry.[20] Louverture then enjoyed victories at San Rafael, Hincha, and San Miguel, which brought his French army into Santo Domingo.[21] Though the capital region was tranquil, that would also change.[22]

Pro-French Black soldiers, now the group able to wield the "greatest strength" on the island, made appeals to enslaved Dominicans. They no longer feared "iron, fire, and blood" and became the "exemplars of general liberty," according to Spanish officials. After years of avoiding serious revolts, Dominican elites watched ideas that had supposedly broken "all respects and ties, divine and human," in Saint-Domingue, turning "beauties into corpses and ashes," enter Santo Domingo.[23] Under the pretense of forestalling subversive influences, officials continued selling Black prisoners.[24] García realized that domestic counterinsurgents would be unable to distinguish friends from enemies among the Dominican majority of color. Clumsy investigations and increased scrutiny antagonized local communities.[25]

Thousands of Black Auxiliaries remained allied with Spain, however, and officials thought that redoubled efforts might be able to prevent further territorial or personnel losses, even after the "disunion" with Biassou that so offended Louverture. Into this leadership breach stepped the "brave spirit" of Charles (Carlos) Lesec, a *mulato* commanding auxiliary troops. Lesec had distinguished himself by heroically defeating *citoyens* at Sainte-Suzanne in early April 1794.[26]

Before daybreak, Lesec's force had faced attack from four columns of "our enemies, the citizens," who tried to overrun and burn their encampment. Within minutes, Lesec's troops killed fifty attackers. The remaining French troops threw aside their equipment to flee, allowing the Black Auxiliaries to capture sixty guns. Lesec also learned that Jean-Baptiste Villate had received serious wounds.

During the battle, Lesec suffered numerous facial lacerations from splintered wood caused by a ricocheting bullet. Though injured, the "valiant commander" meted harsh punishments against Mamba, one of his captains, for hesitating in combat. His vigor impressed Spanish officers who doubted the affinities of the Black Auxiliaries. Lesec's many heroic actions served as an audition for the job of replacing Louverture. Soon, he held rank just under Jean-François.[27] As the Spanish position stabilized, Vázquez even attempted to entice Villate, whom Louverture was by then overshadowing, to defect from France.[28] Spain exalted Lesec as a model of loyalty and accomplishment and as someone who might reverse their myriad setbacks.[29] He even attracted praise from King Carlos IV.[30]

By April 1795, a year after his celebrated victory, Lesec commanded about one thousand of the remaining few thousand Black Auxiliaries. He assumed some of the roles Louverture had vacated, while Louverture, for his part, was busily overwhelming his former allies.[31] That month, however, an informant told Jean-François that Lesec planned to abandon his supposed "love" for Spain.

When Jean-François went to Sainte-Suzanne to investigate, his officer Benjamin Dubison stopped him from entering the camp. Apparently, Benjamin had learned that Lesec had ordered his troops to shoot at Jean-François and his retinue and had set an ambush on their retreat route. Thus informed, Benjamin and Jean-François instead entrapped Lesec. When Lesec realized that his plot had been compromised, he tried to escape on horseback. Benjamin's detachment fired at Lesec, killing him. Details emerged showing that Lesec had planned to deliver forts to Villate, the same man Lesec had nearly killed one year before. Lesec had paid for his dalliances with French republicans with his life.

Lesec's posthumous fall from Spanish favor was precipitous. After his death, a republican official from the nearby town of Trou appeared, likely to conspire with Lesec. Jean-François's troops killed him and arrested two additional republicans with letters. These citoyens carried tricolore cockades for Lesec to wear to show his "patriotism" toward France, outward signs confirming Spanish suspicions of "the union of his soul with his brothers the French." Along with these suspicions came assumptions of internal immorality.

The premeditated betrayal revealed in correspondence between Lesec and French officials shocked García, because "in another time," he had been known "for his loyalty." To curtail more losses to the French, who were offering pay increases, promotions, and notions of egalitarianism, García commended Jean-François for his decisive actions, and García awarded medals to remaining Black Auxiliaries. However, after experiences with Lesec and Louverture, others in Santo Domingo wondered if they could still trust their allies.

Like Louverture, whose Catholic credentials did not spare him from Spanish scorn, Lesec's reputation suffered a rhetorical blow, tarnished by his defection to France. Officials in Santo Domingo demoted Lesec posthumously, depicting his betrayal as a manifestation of innate Blackness defined in correlation to his affinity for republicanism. Documents describing Lesec's betrayal identified him as a *negro*, when he had previously been described as mulato. Conspiring with French republicans had marred his status in the racial hierarchy.[32] Elites in Santo Domingo thus wrote his racial regression, reflexively relegating him from brave mulato to Black in their estimation.

Spanish religious projects meanwhile came under doubt and declined in importance. Fearful of stories from France detailing an archbishop facing arrest, politicians attacking the church, and acrimony against dogma, Portillo implored Dominicans to reject revolutionary influences, and indeed, to abhor them on a supernatural scale. He rebuked the French for sending "Black deputies to Paris to procure themselves liberty." Previously unthinkable Deist alternatives appeared. Portillo pondered his own safety, and, implying holy war, pled with Dominicans to "defend [the nation] with our persons, lives, blood."

The archbishop's rhetoric deepened spiritual and racial divides. He said that Black French citizens were "very indifferent to the religion I profess," and more like "a Mohammedan or idolater."[33] French "libertinage" and the revolutionaries' inability to "guard the Divine . . . [or] respect the sacred churches" had produced anticlericalism, noted José Urízar. Rights discourses had begun enticing Dominicans more than faith professions, he said, and "joined them with the Black general Tusen [sic]." Officials in Santo Domingo, facing more defeats, prayed for retributive punishments of biblical proportions—especially plagues.[34]

Compounding these troubles, later in 1795 British forces began testing a strategy for capturing Dominican territory. Adam Williamson, governor of British-occupied Saint-Domingue, authorized attacks only on towns where the tricolore flew. When French forces captured a Dominican town, the British would then rout the French and raise the Union Jack, often with some local support. Thus, they expanded British influence while technically avoiding war with Spain.[35] This audacious, expedient policy allowed the British to capture large swaths of coveted Dominican lands.

Exhausted, Biassou fortified Bánica to block Dominican enemies from the capital.[36] Besieged, beleaguered priests sang Te Deums over troops and residents, exhorting them to defend their religion, their king, and their *patria*.[37] Dominicans soon had to reevaluate the viability of these invocations.

TREATY TUMULT, FRACTIOUS FRENCH

In August 1795 the ruling French Committee of Public Safety announced a peace treaty that would stun the island. They asked combatants to drop their weapons and let "harmony and friendship . . . reign between the French and Spanish of Santo Domingo."[38] Local French officials received orders to "conquer [their] new siblings" in Santo Domingo through "gentility, benevolence, [and the] purity of our customs." Though Paris promised advice for a prompt cession of Spanish rule, delays beset them for nearly seven more years.[39]

In this shocking reversal, and without recourse, Santo Domingo fell from the front line against France to facing French rule. With significant near-term gains for France, "the famous boss of the Blacks," as papal officials called Jean-François, soon faced banishment.[40] News of the treaty had arrived on Hispaniola by October 1795. Vázquez, who learned of the treaty from a ship at Monte Cristi, informed Jean-François and the 7,500 other remaining Black Auxiliaries.[41] Spanish officials suddenly saw the Black Auxiliaries as possible liabilities and sought their exile before they could "cause us much damage." Newly underemployed, dejected Black troops feared for their futures.[42]

Initially undeterred, Jean-François wanted to persist as a "defender of the cause of the Kings" with a holdout royalist faction against France. Knowing this, French officials sought his immediate exile.[43] Partly to disincentivize British contacts and promote peace, García advocated treating the "multitude" of ex–Black Auxiliaries, some of them saying they preferred "Spanish slavery to French liberty," with gratitude.[44]

Due to the logistical impossibility of mass evacuation, thousands of ex–Black Auxiliaries stayed in Santo Domingo, where many of them had families, some with Dominican partners. Unceremoniously, Jean-François and Biassou traveled toward the coast and permanent exile off Hispaniola. Some of the officers who were left behind, and briefly even Biassou himself, seriously considered British offers to help them continue fighting their despised former French masters, unlike "Toutsaint [sic]."[45]

Jean-François and four hundred of his closest associates, along with some four thousand prominent colonists, had fled by January 1796, mostly to Havana, Caracas, San Juan, and Trinidad.[46] Biassou and his retinue departed from Azua and eventually arrived at San Agustín (St. Augustine) in Florida.[47] Remaining French royalist allies also evacuated.[48] In a distinct divergence from the treatment of ex–Black Auxiliaries, whom Spain began ignoring soon after the ink dried on the treaty, generational benefits of wealth and power followed these families.[49]

Now fully exposed to the revolution, devout Dominicans hoped only to "avoid the guillotine" while keeping the faith.[50] Portillo explained the cessation of spiritual projects to distraught priests.[51] Clergy awaited the imposition of restrictions against Catholics in Santo Domingo like those in France.[52]

Impatient for instruction from Paris, General Étienne Laveaux selected three delegates from Saint-Domingue to visit Santo Domingo and implement his own interpretation of the treaty. For his own strategic benefit, he coveted Dominican resources and new Dominican recruits of color. Elites in Santo Domingo, who already feared that enslaved Dominicans would unite with their liberated neighbors of color, were terrified.[53] Spanish officials rejected French requests for piecemeal delivery of key Dominican locations, which could have allowed the British opportunities to take more territory. Despite considerable costs, Spain continued governing Santo Domingo. Ignoring these contingencies, in late 1795 Laveaux sent the three emissaries to Santo Domingo.

These carefully selected tricolore officials—one Black, one mulâtre, and one white—represented egalitarianism, the three major racial groups, and the blue, white, and red of the new French flag. Aside from this symbolism, the envoys had noteworthy backgrounds. The Black official had survived life on a notorious plantation; the mulâtre was a distinguished revolutionary; and the white man had been a comedian or entertainer in Saint-Marc. Without notice, this group, who "suppose[d] themselves . . . owners of [Dominican] towns," circulated a plethora of revolutionary papers and tried to abolish slavery along their route to the capital.[54]

Whispers of abolition proved a catalyst for Dominican uprisings, and "infinitos cimarrones" fled their owners.[55] Dominicans of color took this opportunity to attempt liberation against systemic grievances. Revolts shook La Vega, Baní, and Cotuí, towns far from the border.[56] Officials scrambled to stop rebels from "incinerating the canefields" like their neighbors in Saint-Domingue.[57] Some enslaved Dominicans killed their overseers, aiding in French intimidation of traditional Hispanic power yet driving many elites toward British protection.[58]

Infuriating Laveaux, officials quickly expelled the French envoys.[59] Attempts to intervene in Dominican law failed, and slavery continued far beyond the treaty deadline for Spanish withdrawal.[60] While asserting that France only recognized "humans" and not slavery, Laveaux sarcastically "forgave" García for his reaction.[61] When concerned Dominican elites visited Laveaux asking him to calm tensions and promote peace, Laveaux instead decided to lecture them on republican virtues. He exhorted them to adopt the "customs, practices, friendship, and fraternity" of the French Republic.[62] France eventually apologized for Laveaux's actions and briefly abandoned Dominican emancipation plans.[63]

Instead, Paris selected Philippe Roume as a "provisional agent" to coordinate with Spanish officials. Roume had experience as a commissioner in Saint-Domingue and had lived in Grenada. He arrived in Madrid without warning.[64] He came at an inopportune moment, however, as, just months before, some disaffected intellectuals and merchants in the city had attempted to install a republic, during the San Blas conspiracy.[65] Additionally, the Treaty of Basel had actually not yet been completed at that point. Spanish officials deplored the idea of a French onlooker without authority meddling in Dominican society.[66] King Carlos IV and his advisers, who had begun to regret the treaty, asked Roume if they could perhaps cede Louisiana instead of Santo Domingo.[67] This attempt failed, and yet Santo Domingo proved "so insignificant that the Republic neglected to take possession" of it for several years. Thus began an era of disjointed Spanish governance over an increasingly revolutionary populace.[68]

The newly empowered French Executive Directory instructed Roume to instill "love" for the republic among France's new subjects, work to end British influence, and prevent a repetition of the Vendée on Hispaniola. French officials sought to dispel years of religious criticism by instructing Dominicans on "eternal truths," as part of an effort to advance the "tutelary muse of the French people" that extended "its wings over both hemispheres." The objective was to "completely Frenchify" Dominicans, including the enslaved, who would become "recognized children." Roume recruited Archbishop Portillo and other clergy to aid in this effort, though his words were tactless and seemed more like self-aggrandizing condescension.[69] The French plans dismayed papal officials.[70]

Roume and other French officials had little understanding of Dominican society, which often made their efforts counterproductive to their stated goals of developing the "virtues and talents" of their "Dominican siblings." Roume alienated many locals. Apart from the religious strife, he realized that among Dominicans, including some of African descent, suspicions lingered about French abolitionism, given the constant tumult in Saint-Domingue. Despite his myriad differences with Archbishop Portillo and Governor García, he believed they would come to love him, and that they would discover that republican values were better than "aristocratic despotism" for Christianity.[71] In Rome, church officials despaired for this "truly deplorable situation of Catholicism on the island of S. Domingo."[72]

DISUNION

Social instability increased as Dominican elites' outward evangelical mission became an inwardly focused fight for Hispanic traditions. Many French citizens of color from Saint-Domingue relocated to Santo Domingo after Roume's entourage arrived on 8 April 1796. In Santo Domingo, pro-French parties commandeered the churches, made pulpits into rostrums for revolutionary rhetoric, and preached a gospel of equality and liberty, scandalizing many locals.[73]

Upon his turbulent arrival, Roume pressed charges against a priest in Sevilla who had insulted his politics en route to Hispaniola. French promises of friendship rang hollow.[74] Officials recoiled at the French intent to "seduce" Dominicans into accepting revolutionary maxims. Though unsuccessful, Roume visited Dominican churches to explain his spirituality and requested the return of Black prisoners who had been resold into bondage. Abandoned by Spain and appalled by France, many Dominicans in the interior towns increased their contact with the moderate British monarchists.[75]

Despite Archbishop Portillo's supplications to believers to ignore Roume, revolutionary precepts did motivate some dramatic Dominican defections.[76] A mulato priest from Monte Cristi, Juan Valerio Quiñones, for example, chose to abandon his vows. In rapid fashion during the summer of 1796, Quiñones called King Carlos IV a tyrant, tried to radicalize other priests, and attempted to cede his parish to France. He earned the nickname "Incendiary," or "Arsonist," perhaps not only as a result of his fiery rhetoric but also because he burned some of the church records. Quiñones had a bad reputation among the locals. He once delayed administering last rites for a parishioner because he wanted to finish playing a good hand of cards. He supposedly read "blasphemous" French texts to the point that "Frenchness" influenced his manners and pronunciations. He wore a tricolore cockade in his hat during a meeting with Archbishop Portillo in Santo Domingo. Shortly thereafter, Roume welcomed Quiñones into his home in Santo Domingo, where the priest proclaimed his loyalty to the French Republic.

Amid the ongoing abolition conflict, Quiñones married a Dominican woman half his age. She may have still been enslaved. A slaveholder claimed that this "bad priest" had fallen for a "good-looking" eighteen-year-old mulata. Others were aware that the two of them had spent nights together. Following a secular French civil ceremony, the newlyweds dined with Roume's entourage as guests of honor.[77] Quiñones departed with the slogan "Liberty, Equality, French Republic" emblazoned on his new citizenship papers.[78] He was not the only one. Others joined the apostate priest in exploring alternatives to orthodoxies.[79]

To stand with "our brothers the Haitians," Roume said, using a term he had adopted to mean residents of the whole island, he wanted an egalitarian marriage to a young woman who adhered to the same revolutionary principles that he did. Thus, only weeks later, he asked Archbishop Portillo for a divorce from his wife of thirty years, claiming that while his own worldview had revolutionized, hers had not. He hoped that this type of politically motivated divorce would become more acceptable in their era of change. Portillo was appalled.[80] The drama of Roume's relationship with the young woman so irritated Louverture that he contemplated skipping the wedding, which took place later in Port-au-Prince. (Portillo did not officiate, however.) Undiscouraged, Roume later fathered a child with his new wife, a mulâtresse, whose racial depictions possibly held revolutionary and pejoratively seductive meanings.[81]

The disintegration of supposedly permanent priestly and marital vows represented dissolution in the surrounding society. Quiñones and Roume serve as case studies for broader metaphors. Ideological awakenings remade both personal preferences and social belongings. Some French republicans were aware that their actions connoted religious warfare. Ritual repudiations of Catholic norms were symbols of sudden disunion in Santo Domingo.

Nevertheless, French officials invited their arch-critic Portillo to remain in Santo Domingo as the Bishop of "Ayti," using the name they said "the native Indians" had given the island, which they believed would be "restore[d] after the handover" following implementation of the Treaty of Basel. This reference to a unified Hispaniola represented possibly the earliest serious attempt to revitalize the name, which would have integrated Dominicans into a blended family of "Haitians."[82]

Portillo was entirely unimpressed with the idea, perhaps because Roume lambasted the Inquisition, sought to limit church properties, and wanted to hold priests accountable to the French Republic.[83] The archbishop also learned of anticlericalism by Black republican troops at the border, who had sacked churches despite the peace treaty.[84] One priest said their leader "talked to me . . . in a miserable state" and took "holy vessels" for his amusement, wearing some as ornaments.[85]

This disregard for Catholicism contrasted with the pious practices of Spain's previous Black allies, and elite Dominicans began to conflate revolutionary Blackness with heretical actions. Portillo advocated "severe censure or armed prohibition" against dissent to avert "anarchy . . . in our populations." Unable to silence the "seditious libel," he felt that "the government [was not] sleeping, but . . . already dead."[86] Though Portillo lamented disloyalty, his excoriation only hastened Dominican disunion.[87] Sensing neglect, vulnerable Dominican towns simply ignored Spanish directives.[88]

With enthusiastic celebrations of Bastille Day in 1796, Roume and other citoyens continued their program of cultural subversion in Santo Domingo, heralding, with raucous applause, what Dominican elites called their "horrible and frightening successes that continue to this unhappy day." The "cleverly tricky" French also mingled directly with the general Dominican populace, accelerating political ferment and flaunting racial conventions. They took homes, opened cafés, and held disruptive funerals with republican motifs as Roume preached the good news of equality and liberty from the pulpit.[89] Confronted by new options, Dominicans reconsidered their own ways of belonging and believing.

Amid the attacks on Hispanic heritage, Spain moved the tomb of Christopher Columbus, the "first Discoverer of the New World," from the Santo Domingo cathedral. With ceremonial pomp, they transferred his bones from a deteriorated old box into a new metal receptacle in a new wooden case draped in black velvet and gold trim.[90] Cut from the vine of its three-hundred-year traditions, Santo Domingo, the symbolic first fruit of the Hispanic Americas, withered. Elite Dominicans, who had long reveled in being the first hemispheric Christian outpost, and in having a capital that Columbus himself had founded, reeled from the loss of the emblems of conquering European whiteness.[91]

BOCA NIGUA

Boca Nigua, the name of both a plantation and the river mouth on which it sat, had long drawn the attention of chroniclers of Hispaniola, such as Gonzalo Fernández de Oviedo and Médéric Louis Elie Moreau de Saint-Méry, for the fertile soil near its banks. The Boca Nigua sugar plantation sat near a sandy beach. Upriver a few miles from the plantation rose a plateau where the river's tributaries forked. This region hosted several of the large *ingenios* (sugar mills) in Santo Domingo and was known for producing "beautiful" sugar.

Boca Nigua, owned by the absentee Marqués de Iranda and operated by Juan Bautista Oyarzábal, was likely the most profitable plantation in all of Santo Domingo. The land around the headwaters, called "gold" for its productivity, also yielded cacao, indigo, and other crops. Perhaps 2,500 people lived nearby, including a "proportional number of Blacks as to what the French [had]," both free and enslaved, also making this region unique in Santo Domingo.[92]

Santo Domingo had not experienced large revolts by the enslaved, like those of Saint-Domingue, for several years. With the influx of "French" Blacks to the capital, who Governor García said "famously hate . . . the white colonists," sweeping changes began to appear in the colony. Feeling besieged, García incited colonists to arm themselves at any sign of unrest by Dominicans of color.[93]

In October 1796, the enslaved at Boca Nigua realized Dominican elites' fears of direct exposure to Black power amid Spanish decline. Initially, the Spanish officials assumed that recent French actions had influenced the rebellion. However, correlation did not equal causation. Investigations revealed that more complex interpersonal factors and cultural networks had motivated the Boca Nigua rebels' drive for liberty.[94]

The revolt at Boca Nigua began on the night of 30 October in a "sudden . . . insurrection of the Blacks on Spanish *haciendas*" led by, in García's biased words, "odious slaves" who had been infected by the "contagion" of "liberty." "Sacrificing all the white class," like the rebels in Saint-Domingue, he said, they had replicated that "theater of horrors." He "could not believe how close this explosion was," and especially that it had taken place at a supposedly well-run plantation. However, the details that emerged would challenge long-standing Spanish conceits of their more benevolent treatment of the enslaved in comparison to the French.

When the revolt began, the rebels pinned the overseer, Oyarzábal, in the main house. He had just moments to react against at least two hundred rebels, including many from other plantations. The insurgents wanted to burn the cane fields, fortify themselves in buildings, kill their oppressors, and enjoy liberty. After repulsing three attacks, he managed to flee and alert neighboring plantations. Oyarzábal arrived in the capital late the next day, overwhelmed by fatigue and desperate to encourage a counterattack. At dawn the next day, the veteran Spanish officer Antonio Barba reconnoitered the area, leaving most of his troops to guard major settlements. Officer Joaquín Cabrera followed with "three pickets of grenadiers" and supplies. He quickly realized that neither cavalry nor infantry would suffice.

Elites in the capital were "dismayed," and many emigrated, with "uninfected Blacks," as they dismissively stated, before more revolts could transpire. García soon learned of the ongoing attacks and worried that the revolt would be the start of an "interminable war." Ignoring the rebels' cognition and agency, however, he dismissed them as "a machine that yields to whatever movement or impression" influenced them. The rebels, meanwhile, apparently planned to extend their uprising to capture the forts at Jayna, hoping to perhaps end all slavery.[95]

After taking Jayna, the insurgents planned, allegedly, to call upon one thousand Black partisans in and around the capital to join in with their revolt. These possible recruits supposedly included many of Jean-François's veterans, some of them men who had been present at Fort Dauphin.[96] The rebels did approach these veterans, but broader plans remained unconfirmed.

On 31 October, dozens of soldiers moved toward Jayna while others approached Boca Nigua, arriving by nightfall. Exhausted by the hot eighteen-mile march, the troops immediately took defensive positions and began collecting operational intelligence. They interrogated an ill Black resident nearby who they suspected had been spying on them. On their approach around nine at night, Spanish troops could hear festivities taking place in the occupied plantation buildings. The rebels had armed themselves with rifles, knives, spears, and two cannons they had taken from the overseers' arsenal for fighting enemy corsairs. Before retreating to wait for morning light, the troops crossed burnt cane fields and met cannon fire from the rebels, whom they disparaged as "poison ivy."

Before dawn, three divisions of troops assembled with a fourth en route to outnumber the rebels. Two plantation employees, Gabriel and Antonio Collar, recruited nearby residents and troops, including Bernardo Bravo, whose father, Manuel, later led the investigations. The Collars assisted troops maneuvering the land to launch a surprise attack. Soldiers captured the river crossing, but as fighting resumed, judging that they were too exposed to rebel fire, they retreated. Bernardo Bravo was injured trying to capture the riverbank's heights. The rebels then outflanked the troops through the forest cover. After exchanging fire for thirty minutes, the rebels retreated behind their cannons. The rebels held other lines of defense and fortified buildings. However, they were outgunned.

Sensing their predicament, the rebels began fleeing for nearby mountains and forests, running through the cane they had not yet burned for cover. The troops advanced to the plantation medic's house looking for bandages, stitches, and medicines for their wounded. They then searched the cane for hidden, injured, and dead rebels. The Spanish troops collected the "ravaged and somber bodies" of the rebels Simón, Marcos, Mecú, Quatro, Diamant, and Elias, the first two near the hacienda, the next three toward Baní, and the sixth in a field three days later. Two holdouts made it as far as Azua, and another fled through the countryside. One wounded rebel, Esteban the blacksmith, later died from his wounds.

Hundreds of prisoners remained, and Spanish officers separated them to begin interrogations. Manuel Bravo began investigating the causes of the Boca Nigua revolt with the overseer, Oyarzábal; a medic, Pedro Anglade; an employee, Simón Yriarte; the distiller, Pedro Abadía; and the *mayordomo*, Antonio Collar, whose brother Gabriel had previously worked there and owned a nearby ingenio. Interestingly, some free people of color had helped certain nearby white people survive.

Bravo accumulated information about two rebels in particular, Tomás Congo from the nearby Buenavista plantation, whom Oyarzábal already disliked, and the primary overseer Francisco Sopó, whom he apparently favored. Officials also interrogated three ex-soldiers of "Jan Fransua" (Jean-François) who lived and worked on the neighboring San Juan plantation and were implicated in the plot. The findings of the investigation were telling and involved both very personal factors and factors involving cultural reciprocity. France may have weakened imperial governance, giving the enslaved an opportunity, and the Spanish officials were contextually poised to blame the French republicans for any form of social dissent. However, in the ninety-six testimonies that the officials gathered, mostly from the enslaved, almost no evidence of French influence emerged. Immediate personal, familial, and social factors instead prevailed in inspiring the rebellion.

In the months immediately preceding the insurrection, two deaths in particular elicited rage among the enslaved at Boca Nigua. An enslaved man named Francisco died after being treated by the medic, who his friends suspected of actually poisoning him. More dramatically, overseers caught another community member, called Benito, with *aguardiente* he had allegedly stolen. Pedro Abadía, the distiller, severely punished him.

Benito, feeling he had lost esteem and honor, became depressed. He told friends that he wanted to return home to his native soil, which he said was not miserable like Boca Nigua. Benito thus made a noose and committed suicide in his home.[97] He was an African *bozal*, likely Kongolese, and possibly believed that his soul would return to his family in spirit. Many Africans enslaved in the Americas conceptualized the afterlife as lying beyond the Atlantic Ocean in their homelands, though such beliefs were less common among the Kongolese than other African ethnicities.[98]

There was a heartbreaking beauty in his yearning to unite with lost kin of the past. Yet his closest kin and friends in the present persisted in plotting a path to liberation and revenge. A cross-plantation Kongolese network mitigated the social dislocations from their natal homes and families.[99] Sopó had adored both Benito and Francisco. He decided to kill Pedro Abadía and told Antonio Carretero, his housemate. They also planned to attack the sugar refiner Simón Yriarte, Oyarzábal, and other white residents at Boca Nigua before starting a broader rebellion across nearby plantations.

These plotters sought to learn from those who had succeeded in revolting against the French. Under cover of night, they met three ex–Black Auxiliaries nearby who were Kongolese *parientes* (kin) "of a same nation." At Boca Nigua, these veterans were highly esteemed representatives of Black power. Sopó and Tomás built trust with gifts of aguardiente and molasses. However, the ex–Black Auxiliaries later claimed they refused to help and discouraged their uprising. Furthermore, they said that on 30 October they tried to warn Spanish officials, yet guards turned them away at the Santo Domingo city walls. Their story of neutrality was difficult to verify. It was also somewhat suspicious, as other parientes that Sopó and Carretero had recruited joined enthusiastically, and there were rumors of a connected plot within the capital.

At dusk, the rebels gathered, rested, passed out plantains to eat, and then closed in around the main house. Tomás Congo and Simón led the enslaved in taking up rifles, shotguns, pistols, swords, machetes, spears, sickles, knives, and spikes to attack Yriarte and Collar, whom they had seen leaving the plantation. Cristóbal César began lighting fires, trying to pin down Oyarzábal. However, despite having planned the revolt and encouraged conspirators all day, Sopó panicked at the last minute and warned Oyarzábal and Abadía. He even helped Oyarzábal escape via secret paths in the hills as Tomás Congo was lighting the *cañaverales* to find any white residents who fled.

The following morning, the rebels feasted and danced in the abandoned main house. Ana María, Antonio Carretero's partner, who directed the festivities, sat upon a makeshift throne under a canopy and enjoyed treatment as a queen.[100] Her affectations of royalty harkened to the establishment of a fugitive African polity common among rebellions by the enslaved. Absent was French-inspired egalitarianism.[101]

Antonio Carretero, Tomás Congo, Papa Pier, and Piti Juan proceeded to arrange defenses. After a huge celebratory meal, the rebels attacked the ingenio of San Cristóbal and incorporated the enslaved there into their rebellion. Antonio told new recruits that those who fought would be free, and those who did not would serve them. On their way toward the capital, they planned to take the fortifications at Jayna and eventually San Gerónimo.[102]

However, the impending Spanish counterattacks ended their uprising, leaving one Spanish soldier dead and six wounded. Spanish troops quickly extinguished the possibility of further "combustion" from the Boca Nigua revolt. Although brief and in some ways an outlier, Boca Nigua reminded Dominican elites of their precarity. It resembled the revolts of Saint-Domingue five years prior, as it started with local grievances, involved lengthy planning amid African ethnic networks, and moved across prosperous plantations.

The investigation named Tomás Congo, Antonio the "King," Ana María the "Queen," Sopó, and Papa Pier as the "authors, chiefs, and principal heads" of the rebellion. Soon after the revolt, the Spanish issued punishments to make examples of them to any aspiring rebels, hanging them then decapitating, quartering, and displaying their bodies on the major roads of the capital. Piti Juan also met with hanging and decapitation. Seven rebels had died from combat. Punishments for others included fifty to one hundred lashes, prison terms, and lengthy sentences to fetters, collars, and chains. Some of the accused were found not guilty and freed, including José Criollo, alias "Viasu," whose nickname was possibly due to his affinity for the exiled general Georges Biassou. Ten of the 103 accused were women. Others faced exile, and some, such as Santiago Espaillat, had to watch the executions of friends.

The roster of Boca Nigua prisoners reveals aspects of their kinship connections and African ethnic backgrounds. Tomás Congo and the "kin" of his "nation" with whom he had organized the insurrection showed that the leadership was broadly Kongolese. Other rebels, such as Lorenso Congo and Pedro Mondongo, were almost certainly from the Congo River region, as were possibly Ambrosio Cita, Ventura Besé, Lorenso Senegui, Basilio Sengui, Benito Matundo, and Melchor Buey. "Sopo," in the Ngombe language spoken between the Mongala and Lopori Rivers, the northern and southern tributaries of the Congo River, respectively, meant "abdomen" or "belly," and could have been a nickname. Additionally, the naming of Antonio and Ana María as "king" and "queen" likely meant they were respected in this kinship group. Outside of the Kongolese leadership, the African regional diversity and creole representation was significant.[103] Far more than the arrival of French influences, love for kin and community trust had driven the liberatory effort.

Provocative conjugal politics soon reappeared. Archbishop Portillo, who had officiated Biassou's wedding, protested the incendiary priest's marriage, and impeded Roume's divorce, speculated that the Boca Nigua revolt was due to the anger of an enslaved lover (Sopó) whose same-sex partner had committed suicide (Benito). In this heteronormative context, Portillo, who likely lacked specifics of the case, seemed to have deliberately miscast

Kongolese solidarities as a manifestation of allegedly unholy passions and African depravity. This distortion had spiritual currency among elites, who rejected responsibility for causing the conditions for social unrest.[104]

UNEXPECTED ALTERNATIVES

Dominican elites' discourses of irreconcilable difference with their more egalitarian neighbors to the west did not develop from conflicts over change and continuity alone. An unlikely alternative to the perceived abandonment from Spain and domestic dissent emerged. That alternative came from the United Kingdom. In the mid-1790s, British interjections enhanced anxious Dominican considerations of exclusive belief and belonging, though scholarship has overlooked the lasting influence of this era to the island's cultural politics.

Since 1791, Spain had worried about a direct British challenge on Hispaniola, a fear exacerbated by the opportunistic British invasion of revolutionary Saint-Domingue in 1793. In 1795, as British officials protested the surrender of Santo Domingo to France, British forces approached the Dominican border. British ships lurked offshore, coordinating with spies and disgruntled Dominicans, and British propaganda circulated throughout Santo Domingo. British agents even attracted interest from Jean-François and Georges Biassou before their exile, and they succeeded in recruiting thousands of ex–Black Auxiliaries who remained on the island under precarious Spanish promises of pensions.[105]

By January 1796, British officials had, "under pretense of procuring some refreshments" at Monte Cristi, contacted thousands of ex–Black Auxiliaries. Many in Santiago also considered requesting British military support to resist French occupiers who had "made themselves particularly obnoxious by prematurely publishing their proclamation giving liberty to the slaves." One "Spanish proprietor of confidence" in Monte Cristi told some of these British assets "in the strongest manner" about the "universal discontent which prevailed" across Santo Domingo.[106]

In response, British officers circulated messages to Santiago stating that Dominicans would "remain in the perfect enjoyment of their property, and in the free exercise of their religion," under British rule, and that their "future prosperity and happiness . . . depend[ed] entirely on the success of the British arms against the French Republicans." They invited "whatever assistance" Dominicans "may afford to the British," implying that British success was critical to Dominican interests.[107]

Shortly after London granted the British officers permission to recruit ex–Black Auxiliaries, an intense young Black officer who despised France, named Titus, joined their cause. His defection promised to be decisive. Pledging to enhance British positions, he prepared to rally disaffected *cultivateurs* (the formerly enslaved still cultivating crops for the French) who were dissatisfied with French promises of liberty.[108] In February 1796, Titus dined with British officers aboard a Royal Navy ship near Monte Cristi. He then orchestrated covert encounters at the mouth of the Río Masacre near Dajabón, where, through signaling with gunshots and flags, a British ship would be able to ferry munitions ashore to Titus's army, which numbered perhaps five thousand men.

Titus assumed the title "Leader of the Blacks," previously claimed only by Jean-François, Biassou, and Louverture. By March 1796, the British settled deals with another former Jean-François protégé, Gagnet, and his troops. As Titus accepted British money and uniforms, García revoked his medal from the king. Emboldened, the British also contacted Black officers fighting for France to gauge their interest in defecting. As Titus maneuvered his considerable force, spies near Santiago engaged numerous Dominican civilians who were supportive of a British takeover.[109]

However, a massive maroon revolt soon convulsed Jamaica. The British redirected imperial troops and resources there, which impeded their new agreements with Black generals. Titus nevertheless amassed his troops along the border, and Spain prepared its defenses against a former ally. The French begged for spies to ascertain Titus's plans. A captured British spy, who had been undercover in Monte Cristi for six weeks, led to the Spanish arrest of other pro-British conspirators. Driven by desperation to calm the Dominican interior, Spaniards assisted Villate in locating and assassinating Titus a few weeks later. And when Gagnet considered new French offers, his own troops killed him. Imperial power on Hispaniola depended upon attracting Black support. On this, the French had accrued a formidable advantage.[110]

Thereafter, the inability to build a local army remained a British strategic regret on Hispaniola, which the governor of Jamaica increasingly disparaged as "a Brigand Island."[111] However, many Dominicans on the ground resisted this outcome, refused to sacrifice their traditions, and hoped to keep long-standing illicit British commerce on the northern coast. British agents continued offering alternatives to their mounting dismay. This coincided with a massive, thirty-thousand-troop-strong British expedition sent that year aiming for a decisive victory in the French Caribbean.[112]

British operatives proved their offers of peace and prosperity on the northern coast by paying good prices for staple foods. Their ability to attract

Dominican support only increased with the construction of barracks in deserted areas of the northern coast.[113] The French recognized this British momentum and judged that, with a large military landing and Dominican support, the British might be able to inflict a coup de grâce in Santo Domingo. This became a major strategic weakness for the French on Hispaniola. Some French officials regretted not having taken Louisiana or Florida instead in the treaty.[114]

With growing Dominican interest, in July 1796 the British general Gordon Forbes issued a mass proclamation in Spanish that empathized with the Dominicans' plight, citing imperial betrayal and French instability. He invited "brave" Dominicans to become British subjects under the purportedly fair, moderate, steady, prosperous governance of a constitutional monarchy. Knowing his audience, Forbes applauded Dominicans as "loyal supporters of the true worship of God," as opposed to accepting the "traitorous" religiosity of the French Republic.[115]

The British drummed up elite Dominican discomfiture by alleging that "Blacks without talent or education" would rule them.[116] A new trend coincided with this message wherein, as Louverture approached a border town, droves of Dominicans would flee, many of them joining the British.[117] A month after Louverture raised the tricolore in Bánica, Las Cahobas, and Hincha, it was announced in Bánica that British forces would take the town.[118] In August 1796, the Dominicans there, including some of color, actively fought French forces, while in Grande-Rivière some ex–Black Auxiliaries, many of them still wearing Spanish cockades, launched an anti-French uprising. Both events likely had British support.[119]

Bánica, a key border town, was a high-priority British target.[120] Perhaps hundreds of Dominicans there accepted British offers of recruitment.[121] The British officer entrusted with Bánica had "articles of clothing" to "distribute amongst their leading people." He used "public money" as part of the broader effort to "conciliate the good dispositions" of disaffected Dominicans in Santo Domingo and Santiago.[122]

French officials lackadaisically dismissed Dominican dissidents as "traitors and treacherous men" afflicted by "simplicity and ignorance."[123] Roume was apoplectic, and to check this unanticipated competition for Dominican support, the French circulated their own proclamation.[124] To counter the British incitement of Dominican fears, Roume denied that Louverture's army was pillaging towns. However, his demands of deference toward the French envoys, who claimed to bring love but mostly castigated the locals and demurred on religious protections, did not suffice. Thus, when British representatives rode into Las Cahobas, the Dominicans there raised the Union Jack.[125]

British efforts to persuade Dominicans partly relied upon covert Dominican supporters, such as the pseudonymous "Mr. Tabares," who inquired about British rule after reading the British proclamation.[126] Tabares delivered intelligence on French maneuvers to British officers, who ridiculed French policy as "so tragic as to be comical." Again deriding the empowerment of Black people, the "most loved race because it is the strongest," British officers again engaged in fearmongering, warning that "African troops" would occupy Santo Domingo.[127] Such statements caused Dominican clergy, including the influential Juan Bobadilla in Neiba, to sway parishioners toward British sympathies. After hearing British overtures, supposedly "all" locals "prefer[red] British dominion."[128]

Into late 1796, Dominican collaborators secretly warned the British about pending French occupations at Monte Cristi and Dajabón and begged for protection. A delegation had secretly sailed from Monte Cristi to Môle Saint-Nicolas to ask for British aid. At night, two British ships near Monte Cristi signaled with rockets to onshore collaborators. Dominicans from Puerto Plata, La Vega, and even Santiago developed similar British ties and sought British support.[129] French commanders responded by establishing limitations on travel to or trade with Dajabón, a supposed hotbed of royalist activity, and sent patrols into Santo Domingo to track Black royalists.[130] British coordination succeeded in delaying French takeovers of Dominican towns.[131]

In September 1796, *The Times* of London published a lengthy article about whole Dominican towns welcoming British protection from French irreligion, anarchy, plunder, and massacre.[132] One Father Márquez, a popular priest in the west, had faced reassignment from Archbishop Portillo because of his scandalous affairs with married women. When confronted, Márquez simply accepted a raise to become chaplain of British Catholic troops, including recent defectors from Spain.[133] In a more telling turn, José Nolasco Mañon, the priest who just one year before had feted Biassou at his wedding, publicly thanked God that local Dominicans could raise the British flag and become subjects of King George III, their new protector of religion from French infidels.[134]

Aside from their anti-republicanism and promises of religious protection, the British had won popularity in part by allowing elite Dominicans to react to French egalitarianism by maintaining their racial and social hierarchies. French scorn and chronic myopia toward Dominican cultural politics also proved counterproductive.[135] The recent executions at Les Cayes did not dissipate Dominican concerns. A captain who hid aboard his ship during "the furies" sailed straight to Santo Domingo, later reporting that for three days the attackers progressed from rifles to swords, and finally to drownings.[136] Disdain for France was not limited to elites. As white colonists fled the island, the British increasingly attempted to persuade free Dominicans of color to join them.[137]

Even if many Dominicans of color ideologically endorsed French egalitarianism, their choices were not so simple. Some lacked racial solidarity with veteran self-liberated armies, could not afford to emigrate, and wanted to protect their homes, religiosity, and livelihoods. Unlike pro-French forces, which sometimes resorted to taking Dominican resources by force, British officers succeeded in unfurling the Union Jack over Dominican territory by treating rural Dominicans with dignity, paying them "superabundantly" for goods, and engaging in trade more than warfare. For many, constitutional monarchy seemed a sane option compared to guns and guillotines.[138]

By the end of 1796, pro-British seditions had infiltrated the capital. On a French tipoff, Spanish officials arrested Francisco Gascue, a prominent urbanite, brother-in-law of the mayor of Santiago, and treasurer and accountant for the Audiencia. Allegedly, Gascue had received the Forbes proclamation and described British intentions to some of his acquaintances in a favorable light. In response, García criminalized the documents that Gascue had admitted to receiving and demanded that Dominicans surrender them. Given his reputation, Gascue's British flirtations shocked city elites, though Spanish officials doubted that he harbored a treasonous intent. The members of the French delegation had busied themselves looking for anti-republic insults. When Gascue had rejected their offers, they had reported him as a British sympathizer. Such theatrics by the "hothead" Roume and the "bad satellites who orbit[ed] him," including a number of Dominicans, such as a priest who wore his holy garb with the tricolore cockade attached, further alienated the residents of the capital. When Spanish courts dismissed the case, García reminded Roume that he was still only a provisional agent.[139] The fact that the evidence against Gascue was limited, though, did not mean that the capital's residents were ignoring British policies, especially in light of their increasing irritation at France.

In December, the British issued a second, lengthier proclamation recounting French anticlericalism in Europe and inviting Dominican martyrs, "successors of the first missionaries" in the Americas, to fight irreligion.[140] To diminish mistrust of state Anglicanism, British officials sent the exiled bishop of Comminges to their territory in Hispaniola. Many priests in Dominican border towns welcomed British protection. The papacy preferred the British to secular France and hoped that a British Santo Domingo might remain as Catholic as Québec had in Canada.[141] As the French general Rochambeau arrived to take Santo Domingo, British agents schemed to take the capital.[142]

"SPANISH HAYTIANS" AND HIS BRITANNIC MAJESTY

In December 1796, Spanish officials arrested a coalition of Dominicans in the interior and in the capital for conspiring with British agents to plot a British invasion. The depositions and evidence reveal an extraordinary amount of detail about the cultural politics and social networks in Santo Domingo. Pro-British activists were adept at appealing to elite Dominicans' sense of spiritual superiority and to their fears that French rule would crush their traditions. The case also unveils critical details about the roles that people of color played in making and breaking the conspiracy. In this plot, many Dominicans pivoted from simple discontent with Spain and France to envisioning the elements of colonial society they wanted to perpetuate into the future.

Domingo Assereto, the informant who revealed the plot, immediately became a suspected coconspirator. The Italian-born Assereto, who eventually fled Hispaniola under suspicion, had served Spain as a military officer briefly in Cuba, and in Louisiana before that, leaving behind a tangled web of court cases and alleged malfeasance. In Havana, he had met Juan Angulo, a local thirty-eight-year-old merchant. After coming to Hispaniola and apparently wandering from place to place for seven months, Angulo arrived in the capital in 1796. He had visited Port-au-Prince, Neiba, and Azua, and had ostensibly looked to trade wood in Jérémie and Gonaïves. Suspiciously, he entered Santo Domingo from British-occupied territory. British officers asked him to inquire about purchasing Dominican horses and cattle for them as he traveled along his route. He had also passed messages for the British. These activities had earned him the nickname "Apostle." Angulo was arrested for spying for the British and was considered the chief spy in the pro-British network, although he excused his odd activities as a search for relatives and attempts to engage in commerce, including in Dajabón and Santiago.

Angulo remained locked in a tower for the time being. At his arrest, he had been carrying cryptic correspondence signed by a British general and addressed to important clergy in Santo Domingo, letters that derided both

123

the French and the Spanish and exalted British stability. Angulo also carried two British passports, a copy of the Forbes proclamation, and additional letters for prominent residents and ex–Black Auxiliaries. He may have burned other secret papers. Further investigation uncovered commercial papers in English within his luggage.

Angulo portrayed himself as having surmounted familial and financial losses to become a merchant of creams, soaps, fabrics, and other goods. He claimed to have stayed with Assereto for just a few days because he didn't know anyone else in Santo Domingo. Angulo denied working for the British, claiming only to be in the capital to protest French harassment of his livelihood. However, he could not satisfactorily explain the papers he was carrying or his actions. If Angulo was a spy, posing as a merchant with British commercial ties and as someone with complaints against French persecution offered a tactful cover.

Former Black Auxiliaries, many of them living around the capital, had become critical players in major events within Santo Domingo. Angulo had also met Pablo Alí and Agustín, two officers who had served prominently under Biassou. In exchange for their crucial assistance, someone had promised them British commissions to replace the salary and prestige taken from them by the Treaty of Basel. Alí and Agustín stood accused as coconspirators.[143] It is possible they had already corresponded with British officials, knew other Black Auxiliary veterans who had aligned themselves with the British, and with Assereto had selected a landing spot for the British fleet at Jayna for a march on the capital.

In their meetings, Agustín, a forty-year-old from Grande-Rivière, had received an enticing pro-British letter, an attractive blue jacket, epaulets, and a golden shoulder braid. Apparently he had recently traveled for several days to visit San Juan de la Maguana and Jayna. Assereto planned to help pay for Agustín and Angulo to travel to Azua. Assereto, who had once lived with one of the few Britons in Santo Domingo, even offered to let Agustín and his wife move into his home, alongside Angulo. Agustín declined because of his many children.

Once he had gained trust, Assereto asked Agustín many questions about how the ex–Black Auxiliaries supported themselves and where they lived. In a related exchange, Pablo Alí said that during his previous visit to Bánica, a British agent had offered him significant pay to join. His colleagues had received similar offers. Alí, then thirty-eight years old, denied receiving letters or knowing Angulo well. He had dealt mostly with Assereto. However, Alí said Assereto had praised the British, stating they would soon arrive in Santo Domingo.

As testimony revealed, "many" Dominicans had become British partisans. Angulo allegedly had several covert coconspirators in Azua, Neiba, and even the capital. Assereto said that Angulo had intended to deliver the letters and that he was carrying messages for the university rector, the mayor, and several religious leaders. Angulo was also reported to have made favorable comments about the British, insinuating that they were more prosperous than the "perfidious" French and might treat Dominicans better. Dubiously, Assereto claimed that he had only participated to try to prevent the conspiracy.[144]

Recognizing his quandary, Pablo Alí decided to flip and confess that there was, in fact, a British "surprise" planned against Santo Domingo. His defense was naïveté, as he claimed that, because of Assereto's rank as a Spanish officer, and hints that the archbishop was involved, the plan had seemed legitimate. Alí confirmed that Angulo and Assereto had cash and secret papers and that he and Agustín had planned to help with affairs near the border.

In renting horses for their trips, Assereto had asked repetitive, odd questions about riding times to towns near British lines and rambled to the stableman about how British forces would easily defeat the French. Agustín confirmed that their trip had involved handling money and scouting locations.[145] In January 1797, Alí and Agustín wrote to García. Describing their years of service and how Assereto had duped them, they requested release after a month of imprisonment.[146] Their testimonies instigated a major Spanish investigation into imminent British threats.

During his arrest, Angulo guessed that the officials suspected him of being a British spy, an odd statement from someone who also declared innocence from any treasonous intent. Questioned again, he claimed his praise for the British had been harmless. Though Angulo denied carrying British papers, on the day of his arrest he had allegedly delivered items to Joseph Sterling, one of the few Britons in the city, who denied any conspiratorial involvement. Another Briton said Assereto had told him Angulo was a British agent. Witnesses from the border said that Angulo had met with many prominent residents en route to the capital, and that he had also delivered letters from Neiba and Azua, including one from Juan Bobadilla, in Santo Domingo.[147] Bobadilla, the respected priest, had drawn suspicion from Spanish officers when they discovered that he and other Neiba residents had received British letters that they had never disclosed.[148]

Angulo attacked his accusers' credibility, calling Assereto a crude man of "impertinent and inconsequential conversations." He claimed to not speak French, and thus denied knowing what Alí and Agustín had discussed.

However, Alí and Agustín confirmed that Angulo had conferred with Assereto in Spanish during meetings.[149] Spanish investigators chipped away at Angulo's story and at his insistence that he had carried the subversive British documents unwittingly. While imprisoned, Angulo met with a woman identified as a free *morena* who managed to visit his cell and circulate messages to and from the outside world.[150] Ultimately, this Dominican woman of color, whom Angulo had previously hired to deliver some of the items he was carrying, in order to evade scrutiny and maintain his own plausible deniability, turned against him.[151]

This intermediary, the thirty-one-year-old Monica de la Cruz Cornejo, had also cooked for Angulo. From jail, Angulo asked her what people were saying about his case and the evidence against him. He apparently told her that all the investigators could prove was his criticism of France and praise for the British. She later testified that Angulo and Assereto would often speak privately in the street and that they had asked to meet some of the Black soldiers she knew. She had confided in a friend, identified as Isabel Ramírez, a morena, who had discouraged her from complying.[152] Angulo had spoken more openly with Monica than he had with others, perhaps because he assumed she would not be a witness, owing to her social position and vulnerability. Monica de la Cruz Cornejo worked for white men who discounted her perceptiveness and agency, and for this she proved an invaluable informant.[153]

Angulo also carried a suspicious number of letters of reference from well-placed people across Hispaniola to help him connect with powerful figures in the capital. Some of the previously unopened letters were politically vague, though one mentioned Angulo's odd interest in French naval positions. Angulo had been unusually connected with Britons in the capital as well as with British officers in Saint-Domingue. In one cryptic intercepted letter, one of the few Britons in Santo Domingo, James Blare, writing after Angulo's arrival, told a possible British agent elsewhere on Hispaniola that he could "visit Santo Domingo soon," and that their friend "Mr. Preston," who fled before he could be questioned, was "always progressing in the entertaining art of speaking alone." Angulo had carried a letter for Preston. These details seemed to provide evidence of a spy network.[154]

Evidence mounted that Assereto was a traitor, too. He often slandered Dominicans, the Spanish, and the French. Roume provided a letter from Assereto that he had written just after Angulo's arrest. In it Assereto complained that the Spanish had not sufficiently thanked him for revealing the plot. Assereto also openly criticized Spain, apparently because he had received some unfavorable judicial decisions in New Orleans and disliked the governor of Cuba. The barber Pierre Echalas, described as a "French Black" whom the Briton Joseph Sterling had sent to cut Assereto's hair, had overheard Assereto say that Spain would soon make him governor of Cuba. Assereto had also told Roume of the plot and claimed, as a native of Genoa, to be a true republican who wanted to serve France. Isabel Pérez, who owned Assereto's quarters, said that his personality was insufferable, repulsive, overbearing, and immoderate.[155] Assereto was an opportunist.

Others called Assereto a "schemer" and a "liar." Roume, eager to preserve a French future in Santo Domingo, reported his personal observations to García, saying that Assereto was unwelcome in his house. At one dinner with French envoys, Assereto, Roume said, had upset the guests by, perhaps in jest, offering his wife or daughter sexually to another guest, the incendiary priest Quiñones. Roume also described the first time they had coincidentally met in Spain. Assereto had told him an unbelievable story about departing from the prime minister's quarters at El Escorial only to be ambushed by a gang. The gang, supposedly sent by his powerful enemies, he said, had left him tied up in a tree. More recently, Assereto had visited the French consulate uninvited, where he had requested French commissions and made anti-Spanish remarks. He had allegedly said, for example, that he had celebrated the Boca Nigua revolt because he knew it meant that Spanish soldiers would die.

Assereto suggested allowing the plot to transpire in order to expose any major players in hiding. He also claimed the high-ranking state and church officials had joined in with the conspiracy, but never produced the documents he claimed would prove this. Officials wondered if Assereto had only revealed the British operation because he feared being betrayed himself. Because of his many strange statements, they suspected that Assereto was psychologically unwell. Closing an unanticipated circle, Charles Gérard, who had faced arrest in January 1792 for destabilizing the Dominican border, was among the French envoys in the capital who verified that Assereto's behavior had been odd. Simply put, Assereto was amoral and sought to sell himself to the highest bidder.

All things considered, officials were unsure what to think of Angulo and Assereto. Roume speculated that while visiting a certain boardinghouse Assereto had overheard specific rumors about British spies in the colony. He wondered if Assereto, who was desperately ambitious, had had this in mind when he had met Angulo, and, in his Spanish captain's uniform, had criticized Spain and France to gain Angulo's trust. Angulo may have thought he had found a coconspirator, while Assereto had accidentally stumbled upon an actual British spy and a conspiracy. In line with recent British ploys, Angulo likely had been given the task of recruiting ex–Black Auxiliaries. Assereto had then sought British employ. However, officials failed to investigate other possible reasons for the first Angulo and Assereto meeting, in Havana, and their unlikely reconnection in Santo Domingo. Perhaps Assereto had already been a British agent. Questions remained, but the pro-British coup with numerous Dominican accomplices was certainly real.[156]

From the outset of their operations the British had astutely plotted to earn blessings from major religious figures in Santo Domingo and thus garner trust among the Dominican populace. Angulo had attempted to speak with and write to specific clergymen and seminarians, who all seemed to know more about British offers than they were willing to divulge to García's investigation. Under scrutiny, one priest dismissed the significance of any letter for him, saying it was likely "fatuous, or errant," just "burning material susceptible to combustion." He denied engaging in any "political slander," he said, with all "the ardor of his heart."[157]

In fact, Angulo had carried secret letters from a British general imploring clergymen to consider joining the British cause. The "disgraced Spanish Haytians," he said, using a historically appealing demonym for Dominicans, would assuredly find religious protection and peace under His Britannic Majesty. The letters praised Dominicans as virtuous and pious, asked them to see the British as allies against sacrilege, and recommended Angulo as an honest assistant who would keep their responses confidential. Suspected religious figures had to stand before court officials to see and explain messages addressed to them discussing the demise of Spain and the Forbes proclamation. Thereafter, Spanish investigators further broadened their search for British sympathizers.[158]

Pablo Alí testified again in April 1797, apologizing for his errors and insisting that he did not know his actions had helped to further a British conspiracy. Agustín, who claimed to speak only the "language of the creoles," added that Alí was more "intelligent in the French language and about white Europeans," and had been more suspicious of Assereto, who had tried to impress them by saying he might become the governor of Trinidad.[159] An ambitious young lawyer for the indigent named José Núñez de Cáceres handled their legal defense.[160]

Once he had taken the case, Núñez de Cáceres collected glowing letters from Spanish commanders commending their "Dear Alí." They said he had been trustworthy, prudent, modest, serious, and honest as a colonel under Biassou, having served Spain with distinction since 1792 (a year before the Black Auxiliaries legally existed). Alí had rejected substantial enticements to fight for France from his former colleague Louverture. He had made decisions that had saved lives, and had once led his troops in moving cannons and munitions by hand over treacherous terrain. He had continued serving Spain even after his beloved Biassou had resettled in Florida. Heartbreakingly, one witness said that Alí had constantly talked about earning his way to Florida to rejoin Biassou, and that someone, likely Assereto, may have promised to make that happen.

Núñez de Cáceres said that Alí's "heroic loyalty" deserved esteem, not a prison term. Prominent Spanish military officials testified on his behalf, speaking forcefully about Alí's intelligence, determination, constancy, and bravery. Núñez de Cáceres blamed Assereto's destructive character for Alí's unfortunate criminal exposure. Quoting from Roman rhetorician Valerius Maximus, he insisted that Alí was rather an "African hero" named as a "friend" by a Spanish general.[161] Having reviewed the evidence, in July 1797 Governor García released Alí and Agustín and endorsed their relocation to Florida. However, circumstances prevented Alí from ever traveling to be with Biassou.[162] He stayed near the capital, working in agriculture to support his mother, wife, and children, and continued to petition officials for permission to relocate to Florida.[163]

Overall, it is unlikely that the astute Pablo Alí did not realize that a British plot was afoot, especially given the recent choices of his peers Titus and Gagnet and prior British recruitment attempts. Alí proved to be the shrewdest actor in the complex situation. He had cover from Spanish officers who vouched for him, yet apparently entertained hedges in case the British prevailed against the French, whom he still detested. It seems he allowed Agustín more direct exposure to the plot and maintained some deniability. The successful defense by Núñez de Cáceres also forged a relationship for Alí that would reemerge in a significant way in the independence era.

Ample evidence indicated that Angulo was a British agent. He was likely not the only one in Santo Domingo. Asked to confess, however, he steadfastly rejected the accusations.[164] Although Juan Bobadilla testified that Angulo was not seditious, the details that Monica de la Cruz Cornejo and others shared prevailed. Angulo received eight years in the *presidio* in Havana and was fortunate to have escaped execution for high treason. Assereto only received more questioning and came under more suspicion as an unscrupulous, untrustworthy opportunist.[165]

Before Assereto fled the island, Monica de la Cruz Cornejo had derided his public reputation compared to her own, saying, after the trial, that Assereto was "the Black, and I am the white." This was likely scathing

sarcasm that derided the supposed moral statuses of imposed racial categories and how, in this case, their individual roles had inverted assumptions.
Compounding the acrimony between them, she accused Assereto of giving her "what I have in my belly," most likely meaning a child.[166] Though
free, she faced uncertainties as to her future employment, health, and social
pressures that the fleeing Assereto would never face.[167] Assereto, taking no
responsibility for the chaos, later traveled to North America, claimed to
have worked with Toussaint Louverture, and served France as a general in
Europe.[168]

This case was the last major campaign for outright British domination on
Hispaniola. The intricacies of the case records reveal an advanced conspiracy
developed by a network of pro-British Dominicans and British agents to
capture the entire colony of Santo Domingo. These events in the capital
were neither isolated nor spasmodic. An attack nearly occurred, and it could
have succeeded. Capital communities, mostly professionals and clergy but
also ex–Black Auxiliaries, explored their imperial options. The plots evince
the extent to which republican violence and the irreligious influences of
a looming French occupation caused many Dominicans to panic. More
importantly, conversations about Spanish insufficiency, French idealism, and
British stability explored the question of what elements of the Dominican
past were worth fighting for and keeping for an unknown future.

UNEASE AND UNREALIZED PROMISES

As Dominican minds became important theaters of competition, the unease
besieging Santo Domingo became ubiquitous. French and British appeals
did not immediately dissipate. However, the British did largely fail to fulfill
the grandiose promises they had made as Spanish rule staggered toward
havoc and insolvency.

By February 1797, the French minister of foreign affairs had acknowledged Roume's negative temperament toward Dominicans and conceded
the inability of French or Spanish forces to stop British advances. García
reiterated that France lacked the forces necessary to successfully occupy
Santo Domingo, complaining that Louverture's army could not complete
the treaty's terms, perpetuating the state of limbo on the island. Meanwhile,
six more Dominican border towns accepted British rule. Hundreds of ex–
Black Auxiliaries still served King George III, and pro-British "cabals and
treasonous plots" still loomed. Though the conspiracies had failed, the Brit-

ish sacking of Spanish ships had halted the evacuation of wealthy residents from Santo Domingo.[169]

The French stood accused of causing chaos and "bloody scenes" wherever they ruled. This helped to ensure growing popularity for the idea of British rule among Dominican elites who wanted "complete freedom of worship, property security, and slaves." Under pressure, as the British navy dominated the coasts, García pondered pooling Spanish forces to fortify the capital, in order to simply allow the British to take the rest of the colony.[170]

García could barely pay employees anyway. Absent Spanish protection, when French-allied Black troops approached Neiba, British troops had offered Dominicans in Neiba a semblance of greater stability. Juan Bobadilla met British officers who convinced him to cooperate and stay. The commander, town officials, and priests of Neiba accepted pro-British sentiment and capitulated.[171] As Azua wavered, San Juan de la Maguana accepted British rule and chose new pro-British officials. However, within weeks, British troops retreated to defend Port-au-Prince. Exposed to the French again, Neiba "entered repentance." Bobadilla explored the idea of reclaiming Spanish subjecthood. "The contagion of the British spirit progressed from town to town," he said, but proved short lived.[172]

Louverture had sent the British into decline across the island. During an April 1797 offensive, he retook the border, rapidly capturing Mirebalais, Grand-Bois, Bánica, Las Cahobas, San Juan, and Neiba and pummeling British defenses at Port-au-Prince and Saint-Marc, which he soon captured. As he cut their connections to Santo Domingo, British casualties from disease also mounted. Tellingly, in Dominican areas hostile to the British, the Royal Navy began stealing livestock rather than paying for it. In Santo Domingo, the long-anticipated British invasion never occurred, and a short-lived British presence yielded few of the promised benefits of commerce and stability.[173] Discontented, pro-British Dominicans had to make amends with both their neighbors and French partisans. As British influence decreased, Dominicans had limited say in the type of French future these factions would install.

Spain transferred Dajabón and Monte Cristi to French forces in the summer of 1797 and allowed French reinforcements at Puerto Plata and Santiago. In July 1797, the Audiencia of Santo Domingo began gradually relocating to Cuba. The French increasingly sequestered private property and government facilities without compensation or due process. Louverture not only dominated militarily, but in August consolidated his political power by ejecting Léger-Félicité Sonthonax from his second term as governor in Saint-Domingue. The only remaining major French officials on Hispaniola were Roume and a powerful *homme de couleur*, the commissioner Raimond.[174]

In January 1798, Roume learned from his counterpart in Santiago that Raimond, then one of the most powerful figures on Hispaniola, intended to occupy Santiago and the Cibao. This greatly concerned Roume, given that Raimond wanted to use Dominican resources for his own strategic purposes in Saint-Domingue. Roume had already told Raimond and Louverture to halt encroachments into Santo Domingo until French troops arrived from Europe.[175] Louverture soon ejected Raimond to France, leaving only his colleague André Rigaud as serious opposition.[176] In each of these instances, García could not prevent Santo Domingo from becoming a new theater for republican competitions in Saint-Domingue.

In mid-1798, the British, having accumulated enormous casualties and debt, decided to withdraw entirely from Hispaniola and signed a secret peace accord. It was not with French officials, however, but with Louverture himself. In exchange for their peaceful withdrawal and access to goods and war materiel, Louverture promised not to export revolution to British colonies.[177] This deal helped Louverture consolidate his power over rivals in Saint-Domingue. This was not the only surprise withdrawal, however, as in April 1798, Archbishop Portillo abruptly departed for Havana. With French occupation looming, he left "this flock" of Dominican Catholics without his "pastoral care."[178]

British strategies pivoted as commercial leverage against their Spanish colonies supplanted warfare. The British thus began offering special trade terms to procure desired goods and destabilize their rivals economically, and eventually politically. With their dreams of dominating Hispaniola dashed, they issued maritime policies to encourage Dominicans to engage in trade in the free ports of Jamaica and the Bahamas. The British listed their merchandise needs, including cotton, indigo, cochineal, medicines, cocoa, tobacco, logwood, dyer's mulberry, tint dyewoods, and leathers. Their new pamphlets and proclamations promoted only trade, however, avoiding any unrealizable promises of protection for the Dominican religion and their traditions.[179]

This newest "atrocious and scandalous invention" of British "perfidy," according to Spanish officials, put the loyalties of some Dominicans, whose "ambition and interest" attracted them to contraband, in jeopardy. The policies also damaged the staid practice of commodity export mercantilism by depleting resources and the local tax base while bolstering already robust British prosperity in ways that were difficult for Dominicans to counter. Over the ensuing years, the policies helped erode Spanish rule in Latin America, eventually playing a role in the development of outright independence movements.[180] A decade later, British commercial strategies facilitated Dominican autonomy.

With Spanish and British power waning, Santo Domingo became more directly tied to conflicts in Saint-Domingue. The ex–Black Auxiliaries Christophe, Dessalines, and their leader, Toussaint Louverture, began charting an anti-imperial future for the island, and Dominicans were drawn by the gravitational pull of these new power players.[181]

CONCLUSION

In the mid-1790s, Dominican society was caught between competing empires, ideologies, and social forces. When news of the Treaty of Basel and the surrender of Santo Domingo to France arrived in 1795, feelings of doom and betrayal surged among many Dominicans. Amid the Spanish decline and the arrival of revolutionary ideas and events, Dominican elites fought to maintain their relationship with Hispanic culture and Catholicism. The Dominican majority of color, statistically enlarged by white emigration, directly engaged with radical ideas, revolts, and empowered counterparts from Saint-Domingue. Across the island, the Spanish, French, and British had all become heavily dependent upon the political support and military acumen of Black populations.

As three centuries of Spanish rule stumbled to an unceremonious end, British promises of moderation and religious freedom enticed Dominican elites as well as small-scale producers dependent upon commerce. Pro-British conspiracies arose as the British seemed to promise greater prosperity than the Spanish, with their stagnant management, or the French, whose self-immolation in Saint-Domingue failed to inspire. Britons also promised freedom of religion and retention of Hispanic culture, which Spain was too feeble to defend and which the French seemed intent on eradicating. By 1798, thousands of supposed enemies within Dominican society had destabilized the already failing status quo.

As Dominicans of color challenged societal norms, both through discourse and revolt, an identity crisis and struggle for sovereignty emerged. Overt spirituality was a litmus test for trustworthiness for Dominicans of color. Those who defied Hispanic Catholic norms fell from grace, just as Louverture had, and passed toward being more French, and possibly more

African, in the process. Elite Dominicans retrenched in virulent defense of their traditions and increasingly defined themselves against revolutionary impiety and Black power. Prominent conjugal politics demonstrated both partisanship and interpersonal symbols of social union and disunion. French efforts to assuage Dominican concerns were tactless, threatening Dominicans' understandings of their place in the universe and causing uncertainty about their legal and religious protections. Even if French rule offered greater liberties, a formidable faction of Dominicans did not want to exchange their supernatural security for de jure distinctions of equality. This turmoil enhanced a growing sense of uniquely local Dominican grievances, interests, and collective belonging in distinction from Spanish, British, or French paradigms, a sense exacerbated by the growing power of Louverture and impending French control.

FIVE

FRENCH FAILURES, 1799–1807

As Spanish control faded, Philippe Roume, the new commissioner in Saint-Domingue, unveiled a new vision of unifying belief for Hispaniola. A series of unique and little-known sources show that in April 1799, during a revolutionary celebration of spouses and children, Roume invited citizens to "gather around the Altar of the Homeland" rather than in a church. He applauded those who had weathered storms on their revolutionary voyage, aided by an "invisible hand" that had guided "them to the port after all hope was lost." He implored islanders to thank this "beneficent Divinity who protected them[,] . . . the Pilot who never left the helm of the ship." This power supposedly superseded the Catholic deity Roume once claimed to follow. The "Supreme Being," whose "power is visible in all that surrounds us" and whose "intelligence . . . governs the universe," merited honor. Unlike prior French iterations, the revived Cult of the Supreme Being on Hispaniola was a novel strategy to reconcile belief and belonging among African, European, and secular traditions.

This newest attempt to conciliate contentions on Hispaniola argued that the "first religion" of humanity was "Deism," as evinced by the fact that every person had a soul, in contradistinction to other animals, a simplicity that holy texts and dogmas had obscured. Important manifestations of both revolutionary virtue and the Supreme Being on Hispaniola were, the decree said, "Vaudou" and Freemasonry. With a rhetorical flourish, it placed the historically significant heroics of Toussaint Louverture alongside the names of Moses, Socrates, Mohammed, and Jesus.[1] From this revolutionary elevation of a Black leader and an African diasporic religion, elites in Santo Domingo feared that a "republic, or kingdom of Africans," would rule "the whole island."[2] Elite Dominicans' worst fears of sanctimonious French secularism and sacrilege, alongside empowered Black citizens enacting emancipatory *égalité*, were upon them.

Though fascinating, this document ultimately failed to have the intended influence. It may have been partly an artifact of Louverture's ascendance, given his unique power, his control over Roume, and his need to offer unifying narratives for the island. In 1801 Louverture would control Santo Domingo against the wishes of French and Spanish officials, including Governor Joaquín García, who still managed the capital and much of the colony, owing to extensive delays in completing the Treaty of Basel. However, because he needed export profits, he left the terms of Black liberty ambiguous on that half of the island and did not promote social revolution. Despite his tempered approach, Catholic professions, and overt conciliation with Dominican beliefs, the presence of Black power and the spread of new ideas amplified paranoia among the Dominican elite. Their accusations of aggression and heresy against Louverture and his supporters represented fears for their lives and afterlives.

The Louverturian era represented the French Republic's zenith on Hispaniola. Meanwhile, France's revolutionary commitment was fading and it was succumbing to a Napoleonic authoritarianism. After French officials formally assumed governance of Santo Domingo in 1802, Dominicans experienced their efforts to "Frenchify" them.[3] The French administrators closed churches, installed pliant clergymen, sold church property, and converted one monastery's belfry into a cannon turret.[4] These actions prompted white flight, cementing a greater Dominican majority of color. Astute Dominican observers understood that Black power in Saint-Domingue was irreversible. Napoleonic attempts to re-enslave the island would inspire irrepressible independence sentiments. The Haitian Revolution culminated in independence for Haiti in 1804, and Haiti became the first universally emancipated state in the Americas.

French rule in Santo Domingo disappointed Dominicans of color who were once receptive to French revolutionary ideals. With time, their interest in their independent Haitian neighbors increased. France had largely ignored Santo Domingo until late 1803, when troops retreating from Saint-Domingue arrived. French rule precipitated a destructive Haitian offensive in Santo Domingo in 1805. Distraction, weakness, and divisiveness characterized French management through 1807, offering a target for a Dominican revolt when Napoléon invaded Spain in 1808, an event that elicited anti-French actions across the Spanish Americas.

Dominican society, now resigned to being ruled by a fading French Republic, recoiled against the French occupiers for a number of different reasons. French reinvigorations of racism and plantation production alienated Dominicans of color. Dominican elites first resented Toussaint Louverture and their entanglement in exogenous conflicts, and later resented French irreligion and ineptitude. Though their nostalgia for Spanish rule remained, confidence in imperial promises had collapsed. In this era, Santo Domingo became the final bastion of French power on Hispaniola. French projects for unifying the island, like the Spanish military campaigns of prior years, failed. Dominicans of all races and ranks debated ideas for a post-imperial future as their contact with the newly independent Haiti increased.

RIGAUD, ROUME, AND FAILED RECONCILIATIONS

Competition for power in Saint-Domingue set the pace for French control over Santo Domingo, which remained delayed for years following the Treaty of Basel. By 1798, four years after defecting from Spain, Louverture controlled French commissioners who were either incompetent or impotent. After the British withdrawal, Louverture's path to unifying Hispaniola opened, with only one rival, André Rigaud and his *gens de couleur* base in Sud, standing in his way.[5] As the strife of recent years expanded, in the late 1790s Santo Domingo steadily became a new resource cache and political venue for competitions in Saint-Domingue.

Starting this transition, on 27 March 1798 General Gabriel-Marie-Théodore-Joseph d'Hédouville, the new "Particular Agent of the Directory," disembarked in Santo Domingo. Tasked with governing Saint-Domingue, he also obliquely oversaw the logistical difficulties of occupying Santo Domingo. García perceived that Hédouville, unlike the French commissioners who had preceded him, wanted harmony. However, Hédouville attempted to ignore certain protections in the treaty. Rebuffed, he departed for Saint-Domingue with his entourage, and the unresolved transfer fell to other parties.[6]

Hédouville faced unhappy partisans in Cap-Français, too. By October 1798, angry citizens of color were besieging his administration. He could not compete with Louverture and his many allies, who even flirted with declaring independence from France. Hédouville sent orders to arrest Moïse, Louverture's adopted nephew and powerful lieutenant, who busily suppressed the opposition in Fort Dauphin. Moïse complained to Louverture, his beloved uncle, who sent his army into Cap-Français to intimidate the French.[7] Thereafter, Hédouville became "a kind of state prisoner . . . completely in the power of Louverture," according to British observers.[8] After suffering calculated forms of public embarrassment, Hédouville, among many others whom Louverture had humbled, fled Saint-Domingue.[9]

As Dominicans watched Louverture consolidate political power in Saint-Domingue, they feared what this would mean for Dominican towns that had previously disrespected him. Soon, García received a contingent of racially diverse visitors from Nord. Their commissions were from Louverture, not Paris. Following the rapid fall of Hédouville, this clique enlisted Roume to become the new commissioner in Cap-Français.[10] The visitors included the Black politician known as Thomany and Colonel Vincent, a white Frenchman. Vincent had become a highly trusted emissary for Louverture, even having defended him several times in person with officials in France. Aside from recruiting Roume, Vincent also wrote a lengthy report on agriculture and resources in Santo Domingo, perhaps as a treatise on its economic value for his friend Louverture.[11]

Louverture, who had also ejected Léger-Félicité Sonthonax from his second stint as a commissioner, reached a cooperation deal with André Rigaud, his main rival. Rigaud, the son of a wealthy French father and an enslaved mother, had been the de facto overseer of Sud since Sonthonax's first ouster in 1793. Geographic isolation allowed Rigaud autonomy from more turbulent areas of the colony. While Rigaud maintained plantation production, irritating *cultivateurs*, he still attracted some Black support. Though white bourgeois French republicans once considered him a threat, he had proved his loyalty in distinguished campaigns against the British. Rigaud eventually became a coveted counterweight to Louverture, and Hédouville even tried to court an alliance with him. However, by insulting Louverture, replacing his troops, and trying to make Rigaud his equal, Hédouville hastened his own departure. To avoid Louverture's ire, Rigaud played it coy.

Nevertheless, Louverture moved to rid himself of Rigaud and control all of Saint-Domingue. Though Rigaud had cooperated with Louverture and sincerely seemed to support *liberté* and *égalité*, Louverture feared that a new commissioner from France would arrive with troops to suppress him. Louverture's erstwhile colleague Rigaud and his wealthy, French-educated gens de couleur subordinates, such as Alexandre Pétion and Jean-Pierre Boyer, could yet betray him.

This War of the South began in June 1799. Personal, racial, and regional rivalries worsened competition for control. Louverture, Rigaud, and their partisans simply bypassed white French pretenses of having control over Saint-Domingue.[12] And to secure new lines of support and supplies, both parties infiltrated Santo Domingo. As this conflict encroached, well-off

Dominicans continued fleeing by the thousands, often taking enslaved Dominicans with them. Those remaining dreaded what direct French rule would mean for their earthly and eternal lives.

Additionally, Louverture managed the agent he had recruited to supposedly quell this crisis, Philippe Roume, who had crossed the island to replace Hédouville after three eventful years in Santo Domingo. Along his route, Louverture incited his partisans to harass Roume. Supposedly to save the new commissioner, Louverture would then send personal messages to calm the crowd. His regular intimidation tactics effectively subverted Roume's authority. Eventually, Louverture even had Roume locked in a chicken coop to force his acquiescence on decisions.[13]

Roume became "no better than a dignified prisoner" of Louverture's when the War of the South began six months after his arrival in Saint-Domingue. As such, observed an American consul, "all the public acts of the agent are in favor of Louverture, and hostile to his rival." Roume would "continue [along this path] as long as he is invested with any public authority . . . [for] he dare not do otherwise." Roume was "privately [supporting] the interests of Rigaud, and Louverture seems well acquainted with this fact." Rather than dismissing him immediately, Louverture had decided that Roume could be useful by "signing such edicts as Louverture dictate[d]." Once he had signed a proclamation, Roume would publish it, but only "reluctantly," and then "strut about the Government House in the costume of agency until something else [was] required of him."[14] This withering portrayal showed a cowed French commissioner unable to prevent an impending civil war that would spill over into Santo Domingo.

In this context, Hispaniola received surprising invocations to unity that only enlivened the paranoia of elite Dominicans, who were anticipating cultural attacks by France. Given their exaltations of Louverture, who managed Roume, the provenance and intent of these decrees are curious. On 4 February 1799, within a month of his arrival, Roume published a philosophical pamphlet requesting that citizens "celebrate . . . around the Tree of Liberty" on the fifth anniversary of France's "glorious" general emancipation, one of the "miracles of the Revolution" that had "avenged Africa from European greed . . . [and the] Machiavellianism of the French monarchy."

The document heralded Louverture and his Black army as the guarantors of this achievement, saying their revolution equaled any French victory in Europe and deserved laurels of admiration. The freed Black citizens would revitalize commerce, rebuilding Saint-Domingue "from its ashes."[15] Louverture graciously received these compliments, ostensibly from Roume, and reciprocated with platitudes about the republic. He praised his officers

Dessalines, Moïse, Clervaux, and Agé for welcoming with him into the "dawn of happiness" for Nord and Ouest, which Sud could also have.[16]

Three months later, Roume published a more shocking decree amid what was widely recognized as Dominican Catholic angst over looming French rule and the religious, racial, and secular factionalism accompanying it. This decree promoted the Supreme Being as a big tent under which Christians, Freemasons, and Vodouizan might unify. It critiqued the "vulgar fables and absurdities" of ancient times that had distorted an innocent form of Deism. Furthermore, it lamented the "magical mechanism of poetry" by which organized religions indoctrinated children with "monstrosities" disguised "as religious principles." These doctrines obscured the "true principles of science and morality." Caught between reason and fanaticism, humans had abandoned their original, simple, Deistic virtue and had been "subjected to the . . . trickery of the wicked . . . under the titles of kings and masters who commanded subjects and slaves."[17]

Dominican elites had long suspected that Roume was a Deist.[18] Roume may have also been connected to Freemasonry, along with Sonthonax, Étienne Polverel, and numerous metropolitan politicians.[19] The Cult of the Supreme Being's brief fluorescence, limited to France, had grafted the loyalties of citizens who longed for a divine purpose onto ideas of public virtue and civic duty derived from rights discourses.[20]

Though Deism, Freemasonry, and secular ideas were somewhat familiar on Hispaniola, the open praise and acceptance of African spirituality was certainly not. The praise for Vodou in the decree contradicted generations of repressive French policy toward Vodou. For example, in 1796 Sonthonax had issued laws against the practice of African-derived spirituality, as he and others viewed *le vaudou* as a separate allegiance that could undermine loyalties or labor discipline.[21]

But the decree went further, lauding "Vaudou, present still in African countries," which it said grew from "mysteries taught by the sages of Ethiopia." It presented other beliefs as pushing toward compatible truths, such as Moses guiding the monotheist Jews out of bondage, Mohammed restoring commitment to a single "Infinite Being," and the powerful figures of Socrates and Jesus suffering and dying for their principles. In total, it argued that "the Supreme Being . . . judged with impenetrable wisdom that it was time to start the seventh epoch of nature," which was entrusted to the French Revolution, a "total regeneration of the human species." And, on the unique journey for Hispaniola, all marveled at the leadership of "this phenomenon, one of the most astonishing of the Revolution . . . TOUSSAINT LOUVERTURE," who fought for an idyllic future.[22]

These unique sources show an inventive effort to unify adherents of Vodou, Abrahamic traditions, and Freemasonry, an attempt to assuage beliefs among Black, white, and gens de couleur contingents all at once. This situational, republican, Deistic promotion of a unifying Supreme Being may have also intentionally comported with other prevalent observances. Specifically, it encompassed the roles of Nzambi (the all-creating, all-knowing deity broadly observed by Kongolese peoples) in nascent Vodou and the *Bon Dieu* (Good Lord) of Catholicism.[23] Even Louverture, who presented himself as a devoted Catholic, sometimes adopted the "Supreme Being" terminology.[24]

Perhaps Louverture used this language to harmonize subconsciously with French Deist trends, or even to take advantage of the moment opportunistically. Yet, when he became the dominant political player on Hispaniola, he promoted Catholicism with state resources and initiated his own persecutions of Vodou, which he had at times earlier ignored in order to maintain a sense of camaraderie. Building on ideas introduced by predecessors such as Sonthonax, he now suppressed Vodou as part of his plan to send the formerly enslaved back to plantation work in order to revitalize agriculture, to quell dissent from forces beyond his manipulation, and to assuage the worries of various parties about his rule, including Parisian politicians, secret British trade partners, and devoutly Catholic Dominicans.[25]

These religious interventions, however, struck Spanish elites in Santo Domingo as "despicable" and great "moral risks."[26] Balancing their influence was the increasing presence of a new French-affiliated elite. In this era, they increased their power, from serving as envoys with little official power to eventually occupying the upper echelons of the colony's political, military, and religious offices.

As civil warfare erupted in Saint-Domingue, Rigaud, who may have been planning to attract Dominican support since 1798, began sending printed manifestos into Santo Domingo, in part because of Louverture's control over Roume. This was only the first attempt by Rigaud to find a new base of support and resources.[27] Helpless, in mid-1799 García had watched as "the Blacks and the *mulâtres* of the French part have already commenced their factions, and harass each other between the parties of Nord and Ouest against those of Sud, whose heads are the Black general Louverture and the *mulâtre* general Rigaud."[28] The barely one thousand remaining Spanish soldiers in Santo Domingo could not impede an eastward-moving conflict.[29]

In a preview of the competition between Louverture and Rigaud in Santo Domingo, García received letters from Governor Johann Rudolf Lauffer of Dutch Curaçao begging for aid against French meddling. The suggestion that an apparent Roume-sponsored and perhaps Louverture-approved republican conspiracy had swept Curaçao piqued García's interest. The Dutch colony had become party to Saint-Domingue's civil war just as Santo Domingo had.[30] Rigaud himself had warned Lauffer of the plot. Two French agents had organized a revolt that would install republicans favorable to politicians in Cap-Français and close extant trade with Sud to undermine Rigaud. More than principle, this was part of a wider struggle driven by practicality to secure more support in the region. Roume had also sent agents to Cuba, Cartagena, México, and possibly other Spanish dominions. However, Louverture secretly outed the agents that had been sent to radicalize the enslaved population of Jamaica in order to honor his covert pledge not to export revolution to British domains.[31]

García understood that score settling between Rigaud's and Louverture's factions in Curaçao foreshadowed rumored plans that both parties hoped to directly manage Santo Domingo. Louverture might control Santo Domingo with or without French approval. Either way, the gradual diffusion of dissent would more fully absorb all of Santo Domingo into the Haitian Revolution.

Dominican elites reviled Toussaint Louverture and assumed he would do away with local racial hierarchies. In Santo Domingo, many partisans who were white or free people of color sided with Rigaud, who was closer to them geographically and with whom they shared more commonalities, especially in terms of socioeconomic class and Eurocentric affects. The French Directory could not prevent the outward spin of civil warfare between "personalities, colors, parties, passions, pride, and ambition" in Saint-Domingue. Likewise, García could not stop more disadvantaged Dominicans, and particularly the enslaved, from favoring Louverture.[32]

TOUSSAINT, *TRIOMPHANT*

"Toussaint is of a different system" than his rivals, a former French planter noted in the late 1790s. Many witnesses recorded similar impressions about Louverture's astounding rise. Eventually, his strategies in the War of the South merged into a campaign to control Santo Domingo. This culminating era of Louverturian power concluded with his triumphant control of all Hispaniola.[33]

With even greater regularity, events on one side of Hispaniola affected the other. For example, when Louverture's former lieutenant Bellegarde betrayed him by handing Môle Saint-Nicolas to Rigaud, Louverture overran the strategic port city. He also cowed Louis-Jacques Bauvais, a powerful mulâtre commanding Jacmel, from supporting his longtime friend Rigaud. Bauvais fled, drowning at sea on his voyage for France via Curaçao.[34] With such treachery and turnover, Roume regrouped available officers, including General François-Marie Kerversau, who briefly served as French agent in Santo Domingo. To replace him there, Roume sent General Antoine Chanlatte.[35]

Despite the governmental disarray impeding his regular pay, Chanlatte developed advantageous political and commercial relationships in Santo Domingo. To ingratiate himself, he consulted with Juan Bautista Oyarzábal of Boca Nigua, who then advised the French on Dominican cultural politics.[36] Overall, Chanlatte appeared to be neutral toward Louverture and Rigaud.[37]

Nevertheless, when Chanlatte arrived in October 1799, he experienced a brusque welcome from Dominican elites, who, between their options, openly preferred Rigaud. García, who had appreciated the "European education, intelligence, and appreciable customs" of Kerversau, spitefully assumed that "General Chanlatte, one of those of mixed bloods, natural of this island," could stoke racial dissent in Santo Domingo. García openly feared Louverture, whose "pretexts" for attacking Rigaud he critiqued. However, García was soon surprised to learn of their shared strategic interests.[38]

A prominent *citoyen* wrote to a Dominican friend stating that "yesterday some mail arrived . . . from the Black general Toussaint Louverture with letters for Agent Roume[,] in which he communicated [his] resolution to take possession of the Spanish part of the island." He implored his friend to flee if possible, as Louverture had allegedly threatened to bring "blood and fire" if the Spanish resisted his impromptu takeover. While this note stirred the capital, it also included the rumor of British and US designs to support an autonomous government of Louverture. Though the author doubted that the slaveholding British and the "southern provinces" of the United States would ultimately support Black power, for the first time debate about unification and independence captivated Dominicans.[39] Officials in Jamaica, in fact, grew increasingly alarmed at the surge of Black power in Saint-Domingue.[40]

Additionally, García had a secret source seemingly close to Louverture who may have once fought in the Black Auxiliaries for Spain. García thus corroborated the independence rumors and Louverture's solicitation of British and US weapons in exchange for commerce in his ports. Giving further credence to the idea that Louverture was angling for autonomy, he had dispatched Colonel Vincent to Paris to retrieve his two children and wrote a provocative message to the Directory blaming French commissioners for the colonial chaos. Further diminishing Roume's ability to prevent this, Louverture regularly intercepted and read French governmental letters not intended for his eyes. Considering this, García was livid at the French for their negligence in not using ciphers in sensitive correspondence about Santo Domingo. By the start of 1800, Louverture wielded pervasive power.[41]

Sensing victory against Rigaud, Louverture pressed forward with his plans. In April 1800, he sent a detachment of white troops under General Agé to formally occupy Santo Domingo. He did so to satisfy treaty terms and appease Dominicans. However, this maneuver lacked consent from Paris and Madrid. His premise to justify controlling Santo Domingo circled around legal complaints against Dominican elites regarding the old "abuses" of selling captured French cultivateurs off the island, as well as the continual outmigration of enslaved Dominicans. Agé's lengthy instructions, likely approved by Louverture, required him to tolerate Dominican religiosity and the public role of priests while encouraging them to comply with republican policies. To expedite the process, Louverture's aides circulated printed proclamations among Dominicans explaining Agé's intentions.[42] This was Louverture's first serious effort to unify the island.

Agé had successfully served Louverture during the civil war. His forces had just captured Jacmel, securing the probable fall of Rigaud.[43] Chanlatte, who had begun to oppose Louverture, suddenly allied with García.[44] To ease tensions, Louverture wrote to García as soon as Agé departed for Santo Domingo with promises to protect Dominican property, keep enslaved Dominicans on plantations, withhold formerly enslaved troops, and respect religious practice.[45] These attempts failed.

Though infuriated by the inconsiderate French and by their treaty violations, costly delays, and theatrical attempts to *francesizar* (Frenchify) Dominicans, García had to acknowledge French concerns about the loss of Black laborers as troops approached. Louverture did not know that Spanish officials had already legislated against selling captives five months prior with support from Chanlatte, and had even prosecuted some Dominicans, albeit half-heartedly. Under pressure to evacuate the colony, García raged at the inability to do so because of the lack of ships and the presence of the surrounding British navy.[46] More assertive attempts to secure Santo Domingo also failed.[47]

García told Louverture that he enjoyed meeting with Agé when he arrived on 13 May 1800.[48] However, two days later, more than two hundred local signatories petitioned Spanish officials to suspend the transfer to France until they could safely depart from the colony. They feared the French "abyss of confusions" and doubted that the new "First Consul Buonaparte" (Napoléon Bonaparte) could prevent "a multitude of Blacks rebelling en masse," spreading "disorganization [and] misfortunes," setting fires, and using knives against Dominicans. Arguably, their fears were exaggerated.[49] Similar letters followed from other Dominican towns.[50] Some claimed to represent all "100,000 souls" of Santo Domingo and appealed directly to Napoléon for mercy.[51] Of course, these occupation orders came from Louverture, not Napoléon, who later seemed to agree with Dominicans and bristled at the assertiveness of his newfound nemesis, Louverture.[52]

Though Chanlatte thought Dominicans were overreacting, the sense of outrage gained traction.[53] García called a conference in his home with Agé and Chanlatte and begged them to wait for a formal commission from France and direct orders from Madrid and Paris. García knew that Louverture managed Roume. He justified resisting sudden demands, as five years had already lapsed since the signing of the treaty. To protect the capital, four hundred residents traveled to Azua to set up defenses, bolstering the garrison of only 1,165 regular troops. García announced the "suspension of the delivery" and then asked Agé to leave.[54] García hoped Louverture would waver.

Certain Dominicans had fixated on terrifying ideas about Louverture, such as that he was an "enemy of the white race" and a "perturber of tranquility." In this they ignored the leniency and humanity he had always shown to white partisans and combatants. Their fear of living under Louverture drove some white Dominicans to threaten Agé, giving him only six hours to leave the capital. Louverture, who had sent a white general trying to avoid such spectacle, was infuriated.[55] Later French accounts said Agé suffered harassment, or even came under attack. Perhaps elites, emboldened by Chanlatte, simply intimidated him. Nevertheless, their actions provided justification for Louverture to directly intervene.[56]

Many Dominican elites felt that they had become orphans from their Spanish family and saw their French neighbors as "a Bloody Lion that by keeping us in its claws threatens us day by day with our fatal end." French troops forced some border towns to fund their occupation, demanded hundreds of cattle and many horses, and paid only one-quarter of the price for the goods they required or sometimes committed theft. Some planters had been disarmed, their weapons passed to local Black Dominicans, who were whispering about insurrection.[57]

Rigaud, also under duress from Louverture, sent a letter in June 1800 complimenting "the character of the Spanish nation." He offered García an alliance "of the highest importance to persecute . . . this plague" of "Black projects."[58] Rigaud also sent an envoy to Chanlatte and García to encourage them to fight the "treasonous" Louverture, whom he accused of being a "genius exterminator and inhuman destroyer." Chanlatte had won Dominican elites' trust. García even considered transferring Santo Domingo to him and his "russet"-colored leader Rigaud to impede Louverture.[59] Rigaud recruited several other distressed Dominican towns near his remaining strongholds.[60] With dwindling hope of prevailing, Rigaud may have even considered Santo Domingo for a new base of operations against Louverture.[61] Despite coordinating with Chanlatte and praising Rigaud, García prudently declined to formally join the civil war.[62] Louverture weathered Rigaud's final efforts, soon placed Roume on a ship bound for France, and thereby enhanced his power.[63]

Louverture had finally defeated Rigaud by August 1800, at which point Rigaud disappeared. In desperation, a detachment of troops affiliated with Rigaud retreated to Neiba and demanded a meeting with the priest Juan Bobadilla. Led by LaFortune, who had once been a rival of Louverture, they hoped to enlist the well-known Maniel maroons. LaFortune, a former Maniel maroon leader himself, knew Bobadilla well and in the 1780s had negotiated peace with Spain. Nevertheless, LaFortune failed to persuade the majority of Maniel maroons to leave the mountains, to which many had returned to elude violence and imperial constraints. Regardless of French emancipation and Black citizenship, they remained suspicious of state power and ambivalent toward rights discourses.[64]

As Dominican society became more entwined with adjacent revolutionary churn, Louverture could more easily reprimand Dominicans for their recalcitrance. In November 1800, Louverture revisited the idea of taking Santo Domingo and complained about the treatment of Black laborers and Agé. During their recent travels, the French officers Pageot and Michel had intercepted runaways from a Dominican plantation. The runaways convinced the generals that they were actually French and had been abducted into enslavement. García dismissed the story, as it seemed designed to benefit both the runaways and French officials.[65] He investigated and claimed that the runaways, three men and one woman, were Dominican creoles.[66] His words did not matter.

Louverture used this issue to justify controlling the east and rallying Dominicans of color. The French also cited the accusations when imposing new agents in Santiago and Azua. By the close of 1800, Louverture was presiding in Saint-Domingue after installing himself as the chief French agent on Hispaniola. Dominican elites watched as retributions were carried out against Rigaud partisans in Sud, including executions in Jérémie and elsewhere as Dessalines and Laplume consolidated power. However, halcyon hopes of more *liberté* for the Black population across Hispaniola faded. Drawing upon the restrictive labor policies of previous French commissioners, Louverture initiated unpopular new imperatives to send Black citizens back to work on plantations as cultivateurs in order to revitalize commodity exports and fund his government.[67]

Capping the shift from fearing the French Republic to fearing Toussaint Louverture and Black citizens that began in the mid-1790s, elites in Santo Domingo panicked as Louverture began marching toward Santo Domingo in January 1801. However, neither mass uprisings by the enslaved nor rampant labor absenteeism followed the transfer of power. Louverture needed the laborers, too, as did the French Empire, much to the disillusionment of Dominicans of color, who recalled the once robust rhetoric of Roume and Sonthonax. Also, Louverture's perceived usurpations of French imperatives attracted the attention of Napoléon Bonaparte. Formal French metropolitan management of Santo Domingo did not commence until 1802, with the arrival of General Charles Leclerc, who was sent to curtail Louverture and Black power seven years after parties signed the Treaty of Basel. That year, Napoléon, who was also interested in revitalizing Saint-Domingue's exports, pondered even more drastic labor politics: re-enslavement.[68]

TOUSSAINT, *DOMINICAIN*

After his triumph in Saint-Domingue, Louverture's Dominican governance, albeit brief, brought change for Dominicans of color and ushered in rule by a French Republic undergoing authoritarian reversals. In early January 1801 Louverture began issuing proclamations to Dominicans stating that they would not "insult the Republic a second time" after their rejection of his envoy Agé. He told them, "I have dispatched the armed forces, and I will come myself."

However, he also hoped to disprove the propaganda against him. For example, Louverture promised "security, protection of property, and respect for proprietors," to preempt panicked resistance from Dominican elites. He exhorted them "to revert from their error," as France "only asks for your hearts." In one of many prudent tributes to Dominican culture, Louverture professed that "religion and humanity" had compelled him to approach in "peace and the happiest tranquility."[69]

Many elites remained unconvinced. Implying that Louverture was simply pandering, García aggressively questioned his purported religious motivations. He begged Louverture, his former ally from the Black Auxiliaries, to prevent acts of retribution by his large army. Many of Louverture's soldiers had once fought for Spain.[70] Louverture soon entered the colony with twelve thousand troops. He sent an additional five regiments to Santiago, and rumors circulated that five thousand more troops might disembark at Boca Nigua, ferried by the British, who wanted to open rival colonies and thought their covert cooperation with Louverture might coax a break with France. As Louverture's army passed through Azua, Ocoa, and Baní, residents who did not immediately surrender were threatened with losing their homes.[71]

Louverture held these towns as leverage to pressure García to acquiesce. He paused in Azua to send two locals, Nicolás González and Gerónimo Díaz, with special messages to the residents of Baní, a town between his army and the capital. Through these Dominican messengers, Louverture reiterated his peaceful intentions, but he also said he was perturbed that elites in Santo Domingo were insisting on an officially sanctioned French army to receive the colony.[72] García and the Cabildo of Santo Domingo received similar messengers from Louverture, but in response they refused to apologize for how they had treated Agé and instead blamed Chanlatte and his Dominican friends.[73] Louverture sent out similar messages of peace to La Vega and Cotuí, two key towns in the Cibao, and even to Monte Plata and Bayaguana north and east of the capital. His method of selecting Dominicans along his path to mediate for him succeeded in producing some peaceful capitulations. Compliance was preferable to annihilation. To reduce tensions and retain laborers, Louverture, intriguingly, avoided mentioning slavery and abolition in his introductions.[74]

Louverture continued tightening his grip on Santo Domingo through January with the southward push of Moïse's army through the Cibao and toward the capital. Along the way, Louverture counteracted pockets of non-compliance with proclamations and exhortations more than violence. He subtly attempted to mollify fears of a race war among Dominican elites.

After taking Baní, Louverture sent his formerly enslaved troops to plantations around the capital to gain support from local Dominicans of color and acquire food. Moïse approached from the north, where he met with minor resistance in Santiago and executed an uncooperative Dominican officer. After that, La Vega, Cotuí, and towns just north of Santo Domingo organized orderly surrenders. Surrounded, García began planning to deliver Santo Domingo. However, at the mouth of the Nizao River near Baní about one thousand Dominicans, led by Chanlatte, pitched a battle against Louverture's army, resulting in deaths on both sides. García did not endorse them, and he feared the incident would provoke reprisals from Louverture. Realizing their defeat, the militia retreated to the port in a panic and fled by ship. This was also, in part, a final battle of Louverture's war with Rigaud.

To prevent further needless bloodshed that would only delay the inevitable, García sent a delegation to entreat with Louverture. The negotiations produced the transfer of Jayna on 25 January 1801, and then Castillo San Gerónimo the next morning, followed by the capital, Santo Domingo, in the afternoon of 26 January. Despite Louverture's restraint, many Dominicans crowded the docks. However, only ships with women and children could leave, and a naval blockade by ships affiliated with Louverture and his British allies ensured this would be the case. Noncompliant vessels were warned not to continue.[75]

Almost immediately upon his arrival, Louverture issued a flurry of governmental directives. He tried to reorganize the currency, stimulate commerce and agriculture, change the bureaucracy, and alleviate trepidations. To maintain personal oversight, he sent his brother to manage Santiago.[76] His practical, measured policies contrasted with the massacres some expected.

Unlike his predecessor, Roume, the Deist, and later French officials who antagonized Catholics, Louverture kept the churches open, allowed the clergy to remain active, and repeatedly affirmed his own Catholicism.[77] To build social trust and political legitimacy, he held sanctifying Masses after his arrival in Santo Domingo. For example, Louverture arranged priestly blessings over his receipt of the keys to the city. Surrounded by prominent Dominicans and Spanish officials, he savored the political capitulation of former allies turned rivals, all the while showing his own trustworthiness to the community by humbly deferring to their shared Deity.[78]

Louverture could have violently occupied Santo Domingo. He did not. Rather, he knew elite Dominicans' reverent religiosity well from his former alliance with Spain and chose to present his own faith. Wisely, he told Dominicans of his intentions to pay homage at the chapel of Nuestra Señora de Altagracia, the shrine to their patron saint, located hours away in Higüey.[79]

However, elite Dominicans' diatribes continued. They ignored Louverture's actions and rejected the idea of "trust[ing] in the humanity of a conquering barbarian without faith, and without honor."[80] They cowered from Louverture's Black soldiers, whom they unflatteringly described as "hungry, naked, licentious, and rapacious," with a "strange language and nasty character." Racist insinuations aside, Louverture's thousands of troops were in fact famished. Moïse took the keys of a storekeeper and raided Spanish provisions, and then plotted to distribute the riches of the Spanish royal treasury. With racist appraisals of Louverture and his men as "petulant" occupiers, García himself finally prepared to leave the island after well over a decade as governor, including many years of waiting, from a weakened position, for the long-delayed Treaty of Basel to be fully approved and go into effect. He continued to insist that Louverture and the French had yet to legally fulfill the terms of the treaty.

Thus began the next phase of conflict resolution. Dominican elites insisted on emigrating with enslaved people. Louverture tried to stop them upon principles of the French Republic, with the apparent exception of the enslaved wet nurses who were permitted to leave with young white families. Many elite Dominican families complied with Louverture's rules before departing, some signing freedom papers for the enslaved they had tried to take with them. Their manumissions raised questions about the emancipation efforts Louverture attempted. In his unpopular labor policies in Saint-Domingue, he had sought to retain laborers, and he took the same approach in Santo Domingo. He made no clear abolition declaration upon his arrival there.[81]

With careful wording, Louverture insisted that France did not recognize slavery. This was distinct from implementing freedom for the Dominican enslaved. And while Louverture perpetuated Dominican production, cultivateurs in Les Cayes soon revolted against Dessalines and Laplume for enforcing labor standards.[82]

After years of elite Dominican paranoia and popular hope, Louverture tactically left the terms of Black liberty ambiguous. Though his influence was greater than during Laveaux's failed emancipation attempt years before, Louverture's brief stay in Santo Domingo and roughly one year of management became entangled in an array of concerns that impeded the simple extension of policy precedents from Saint-Domingue. His focus was diffused across the island. Records show that most enslaved Dominicans persisted in slavery or something similar. In fact, actions by Louverture in seeking self-sufficiency gradually eroded his own popularity among the majority of color across the entirety of Hispaniola.[83]

Louverture calculated that "the extraction of the people devoted to the work of cultivation" would result in "the annihilation of this country." In other words, his government required a robust export sector in order to survive, so it needed agricultural laborers. He also attempted to encourage elite Dominicans to remain, perhaps to retain capital or expertise. He was furious about the departure of cultivateurs. This, he said, represented "stealing from agriculture the arms devoted to it." He estimated that three thousand such cultivateurs had left and said that many of these captives "were Blacks robbed from the French part." Their loss compounded the losses for all of Hispaniola. Feeding Hispaniola and selling commodities were priorities and would help to sustain his governance.

Oyarzábal gave Louverture a "shocking example" from Boca Nigua of agricultural laborers under his management leaving and the land going untended. Because of their departure, the "most beautiful habitation," he said, would "fall into ruin and turn . . . into forest." If the Boca Nigua plantation had purchased captives illicitly from Saint-Domingue, as Louverture had broadly alleged, then Oyarzábal was implicating himself. This could explain the several francophone names in Boca Nigua court records. Also, Oyarzábal was likely referring to those who were still legally in bondage as cultivateurs to mirror French nomenclature.[84] If the Boca Nigua owner Marqués de Iranda had asked to export the enslaved, then under Spanish law and the protections of the Treaty of Basel, they claimed that nothing illicit had occurred. Oyarzábal's perhaps opportunistic presentation of the situation more likely indicated his inclination to protect profits and Boca Nigua under French rule than any political conviction.[85]

As part of his effort to halt the outmigration of laborers, Louverture investigated a "certain frigate . . . anchored in . . . port [that was] ready to depart." A number of Blacks had apparently been taken to the ship "by force." But a man had been intercepted fleeing with some of these laborers, and it turned out to be Pedro Abadía, the same employee whose heavy-handed punishments had sparked the 1796 revolt by the enslaved at Boca Nigua. Louverture demanded their return and insisted that they rejoin Oyarzábal to work at the Boca Nigua plantation.[86]

García complied with Louverture in this case, ordering the disembarkation of Oyarzábal's laborers and their return. However, he rejected the statement that three thousand laborers had been taken from Santo Domingo. He requested that Louverture allow those who were not cultivateurs—such as the "domestics" that García himself owned—to leave, citing the Treaty of Basel's provision allowing "goods" to be taken. "Goods" included the enslaved under Spanish laws. Some planters ignored Louverture and were immediately intercepted by the British navy. Louverture also heard rumors that some Dominicans had sabotaged their own plantations before leaving in a plot to undermine him. Such news frustrated Louverture. In response, García sarcastically appealed to Louverture's professed sense of virtue and religion.[87]

By then, as many as forty thousand Dominicans had fled, which put a financial strain on other Spanish colonies.[88] The majority of the emigrants were white Dominicans from the capital. Even if Louverture overestimated the number of the enslaved who departed, certainly thousands had left. Sánchez Valverde estimated that as many as fourteen thousand enslaved people left, and it is unlikely that this loss could be compensated by natural increase or by the illicit trade with Saint-Domingue of small numbers of captives. An overall decline would follow, with the falling numbers due to forced emigration, natural deaths, and manumissions. These declines among both the white and enslaved populations meant an even larger free majority of color in Dominican demographics.[89]

García finally departed from Santo Domingo, arriving in Maracaibo on 22 February 1801. Other officials evacuated to Puerto Rico and Cuba.[90] García moved to Havana, where at the end of September he finally received formal permission from Spain to transfer Santo Domingo to sanctioned French officials, not the allegedly "brusque" Toussaint Louverture.[91]

García and Dominican exiles kept informed of a new, massive French expeditionary force in 1802 as the Spanish ambassador in Paris used their reports to claim damages, adding to the French distaste for Louverture.

FIGURE 5.1

"Court Martial," in Marcus Rainsford, An Historical Account of the Black Empire of Hayti *(London: Albion, 1805), John Carter Brown Library, Archive of Early American Images, D805 R158h / 1-SIZE. Instances of newfound official Black governmental power resonated throughout the Americas.*

They watched Leclerc regularize Napoleonic rule in Santo Domingo and attempt to restrict Black power in Saint-Domingue.[92] In a fitting finale of an era on Hispaniola, García went to Madrid in 1803 and returned two silver and four gold medals, rewards intended for the long-disbanded Black Auxiliaries. Indeed, they were like the one from Spain that Louverture had once proudly worn.[93]

TOUSSAINT, *DÉNOUEMENT*

In the Spanish Caribbean, rumors already circulated "that they had sworn Toussen [*sic*] as King" on Hispaniola.[94] These rumors approximated reality, as in mid-1801 Louverture promulgated a new constitution that envisioned a more autonomous relationship with France and made him governor for life. Colonel Vincent delivered this document to Napoléon by hand. Countervailing Louverture was Roume, who regaled Napoléon with tales of Louverture and his defiance of France. This, and Louverture's absorption of Santo Domingo, outraged Napoléon. His brother, Lucien, admitted to Spain that French officials thought Louverture's actions were irregular implementations of the treaty.[95] Further, Lucien and Napoléon were already drafting plans for their new French Santo Domingo.[96]

Regardless of what Madrid or Paris had preferred, Louverture had used the delayed Treaty of Basel to unite Hispaniola for the first time in over a century. Though it was fleeting, the unification was ostensibly for France, but certainly for his own political advancement. Aware that he could become a Napoleonic target, the calculating pragmatist Louverture yet busied himself managing labor, trade, and security across Hispaniola.[97]

Louverture installed his brother, Paul, to oversee the capital region. Paul was also put in charge of increasing cross-island trade and assessing repayment claims for confiscated crops. Together, they enlisted troops that Louverture knew from his time with Spain and drafted additional Dominicans for defense forces.[98] However, citing biblical scriptures, Catholic history, and theology, priests in the northern parishes protested the imposition of new bishops who were aligned with Louverture or France.[99] Such ecclesiastical shuffling also concerned the pope.[100] Supposedly to support Dominican piety, Louverture had tried to install a possible ally, the new bishop of Sud, Guillaume Mauviel, as archbishop for Santo Domingo. However, the capital rejected Mauviel, and far more turbulence followed.[101]

On 29 January 1802, barely a year after establishing his impromptu government in Santo Domingo, Toussaint Louverture stood on the northeastern

Dominican coast at the Samaná Peninsula. He scanned the horizon, having received intelligence of a French expedition approaching with the aim of ending his authority. Where the sky met the sea, he saw the sails of some fifty ships, carrying a force that would eventually surpass forty thousand of Napoléon's finest troops. They were commanded by his brother-in-law, General Charles Leclerc. Most of these new challengers would perish soon after their arrival. They were only part of the more than seventy thousand total French troops sacrificed fighting first to protect slavery, then to secure abolition, and finally to reinstall slavery and reverse Black power.[102]

As Leclerc departed France, Napoléon wrote to the Spanish court to explain his plan to undermine Louverture, complete the Treaty of Basel, and give Dominicans formal French administration.[103] Neither France nor Spain acknowledged the fulfillment of the colony's transfer until the Leclerc expedition controlled Santo Domingo.[104] En route, Leclerc even unsuccessfully suggested to officials in Cuba that they conduct a commission to formally cede Santo Domingo to France, in order to finally fulfill all the terms of the lingering Treaty of Basel.[105] With peace in Europe, Napoléon selected forces to dominate the Americas, explicitly including the extrication of Louverture from Santo Domingo as part of their mission.[106]

At first, Leclerc outflanked and outgunned Louverture's forces. François-Marie Kerversau, the former French agent in Santo Domingo who had fled from Louverture with Chanlatte, retook the capital from Paul Louverture, who joined Leclerc, betraying his brother Toussaint. Kerversau declared draconian labor and vagrancy rules. He then captured Santiago without a fight. He became the Paris-sanctioned French governor exercising day-to-day management in Santo Domingo.[107]

One of Kerversau's least popular acts during his unremarkable year governing Santo Domingo was the closing of Dominican churches. He took this step in order to punish locals for again not accepting Guillaume Mauviel, who saw Leclerc's expedition as another opportunity to become archbishop. Yet, as conditions deteriorated across Hispaniola, Mauviel fled.[108] The pope, like Dominicans in the capital, did not trust him.[109] However unpopular, the French bureaucrats who were present did permit Dominicans to pursue legal claims, account settlements, and criminal cases from ten years of direct involvement in the Haitian Revolution, proceedings that would continue for the duration of French rule in Santo Domingo.[110] The fact that exiles were now scattered across the Atlantic only complicated these cases.

Jean-François, the famous retired Black general, was a witness for a case lingering from the 1790s. Once one of the most important figures of the entire revolution, his health and career had since declined in isolated exile with a few officers in Cádiz, Spain.[111] His past collaborator Biassou had already died in poverty in Florida. Jean-François's reward for his remarkable dedication to Spain was a similarly depressing, albeit lengthier, demise in Andalucía.[112] In one of his final official statements, Jean-François defended the reputations of his troops and praised their service for Spain.[113]

The priest José Vázquez, Jean-François's former esteemed adviser, had rebuilt his career in Cuba, having emigrated, like many other Dominicans, to flee French rule.[114] By 1803 he had become the treasurer of the cathedral in Santiago de Cuba, where he ministered to the numerous Dominican exiles.[115] Like Jean-François and the late Biassou, Vázquez had also experienced poverty. They had all been forced to beg for additional support from Spanish officials who had forgotten their exemplary service. Culturally distinguishing from the royalist and religious Black Auxiliaries, Vázquez lamented that Dominicans had resided under "the Republican Africans."[116]

From opposite sides of the Atlantic, the once inseparable Jean-François and Vázquez watched the unthinkable happen. As Spanish rule collapsed, their old friend Louverture rose to power in Hispaniola. In another stunning arc, post-revolutionary France reversed emancipation.

Dramatically, General Leclerc perished from yellow fever, one of the many French dead by November 1802.[117] King Carlos IV offered Napoléon his personal condolences for the loss of his brother-in-law.[118] As French resources focused almost entirely on the significant struggles in Saint-Domingue into 1803, many Spanish officials assumed that Santo Domingo's return to Spain was only a matter of time. Spain thus sent an agent, named Francisco Arango, to negotiate with French officials in Saint-Domingue about claims pertaining to Santo Domingo and to collect intelligence.[119]

Arango arrived on French Hispaniola in March 1803 in time to witness the final months of the Haitian War for Independence.[120] He and others of his social position across the Spanish Empire watched as French peers lost their possessions after having supported imperial policies. One planter asked poetically if his own excesses and exploitations, which had only afforded him the price of a farm in France, had caused the conditions for social revolution. Apparently, it had taken a revolution for him to realize and accept that he did not need a beautiful home built from the labor of others, just good soil to feed his family.[121]

Arango requested permission for Dominicans to transit the island. He also asked for recompense for Louverture's takeover of Santo Domingo, as well as for Spanish access to Dominican ports. Meanwhile, he covertly evaluated the morale of the remaining Dominicans, the condition of agricultural properties, and the stability of French rule in Santo Domingo.[122] By asking why French ships had recently sold illicit cargoes of Black captives in Cuba, he learned more of the Napoleonic re-enslavement campaigns.[123]

Arango departed two months later with intriguing reports.[124] General Rochambeau, who had assumed command from Leclerc, had moved against Black power in a gesture favoring the Dominican elites, signing a French apology for Louverture's actions and promising to pay damages to aggrieved Dominicans.[125] He also negotiated the release of hundreds of troops who had previously been forced to join Louverture in Santo Domingo. Some of them had experienced two years of combat. However, the "poor Dominicans" would have to guard Santo Domingo's borders for France against armies to their west. Kerversau organized a militia force of two thousand Dominicans. Though he was prevented from visiting Santo Domingo himself as a result of the inland violence, Arango had gathered intelligence from his Port-au-Prince base suggesting that although there was peace in Santo Domingo, economic dislocations were prevalent. In Port-au-Prince, Arango met displaced Dominicans. Many of them said they wanted to leave because the island's commerce had come to a grinding halt.[126]

France had failed miserably in their brutal attempts to reanimate exports. Most of the properties sat empty or were charred by fire. The massive French army had been decimated by disease and war. Summarizing the imperial perspective, Arango wrote, "The plume falls from my hands when I try to begin the sad painting" of what had befallen Hispaniola.[127]

Though the French expedition effected Louverture's demise, liberatory resistance against France intensified exponentially once their intentions to restore slavery became clear. Louverture's remaining officers, figures who had first risen through the ranks of the Black Auxiliaries, led this final stage of the struggle. This war for survival escalated into an unambiguous independence project by 1803.[128]

Arango concluded that the French knew very little about the independence army, only that "the Black De-Salines [sic] was recognized as successor of Toussaint when he made the last insurrection public and divided the command of the colony among the rest of his generals." Dessalines had "established his headquarters in Gonaïves, and there subsists well-fortified, and with a corps of 3,000–4,000 troops." Only 14,000 French troops remained in June 1803, and they were outnumbered five to one. By then, a mulâtre named Alexandre Pétion, who had once been a colonel for France and an understudy to Rigaud, was governing Sud almost independently.

The systemic, "atrocious" actions of the French included ruthlessly shooting, stabbing, torturing, blinding, and drowning Black prisoners. This shocked Arango. He even learned of a female prisoner who had been killed by dogs in a public spectacle, and worse, that this had become a regular form of execution. Arango believed that these practices were not only counterproductive, but that the war would be "interminable if they take from the rebels the hope of capitulation or pardon." One citoyen had already accepted that the subjugation of the Black population was impossible, and the French should instead try for a "chimeric project of union and commerce with them." However, Arango was skeptical that the colony could ever recover. Rochambeau, who wanted to annihilate the entire Black population, proposed introducing "new Blacks" untainted by revolution to the island instead. Rochambeau was in denial about France's fate. And, aside from two Black companies in the Cul-de-Sac that remained

FIGURE 5.2

"Blood Hounds Attacking a Black Family," in Marcus Rainsford, An Historical Account of the Black Empire of Hayti *(London: Albion, 1805), John Carter Brown Library, Archive of Early American Images, D805 R158H / 1-SIZE. Juxtaposed to demands for Black dignity were the desperate and despicable methods of dying empires.*

pro-French, almost all other Black people, including women and children, had become avowed anti-French fighters. A French general who had been their prisoner for two months was convinced that it was impossible for France to prevail.

Arango wondered if "these warriors of twelve years, already respected and feared by the soldiers of Bonaparte[,] . . . [might] pass someday to our colonies to make our slaves adopt their disastrous maxims." He feared a new era of Black "filibusters and buccaneers" along Spanish coasts and recognized that a tide of abolitionism was rising. This, he said, even included the "philanthropy of the Quakers who in North America have pursued abolition," who he believed would not hesitate to support those in Saint-Domingue who sought their freedom. Spanish observers well knew that the British had begun debating how long they could continue slavery. As these forces combined, those seeking autonomy in the Spanish Caribbean colonies would gain new allies. With Black independence and international recognition of independence on Hispaniola a real possibility, Arango suggested supporting the "Spanish Dominicans" who had suffered French neglect.[129]

HAITIAN INDEPENDENCE

In November 1803, the Black independence army of Jean-Jacques Dessalines, once Louverture's closest aide, definitively defeated French forces. Dominicans at home and in exile closely watched the French collapse. Dessalines declared independence at Gonaïves on 1 January 1804.[130]

Absent were the main generals of the early Haitian Revolution who had once fought under Spanish flags, including Louverture. Having acquiesced to retirement after France held his children in France as leverage, Louverture was accused of wielding insurrectionary influence over the populace. In June 1802 he had been arrested and deported. Imprisoned, alone, and cold in the French Alps, Toussaint Louverture died in April 1803, only nine months before independence, his body buried in an unmarked grave. For this new state, Dessalines reclaimed the Taíno name for the island, Haiti. Once a term used colloquially across Hispaniola, it soon became an Atlantic axiom of anti-colonialism and anti-racism.[131]

In Cádiz, Jean-François, eight years into his exile, watched as his former acquaintance Laplume arrived for his own exile in Andalucía.[132] Laplume had once skillfully helped Louverture rout Rigaud in Sud.[133] However, when Leclerc arrived, Laplume had joined the French. During the war for independence, Laplume remained a pro-French impediment to Dessalines. Even when Rochambeau demoted him and other Black officers in favor of white leadership, Laplume remained loyal to France.[134] In another French imposition upon their Spanish allies, they forced Laplume into exile in Cádiz after the war. When Laplume died in September 1803, the French consul in Andalucía asked local officials to assist in a lavish military funeral. They complied and buried the recently arrived Black general on Spanish soil with pomp and ceremony. These honors contrasted, of course, with Spanish treatment of Jean-François and French treatment of Louverture.[135]

Spain had largely withheld promised resources from the ex–Black Auxiliaries in Cádiz. Laplume's name, unlike those of prominent ex–Black Auxiliaries who died in Cádiz, appears on the cemetery registry. In this dismissive context, Jean-François watched disbelievingly as his former subordinates Dessalines and Christophe founded a new antislavery nation in a slaveholding hemisphere. Briefly, Spain considered resurrecting Jean-François's career by returning the charismatic leader to the island to challenge Dessalines. This plan never materialized. Despite Dessalines's efficacious audacity, Jean-François, perhaps because of some mix of astonishment, regret, and jealousy, remained outwardly unimpressed with Haitian leaders.[136]

Before Haitian independence, Dessalines asked Rochambeau's withdrawing officers about the status of Santo Domingo. His questions revolved around whether the French surrender included the whole island, whether Spain would resume its colonial rule in the east, and whether the newly concluded Louisiana Purchase with the United States had included Santo Domingo. Dessalines's uncertainty was quite understandable. However, France not only kept Santo Domingo, but its general Jean-Louis Ferrand merely retreated eastward with his troops and claimed the governorship of Santo Domingo.[137] Soon, Napoleonic emissaries were asking the Spanish colonies to arrest any visitors from Haiti as suspected revolutionaries sent by Dessalines.[138]

For three years, Santo Domingo had been secondary in importance to the French defeats in Saint-Domingue. Santo Domingo's significance now suddenly changed with the French retreat across the Americas. Though the French were most actively focused on Santo Domingo from 1804 to 1807, their presence had lasting implications for Dominicans. The Dominicans did not enjoy this sudden change in status as French power faded in the Americas.

How Santo Domingo received its longest-lasting French governor was also haphazard. Among many other humiliated French officers, General

Ferrand had abandoned his French positions and retreated from Dessalines. When he arrived at Santo Domingo, he realized that he outranked other French administrators and rallied his troops to oust Kerversau. As more French troops retreated there, Ferrand secured Santo Domingo for France by military means. These events took place mere months before Haitian independence. To many elites, the French troops seemed to have abandoned the remaining white French residents in Haiti even as many of them were being executed by Dessalines.

Ferrand was not necessarily popular in Santo Domingo. From their campaigns in Saint-Domingue, French personnel brought with them the ethos of curtailing rights, reversing Black liberties, and eliminating resistance. Antagonizing Dominican Catholics, Ferrand liquidated church properties to raise cash, using a broker from nearby Danish colonies to fetch higher prices. Perhaps to counter critics, Ferrand publicly announced that he had asked for the blessing of Father Vázquez, whom some locals basically venerated.

In 1805, one year after most chronologies of the Haitian Revolution end, Dessalines's concern about a French counterattack exposed Dominicans to a continuation of independence struggles. That year, Dessalines, with his officers Christophe and Pétion, directed military forces into Santo Domingo and besieged the capital. Some in the Cibao, angered at France, even assisted in an attack against French personnel. The colony suffered as Haitian soldiers punished French positions and, by extension, Dominican towns. Hundreds of Dominicans died. Ultimately, arson nearly destroyed Santiago, La Vega, Cotuí, and Moca. This siege only lifted when Dessalines, having sighted French sails at sea, abandoned his Dominican campaign to defend Haiti from French invaders.[139]

For Dominicans, Dessalines's invasion further illuminated French deficiencies. For the elite families cooperating with France, this warfare caused growing mistrust of Haiti. While he and his state favored emancipation, their foray into Santo Domingo, compared to the events of 1795 and 1801, were ineffectual, and he failed to secure abolition for Dominicans. Hostility was directed primarily at the French, and not at the Dominicans caught in between. Nevertheless, events seemed to prove to certain observers that Haitian influence was always correlated with destruction. Some even feared that Dessalines might force Dominicans into agricultural labor in the west, and rumors claiming that this was his intent circulated throughout the colony.[140] French officials warned Dominicans against potential "domination" by Dessalines with language calling him a "Black slave" and a "cannibal."[141]

In sum, the aspersions cast upon Dessalines and the events the Dominicans witnessed added another layer of wariness toward Haiti among the
population. Haitian leaders spent the next two decades attempting to
change these impressions. Further, Dessalines had become Emperor Jacques
I of Haiti in October 1804 and established a new constitution in 1805 that
did not offer Catholicism protected status. It also said that the island was
Haitian and named all citizens as Black. In some ways it was a radical document. Along with Dessalines's military actions, it challenged the privileges
and preferences of Dominican elites.

Months after Dessalines's retreat, Jean-François died in Spain. Although
the new Black nation-building project exceeded Jean-François's ambitions,
the promise of rights for all had extended from the heavy-handed per-
sonalist politics that emerged in Haiti. For this and other reasons, after his
death Jean-François lived on as an emblem of enslaved resistance and Black
empowerment in the Spanish Caribbean.[142]

And the ongoing French threats were not Dessalines's only problem. He
had to rehabilitate a workforce and economy that had been decimated by
well over a decade of war, handle gens de couleur opposition, and build
a capable military. He even considered Protestantism as a state religion to
forestall the perceived corrosive influences of the priests on some revolutionary figures.[143] However, Dessalines was assassinated by his opponents
in 1806 before he could build the Haiti he envisioned. In another twist of
history, it is Dessalines—not Boukman, Jean-François, Louverture, Christophe, or Pétion—who sits atop the Haitian national pantheon. His brief,
decisive rule enshrined him as a Vodou *lwa* (spirit), and his name lives on
in the title to Haiti's national anthem, "La Dessalinienne." After his death,
the co-claimants Christophe and Pétion divided Haiti into two governments, based in Cap-Haïtien (formerly Cap-Français) in Nord and Port-
au-Prince in Sud. Ouest became a battleground, with both leaders tapping
their neighbors, especially Santo Domingo, for support.[144]

They found ready audiences. Many rural Dominicans outside of the isolated urban pockets of French power were livid when Ferrand attempted to
end all trade with Haiti. The massive Dominican cattle industry depended
upon Haitian markets. Economically, French rule threatened colonial economics, and few Dominicans cared to defend Ferrand. Socially, enslaved
Dominicans and the free majority of color never enjoyed the once-vaunted
French liberties. Rather, they endured regressive Napoleonic racism dic-
tated from the other side of the ocean, though, all the while, Black citizens
on the other side of the island welcomed Dominican commerce and collaboration. Culturally, Dominicans largely rejected attempts to "Frenchify"

them and diminish church power. Politically, widespread irritation with France soon exploded into rejection and then open rebellion.[145]

CONCLUSION

Diminishing imperial power caused Dominican society to grow even more entwined with Haiti. The process started with Toussaint Louverture's consolidation of Hispaniola in 1801 and it continued through the final Haitian War for Independence ending in 1804, through Dessalines's Dominican campaign of 1805, and through the civil conflict between Henry Christophe and Alexandre Pétion that began in 1807. At first reconciled to rule by a fading French Republic, Dominicans then came to reject their new occupiers for a variety of reasons. Many Dominican elites resented French irreligion and economic inefficiencies. Many Dominicans of color were alienated by the renewed racist French restrictions on them, which were intended to increase plantation exports.

In the absence of Spanish support and with thousands of Dominican elites in exile, many in Santo Domingo willingly accepted Haitian support in their struggle against their common French enemy. Though they began by simply undermining the French, when Christophe and Pétion began to collaborate with Dominicans their collective paradigm shifted. Dominicans of many backgrounds situationally welcomed new collaborators of color who were willing to help them undermine European empires. Moreover, they now had two Haitian states engaged in competition for their affiliations.

Saint-Domingue's metamorphosis from white plantocracy to Haitian state shocked the slaveholding Americas. However, the society most impacted by Haiti, and most entwined in its growing pains, was Santo Domingo. The exceptional struggle that brought Haiti into being was comparatively more distant to people of color around the hemisphere. However, to Dominicans of color, it was adjacent, concrete, and very familiar. Haitian independence itself had formed an important part of the revolutionary contours that Dominicans had experienced for well over a decade. However, it was Haitian collaboration that would become a catalyst for change over the ensuing decade.

SIX

CROSS-ISLAND COLLABORATION AND CONSPIRACIES, 1808–1818

In the early 1810s, fearing Napoleonic invasion, the Haitian leader Henry Christophe astutely asked his "brethren, the Spanish Haytians," the "inhabitants of the same soil" as his compatriots, to join their fight against imperial impositions. He expressed a similar ethos and language using familial appeals in calling for unification a decade later. Christophe had just strategically supplied ample guns and funds for the ouster of the French from Dominican occupation. Nearly three decades after insurgents had involved Santo Domingo in the Haitian Revolution, Dominicans and Haitians collaborated to topple the last French stronghold on Hispaniola.[1] New ideas of national belonging permeated the island.

To enhance relationships in the east, Christophe also built new, mutually beneficial forms of commerce with Dominicans and engaged in correspondence with Juan Sánchez Ramírez, who had led a Dominican *Reconquista*, or reconquering, of Santo Domingo against France. Christophe recognized Dominicans as potentially pivotal partners not only against France, but also against his rival Alexandre Pétion to the south, who had sought allies in Santo Domingo as well. From 1808 to 1818, Dominicans considered alternative sovereignties. Several prominent conspiracies developed. Some were connected to Pétion. Others were connected to revolutionary projects in mainland Latin America. Certainly, many Dominicans were unwilling to entertain options that would incur even more changes following their years of turmoil. However, growing numbers of Dominicans were willing to cooperate with Haitians to build a more integrated island, relying upon shared interests to pursue mutual benefits.

Dominicans eager to cast out the French occupiers planned a Reconquista in 1808, adopting their title from Catholic campaigns to evict Muslims from Iberia centuries earlier. In the name of the deposed king, this final ejection of France from Hispaniola was in part in response to the Napoleonic ouster of King Carlos IV and the exile of the rightful heir, King

Fernando VII, in Spain. Histories of the era typically emphasize that many Dominicans yearned for the return of Spanish rule and traditional beliefs. The subsequent recolonization, usually called *España Boba*, or "Silly Spain," focuses on Spanish ineptitude. Certainly, some Dominicans did prefer Hispanic cultural norms, and Spanish imperial disorder was real.

However, a more important and powerful force, though undoubtedly less well known, was that of cross-island and regional cooperation, which did not simply stop with the Reconquista. Moreover, though the name of Juan Sánchez Ramírez persists in Dominican national memory, the majority of the dissidents against imperial constraints were of African descent, and their names remain virtually unknown. Further, direct collaboration with the Haitian leaders Christophe and Pétion and their competing Haitian agents played a crucial role in events. Paradoxically for elites, the Reconquista and the restoration of Hispanic ties relied upon Haiti's assistance. Cooperation between Dominicans and Haitians involved routine direct contact that increased over the course of the next decade. Indeed, the Dominican majority eventually explored various possible futures far beyond the ambitions of the Reconquista.

The size, frequency, and goals of the conspiracies changed over time. A deluge of anti-imperial, cross-island cooperation and conspiratorial activity increased throughout the 1810s as Dominicans and Haitians cooperated to challenge empires. The plots, which varied in terms of their ideological associations, nevertheless converged on the need for emancipation, citizenship, and independence in Santo Domingo. In this era, for many Dominicans, Haiti became synonymous with liberation and citizenship.

Aside from local particularities, Santo Domingo's experiences held some broad similarities to those of many mainland South American Spanish colonies in the 1810s. After returning to nominal Spanish rule, Dominicans had extensive autonomy under the liberal Cortes de Cádiz, which established a short-lived constitutional monarchy with the Constitution of 1812. Santo Domingo and mainland colonies were also alike in that they all experienced increased popular political participation and frustrations with the 1812 Constitution, which excluded people of African descent from many of its provisions. After the restoration of King Fernando VII in 1813, the king's more restrictive policies further alienated them. Also, after a decade of French cultural influences attempting explicitly to change Dominicans, questions remained about which old traditions Dominicans should try to restore and what new traditions they should begin to build. Conversations about continuity and change pervaded the hemisphere. However, a unique layer existed for elite Dominican narratives of difference. Many Dominicans believed that Spain had neglected re-evangelization and recolonization, and that unwanted foreign intrusions had been allowed to contaminate a supposed Iberian and Catholic essence in Dominican culture. This notion influenced the ensuing debates over independence and Haitian influence.[2]

Such attitudes did not keep Dominicans of color from engaging with Haitian agents, however. Nor did they keep Haitians from pursuing their interests in a decolonized Hispaniola. Instead, Dominican society became more defined by Haitian affairs and the influence of Dominicans of color increased. As imperial oversight during the era declined, generally yielding greater autonomy for Dominicans, space opened up for regular and ambitious antislavery or anti-imperial plots. Cultural competitions intensified over Hispanic traditions, liberal self-rule, and the adjacent, tangible Haitian example of anti-colonialism and Black power, leading toward multiple independence projects in the 1820s.

RECONQUISTA

In 1808, Napoléon forced King Carlos IV to abdicate and made his heir, the would-be King Fernando VII, a de facto prisoner. The French invasion of Spain provoked anger across the country, giving rise to *guerrilla* warfare. Massive anti-French demonstrations ensued across the Spanish Americas, including among a Dominican populace weary of French rule. Juan Sánchez Ramírez, one of many Dominicans exiled in Puerto Rico, discovered that his family's cattle business was struggling. A "strange combination" of economic malaise and patriotism amid the Peninsular War inspired him to attempt to end French rule in Santo Domingo.[3]

The Spanish Americas ignored pleas for loyalty from Joseph Bonaparte (King José I), usurper to the Spanish throne and Napoléon's brother.[4] Spanish loyalists in Iberia could not offer support to conspirators. Rather, some aid came from Governor Toribio Montes of Puerto Rico and Dominican exiles. Sánchez Ramírez, identified as a *mulato*, covertly traveled to Santo Domingo to summon popular support against France. In exchange, he promised to send sufficient supplies of mahogany to Puerto Rico to cover costs.

The nascent Dominican uprising temporarily united the two new rulers of divided Haiti. At that time, Alexandre Pétion presided over a republic of the south based in Port-au-Prince, and Henry Christophe ruled over what had become a kingdom in the north with its capital in Cap-Haïtien (formerly Cap-Français). Both Christophe and Pétion pledged support.[5]

In Santo Domingo, a Reconquista effort to expel the French quietly coalesced. It was deliberately named after the religious warfare of Christian campaigns to evict Muslims from Iberia centuries before. It also pushed Dominicans toward more autonomy beyond imperial strictures. Dominicans faced a choice about which aspects of their Spanish heritage to reclaim and perpetuate, particularly when it came to religion, monarchism, and racial restrictions. This domestic Dominican tension intensified as Haitians voiced shared detestations of French presence on Hispaniola. Nevertheless, various Dominican and Haitian groups found enough common ground to allow for extensive cross-island cooperation. In short, the Dominicans successfully courted a temporary, situational alliance with Haitian officials.

In August 1808, the makeshift French governor Jean-Louis Ferrand finally realized that Spanish loyalists had formed a holdout junta against Napoléon and that many Spanish Americans considered themselves at war with France.[6] Dominican rebels, buoyed by avid support from anti-French clergy, networked with discontented rural Dominicans. To dissipate this threat, Ferrand issued a proclamation extolling friendship. He claimed that French protections of their customs and Catholicism had succeeded and that divine providence had given them a better path than that of European nations embroiled in conflict.[7] Ferrand discounted the idea that Dominicans would actually revolt.[8]

The Reconquista began in September 1808 when Salvador Feliz, who also collaborated with Montes, arrived at Barahona near the border with Haiti. There he joined Cristóbal Huber, who built ties with the anti-French rebels Ciriaco Ramírez in Azua and Manuel Jiménez in Neiba. Henry Christophe gave the Dominicans prompt, generous, and needed support in the form of three hundred troops and hundreds of guns, boots, and swords. In return Christophe only asked for open commerce, commensurate with his attitude of peace toward Spanish subjects. Governor Montes of Puerto Rico soon sent goods to Cap-Haïtien, topping them off with a fine watch and a cane as personal gifts to Christophe. At the cost of Dominican cattle, Sánchez Ramírez cooperated with Alexandre Pétion, who feared spillover from the war.

On 12 October, the Dominican rebels routed French regular troops under Colonel Aussenac at Mal Paso (Mallepasse) at the border. Ten days later, Aussenac and his troops faced an ambush near Azua. Furious, he burned many Dominicans' homes to the ground, while Ferrand put a bounty on the heads of rebel leaders. Rather than taking him up on that offer, Dominicans in San Juan de la Maguana assassinated a French officer, took the town, and immediately appealed to Pétion for aid. As Dominican towns continued to fall, including ones in the east such as El Seibo and Higüey, Ferrand departed from the capital with five hundred troops to quell the uprising.[9]

That same day, French officials in Santo Domingo tried to rebuff rumors of support from Haiti and nearby Spanish colonies and lamented that Dominicans had not heeded their "fatherly counsel."[10] Furthermore, they published an open letter from prominent Dominicans in the capital who worked in their government. They implied to their fellow Dominicans that a rebellion could invite interventions such as those spearheaded in the past by Toussaint Louverture or Jean-Jacques Dessalines.[11] In a further attempt at turning capital opinion against the Reconquista, the French newspaper published intercepted communiqués from an officer of Pétion to the rebels Huber, Feliz, and Ciriaco Ramírez detailing Haitian support.[12]

It was clear that many Dominicans were ignoring his repeated pleas to drop their weapons. Ferrand approached El Seibo on 7 November 1808 and the next day launched an all-out attack on the Dominicans' position in an area called Palo Hincado. The Dominicans routed Ferrand's army. Due to casualties and desertions, reportedly only forty of the five hundred French troops returned to the capital. Ferrand, after hours of fleeing his pursuers, fatally shot himself. After recovering his body, Dominican rebels may have put his head atop a pike and shown it to British officers who supported them. On 10 November, the British navy accepted the French surrender at Samaná.[13] Ferrand would never realize his detailed plans for a "Port Napoléon" on Samaná Bay, which he had intended as a new hub for French naval and plantation activity.[14]

By December, the Dominican Reconquista was entrenched around the capital. As the French arrested suspected conspirators within the city walls, Puerto Rican ships resupplied the Dominican rebels. At the end of December, Juan Sánchez Ramírez became "intendant general" of a provisional Dominican junta loyal to the deposed King Fernando VII. The rebels enjoyed abundant support from both Haitian leaders. Sánchez Ramírez insisted on paying Christophe for his aid. He was suspicious that his Haitian ally might incite subversion among darker-complected Dominicans working with him.[15]

For the second time in four years, the residents of the capital of Santo Domingo endured a siege because of their French occupiers. Dominican residents quickly tired of eating mules, rats, pigeons, and even leather. The rebels sufficiently withheld resupply from the French with a blockade by British allies to further damage their imperial rivals in the Caribbean. Despite minor victories in late January 1809, the French could not break the Dominican cordon. With only sparse provisions and dwindling ranks, they promised liberty to about one hundred enslaved Dominicans if they would help them against the Reconquista and fight for France for another eight years. This quid pro quo deal was a mockery to unfulfilled French promises of liberty for all Dominicans a decade before.[16]

International newspapers spoke admiringly of the "Spanish Dominicans" and their cause. The Reconquista was truly an international effort of Hispanic Caribbean, Haitian, and British collaboration. In this spirit, Sánchez Ramírez entreated with British officers in Jamaica for more support to finally expel the French. Henry Christophe continued to eagerly supply aid through his military officers, which Sánchez Ramírez attempted to accept without angering Pétion.[17]

The French had sent five agents to connect with Pétion and request peace and relief for their depleted positions. To preempt this connection, Sánchez Ramírez, in the midst of planning a final assault on the capital, immediately sent letters to both Pétion and Christophe proposing a humanitarian ceasefire.[18] Such contacts revived ongoing competition among the Haitian leaders, underscoring the fact that the Dominican Reconquista was partly a proxy war. Once Haitians were tied into local cultural politics, Haitian connections would exert a pull on Dominicans for years to come.

The arrival of a substantial British fleet in May was the coup de grâce for the French occupiers.[19] With this new pressure, the French finally surrendered in the first week of July 1809. The allies advanced from their nearby encampments, including at Boca Nigua, to accept the capital on 9 July.[20]

One of the final acts by a French official on Hispaniola was to publish a governmental almanac for Santo Domingo in 1809. It dramatically marked the thousands of years since the construction of Solomon's Temple and the first Olympiad. It referenced Columbus arriving in the Americas 317 years before and the three subsequent centuries of Spanish rule in Santo Domingo. Ironically, it marked the invention of gunpowder 471 years earlier. Eighteen years after the Haitian Revolution began and 112 years after the Treaty of Ryswick, the almanac celebrated the seventh year of French rule, which proved to be the last.

Around the edges of a personal copy of this 1809 almanac and next to printed text listing major historical moments, an anonymous and dutiful French official wrote marginalia about the Dominican uprising, including Ferrand's suicide, the opposition of most of the clergy, and the desertion of an Italian-born lieutenant named Emiglio Pezzi. Along with other Italians in French service, Pezzi had apparently defected. These were personal travails in the midst of an ignominious, rapid decline of French rule for French holdovers. Those who were unable to prevent the founding of Haiti in 1804 now witnessed the finale to a protracted French demise on Hispaniola. Thus a period that began in Saint-Domingue in 1791 now ended in Santo Domingo in 1809.[21]

RESTORATION

Sánchez Ramírez jubilantly unfurled Spanish flags over the Santo Domingo walls on 11 July and praised "those good Spaniards" who had achieved the Reconquista.[22] After "so much pain for its natives having been torn from its bosom," Santo Domingo had been returned to Spain. Sánchez Ramírez, thrilled by having won in the name of King Fernando VII, was "heartbroken" that the Bonapartist usurper was still on the throne.

Santo Domingo was still in difficult straits. In the recent warfare, Dominicans had suffered razed fields, stolen cattle, burned towns, and death. Financially destitute, Sánchez Ramírez continued to rely on aid from neighboring Spanish colonies. He appointed "patriotic" colleagues to government posts, while remaining Italian and Puerto Rican soldiers guarded 1,500 French prisoners.[23]

The British allies finally departed on 24 August 1809. Unbeknownst to Sánchez Ramírez, this was only after the British had drafted an extensive new plan to capture Santo Domingo, similar to their designs of the 1790s. They had analyzed Santo Domingo's soil and judged it to be far better than Jamaica's. They even considered a campaign against independent Haiti. Rather than immediately taking this risk, the British instead compelled Sánchez Ramírez to sign a free trade deal that would permit British merchants in Santo Domingo's ports, waive taxes associated with commerce, and lift restrictions beyond those otherwise equally imposed on Spanish ships. British subjects would also enjoy protected status in Santo Domingo. To Sánchez Ramírez, it seemed prudent, and even necessary, to sign the agreement, given the colony's material deprivations. He acceded without consulting with Spain, amplifying Dominican autonomy.

Sánchez Ramírez thanked British officials and the neighboring Spanish colonies profusely for their support. Notably, however, he excluded Haitians from public expressions of gratitude.[24] This was a calculated slight against Christophe, who had arguably been the most invaluable and unflinching supporter of the Dominican rebels. Beyond his likely racism, Sánchez Ramírez may have also been hedging against making himself a target of Haitian domestic divisions, as he had grown somewhat suspicious of Pétion.

After promising support, Pétion had equivocated in supplying it. Many French evacuees had fled to his domains after their defeat in Santo Domingo. In a principled act, Pétion's navy also intercepted Dominicans returning from Cuba and forced them to disembark enslaved passengers. Pétion had sent his armies through Dominican territory without permission, ostensibly to launch surprise attacks on Christophe. Sánchez Ramírez suspected that Pétion was testing the fragile Dominican stability. Perhaps Pétion's fleeting tactical support had been a strategic ploy to restore weak Spanish colonialism to his east.[25]

For the new Dominican administrators reviving Hispanic rule, new opportunities to interact with Haiti abounded. They also had to negotiate with remaining Black troops. Some of them had apparently served the "Black Tousant [sic]."[26] One of the figures who returned to a prominent role in the capital's community of color was none other than Pablo Alí, the officer who had fought with Biassou, and who had been acquitted in the British conspiracy of 1796. After briefly living in Puerto Rico, he had returned to fight his former peer Dessalines in 1805. He quickly joined the Reconquista and sustained a severe facial wound during combat.[27]

Those attempting to re-evangelize the Dominican populace had to first face the fact that French soldiers had turned the Convent of San Francisco into an armed garrison. For strategic and possibly symbolic reasons, they had mounted artillery on the chapel roof.[28] Sánchez Ramírez selected Juan Antonio Pichardo, a priest who had also spent his time in exile in Puerto Rico and returned to serve the Reconquista forces, to lead this effort. In ensuing years Pichardo factored prominently in cultural politics with Haiti.[29] The effort to pursue a religious restoration underscored dominant definitions of being Dominican as inextricably Catholic and royalist. The question would be whether the Dominican majority would agree.

By this time, Dominicans were accustomed to being caught between vying interests, which at times enhanced a sense of vulnerability, but could also offer opportunities to play one side off the other. To an extent, Dominican leaders navigated this issue again during the Reconquista and early restoration. However, with two competing leaders of independent Haiti looking eastward for new opportunities for commerce and allies, the question remained whether officials could govern a majority of color that was still uniquely disappointed by the unfulfilled promises of the revolutionary era. The distant and weak loyalist Supreme Central Junta in Spain vaguely promised more troops, economic concessions, a reestablishment of the archdiocese and cathedral, and help for Dominican exiles.[30] However, unlike in the 1790s, Dominicans now negotiated these new challenges mostly apart from the imperial framework.

IMPINGING EMPIRES

The loyalist Junta officials in Spain heralded Santo Domingo as "the first possession of our glorious acquisitions in the Indies" by Columbus, a historic city that had once "justly" housed "his illustrious ashes, the seat of the primate of both Americas, [and] a royal Audiencia." Dominican elites, infused with more recently arrived French families who stayed, savored the return of such distinctions. Optimistically, the Junta concluded that Santo Domingo would prosper. Its soil was "healthy, in good condition, and capable of rich and abundant production."[31] However, with Napoléon's brother Joseph on the Spanish throne, the Junta only loosely managed Spanish colonies, including Santo Domingo. Though the Junta congratulated the patriotic Dominicans for their heroism and assured them of King Fernando VII's "paternal love," their promises of support rang hollow, and Santo Domingo remained financially insolvent over the next decade.[32]

Spain simply could not address major Dominican structural problems.[33] Burdened with new responsibilities for which he was unprepared, Juan Sánchez Ramírez tried to rebuild the colony. The colony was soon full of "unhappy Dominicans who, after having suffered all the horrors of exile . . . have returned . . . laden with misery, and find nothing in their homes other than desolation and [the] debris of their old fortune[s]."[34] Absent imperial oversight, Sánchez Ramírez improvised by necessity. On commerce he relied upon the British agent William Walton, who had fomented anti-French sentiment in 1808, helped Sánchez Ramírez gain British supplies, worked with London on policy, and facilitated the surrender of Santo Domingo. To procure the supplies his "patriots" needed, Sánchez Ramírez drew closer to Jamaica, selling to Jamaican merchants the lumber he had confiscated from the French.[35]

This new and growing British trade gave Dominicans access to canvas, cotton textiles, glassware, ceramics, and other items in exchange for coffee, sugar, and timber. The level of British-Dominican trade perplexed the Junta in Spain, which was, however, incapable of stopping it.[36] To rebuild ruined towns, Sánchez Ramírez needed cash infusions. México offered limited support, but colonial México would soon itself erupt in social revolution.[37] Distracted officials seemed to be simply ignoring the needs of the

Dominicans, and this heightened the majority's engagement with Haitian influences.

Absent Spanish policing, Dominicans' illicit trade with Haiti and sometimes other nearby islands flourished, obviating agricultural concessions offered by the Junta. This was an unresolvable conundrum. Dominicans desired markets, but officials feared that in building connections with the "two independent states of people of color" in Haiti, some Dominicans might be "seduced or dazzled" by their ideologies.

Haitians, after helping Dominicans rid Hispaniola of the French, might also tire of the Spanish imperial presence, the return of planters from exile, and their exploitation of the enslaved to work the *ingenios* and *cafetales* (coffee farms). Also, opening free ports to stimulate trade would encourage the independent Blacks and mulatos of Haiti to visit, and they would be likely to dominate trade, perhaps "winning among them some partisans," which might jeopardize Dominicans' loyalty to Spain. Portending future events, the Junta realistically recognized that "when the Santo Domingo natives rose up against the French government, they had no links to bind them to Spain"; thus, "Who would be able to censure them if they declared independence?"[38] Sentiments favoring independence soon swept not only Santo Domingo, but most of the Spanish Americas.

At times, Haitian politicians, still credibly concerned over possible European attempts to undermine their independence, nurtured these sentiments among the Dominicans. For example, in 1810 Christophe's secretary of state reported that "the famous Rigaud has just recently come from France." Rigaud had stopped in Philadelphia before coming to Haiti, however, to seek support from the French consul to the United States. Christophe suspected that Pétion, whom Rigaud had mentored, was perhaps involved, as some of the French who had been expelled from Santo Domingo had taken refuge in southern Haitian ports. Christophe also discovered that Dumoiland, another subversive French agent, had visited México and South America to raise favor for King José I, the Bonapartist usurper.[39]

With hope for mutual preservation, Haitian officials from the north called for unity, proclaimed the honor of both Henry Christophe and "Don Juan Sanches [sic]," and called attention to "the approach of Rigaud." French corsairs reappeared in southern Hispaniola. To attract British naval support, Christophe reminded the British that Jamaica could be also under threat and that Pétion's and Rigaud's forces had shed British blood in the 1790s at Jérémie, Tiburon, and Léogane. Christophe suggested that together they could crush Rigaud, "destroying the root of evil on the spot, [and] expelling the . . . party of the Corsican Emperor." Whatever the actual threat, a Rigaud invasion empowered Christophe to rally his allies and again attempt to unify Haiti under his government.[40]

Concerned about French subversions, in part because of his own reliance upon the expertise of a few French defectors, Sánchez Ramírez supplied Christophe with more intelligence regarding Rigaud. Priests with Rigaud appealed to religion in an attempt to sway Catholics on Hispaniola to the Bonapartist side. Christophe was convinced that Port-au-Prince was a target, given recent French seditions there. With his armies on high alert, Christophe resolved that the "impregnable *Citadelle*" he had built would protect Hispaniola, and again offered his Dominican neighbors a joint defense agreement.[41] Whereas Christophe presented the Dominican leaders with favorable terms for their assistance in rejecting European interference, Pétion soon provided the wider Dominican populace with more radical solutions.

OPENING OPPOSITION

Transnational tensions arising from Haitian, French, and British efforts to attract Dominicans once again washed over Santo Domingo. The arrival of Rigaud caused the temporary truce between Christophe and Pétion to deteriorate, and the disruptions cascaded into Dominican society, deepening domestic divisions. Despite having granted liberty to some enslaved Dominicans who fought against France, Sánchez Ramírez continued to support slavery and failed to soothe the seething social strife. With greater regularity than in previous periods, and with greater clarity concerning racial solidarity and their anti-colonial intents, Dominicans of color became primary organizers of the emerging conspiracies and coups, often with direct linkages to Haitian agents.

In a suitable opening to the churning 1810s, Cristóbal Huber and Ciriaco Ramírez, two of Sánchez Ramírez's closest associates in the early stages of the Reconquista, faced arrest. They and the Reconquista veteran Salvador Feliz had apparently become "dedicated . . . to the party of Pétion." In July 1810 they were suspected of plotting a revolt on Santo Domingo's southern border with Haiti.[42] By September, they were connected to a more ambitious plot centered in the capital. Their plans included several Italian troops, led by the Sardinian officer Emiglio Pezzi, who had previously defected from the French, and several veterans of the Black Auxiliaries, including Pablo Alí.

Two other key conspirators were identified as the mulatos Santiago Foleau, who was originally from Saint-Domingue and had military experience (and a Dominican family), and José Castaños, from Caracas. Castaños brought news from Venezuela, where months earlier their Junta Central had forced the Spanish-appointed captain general to resign. The Junta had installed an autonomous ruling committee in his place and started on a path toward the first declaration of independence in the Spanish Americas. That declaration came a year later. In Santo Domingo, the conspirators' plans were similar. They wanted to oust Sánchez Ramírez and install a new government. They had asked Pétion for support, and he had agreed. Sánchez Ramírez saw that trials, sentences, and executions related to conspiracies were concluded in less than three weeks in order to deter any future plots.[43]

During the Reconquista, Sánchez Ramírez had fallen out with Huber and Ciriaco because of their suspicious behavior.[44] Also, British officers had reprimanded Foleau during the handover of the capital for antagonizing the locals.[45] Sánchez Ramírez was inexperienced and unsuited to daily governance, and his flaws alienated potential allies. In such a lightly defended colony, any modest mobilization had an opportunity to succeed, particularly with some *afrancesado* (Frenchified) sympathizers remaining. Well-placed officers and artisans, displeased with the tepid climate of social and economic change under Spanish recolonization, who designed the plot, found perhaps hundreds of multiracial coconspirators.

Letters later presented in court demonstrated that Pétion had promised to support the rebellion. Not only were several veterans of the legendary Black Auxiliaries accused, but the plotters may have even contacted the maroons of Maniel. When investigators inquired, Pablo Alí, who was ever present at major flashpoints in Dominican affairs, denied having aided the plot, though he apparently also refused to reveal it to officials. Though they were complicit to varying degrees, Alí, his troops, and most of the Italian soldiers avoided punishment. Four men were eventually executed, but they did not include Huber or Ciriaco, likely because of their formerly close ties to Governor Montes of Puerto Rico.[46]

Discovery of the plot confirmed Sánchez Ramírez's suspicions about Pétion's revolutionary intents. Fortunately for Sánchez Ramírez, Pétion could not send the necessary aid to the conspirators in a timely manner, as the return of Rigaud, his former mentor, who attempted to take power in Haiti, distracted him.[47] Pétion's anti-imperial positions during the Reconquista and Spanish recolonization period perhaps primed his support for Simón Bolívar's independence project in South America when the latter requested it in 1815. Spain understood Pétion's importance and discouraged him from supporting Latin American independence movements.[48] Before Bolívar, Pétion styled himself as a hemispheric liberator on par with anyone in the independence pantheon of the Americas.

Managing the investigation became one of Sánchez Ramírez's last major acts in office, as he died in February 1811, thrusting the colony into greater instability. Juan Caballero assumed charge of military affairs in Santo Domingo.[49] Before his death, Sánchez Ramírez implemented new procedures for scrutinizing any who entered, transited through, or resided in Santo Domingo, replete with regulations about passports and permissions.[50] In conducting intelligence about French people in transit, Caballero scoured this paperwork for possible fake documents and cracked down on nearly all immigrants.[51]

Compounding the problem, officials worried that Haitians or Venezuelans might seek to undermine Dominican society. Also, some worried that the "tyrant Napoléon Bonaparte" might commit "iniquities" by trying to entice disunion on Hispaniola. Caballero, supplied with the names of supposed subversives, intercepted those entering at ports and on the border and interrogated them.[52] Over time, this kind of policing and the preoccupation with legal papers represented the wishes of fewer and fewer Dominicans. Nevertheless, paranoia about controlling who was present would only grow.

NEW RULES, OLD RESTRICTIONS

The Cortes de Cádiz, a legislative body loyal to Fernando VII founded upon the liberalizing promises of September 1810, also failed to deliver more effective government in Santo Domingo, just as the provisional Junta had before it. Even before the death of Juan Sánchez Ramírez, politicians in Cádiz sent Francisco Xavier Caro to oversee the colony. He arrived from Las Canarias to find the colony in decay, with crumbling buildings, empty fields, and limited supplies. There was a garrison of only two hundred troops, and no military discipline. The number of enemy ships in local waters had increased, and Haiti's influence had grown.[53]

Vying for influence with Sánchez Ramírez, Caro began informing Spain about Pétion's rejection of Rigaud, after it was clear that Napoléon Bonaparte had sent him to foster French recolonization. For this reason, Caro urgently requested more troops from Puerto Rico or Las Canarias. In Hispanic patriotic solidarity, the archbishop in México even volunteered to raise troops. Officials feared that underpaid militiamen and only a small number of soldiers had no chance against the alleged "perfidy" of the mulâtres in Haiti, presumably meaning Pétion, or the neighboring "disciplined and hardened army of Blacks," likely referring to Christophe's forces.[54]

However practical his advice might have been, elites rejected Caro's suggestions and criticisms.[55] Rebuffed, Caro became an elected representative for Santo Domingo in the Cortes de Cádiz formed under the new Constitution of 1812. This code extended more rights to many Spanish subjects in the empire.[56]

Elite Dominicans launched public celebrations of this new constitutional monarchy, which elevated their status in a more participatory Spanish Empire. However, the festivities stressed only the de jure exclusion of most Dominicans. Initially promising language of liberalism and inclusion proved an illusion, with the Cortes granting rights only to male subjects of European and Indigenous descent, and excluding those of African descent. After the Cortes decreed its new civic restrictions, the Haitian model of citizenship became more appealing to disaffected Dominicans of color.[57]

Taking a step toward future political prominence by complaining about the inadequacies of the Cortes, José Núñez de Cáceres started building a public reputation in this era. Núñez de Cáceres had previously gained visibility with the acquittal of Pablo Alí in 1797. By August 1811, he had assumed new governmental roles. He began writing regularly to officials in Cádiz making his own policy recommendations for relieving Dominicans' misery and for dealing with worries about Haitian or French influence.[58] He also exhorted clergy to promote Spanish initiatives to their "good vassals" in order to protect values and empire.[59]

Of "whites, Blacks, and mulâtres," Núñez de Cáceres was unsure "which of these three races has been more ominous and desolating for this hapless land." Favoring commercial liberalism, he hoped that exceeding the recent concessions from Cádiz on agriculture and British commerce could entice more foreign trade to Santo Domingo to rescue it from its "universal shipwreck." With more trade, the colony could "rise from the tomb." Perhaps Dominican mahogany could play a role here, he suggested. Dominicans, who continued to return from exile, "attracted by sweet love for the homeland," only encountered decay. Those who stayed joined a group jaded by "French tyranny, [who had suffered] invasions, fires, deaths, and havocs."[60]

Perhaps portending his dramatic role in independence struggles a decade later, he criticized the "anarchy" of Dominican colonial governance and said he favored stronger rule. This was a problem that, implicitly, the distant, decentralized, distracted Cortes could not rectify. Núñez de Cáceres also cataloged the continued subversive plots in morbid prose. After some "French of color" (that is, Haitians) formed a plot at Samaná, he insisted that "those colors" required urgent scrutiny before they killed the "almost cadaveric body" of the Dominican polity. Considering that Louverture and Dessalines had attempted "successive revolutions . . . on [Dominican] soil," he noted that Santo Domingo could not impede Haitian armies. He and other professionals in the capital were also unimpressed about the possibility of the new captain general, Don Carlos de Urrutia, stopping the "gangrene."[61] Though Rigaud soon died, prevalent perceptions of the challenges faced by those in charge of governing Santo Domingo were fairly accurate.[62]

For many Dominicans, spiritual matters and supernatural interventions still rivaled social and structural considerations in importance. The re-evangelization of Dominicans began immediately after Spanish recolonization began. In 1810, officials had prioritized reestablishing convents and seminaries and recruiting clergy.[63] Many monks petitioned to return so they could minister to the masses and restore Spanish Catholicism and colonialist culture. A group of Capuchins who had once worked in Santo Domingo wrote from exile in Jalapa, México. They anticipated that their earlier service in francophone Louisiana had prepared them to deal with French partisans. These Capuchins and other clergy could reawaken the faith for Dominicans who had been exposed to secularism during seven years of supposedly impious French rule. Dominican officials apparently accepted their offers.[64]

The almost frantic re-evangelization efforts that followed coincided with a period when fears of French corruption were rising, particularly with Napoleonic occupation in the metropole.[65] By 1813, a robust Catholic reeducation program was underway, and many religious orders were fully operational. Pedro Valera, who awaited consecration as the new archbishop, began rebuilding church influence in Santo Domingo.[66] He also tried to revive and expand the archdiocese's efforts in the area of education.[67] The Poor Clares, exiled nuns in Havana, wrote asking to return.[68] Clergy who had resisted the French before fleeing also returned, many of them helping to recruit more priests.[69]

However, Catholic practice had become lax with the spread of revolutionary ideas in the Hispanic Americas, including among priests in the Mexican Independence War, and local clergy struggled to adapt. To help, Urrutia suggested renewing the Inquisition in the Caribbean. This idea was unpopular.[70] In Santo Domingo, parishioners accused one priest, Manuel

Marqués, who ran the capital's Catholic school, of committing "infamous vices and criminal offenses." He had scandalized them with his "audacious" and "perverse" forms of "libertinage." He was not the only one. Some said it had become a "fatal epidemic."[71]

Amid this reconstruction of organized religion in Santo Domingo, a rapid reversal of the barely implemented Constitution of 1812 transpired in Iberia, where Napoléon neared defeat in December 1813. The restoration of the Bourbon heir King Fernando VII resulted in a thorough repeal of the liberalizing gains that had been made under the constitution.[72] The majority of Dominicans had already been alienated by their lack of inclusion in the document, so these reversals meant little to them. Nor did they matter for the troops of color on whom the colony relied, including Pablo Alí. Within five years of the Reconquista, more Dominicans were discontented than ever before with Spanish rule, especially its feeble recolonialization effort. Elites and professionals began to join Dominicans of color in associating promises of freedom and rights with nearby independence projects and not Spain or France. The desire for an anti-colonial sovereignty increased.

DOMINICAN DISSENT

A post-emancipation, post-colonial world was less abstract in Santo Domingo than it was for its regional neighbors. While perhaps most of the colony's population associated citizenship with being Haitian, more *criollos* in the capital followed their peers who were leading arguably more moderate independence movements on the more distant mainland of South America. The Dominican polity became a colorful palette of loyalties manifested visually in racial divisions and contending national flags. Bypassing old metropolitan affiliations, a spectrum of sovereignty options enhanced local competitions for control.

Even before the restoration of Fernando VII could stir up more turmoil on Santo Domingo, Pétion and Christophe had turned their interests eastward. While the former sought subversion and the latter stability, both envisioned an integrated Hispaniola. They competed for Dominican loyalties as vying factions from western Hispaniola had for two revolutionary decades.[73]

More Haitian agents entered Santo Domingo. Because of Haiti's proximity, its promises were already influential. Whether by land or sea, Dominicans could access published items from Haiti such as constitutions, speeches, and laws, which were often smuggled in to avoid censure from Dominican authorities.[74] Due to this influence, Núñez de Cáceres increased Dominican scrutiny of all foreigners.[75] The 1810 plot by Huber, Ciriaco, Foleau, Castaños, and Pezzi proved to be only the first of many.

Some of the events resulting from the unrest took place relatively far from the border, showing the reach of anti-colonial angst. At the end of 1811, a conspiracy fomented by "French of color" (Haitians) was uncovered at Samaná. To combat the plot, desperately needed agricultural laborers from outside the capital were conscripted to form militia troops.[76]

In August 1812, officials uncovered a more significant plot led by the Dominican José Leocadio, who traveled near Monte Plata and may have recruited several enslaved and free Black residents. In a counterproductive overreaction, Núñez de Cáceres suggested arresting any supposedly suspicious Black person anywhere in the colony. Such policies would not earn officials any popularity, including among the soldiers of color who had to carry out the orders. The Cortes had marginalized them, too.[77]

Leocadio had collaborated with Pedro de Seda, Francisco Abad, Pedro Henríquez, and supposedly many others in a plot to capture plantations and execute their overseers, gathering weapons along the way. They were motivated by the exclusions of the Cortes de Cádiz as well as the restrictions enforced by local officials. Seda had written "inflammatory papers" to Núñez de Cáceres that March. Spanish officials executed Leocadio, Seda, Henríquez, and another plotter. Others faced torture, whippings, or exile.

Once again, Pablo Alí and his affiliates faced scrutiny as suspected coconspirators. Shocking rumors also surrounded the recently returned Gilles Narcisse (or Gil Narciso), a former officer in the Black Auxiliaries under Jean-François. Supposedly, Narcisse would have become the "legitimate governor" after the revolt. Alí and Narcisse denied involvement and claimed that others had used their names to attract recruits.[78]

The involvement of Gilles Narcisse was provocative. He had just reappeared from exile. When in transit through Havana only months before, he and his entourage had faced severe interrogation as possible coconspirators in the Aponte Rebellion of March 1812. Hilario Herrera from Azua had also been a suspect in Cuba and had possibly fled into Santo Domingo. Across the Hispanic Americas the enslaved were aware of debates over slavery's future in the Cortes de Cádiz and anticipated new rights.[79]

Despite their regular appearance in credible court testimony focusing on the conspiracies, the troops of color in Santo Domingo, many of them veterans of the Black Auxiliaries, remained quite socially visible and militarily important. Their families did, too, as the group later supported the petition for a Spanish pension for the widow of Gilles Narcisse.[80] Two years after the Leocadio conspiracy, and roughly coinciding with the one-year anniversary of the restoration of Fernando VII, the "battalion of *morenos*" in Santo Domingo under Pablo Alí wrote to the monarch. They expressed their "pleasure for the happy return of Your Majesty to Spain to occupy with dignity the royal throne of your elders."[81] Pablo Alí, again averring his innocence, became more prominent in the capital and more indispensable to Spanish rule. He soon began applying for meritorious promotions.[82] By 1815, he had advanced to the rank of captain.[83] Despite scrutiny, he and his colleagues were still upwardly mobile. Spain could not risk losing their invaluable service in a colony in which revolutionary plots were undeterred.

In November 1812, an arrest order circulated for Domingo Ramos. This twenty-year-old enslaved Dominican was "not very dark," had braided hair, and spoke colloquial Spanish. He had a reputation with local officials. Ramos stood accused of organizing a revolt in the northeast at Cotuí and Samaná.[84] It is unclear whether he was affiliated with earlier plots. As anti-imperial, antislavery dissent by Dominicans intensified, so did its pro-Haitian tones. Considering elite fears of Haitian influence and social unrest, it is telling that Ramos's accent featured in his arrest warrant.

The paranoia was not baseless. The next major conspiracy demonstrated the diffusion of pro-Pétion sentiments specifically throughout Hispaniola. In Chavón near Higüey at the far eastern end of Hispaniola, far from the border, the resident Juan Pedro Estudillo, a fifty-year-old carpenter and timber merchant, claimed to have found out about a conspiracy by the "French *mulâtres*" of the area in February 1813.

One evening, an older, short, possibly enslaved man who spoke colloquial Spanish, and who may have originally been Haitian, had appeared at Estudillo's home asking for a shot of liquor and a small amount of cash in exchange for information. After agreeing, Estudillo learned that some neighbors were well armed and over the preceding months had been organizing via a chain of letters that linked them to Port-au-Prince. Though Estudillo knew little about the alleged plot, an arrest warrant was immediately issued for a person of Haitian birth whom Dominicans called Duson Montas. Montas faced suspicions of hosting Black conspirators and visitors from Haiti and trafficking in letters that were part of the subversive scheme. "Duson," an atypical name, could have perhaps been a nickname Hispanicized after Toussaint Louverture.

José de Castro, a sixty-year-old carpenter, likely of African descent, was interrogated for having commented that the "French *mulâtres*" had enough money and people to revolt if they chose to do so, and that at least one of

CROSS-ISLAND COLLABORATION AND CONSPIRACIES, 1808–1818

them had visited the capital, perhaps on a mission to collect information. The local priest, Mariano Herrera, had apparently met the supposed conspirators, who had asked seemingly innocent questions, perhaps to gather details about Spanish governance. Two others, when questioned, namely, Pepe Bernaber and Casimiro Castillo, denied knowing anything.

Officials sent the suspects to the capital for questioning. Investigators focused on those who had visited Marie-Claire Morel, as the accused conspirators had perhaps used her home to evade suspicions. Given the "French *mulâtres*" own backgrounds, it is no surprise that most of the Dominicans they trusted were of similar social, racial, and occupational statuses. The suspects had primarily engaged free people of color or the enslaved, groups that were excluded from citizenship by the 1812 Spanish Constitution, whom they allegedly influenced with their secret, anti-colonial sentiments.

Estudillo claimed that he had already suspected the "French *mulâtres*" somewhat, as they carried themselves peculiarly and their travels were suspicious. However, when he encountered skepticism for not revealing the rumor more quickly, he defended himself by saying he was reluctant to trust provocative words from someone he did not know, who was also drinking. The night before Estudillo made his claim, four of the accused had ridden into town without any cargo late at night and gone to the Morel house. Each had departed with cargo and had taken to the road instead of going home. Two of these suspects were the brothers Jean and Barthélemy Riche, both from Haiti. Their brother-in-law, a baker, moved about the town at night, taking an unusual route, perhaps to produce or deliver his goods. Their associate François LaPlen, who was from Mirebalais, also visited the capital regularly, apparently, he said, to check on his wife's inheritance.

This behavior could have been attempts to hide the trafficking of letters or weapons. The conspirators in 1810 had done something similar. Morel, who hosted their meetings, said that two "French soldiers" had arrived on horseback in February and asked to visit her. She claimed that these men, Philippe Jeriso and Barthélemy Riche, had only traveled there for a wedding and to buy yuca and rice. Other suspects, such as Tibney and Pilié, a shoemaker and a saddler, respectively, were also from Mirebalais and had military experience.[85] Although it was unclear what their plans intended, Núñez de Cáceres and Urrutia decreed that the enslaved informant had worked for the plotters against *la patria*. They demanded a thorough investigation of the alleged conspirators' homes. Dominican officials removed many French speakers or suspected Haitians from the coasts and heavily restricted their travel.[86]

Compounding this reactionary malfeasance, imperial stability in Santo Domingo broke down further as neighboring governments in the Hispanic Atlantic contended with the return of Fernando VII, the end of the Constitution of 1812, and independence wars. Pro-independence infiltrators appeared more regularly. One of these was Caracas native Francisco de Miranda, who had fought with republicans during the French Revolution. He had participated in independence movements, including in Venezuela in 1806 and the movement that achieved a short-lived independence with the establishment of the First Republic of Venezuela in 1811. He was closely affiliated with several British politicians, who were interested in supporting his vision for independence across the Spanish Americas. During a respite in Jacmel, Haiti, in 1806, he had reportedly first raised the flag that would represent Gran Colombia.[87] Compared to nearby wars, however, the Dominican disturbances were minor, and officials remained complacently pleased that the conspiracies had been manageable.[88]

HAITIAN REALPOLITIK

Surveillance ultimately proved incapable of preventing Haiti from influencing Dominicans. As Dominican officials stressed over conspiracies, both Haitian states crafted highly effective regional military positions and international diplomatic programs that enhanced their long-term power on Hispaniola. In May 1815, a British ship arriving in Cuba from Port-au-Prince reported that "the two *caudillos*," Christophe and Pétion, had resolved that if France invaded, they would enter a truce to repulse the common enemy. Their well-armed forces were a deterrent.[89]

Officials in Spain passed these details to the French, conferring with the Duke de Richelieu, who represented the newly restored Bourbon king, Louis XVIII.[90] They regularly traded intelligence about "the part that the Blacks dominate." This reference arrogantly ignored the name "Haiti," implying rightful French rule and undermining Haitian sovereignty. France urged caution. Christophe had the superior military. The French had paused an invasion, still hoping to win over Pétion, who still faced a long-standing rebellion by his rival Goman in the southern peninsula.[91] These imperial exchanges threatened Dominican interest in more trade with Haiti.

Haitian markets remained a critical component of the Dominican economic recovery. Imperial officials who disliked this fact offered insufficient support or alternatives. However, practical local administrators sometimes overlooked formal attempts to ban exchanges with Haitians.[92] For example, in 1815, officials in Santo Domingo requested instruction on how to handle such enormous volumes of cross-island trade, particularly with Christophe. The severely delayed response from Spain advised that, though it was not ideologically pure or jurisprudentially prudent, retaining Santo Domingo required tolerating trade indiscretions and appeasing Haitian leaders.[93] However, French officials complained about the extralegal Dominican ties to Haiti.[94]

Pétion rightly concluded that Dominican elites were more aligned with Christophe on many issues, including his monarchical preferences. This complicated Pétion's normalization of relations with France and his support for hemispheric independence. Although partial to Christophe, Spain wanted to avoid conflict, as both Haitian leaders could influence the Spanish colonies. Metropolitan officials even worried about how to respect the Haitian legal system in Santo Domingo. Normalized Haitian relations with Europe could have eased tensions in Santo Domingo.[95]

Formidable Haitian forces supported Haiti's regional clout. By 1816, the presence of naval vessels affiliated with southern Haiti or with South American rebels tested Dominican shipping, and even forged relations with the maroons of eastern Cuba.[96] Pétion and Christophe both had navies of about ten vessels.[97] Christophe, who bought British ships, had once even hired Royal Navy officers to staff his fleet, though these ties tensed after Christophe mistreated a Briton working for Pétion.[98] Also, Pétion convinced French officials that it was not "a suitable time to employ forces against the Blacks," because "they want[ed] to negotiate." Unlike Christophe, he created space by allowing France to hope for some unlikely reconciliation.

Pétion used the greater international and domestic stability his state enjoyed to expand its support for hemispheric independence. For example, he provided refuge for independence leaders who threatened the Spanish Empire, such as Simón Bolívar in Les Cayes in 1815. Through 1817, Pétion allowed dozens of revolutionaries from the Hispanic Americas to gather in Port-au-Prince, which they used as a base from which to plan expeditions. These agents of subversion also operated in Santo Domingo. Resuming its status as a long-standing theater of anti-imperial struggles, Pétion renewed his efforts to incite a Dominican revolution.

With limited protections from Spain, Dominican elites considered myriad reasons to break with Spain and preempt possible Haitian unification. Some professionals in the capital closely followed moderate independence projects. This specifically included Bolívar's, who, ironically, was backed by Pétion. Complicating their curiosity, in June 1816 Bolívar began offering emancipation to combatants against Spain, a condition Pétion had demanded.

In December 1816, a pro-Pétion and pro-Bolívar agent attempted to rouse disaffected Dominicans to stage an independence war. Fermín Núñez, a twenty-nine-year-old from Cura, near Caracas, had networked in the capital after apparently also recruiting coconspirators in Puerto Plata. Deponents noted that he had opened seditious conversations, and he demonstrated his own connection to, and protection from, Pétion. He whispered about the financial support that South American rebels had received while in Les Cayes. Undercutting possible support for Christophe, Fermín Núñez also stated that Pétion was assembling resources to unite all of Haiti. He claimed they had the unusual support of the former king of Spain, José I, the deposed usurper Joseph Bonaparte, who then resided in the francophone expatriate community around Philadelphia.

Pétion had grown to see Dominican officials as enemies because of their close military, diplomatic, and commercial ties to Christophe. Their perpetuation of the Spanish Empire and of racial hierarchies contributed to an ideological chasm. Apparently, as Bolívar won on "Costa Firme," he and Pétion could settle perceived scores with those in Santo Domingo who were impeding their respective national projects and had foiled earlier conspiracies that had aspired to a Hispaniola without empires.

The Fermín Núñez conspiracy, like others, targeted the battalion of morenos as possible collaborators. One of their officers, Jean Fantaisie Gaston, was a longtime associate of the previously accused Gilles Narcisse. Gaston had secondhand knowledge that a *caraqueño* (Caracas native) was building a rebellion and alerted officials. Núñez had spoken to one of his colleagues, Ceri, who was originally from Port-au-Prince. The first time they had met, Núñez had chided Ceri for removing his hat out of politeness, saying that the gesture was unbecoming of a good republican. Núñez hinted that he could give his moreno troops raises and higher ranks in exchange for helping take the capital. He carried a pouch that included two silvery braids and a clip, perhaps an epaulet, to place them on a makeshift uniform as leader of an insurrectionary army.

Pedro Figueroa, a shoemaker, had learned from someone nicknamed "Guavina," who in turn had heard rumors, that in the house of an "admiral," Núñez had conspired with José Joaquín de Coca, José Diez, a man named Moren, and some "French." They announced their meetings by placing lights in certain windows and talked behind guarded doors. Once, they reviewed the city walls together. Though he claimed to investigators that he had only been posing as a supporter, Figueroa had talked with Núñez about the meetings, the independence wars, and the funds that conspirators had stashed on the Danish island of Saint Thomas.

Núñez, who had promised to prioritize helping oppressed people of color, was very cautious about which white criollos to engage. He forbade his collaborators from talking to *peninsulares*. Among those with whom Núñez conversed was Luciano, a close associate of Pablo Alí, as Alí kept his distance. Coca, a tailor, and Diez, a distiller, claimed that their talks with Núñez were about trivial matters. They eventually were released from custody, as was Figueroa, who may have been guiltier. Ultimately, Núñez received a death sentence, which was later commuted to a long stay in a North African *presidio*.[99] Pétion's regular attempts at subversion prompted officials to consider sending spies to infiltrate Haitian political circles.[100]

Pétion's strategies converged with unexpected factors from across the Atlantic. Spanish officials deduced that France, holding imperial remnants and unlikely to retake Haiti, quietly welcomed independence struggles in the colonies, as the British had after losing the United States.[101] The British had long projected that Spain's "despicable" governance and engagement with the United States would incite independence across the Hispanic Americas.[102] Spanish officials queried their Parisian counterparts about the travels of suspected rebels in South America, in France, and in the illicit trade hub of Danish Saint Thomas.[103] Sebastian Kindelán, the new governor of Santo Domingo, said that Hispanic American dissidents in London had circulated critical newspapers into the colony.[104]

Given the threats to Spanish rule, Kindelán increased censorship and scrutiny of visitors.[105] These policies were unpopular. Even if their island existence made certain external influences seem distant to Dominicans, it magnified their connection to abolitionist Haiti. Promises of emancipation circulated in a number of nearby anti-colonial movements. Spain even signed a treaty with the British to abolish trading the enslaved.[106] Dominican slaveholders nevertheless remained recalcitrant and disliked the idea of change.

Elite inflexibility and the strategic interests of competing empires amplified Pétion's extant project for the Americas. Christophe, whose economic presence was stronger than Pétion's, and who might have eased many Dominicans into viewing Haitians as partners in some areas, supported Spanish officials instead. Christophe's comparative lack of antislavery and republican plans for the island, partly a pragmatic choice in the interest of preserving certain alliances and his own monarchical power, made Pétion's plans more distinct and appealing to Dominicans who wanted change.

Considering its ties to Hispanic American rebels gathered in Les Cayes and Port-au-Prince, and its active engagement in Caracas and beyond, the failed Fermín Núñez plot appears to have been a collaborative effort by Pétion and Bolívar partisans working for their mutual benefit. Furthermore, a ship supposedly passing from Haiti to Saint Thomas was suspiciously found at Santo Domingo with revealing documents. They detailed how the Senate of Haiti had confirmed Pétion as president for life, revealed Pétion's negotiations with Christophe and France, described Bolívar's victories and his Haitian support, and gave evidence of Pétion's support for hemispheric independence.[107] Pétion's priority was to gain an adjacent ally that would stand with him against Christophe and attacking empires. His interest in unifying Hispaniola seems to have been flexible, and perhaps subordinated to broader anti-colonialism. Haitian views soon changed.

Pétion died from yellow fever in March 1818 at the age of forty-seven. His years of outreach to disempowered Dominicans of color, which differentiated him from Christophe's positive relations with officials in Santo Domingo, would prove helpful to his successor, Jean-Pierre Boyer.[108] Pétion's acolytes eulogized him as the cofounder of Haiti with Dessalines, as well as the co-liberator of the Hispanic Americas with Bolívar, who they claimed had compared Pétion to George Washington.[109] North Americans, loath to praise the revolutionary Haitians, ironically enough, later bestowed this honorific on Bolívar instead. With time, Pétion's eagerness to build transnational collaborations with Dominicans to oppose slavery and colonialism achieved results he would never see. His efforts in the 1810s would culminate with Boyer's achievements in the 1820s.

CONCLUSION

For the Dominicans, years of imperial turmoil, ties to nearby revolutions, and eventually participation with their Haitian neighbors introduced a new era of relative autonomy and antislavery possibilities in Santo Domingo. The anti-French, pro-Spanish uprising that erupted after Napoléon invaded Spain in 1808 became an opportunity for Haitian leaders to bankroll an amenable Dominican Reconquista. The determining factor thereafter was not simply lackluster Spanish recolonization, but regular, ambitious plans among Dominicans of color as they sought a liberatory future.

In the 1810s, Dominican elites returned to their ruling roles in a nominal Spanish restoration with little metropolitan oversight or aid. Their restitution of Hispanic cultural symbols and Catholic evangelization did not ameliorate their weakened structural and social conditions. Slavery persisted despite years of emancipatory potential, and free people of color were deliberately excluded from the liberalization and democratic experiments of the Cortes de Cádiz. The restored Spanish king, Fernando VII, later exacerbated strife by erasing new colonial autonomies.

Awash in recent French and Spanish failures to address the roots of racial strife, Dominicans increasingly engaged with Haitian visitors. They also read a variety of printed texts advancing revolutionary ideas. These influences resulted in regular attempts at popular revolt in the 1810s.

Some Dominicans and Haitians began collaborating in a way that reflected both the trust and the occasional tensions of a family, their interactions increasingly resonating with shared interests that the Age of Revolutions had made apparent. Constant vigilance and arrests uncovered agents of Pétion, and occasionally Bolívar, conspiring with Dominican collaborators. These plots had overarching anti-colonial aims that exceeded those of the revolts of previous eras. Beyond abstract Enlightenment principles, Haiti posed a tangible example of emancipation, liberty, and citizenship for Dominicans of color. The 1810s set the stage for an intense confrontation among those favoring the preservation of Hispanic traditions; those envisioning a more liberal self-rule, like the new independence movements on the mainland; and those who admired the nearby, tangible, radical Haitian experiment with Black power and anti-colonialism. In the early 1820s, the preceding four decades of revolutionary churn yielded a crisis of imperial sovereignty that featured two conflicting national projects.

SEVEN

THE "SPANISH PART OF HAITI" AND UNIFICATION, 1819–1822

In November 1821, several Dominican towns announced their desire to join Haiti. The Haitian president, Jean-Pierre Boyer, read a letter dated the "first year of the independence" from military officers at Dajabón who regularly interacted with Haitians. The note stated, "We respectfully announce to you . . . that we have started the reunion, and that the banner of Haiti has been planted in our city." They requested "munitions of war" in case their "cause of Independence and Liberty" required it.[1]

The border town that had bridged many pivotal moments of the preceding revolutionary decades claimed independence from Spain via unification with Haiti. Dajabón was not alone. Boyer also received a letter from Monte Cristi, whose residents also "thought it appropriate to display the Haitian banner." The town, which sent three commissioners to engage with the Haitian state, hoped Boyer would "protect this city which today becomes a portion of the Republic of Haiti."[2]

Beyond abstract Enlightenment principles, failed French promises, Spanish malfeasance, or distant and white-led independence projects in South America, by the 1820s Haiti presented the most tangible and robust example of liberty and citizenship. Capital elites could not prevent demands for unification and panicked.[3] In reaction, just over two weeks later, in December 1821, José Núñez de Cáceres and a cadre of disaffected professionals proclaimed the "Independent State of the Spanish Part of Hayti" and pleaded with Simón Bolívar for union with Gran Colombia. This declared nation, without many supporters, without clear nationalism, but still with slavery, represented a maneuver by certain capital elites to forestall Dominican unification with Haiti.[4]

While Haiti's example had inspired liberatory struggle across the Americas, Dominicans' collaborative experiences with Haitian citizens had increased in the 1810s, a period that had followed constant contact from the 1790s. By the 1820s Dominicans had welcomed myriad forms of direct involvement with Haitian agents. All of this culminated in popular demand for independence from Spain and unification with Haiti in 1822. In an era marred by violent, costly independence wars across Latin America, this new sense of familial belonging signified perhaps the most peaceful, amiable, and ambitious nation-building project in the region.

Haitian influence abounded without interruption, partly because, after years of tenuous cohesion, capital professionals and elites began to split on how to preserve their status, wealth, and traditions. Some royalists remained. Most Dominican elites were contented with retaining racial hierarchies, Catholicism, and an Iberian heritage. They balked at subservience to a distant, restrictive, and negligent Spanish crown and began considering sovereignty options. Increasingly, young professionals admired the comparatively moderate, white-led independence movements in South America, and they now pondered affiliating with them to preserve their social status quo and preempt Haitian power.

Boyer, who had succeeded Alexandre Pétion in 1818, unified Haiti after Christophe faced discontent, suffered a stroke, and ultimately committed suicide in 1820. While repairing Haitian divisions, Boyer began sending emissaries into Santo Domingo to explore the discontent with Spain and reinforce trade. Beyond the well-known Haitian stances for emancipation and citizenship, Boyer appealed to a wider segment of the Dominican populace. He did so in part by challenging extant Dominican elite concerns about Haitian religiosity and by showing the cross-island compatibility of beliefs. For example, Boyer asked to pay for priests from Santo Domingo to minister to and educate Haitians and stated his desire for a papal concordat. Whatever Boyer's own convictions, his cultural politics conveyed his congruity with Dominicans in terms of religiosity and values. He moved to accomplish what Toussaint Louverture and Jean-Jacques Dessalines could not—a unified, universally emancipated island impervious to European imposition.

In 1820, Boyer also began peaceably asking Dominicans if they were interested in "the whole island of Hayti" uniting as one citizenry with one government.[5] By 1821, pro-Haitian and anti-Haitian movements for independence from Spain gripped Santo Domingo. This project was rather reactive, held little territory, began later, and fell quickly. Nevertheless, José Núñez de Cáceres and his capital colleagues remain wistfully commemorated in selective Dominican historical memory today. In December 1821, Núñez de Cáceres's printed independence decree complained about metropolitan neglect, want for treatment as "legitimate children," and the maximization of "fertile soil" on the "Spanish part of the Island of Hayti," echoing some concerns of Antonio Sánchez Valverde nearly four decades prior. Though he used some popular anti-imperial terms, his proposals impacted a select group, did not address slavery directly, and sought union with Gran Colombia.[6] Hopes to avert Haitian unification faded when Bolívar never responded. Unlike this moderate mainland leader or a distant white king, Boyer and the Haitians were present collaborators of color who supported ambitious popular demands. As pro-Haitian sentiment spread, Boyer noted that Bolívar himself had relied on Haitian aid for his movement, making Haiti the true vanguard of hemispheric independence.

Through proclamations and letters, Boyer claimed, with references to Taíno legacies, that the island should no longer suffer under European extractions. He proposed a unified island founded on anti-colonial, geographical, commercial, security, and, implicitly, some Catholic commonalities. In early 1822, with Dominican towns inviting Haitian rule and Núñez de Cáceres diluting Hispaniola's sovereignty by seeking Gran Colombian affiliation, Boyer entered Santo Domingo. Individual towns accepted the Haitian army and wrote to the capital about Boyer's conciliatory intents and demeanor. He assuaged elite concerns and offered Spanish-language representation in Port-au-Prince. Support from thousands of Dominicans, many of color, compelled Núñez de Cáceres to hand Boyer keys to the city in February 1822. As siblings of soil, newly emancipated Dominicans, old Spanish families, and Haitians became co-citizens. Unification began one of the most remarkable, and forgotten, nation-building projects of the Age of Revolutions.

INTEREST

In 1819, Sebastian Kindelán, newly chosen by Spain to govern Santo Domingo, was steadily tested by Hispanic American rebels and rival empires.[7] Though mainland independence wars succeeded, the key trial for Spanish rule was rising Haitian influence. For years Haiti had been consumed by domestic divisions, distractions that soon resolved with dramatic effects for Dominican society.

In 1820 Henry Christophe suffered a stroke. Seeing his unpopularity with his subjects and the army, and the rise of Boyer, he killed himself in his palace at Sans-Souci. Christophe's son and heir, Jacques-Victor, died by assassination. Jean-Pierre Boyer then rapidly unified the two Haitian states.[8]

A Haitian commemoration framed this process as divine providence reconciling estranged relatives, saying that "the time marked by Heaven for the reunion of the Haitian family had arrived" when "brothers . . . finally felt that *union alone* could preserve them." This "pacification of the north . . . was bound to bring together to the family the inhabitants of the eastern part," as already "their eyes [had] turned to the Republic of Haiti." Inextricably linked to Haitian prosperity and security, the next step of unification entailed welcoming Dominican supporters as co-citizens.[9]

Many still doubted Boyer. Christophe partisans thought he did not understand the interests of the formerly enslaved masses and was too conciliatory toward France. Prince Saunders, an African American intellectual who advised Christophe, told the noted abolitionist Thomas Clarkson, "It is my sincere and candid opinion that I have heard King Henry develop more just and rational ideas . . . in fifteen minutes than I have ever heard from Gen. Boyer and his whole administration."[10] Boyer also had to contend with a legacy of Haitian leaders who had promised to protect gains from the Haitian Revolution while contradictorily wielding authoritarian state power that limited Haitian freedoms.[11] In contrast, Boyer enjoyed leeway as a new and unifying figure. After years of collaboration, Haiti remained a symbol of emancipation to oppressed Dominicans.

Defying his critics and contextual constraints, Boyer steadily began integrating Hispaniola into a unified whole. He started by listening to Dominican independence sentiments. In response, as early as November 1820, Kindelán pleaded for friendship.[12] Independence conversations increased after Andrés Amarante and Francisco Esteban, Dominicans who had sold cattle and tobacco to Christophe's old domains, visited northern Haiti from Monte Cristi. There, they told the officer Charles Arrien that some Dominicans had discussed ejecting Spain and petitioning Gran Colombia for annexation.

This was a turning point. Boyer's own mentor, Pétion, had previously welcomed plots aligned with Bolívar in Santo Domingo. At first, his advisers debated whether they should encourage the pro-Bolívar group, including offering arms and arranging support from pro-independence sailors who had once fought in South American struggles and regularly visited Manzanillo Bay. A long-standing alternate perspective was that the Haitian Constitution rightfully aspired to sovereignty over the whole island. To avert a pro–Gran Colombian uprising in Santo Domingo, Boyer attempted to convince Amarante and Francisco Esteban that peacefully joining Haiti would benefit Dominicans far more.

Joseph Balthazar Inginac, a close adviser and diplomat for Boyer, who supported this plan, asked Arrien to travel to Santo Domingo in late 1820 to try to persuade the conspirators to choose independence through unification with Haiti. Sending an army without an invitation would violate the 1816 Haitian Constitution. Keen to avoid war with Spain, Boyer also needed the many Dominicans that he knew admired Haiti to show support for unification. By 1819, Boyer knew Spain had been unable to protect Dominicans from poverty and piracy and that, if challenged, it would be unlikely to be able to fend off French recolonization. The fear of instability in the east also motivated Haitian officials. Arrien quickly attracted Dominican towns and militias, with commitments as early as November 1820, and Spanish officials expelled him.

As Boyer considered his next move, José Justo de Silva arrived with secret permission from prominent Dominicans to ask Boyer about the specifics of possible Haitian unification. Boyer explained that he would only enter Santo Domingo if more Dominicans made their wishes for Haitian unification publicly clear. He even dissuaded Commodore Aury, a naval mercenary who had fallen out with former ally Bolívar, from intervening against the pro–Gran Colombia party. Instead, Boyer sent Désir Dalmassy, an officer carrying a deliberately modest travel passport, to talk with many of his contacts in Santo Domingo about vocally supporting Haitian unification.[13]

Spanish officers at Las Matas de Farfán notified the capital that Dalmassy had appeared from Las Cahobas and was suggesting that Dominicans voluntarily join Haiti. Dalmassy proposed benefits to those who welcomed the relationship. In many towns, few rejected the idea, thinking there was more to gain by accepting what seemed an inevitability. By the end of 1820, Dalmassy had contacted towns farther to the south and east, including San Juan de la Maguana, Neiba, and Azua. Kindelán pondered the timing of such overtures from Haiti and demanded that Boyer explain his intentions.

One of the major figures in Santo Domingo targeted by these agents was, again, Pablo Alí. They called him a natural Haitian and promised him prosperity for his allegiance. Additionally, Haitian agents proposed that Dominicans would be able to send their own locally selected representatives to the Haitian national legislature.[14] Dalmassy, his colleague Charles Arrien, and other, less visible Haitian agents did not realize immediate results.[15] Nevertheless, they forced thousands of Dominicans of all backgrounds to talk with each other about whether they should join or resist Haitian neighbors.

FIGURE 7.1
*Jean Pierre Boyer, "Président d'Haïti," Paris, Guérin, 1825, John Carter Brown Library,
Archive of Early American Images, E825 R112r.*

When confronted, Dalmassy carried no written orders to show Spanish investigators. He claimed, rather, that Boyer had personally asked him to undertake this exploratory visit as a peaceful mission.[16] Boyer maintained plausible deniability about Dalmassy's travels, simply stating that he was a trusted, prudent colonel who had lived and traded for years in Santo Domingo. He asserted honorable intentions and his interest in being a "consoler and pacifier."[17]

DEBATE

Haitian officials also knew that to succeed in enticing Dominican sympathies their appeals had to exceed those of emancipation or racial solidarity. Their stance on slavery was already widely apparent. As regional "race war" fears abounded, this position was muted in conversations about unification. Furthermore, only several thousand enslaved Dominicans remained, and Haiti expected their support. Also, many Dominican merchants, especially in the west and north, had vested interests in maintaining cross-island commerce. Instead, Boyer needed to convince the much larger free population of color and of Iberian descent, especially in the capital, to join.

Thus, in part to demonstrate goodwill and piety, Boyer asked the Dominican church to send priests to minister to the Haitian populace.[18] Showing the political value of this gesture, Kindelán supported the archdeacon of the cathedral, Santiago native Juan Antonio Pichardo, in his move to Nord and to become the "vicario general" of the "Republic of Hayti" in December 1820. Other priests departed to minister to Haitians as well. The Spanish government even gave some financial aid to support this endeavor.[19] The 1816 revision of the Haitian Constitution, unlike previous charters, said that "the state and its ministers" would "protect" the Catholic religion as "being that of all Haitians." Of course, not all Haitians, or even all Dominicans, were Catholic. But such language, compared to earlier secular documents, assuaged the fears of some Catholics in Santo Domingo.[20]

This compliment to Dominican spirituality and the idea that the priests would increase their influence in Haiti also placated Dominican elites. Perhaps Boyer wanted to undermine Christophe's old power networks, better integrate Nord, and diminish the comparatively more pronounced regional influence of Vodou.[21] However, Boyer's pro-Catholic politics were complicated. Pichardo had been suspended that year for insubordination. After the archbishop recalled him from a previous visit to Haiti, a scandalous anonymous pamphlet appeared calling the archbishop tyrannical.[22]

In Haiti he joined other priests whose standing in the church was suspect. In early 1821, Boyer informed Dominicans that the pope would send the bishop of Macri, Pierre de Glory. This seemed a momentous occasion for Haitian international standing until Boyer received concerning letters from the abolitionists Abbé Grégoire and Thomas Clarkson. The bishop had arrived with peculiar papers printed in Paris and an offer of French affiliation. He had been given only *in partibus infidelum* status, a titular role carrying less authority. In short order, this titular "bishop" insulted the Haitian Constitution and banned the irregular clergy, which divided Haitian

Catholics. He soon departed, only to drown at sea. Boyer's work toward a papal concordat and his effort to gain the confidence of devout Dominicans was clever, yet the objective had not yet been met.[23]

In January 1821, while Boyer was occupied with elevating Catholicism and reintegrating Nord into the Haitian state, across Santo Domingo open debates emerged over whether Dominicans should align with Haiti or Gran Colombia. Conversations in Monte Cristi, Puerto Plata, and even Santiago leaned toward unifying Hispaniola. Boyer soon visited the border region in person. In Ouanaminthe, he learned of growing Dominican support for Haiti.[24] There were even rumors in the Spanish Caribbean that a force affiliated with Bolívar and supported by London might invade Santo Domingo.[25] Nevertheless, as his conversations with Dominicans continued, Boyer again disavowed rumors that he would intervene militarily.[26]

As Kindelán learned of the seriousness of the competition for Dominicans' loyalties, he proposed "*guerrillas* and ambushes," and even a scorched earth policy, to stop Haitian unification.[27] He told Dominicans to reject "infamous inductions" and "wicked wiles" and to "defend their homes and homeland." This, he said, is what would earn "Spanish Dominicans" the "greatest glory."[28] Boyer reminded Kindelán, who even published some of their letters for Dominicans to read, that "almost all parts of the world are the scene of liberal revolutions," and that people eager for prosperity had "communicate[d] with the rapidity of lightning." Boyer thus justified the conversations about Dominican independence as a trend of the times with historical impetuses beyond either his or Spanish control.[29]

Kindelán realized that most Dominicans had likely turned against him. Even white Dominicans who had supported Spain were now extremely disappointed by governmental fragility and their inability to keep Haiti from growing in influence. In the capital they increasingly voiced their frustrations. King Fernando VII was distant and distracted by major wars in México and South America, where his armies were mired in combat. Boyer openly tried to influence Santo Domingo, but as he awaited more overt support from the Dominicans, he was careful to avoid violating Haitian or international law.[30]

In response to these developments, Spanish officials founded the *Telégrafo Constitucional*, a pro-colonial newspaper intended to stem the intellectual tide. Unsurprisingly, its first issue exclaimed the supposed benefits of thoroughly policing politics.[31] This newspaper was a late-stage royalist bastion for "illustrious Dominicans" to rediscover the "luminous principles . . . [and] sublime views" of the Spanish monarchy, which it said promised them "justice and manhood." It said that Spain would not "abandon" Santo Domingo to "another catastrophe."[32] Kindelán even tried to explain the Spanish inter-pretations of liberty and equality to the masses and asked priests to do the same from their pulpits.[33] He tried to dismiss past citizenship exclusions for people of African descent, scolding protest against racial discrimination as the real cause of social ills.[34]

Kindelán begged "Spanish Dominicans" for their loyalty.[35] However, such proclamations for Spain against Haiti were ineffective.[36] In fact, a small, mostly white clique of professionals in the capital had founded "patriotic societies" to seriously discuss independence from Spain and a Bolívar-style, elite-managed republicanism.[37]

Boyer received regular updates from José Justo de Silva on these discus-sions about a "République Domingoize." He asked the Haitian president about unifying the island. In turn, Boyer expressed concern about this insular Dominican idea.[38] The "eagerly desirous" Silva also conferred with other Haitian officials, who were concerned that Dominican society torn by competing ideas for the future might descend into anarchy. Boyer, still hoping for more evidence of pro-Haitian sentiments in Santo Domingo, welcomed calls for unification in at least Dajabón and Monte Cristi.[39]

In a letter from January 1821, Silva reported to Boyer, "I have been instructed to make to Your Excellency . . . on behalf of my compatriots . . . [an] account of the result of the mission." He had explained Haitian terms to his Dominican colleagues. Thereafter, his "compatriots, and other people in great numbers," were "very satisfied." However, Boyer also heard details about the opposition of Spanish officers, on whom Kindelán increasingly relied, and learned that the French were willing to provide naval reinforce-ments from Guadeloupe and Martinique. Boyer still had to avoid a war and avoid further jeopardizing Haiti's fragile foreign relations. Importantly, Silva's Dominican allies intended to send Boyer letters detailing their posi-tion. Formal appeals justified his decisions and appeared in print years later to show a wider audience the reasons for Haitian actions.[40]

Rumors of French backing for the outmatched Governor Kindelán piqued Boyer's attention. In response, Boyer reminded his growing base of Dominican supporters of shared cross-island hardships under French rule and their common interests in commerce and co-fraternity. By this time, perhaps only one-quarter of Dominicans claimed whiteness. Among this shrinking class, panicked questions swirled about Spanish neglect and how to preserve Iberian religiosity and culture. However, they had little sup-port. For example, the "rustic people" of the interior, peasants and ranchers who had aided in Spanish recolonization a decade before, began to favor Haiti.[41]

ACTION

Key Dominican towns began announcing their commitment to a Haitian future in November 1821. Boyer received a letter asking him to accept and protect Monte Cristi as part of the "Republic of Haiti." Residents displayed "the Haitian banner" and sent three commissioners, Díaz, Domingo, and Escarfulez, to collaborate with Boyer.[42] A letter from military officers at Dajabón stated, "We respectfully announce to you, General, that we have started the reunion, and that the banner of Haiti has been planted in our city." They requested arms in case they needed to protect their "cause of Independence and Liberty."[43] The Haitian press announced that Amarante had helped raise the Haitian flag to join the republic.[44]

As news of public support for unification arrived, Boyer continued monitoring the pro-Bolívar preferences in the capital. Appealing in familiar terms, he asked these Dominicans if they would join their "western brothers" instead.[45] Some refused. The capital knew that pro-independence partisans at Monte Cristi and Dajabón had requested Haitian rule.[46] As towns near the border welcomed Haiti, anonymous white politicians in the capital began writing to South American leaders, including Bolívar, at the end of 1821.[47]

Partly, the appeal of joining Gran Colombia came from the notion of being able to integrate clergy into their independence struggle, as expressed in pamphlets sent by an anonymous "Caracas native to his Dominican compatriots." The author suggested that they could thrive economically as the "Spanish part of Hayti," an intriguing word choice that Henry Christophe and others had also used. They only needed someone like "Washington in the north" to extol civic virtue, or "Tupac Amaru I" to expunge Iberian injustices. Perhaps ironically, Dessalines and his independence army also called themselves "Incas" avenging European desolation. This supposed *caraqueño* suggested that Haiti could assist them in gaining independence and provide a mutual defense yet remain a separate state. This approach would perhaps appeal to Dominicans who wanted to avoid antislavery movements or Black power sentiments in Santo Domingo. This concern tied into a paranoid race-war trope common in this era.[48]

Some intently absorbed these suggestions. At some point in 1821, the ambitious official Núñez de Cáceres, who had failed to ascend the colonial hierarchy, joined white, anti-Spanish critics in the capital.[49] His suppression of other South American–linked conspiracies in recent years had hampered his belated defection. While their pamphlets hinted at support from Bolívar, it is unclear whether he was actually aware of their current plans for Hispaniola. That year, Bolívar was busy defeating Spain, building Gran Colombia, marching to Ecuador, and expanding his coordination with rebels from southern South America. His focus was not on the Caribbean Basin.

Nevertheless, on 1 December 1821, Núñez de Cáceres and a cadre of disaffected professionals in the capital proclaimed the "Independent State of the Spanish Part of Hayti" and appealed to Bolívar for affiliation with Gran Colombia. Although they were open to a treaty of mutual defense with Haiti, their actions were as much to oust Spain as they were to secure their continuity of control in Dominican society, a move inimical to the racial egalitarianism of Haiti. Their constitution sanctified the role of the church. Archbishop Pedro Valera, reluctant to support the new state, cooperated to avoid bloodshed. However, the constitution also defined their own terms of liberty without approaching abolition. Their tactless response to sharply rising pro-Haitian sentiment across the colony was to allow capital elites to keep their enslaved laborers.[50]

By then, Pablo Alí had served Spain for nearly three decades. When he and other Black veterans applied for Spanish citizenship, Alí cataloged his illustrious service from the Haitian Revolution through the 1810s. However, despite his skill, his bravery, and the praise he had received from white officials, Spain denied Alí citizenship. In 1821, the last pillars of Spanish power in Santo Domingo, such as Alí, collapsed. At first, Alí joined the more moderate independence movement. He may have leaned this way because of his location in the capital, or because of the position he had earned in local society, or even because of his longtime relationships with officials, especially Núñez de Cáceres.[51] In any case, Alí apparently remained loyal to Spain until Núñez de Cáceres himself presented him with the papers rejecting his citizenship request.[52] Alí then helped Núñez de Cáceres expel the new governor, Pascual Real, at bayonet point.[53] Alí got his citizenship, albeit in a state that barely lasted two months, and that did not convincingly control significant territory beyond the capital.

However, many other Dominicans were uninterested in a Hispaniola that would be perpetually divided by lingering European distinctions, linguistic differences, or governments across the sea. As enslaved Dominicans "continued to groan under the yoke," Santiago protested this new republic, followed by Puerto Plata, La Vega, San Juan, Neiba, Azua, and Samaná. The "Haitian banner" spread.[54] Haitian officials monitored capital politics via correspondence with interested Dominicans. In January 1822, Boyer mobilized his army. Dominican appeals for Haitian unification had appeared publicly, and he feared a sovereignty crisis, military conflict, and French intrusion.[55]

Nevertheless, some Dominican officials remained dubious and dismissive of popular Dominican sentiment. One general argued that "towns adjacent to the French part are dedicated to the government of Boyer, because their population today consists for the most part of *mulatos* and Blacks." He said that Haitian solidarity arose because they wanted "liberty, prosperity, and dominance over whites."[56]

Meanwhile, in the capital some were portraying Núñez de Cáceres as having experienced some sort of mania or a nervous breakdown. Some thought he had cycles of extreme anxiety and subsequent withdrawal, at which time he soaked in hot springs, correlating to a suspected family history of mental illness. Beyond his politics and seemingly erratic behavior, others thought he had been personally motivated by insecurity about his modest family origins and his annoyance that many officials who were peninsular Spaniards yet seemingly less qualified and less intelligent than him held more powerful positions.[57] His unpopularity was compounded by the fact that he had long been known as someone who enforced restrictive or even racist Spanish imperial edicts. Politicians with such imperial careers had difficulty transforming into credible independence leaders.

Boyer's popularity was, however, growing. He had received letters from across Santo Domingo. A newspaper in Port-au-Prince printed a message from leaders in Santiago saying they favored unifying the island and rejected Núñez de Cáceres's notion of a "Spanish Hayti" in the capital.[58] In Santiago, "the undersigned patriots," were "moved by unequivocal sentiments" to reject the "Constitutive Act of December 1 relating to Dominican Independence" and affiliation with Gran Colombia. These Santiago citizens thought Núñez de Cáceres had "establishe[d] distinctions between the peasant and the military, between the poor and the rich, between the different districts of this part," and that he "maintain[ed] slavery in defiance of the fundamental bases of all political society." To them, his capital project would make "some individuals prosper by sacrificing thousands of respectable family fathers." Santiago sent deputies to meet with Boyer, and they reminded him of his promises to be "peacemaker and friends of the inhabitants of this part." They asked for "help to reach independence" and for "general liberty of the slaves" under the Constitution of Haiti "in union and fraternity."[59]

The residents of Puerto Plata also sent letters and deputies, and they, too, "flaunted the flag" of Haiti. They hoped their "deference" would lead to the "welfare of the inhabitants, their individual safety, and the preservation of their property," as they now considered themselves to be "under the laws of the Republic of Haiti."[60] They "took the oath" to "preserve the public tranquility" and called Boyer a "philanthropist."[61] The Puerto Plata junta thought that this statement would "put an end to the unrest and discontent that [had] followed, throughout the Spanish part, the publication of Dominican Independence united to the Government of Colombia." They invited Haitians to "act together . . . as brothers."[62]

UNIFICATION

Familial language suffused both Haitian and Dominican unification language. In January 1822, concluding that the "entire island has only one family," residents of San Juan de la Maguana issued a "cry of long live the Haitian Republic, long live President J-P Boyer."[63] The citizens of Neiba "hasten[ed] to make known" the pleasure they took in accepting Haitian laws and asked Haiti to accept them "among its children."[64] Some in Neiba said they were "ready to die for the defense of our father and benefactor," Boyer.[65] La Vega's citizens notified the "generous" Boyer that they, too, were flying the Haitian flag.[66] Azua welcomed Haitians with ringing bells and celebratory artillery fire.[67] Cotuí, San Pedro de Macorís, and Samaná joined soon thereafter.[68] In Samaná, officials reassured locals by saying that "peace and concord follow[ed] [Boyer's] steps," adding that Boyer would "embrace us like a tender father, a faithful friend, a good brother." They promised that their "reward" would be "liberty and equality."[69]

The Haitian press also offered ideas. One newspaper found it peculiar that the "Dominican Republic"—one of the first uses of that name to distinguish "Spanish Hayti" from the Republic of Haiti—would ask Gran Colombia to intervene in governance or defense from across the Caribbean. Rather, the newspaper said, Dominicans should "remember the support that the Haitians have sent them . . . to help them in the liberty of their territory," as "when they found themselves occupied by the French forces." It argued that Haiti was obviously their closest and most natural ally.[70]

Prudently, Boyer remained aware of both domestic laws and the possibility of confrontation with Dominican elites in the capital. He thus asked the Haitian Senate for its opinion. Precedents included previous treaties and legal interpretations, such as Toussaint Louverture's 1801 view of the Treaty of Basel, Haitian assertions to retreating French generals at independence, and Dessalines's 1805 Constitution, which asserted unity for the island and

said that all Haitians were "brothers." The revised 1816 constitution identified the "island of Haiti" as rightful territory of the republic. Though it did
not explicitly claim Spanish-controlled Santo Domingo, the colloquial use
of "Haiti" by all on the island, including Dominicans, made the Senate's
interpretation, that only one republic could exist in their land and that the
entirety of Hispaniola could fit definitions of Haitian territory, viable.[71] Of
note, Núñez de Cáceres had located his republic in Haiti, only distinguishing the "Spanish" part.

In a direct letter to Núñez de Cáceres, Boyer elaborated his concerns
regarding the instability of "Spanish Hayti" and explained rising interest
in unifying the island. Boyer professed to be a pacifier and conciliator, not
a conqueror, and said he hoped that soon all Dominicans would raise the
Haitian flag. He noted that Dajabón, Monte Cristi, Santiago, Puerto Plata,
Las Cahobas, Las Matas de Farfán, San Juan de la Maguana, Neiba, Azua, La
Vega, and other towns had already accepted unification. Boyer wanted to
cooperate, unlike Bolívar, who had never replied to Núñez de Cáceres.[72]

Núñez de Cáceres responded to Boyer by the end of January. He conceded that his advisers had "all unanimously agreed to be under the laws
of the Republic of Haiti, and to fly the flag in this city." He hoped to find
in Boyer "the brother, the friend, and the father" that would bring peace.[73]
That day, Núñez de Cáceres had announced to all "Loyal Dominicans" that
he was taking a stance of peace and passivity toward Boyer and his army,
because he was coming as a "father, friend, and brother" to blend the island
under one constitution with a participatory government that would benefit
all. He asked resistant Dominicans to "open your hearts," to "reciprocate
with union," and to ignore "the echoes of old worries" about Haiti.[74] Popular consent and political conciliation thus left Boyer's thirty thousand troops
idle, although their readiness had hastened resolution.[75]

When Boyer entered the city of Santo Domingo on 9 February 1822, he
faced no resistance to the idea of securing Dominican independence from
Spain by unifying Hispaniola. Many Dominicans saluted the Haitian flag.
Boyer asked the capital not to see him "as a conqueror," but as "a father, a
peacemaker, [and] a friend." He was ready to repair their "isolation from the
Haitian family" and invited them, as "citizens of Haiti . . . to live forever free
and independent or die."[76] Dominican slavery had finally ended.

Boyer made a public appearance upon his arrival in the city of Santo
Domingo on 9 February 1822. Ceremonies had been arranged to greet him.
Núñez de Cáceres symbolically relinquished his claims to power by handing Boyer the keys to the city. Núñez de Cáceres gave a speech saying that
the Haitians who had "incorporated themselves into the Republic" were

worthy of protection. Tactfully, Boyer chose to minimize the pomp, saying it did not comport with his modest sentiments. To calm the capital elites, he avoided presenting himself as an arrogant conqueror. He expressed regret at not speaking Spanish well and also mentioned his previous professions of faith. He later visited the cathedral for a Te Deum of gratitude for their peaceful union.

Echoing the sense of kinship that had defined unification efforts and many moments of the revolutionary era that had preceded them, Boyer portrayed himself as "a father, a brother, a friend, who [has come] to kiss with all the effusion of the heart the new Haitians who [have] joined the family." He was pleased that so many Dominicans knew the "righteousness of his intentions," which included the desire "to guarantee their future security and their inner tranquility." Concluding the festivities that day and the revolutionary trends that had driven Dominican and Haitian collaboration for decades, the audience in Santo Domingo exclaimed, "Long live the Republic of Haiti! Long live independence!"[77]

CONCLUSION

Unification with Haiti was by invitation, not a result of aggressive invasion. This successful culmination of long-running cooperation between Dominicans and Haitians empirically contradicts historiography that projects later incompatibilities exacerbated by Dominican nationalism onto the past. Such depictions have distorted the nature and origins of Dominican identity to deleterious effect across generations. Dominicans who wanted to join with Simón Bolívar's Gran Colombia had multiple years in which they could have done so, including during Bolívar's stay in Haiti, and then later with his spies. These options seem to have only become more popular with rising pro-Haitian support among Dominicans. The ample popular conspiracies with Dominican participants in the 1810s and the numerous towns that wrote letters asking to join the Haitian state in 1821 and 1822, against the wishes of capital elites, show growing collaboration and support for unification.

Among the exceptional influence of Haiti in the revolutionary Atlantic, by far its greatest impact was in adjacent Dominican society, where Dominican and Haitian collaboration shaped an independence movement entirely unique in the Americas. The immediacy and practicality of a Haitian future countervailed French radicalism and retraction, Spanish liberalism and reaction, and ineffective alignment with mainland Latin American independence projects. The end of the imperial era in Santo Domingo came peacefully, contrasting with the chaos and warfare taking place elsewhere in the Americas.[78]

Unlike mainland Spanish colonies that broke away with elite-led movements, marginalized people won this anti-imperial contest. Dominican elites were yet unable to articulate a national identity that appealed across society. Later dissenters against unification defined an identity oppositional to being Haitian that revolved around a Hispanic past, the Spanish language, staunch Catholicism, and cultural and racial fears built from skewed depictions of the Age of Revolutions.

Thousands of Dominicans' dreams of liberty, equality, and national belonging became a reality with Haitian citizenship. Unification ended Dominican slavery, unlike in neighboring Cuba or Puerto Rico, or, for that matter, in the United States or Brazil. Unlike their counterparts around the Americas, Dominicans also evaded immediate racist curtailments of post-emancipation civil rights. For their initial independence from Spain, very few Dominicans perished, unlike the hundreds of thousands who died over many years of destructive warfare in México and across South America. The protection of Haitian defenses deterred Spanish, French, or British interference. As a constituent region of the republic, Dominicans who wanted to maintain their identities as Catholics, Spanish speakers, and Iberian descendants had approval to do so. Haiti also printed official documents in Spanish, and Dominicans took governmental jobs in Port-au-Prince.

Their explicitly multiracial, multiethnic, multilingual nation-building project ranks among the most ambitious in the history of the Americas. In their first day as Haitians, Dominicans gained a more inclusive and stable state than any other new independence project in the Americas had been able to achieve. The unique dynamics of racial formation and religiosity from the 1790s through 1822 made this one of the most interesting contests over national belonging in the Age of Revolutions. Dominican unification with Haiti in 1821 and 1822 represented perhaps the most peaceful and innovative independence in Latin America, secured by popular demand and invitation, not invasion. Although Boyer recognized the difficulty of their project in 1822, he and other Haitians tried to cooperate with Dominicans as "their siblings of soil."[79] Once upon a time, many Dominicans wanted that, too.

BECOMING DOMINICAN IN HAITI

Who succeeded in ending the colonial era and who should be the face of Dominican independence? Was it Jean-Pierre Boyer? And how should earlier figures, such as Jean-François, Georges Biassou, Toussaint Louverture, Henry Christophe, and Alexandre Pétion, appear in the anti-imperial pantheon? What do selective memories about José Núñez de Cáceres, and later Juan Pablo Duarte, who led Dominican separation from Haiti in 1844, reinforce? Whom do they exclude? Including extensive Dominican involvement in the Haitian Revolution, should independence narratives encompass all of Hispaniola? Some answers to these challenging, complicated, and contentious questions appear in the preceding chapters. Evidence and analysis present many faces of independence, both Dominican and Haitian, and many of color.

Across decades of complex contingencies, those who were not easily conscripted into prevailing Dominican national stories were most responsible for building an era of cooperation. These figures included both famous and lesser-known individuals whose portrayals have long influenced cultural politics on the island.[1] For example, the lightly supported, geographically confined, short-lived project of Núñez de Cáceres remains the initial form of independence, wistfully evoked by Dominican nationalism and prevalent historiography. Such narratives anachronistically impose the supposition of an inevitably separate Dominican state onto the past. This interpretation of history ignores formative appeals of revolutionary Haiti, cross-island kinmaking and cooperation, and historical Dominican demands. At times, these denials and accusations of Haitian aggression have bolstered the Dominican state's "historical" justification of corrosive national and racial exclusions. Rather than allowing anti-Haitian holdouts then or anti-Haitian nationalists now to define the past, unification in 1822 must be framed within decades of popular anti-colonial, anti-racist collaboration built from shared interests.

AFTER 1822

At the outset of unification, Haitians attempted to deliver on promises of good government. Many local officials stayed on under Boyer. Many residents esteemed the Haitian commanders, among whom was Pablo Alí, who had agreed to Boyer's terms and donned the Haitian army uniform.[2] For years Alí remained commander of defenses in Santo Domingo and a leader in the Dominican community of color.[3]

The blended family seemed advantageous to many Dominicans and Haitians. Haitian officials arriving in the capital noticed that "the place was destitute of all pecuniary resources, and even of provisions," conditions they sought to ameliorate. Among other factors, local economic malaise had driven Dominican demand for access to Haitian markets that could support their livelihoods. Boyer tasked Joseph Balthazar Inginac with "organizing . . . the justices of peace, installing the civil court of Santo Domingo, and also organizing . . . finances." Inginac immediately visited Dominican schools, as Haiti had provided more support to public education. However, the undercurrent, "that the aristocracy . . . had only submitted to necessity," implied that circles of well-off Dominicans complied only due to pressure, an issue that remained a long-term challenge to integrating all Dominicans.[4]

The gradually growing complaints by the elite few paled in comparison to improvements for the many who joined the antislavery, anti-imperial experiment that inspired the Black Atlantic. Early in the unification period, newly freed Dominicans mocked their former owners and eagerly assisted Boyer's government. However, the Dominican majority refrained from starting a retributive race war, something the elites had feared. Boyer himself modeled moderation and tact, earning a modicum of begrudging respect from many who had opposed his campaign of persuasion of Dominicans through his agents and published texts.

Perhaps, as Boyer expected, trust in Haiti among some elite Dominicans began to erode early in unification. Their Catholic beliefs remained a rallying point of Dominican *hispanismo* identity against supposed Haitian depravity, and therefore against unification. Though Catholicism officially predominated, unified Haiti was a more pluralist society. That pluralism tested ideas of superiority festering among elite Dominicans, and some of them revived old worries about the supposed innate racial, cultural, or religious incompatibilities between them and Haitians rooted in the fears of decades past. Many Dominicans felt affronted by the lack of Catholic practice among some Haitian citizens and soldiers.[5] Haitian officials were also somewhat surprised at the level of Catholic devotion throughout the

Dominican populace.[6] As many neighboring colonies gained independence, and eventually started pursuing papal relations, vociferous Dominican Catholics felt isolated, as Haiti lacked a concordat or normalized diplomatic or commercial relations.[7]

Exaggerating existential threats, within months of unification white Dominicans in Samaná and elsewhere began courting French and Spanish interests for recolonizing Santo Domingo. They fortified Samaná as a royalist refuge, raised the Spanish flag, and begged for aid from Puerto Rico and Martinique to help them shed their supposed "African yoke."[8] A French naval ship just happened to appear at Samaná to receive their request. Boyer, learning of the uprising and fearing a new French invasion, marched on the peninsula. When ten French ships arrived and briefly disembarked hundreds of troops, Boyer responded with force.[9] Dominican narrations of this era typically do not contextualize such events. In fact, punitive actions of this sort by Haitian forces were uncommon.

Anti-Haitian resistance, though not significant, did not end.[10] When white dissenters attacked Haitian interests, Boyer responded with several executions and dozens of expulsions, including, on both counts, of anti-Haitian priests.[11] Boyer, who knew that Spanish agents had incited elite Dominicans to pursue recolonization, allegedly threatened anybody displaying the Spanish flag with execution for treason.[12] To avert invasion, he also had spies throughout the region, a network that caused empires to fear that people of color across the Caribbean might welcome a revolutionary Haitian archipelago.[13] Unlike the elites, who engaged in much hyperbole when expressing their fears, many thousands of Dominicans and Haitians reasonably feared re-enslavement.[14]

Boyer could not persuade an "anti-liberal minority" to tolerate pluralist Haitian society or stop plotting an imperial return. Furthermore, Boyer's understandable policy of conscripting Dominicans, along with poor pay for soldiers, eventually frustrated even his supporters. Land redistribution of old plantations initially benefited Haitian officers, not necessarily working Dominicans. Beset by the many annoyances he encountered in managing Santo Domingo, Boyer later reconsidered the sequence of actions he had taken. Regarding the tactics in 1820 and 1821, it seems that he may have considered a more gradual unification process before he perceived that Núñez de Cáceres was jeopardizing Hispaniola's security. Núñez de Cáceres had thus forced Boyer to engage Dominican elites before he had intended.[15] Resolution of the problem after unification proved elusive.

Meanwhile, Bolívar envisioned post-independence Latin American integration and debated forms of confederation and cooperation at the Congress of Panamá. Bolívar simultaneously used fears of race war to justify exclusions of people of color, and undermined anyone organizing against oppression by framing their actions as attacks against social harmony. For the congress, Bolívar explicitly rejected inviting Haiti, the state that had most supported his own survival and social promises when his movement was on the verge of failure a decade earlier. Though the United States and Brazil were invited, Haiti was considered too Black and, ignoring Santo Domingo, not Hispanic enough.[16]

This exclusion was myopically ironic, as dozens of *mulato* and white politicians from Santo Domingo had served local interests in Port-au-Prince and contributed to Haitian policy. Hundreds more had staffed Haitian governmental roles in the east.[17] Haitian treatment of Dominicans, albeit flawed, represented a majority Black state attempting the most ambitious and peaceful integration of racially plural citizenry to date. Yet despite shared interests and access to critical Haitian markets, Haiti's diplomatic hurdles impeded Dominican ties to new Hispanic American solidarities and prevented the formation of close ties to Cuba and Puerto Rico, which remained Spanish until 1898.[18]

LEGACIES

Anti-Haitian ideas of innate incompatibility and outright racism both emerged during and laid claims upon the Age of Revolutions. Intense Dominican and Haitian collaboration was the backdrop to complex discourses and have shaped long-lasting consequences for Dominican cultural politics and policies. The most corrosive cases of Dominican nationalist assertions of difference draw upon a series of grievances against Haiti rooted in selective memories of colonial endings and early national beginnings.

In the mid-nineteenth century, Dominican elites restored an exclusivist hispanismo identity and harsh critiques of Haitians from the revolutionary age. Recently, the Haitian unification era has received necessary analysis that moves beyond frameworks and sources that simplistically imply Haitian imposition or domination over Dominicans.[19] Elite Dominicans displeased with the Haitian indemnity to France, and also losing slavery, social prestige, political power, linguistic dominance, and Catholic influence, began organizing resistance through renewed royalist rhetoric.

By 1833, they considered engineering Spanish recolonization or perhaps a second attempt at a Hispanophilic republic distinct from Haiti.[20] Application of Haitian law was uneven, though in locales such as Higüey, far in the east, public life changed little in the first years of unification. Aside from protections for newly freed laborers, the greatest friction came from local elites having to acquiesce to Black Haitian leadership.[21]

Dominicans who were newly emancipated after enduring the multiple failed promises of the revolutionary era benefited greatly from Boyer's concrete liberation policies. Dominicans of color also seized upon newfound protections to assert property claims as Haitian citizens. However, sudden co-citizenship with people of African descent caused elites to redouble their racist rhetoric. Over time, Boyer's failed program of land redistribution and coercive labor policies also dampened support for him from Dominicans who had once championed unification. By the 1840s, Boyer had lost popularity in the west as well because of his increasingly authoritarian tactics. Cross-island alliances, commerce, and social accommodations formed amid unification came into jeopardy.[22]

In the independence era and continuing even to the present, disdain for Haiti from Dominican elites and public figures has simmered in loosely historicized claims, often accompanied by attempts to diminish and debunk copious evidence of popular support for Haitian unification. Once this whitewashing had obscured the fact that unification was driven by popular demand, a narrative of Haitian aggression and invasion could prevail.[23] Indeed, emotive exaggerations about the events of 1822 and the years preceding it were key to certain forms of Dominican identity and to longstanding anti-Haitian themes.[24]

Dominicans told a recurring story encapsulating fears about the Haitian presence in the east. It recounted the alleged brutal assault and murder of three young sisters within weeks of unification. Though it was never definitively proven that Haitian soldiers perpetrated the attack, and despite evidence of Dominican involvement, a moral panic about racial violence and contamination erupted. Dominican public figures retold this story throughout the nineteenth century, and these "Virgins of Galindo" became nationalist martyrs symbolic of the misery brought upon the Dominicans from supposedly unwarranted and unwanted Haitian occupation.[25] Along with understanding past acts of solidarity between Dominicans and Haitians, empirically reckoning with or contextualizing negative, whitewashed narratives can help dismantle the distortions that have justified oppressive actions. Such legacies influenced eventual Dominican separation with Haiti, cast Haitians as depraved or unmodern, and gradually spread across Dominican society.

INEXTRICABILITY

Aside from blame, narrating separation from Haiti and determining who to heroize has proven complex for many Dominican nationalists. Boyer fell from power in 1843 amid a flurry of discontent on Hispaniola over his autocratic rule. A costly indemnity payment to France in exchange for French acknowledgment of Haitians' freedom and independence and the normalization of relations also played a role. There were valid reasons for discontent with Haitian governance across the island. Not all the reasons for Dominican discontent were tinged with racism.

Capitalizing on the disarray of the Haitian state and on real dissent against some of the policies impacting certain Dominican sectors, a mostly white Dominican cadre, led by Juan Pablo Duarte, eventually reacted. A group descended from landowners, slaveholders, and colonial professionals, and representing only a small percentage of the populace, reformulated colonial nostalgia and staid anti-Haitian tropes honed from the revolutionary era to rally ethnic grievances in support of separation from Haiti in 1844.[26] Even then, the possibility of a French protectorate preceded and encouraged Dominican autonomy from Haiti. Despite these Dominicans' paths through contingent futures, heroic stories persist.[27] The new narratives of independence not only demoted Boyer, but almost turned him into a villain.

Since 1844, Dominican leaders have looked for independence heroes who embody Dominican virtue and exhibit anti-Haitian credentials. Powerful politicians have looked for such heroes in intriguing places. To the present day, this process has produced under-researched details that might complicate nationalist uses. Some figures with questions about their Haitian ancestry have earned redemption as being more Hispanic by emphasizing their protection of a fledgling Dominican nationalism based in parts on cultural exclusion, religion, and virulent opposition to Haiti. In such Dominican discourses, claiming these beliefs has proved national belonging.[28]

For example, Jean-Claude Montas Cleride, otherwise known as Duson Montas, was among several Haitians, or "French mulâtres," from Mirebalais who settled near El Seibo and Higüey and came under suspicion in the 1810s for plotting an anti-Spanish coup with support from Alexandre Pétion's administration.[29] A warrant was issued for his arrest in 1813, but Montas's connections to the Haitian state were too murky to punish as treason against Spain. By the 1820s, his sympathies were no longer in question, after he became a Haitian justice of the peace in San Cristóbal, during the unification period. During his life in Spanish and Haitian Santo Domingo, he fathered a multiethnic family, common for so many on Hispaniola.

Rosa Montas, Duson's *hija natural* ("natural daughter," likely meaning born out of wedlock), also featured prominently in the Haitian state. Her mother was Dominican and lived near Higüey, where pilgrims from Port-au-Prince occasionally came to visit the shrine at the chapel of Nuestra Señora de Altagracia. In August 1831, Rosa married Antoine Duverger (His-panicized to Antonio Duvergé), a Haitian colonel whose mother was from Croix-des-Bouquets, and whose father, like Rosa's, was from Mirebalais. When their first child was born five months later, Duson served as *padrino* (godfather). Another of Antonio Duvergé's children, the *hijo espurio* ("spu-rious son," likely meaning born out of wedlock) José Daniel, was born as a free Haitian citizen, possibly in 1838, the year a pro-separation Domini-can group called the Trinitaria formed. His mother, Bartolina del Maniel, merged these families with those of the maroons.[30]

At Dominican separation in 1844, the Montas and Duvergé families sided with the Dominican rebels and stayed in the east. Duvergé com-manded famous victories at Azua and Cachimán in support of Juan Pablo Duarte, fighting against Haitian efforts to stop the rebellion. Whereas the first Haitian flag had cut white from the French *tricolore* and sewn together the blue and red to symbolize Black and *gens de couleur* solidarity against France, Duarte's first Dominican flag took the Haitian national flag and emblazoned it with a white cross.

Notably, though Duarte himself is not known to have espoused racial motives for separation, many of his supporters did. For example, the Domin-ican leader Pedro Santana, who would have Duvergé executed in 1855, coordinated with a new Dominican agent in the United States. They asked the staunchly pro-slavery secretary of state John C. Calhoun to support the "white men" of Santo Domingo, who they said were standing up to "Hai-tian negroes." This was one of many instances in which Dominican nation-alists presented their struggle as white survival against racial invasion.[31]

In Dominican nationalist lore, the genealogies of Duvergé and Montas are as obscure as their reasons for relocating to Santo Domingo in the first place. Haitian chroniclers who lived through these events said Duvergé was originally Haitian, and that his father was perhaps of partial African descent.[32] Some Dominican hagiographies say that Duvergé's grandfather, or perhaps his father, was a military officer who had notably fought against Toussaint Louverture. This description may have strictly been true, as some-one named Duverger had aligned with the gens de couleur officers who supported Rigaud in 1799.[33] It seems they entered exile in Puerto Rico, where Antonio was born after 1805. Additionally, a Haitian officer named Duverger apparently ordered assassins to fire at Dessalines the day he died in October 1806, perhaps in coordination with Pétion.[34] If these were actions by members of the Duvergé family, they may have had few options on where to settle, and they may have harbored long-running, more complicated discontentment against the Haitian state.

Nevertheless, the Dominican state has exalted Rosa Montas de Duvergé, nicknamed "Madame Bois," as a founding heroine. For her and her family's national service against Haiti she received a pension until she died in 1895.[35] Duvergé is now a revered name that appears in street names, neighborhood names, and names of towns throughout the Dominican Republic. This valorization mostly transpired after the general's publicized reinternment from Higüey to the Chapel of the Immortals at the Holy Cathedral of Santo Domingo in 1911, perhaps in part a pantheon for the hallowed defenders of Dominican Catholicism and Hispanic values who stood against supposed Haitian impurities. Over a century after his death, moving elegies from Joaquín Balaguer hallowed Duvergé as the heroic "Sentinel of the Frontier." In a book that Balaguer completed following the assassination of Rafael Trujillo, who had held a thirty-one-year dictatorship—and just as his own twenty-four intermittent years of autocratic dominance began—Balaguer claimed that the "Virgins of Galindo" case of 1822 had infuriated Duvergé, and that he had learned of supposed Haitian atrocities from his family.[36] Today, Dominican media project nationalist virtues upon the lives of Duvergé and Montas.[37]

Balaguer's statement was unintentionally ironic, given that both the Duvergé and Montas families had crossed that same border into Santo Domingo, were likely tied to Haitian revolutionary events, and probably stayed and supported Dominican separation due to expediencies other than hispanismo. Trujillo, who as a future dictator exuded anti-Haitian vitriol, was born in San Cristóbal just decades after Duson Montas had relocated there with his multiethnic family to serve as a Haitian magistrate. Many other Dominican-Haitian families with a blended cultural and racial lineage resided there as well. Trujillo's own maternal grandmother, who taught him to read at a young age, had darker skin than him and was from the Haitian Chevalier family, which had crossed the island during unification.[38] One prominent Haitian officer in this era, who this family likely would have known by reputation, if not personally, was none other than Pablo Alí. After five decades of prominence across Hispaniola, Alí died in Santo Domingo in the 1840s as an esteemed member of the cross-island cultural, political, and biological families he had fought for decades to create.[39]

The Boyer administration was right to appeal to Dominicans as siblings. The Age of Revolutions was but one chapter of a family history that still features Dominicans and Haitians perpetually converging into the yet unknowable future. Rebuffing these connections, Dominican elites often honed ideas of irreconcilable differences with regular affirmations of hispanismo, relics of Spanish culture, belief, language, and appearance prefigured as antithetical to Haiti. Broadening the cultural terms of Dominican inclusion along with anti-Haitianism expanded national belonging across social and racial strata to new participants in this narrative, augmenting a collective Dominican identity that often included a sense of superiority against their "Black" neighbors.

In the two decades following separation from Haiti, the two most dominant early Dominican heads of state, Pedro Santana and Buenaventura Báez, were both phenotypically men of color. White elite circles in the capital accepted them without racial scorn because of their mutual practice of hispanismo. Despite constant turnover in the presidency, the Dominican elite benefited from building a republic self-defined as a superior civilization to Haiti. Displacing racial angst against an external other, especially when Dominican ideologues depicted Haitians as assailants, provided a collective sense of identity despite drastic social, wealth, and regional differences. All the while, Dominican politicians knew that with any threat of re-enslavement Dominicans of color would rush to collaborate with Haiti.

The tropes of laziness, lax morals, and unorthodox religious beliefs and practices first honed during the Age of Revolutions now reemerged. Anti-Haitian markers of national pride coincided with an elite interest in selling off the new state to Atlantic powers with compatible anti-Haitian traditions, in hopes of gaining monetary or status rewards along with greater insulation from Haiti. Báez, the grandson of the famous writer and priest who stepped out on his vows, Antonio Sánchez Valverde, and son of a formerly enslaved *mulata*, schemed continually to cede the new Dominican Republic to the United States. His rival Pedro Santana returned Dominicans to Spanish colonization from 1861 to 1864. Around the time that his coterie sacrificed Dominican sovereignty in exchange for the supposed restoration of hispanismo, someone toppled the Tree of Liberty that Boyer's administration had planted in Santo Domingo in the 1820s. Nevertheless, when Haitians helped the majority of Dominicans once again eject Spain, the terms of familial solidarity briefly returned.[40]

BELIEFS OF NATIONAL BELONGING

As the preceding chapters show, at the end of the eighteenth century, Dominican elites convinced themselves that new "Black Codes" would resurrect their plantations, restoring production levels and profits. This financial boon would be driven by a severe form of slavery and by a growing slave trade. Associations of Blackness with criminality informed additional revolutionary-era racial conflations with radicalism, heresy, and violence. The Black Auxiliaries' piety reinforced a supposed process of racial redemption via sufficient religious profession. However, when many of these allies defected to the French Republic, elites added duplicity to their ideas of Blackness. These concepts hardened across the early nineteenth century. Dominican descriptors for skin tone are not binary, as in the United States, but instead fall along a spectrum. This spectrum derives from this past and in particular from a Spanish colonial schema. However, that did not preclude negative ideas about what it meant to be Black, a category that eventually tied directly to being Haitian, a cultural arc that requires scrutiny.

This past speaks to and has consequences for the present. In recent Dominican culture, Blackness still exists along a racial spectrum inherited from the Spanish colonial era. As a discrete ethnicity or racial solidarity Blackness is less evident than in some areas of the Americas. This diasporic divergence continues to evolve in dialogue with immigration and emigration. Along with its cultural associations with slavery, Africanness, and Haiti, being "Black" could also have unwanted connotations.[41] Interest in accepting a multiracial heritage (*mulataje* or *mestizaje*), rather than Blackness, coincided around the turn of the twentieth century with writings and commemorations compatible with distinctly Dominican notions of *hispanidad*. One iteration, espousing *indigenismo*, revalorized genealogy or Dominican culture as supposedly more indigenous, an assertion that does not withstand scrutiny.[42]

Trujillo promoted hispanismo, indigenismo, and Catholicism as state-sanctioned markers of Dominican belonging. Without necessarily needing to use overtly racist language, he crafted harshly anti-Haitian policy in a context of a supposed new Haitian invasion or cultural corruption. This was part of Trujillo's redoubled scrutiny of Dominicans of darker complexion and of African cultural symbols. The mass murder in 1937 of twenty thousand Haitians and Dominicans of Haitian ancestry, sometimes called the *perejil* (parsley) massacre, occurred most intensely along the same border near Dajabón that had served as perhaps the most important throughway for cultural politics linking the island in the revolutionary era.[43] This massacre followed hopes by Haitian diplomats earlier in 1937 that "fraternal union" would help resolve tensions along the border.[44]

Many Dominican writers have rejected colloquial uses of "Hayti," including by people such as Núñez de Cáceres. In another rejection of Haiti, they have adopted the lesser-known Taíno toponym of Quisqueya for the Dominican Republic.[45] Along with overt actions, tacit modes of cultural superiority and anti-Haitianism have also impeded the sort of race-based political organizing common among neighboring nations.[46]

To be clear, of course not all Dominicans endorse these narratives. This is neither simply a case of Dominicans denying their own African ancestry nor a narrative that all Dominicans unthinkingly accept. Descendants of San Lorenzo de Los Mina and the Maniel maroons did not forget that they had African lineages; nor did the formerly enslaved forget that their ancestors had been in bondage. Nor do the Congos de Villa Mella and the observers of Las 21 Divisiones today ignore the African origins of the cultures they celebrate. Some thoughtful Dominican thinkers, journalists, and activists have certainly critiqued anti-Haitianism, denounced past racial exclusions, and presented the 1822 unification and wider revolutionary era with nuance. Many Dominicans aided Haitian earthquake victims in 2010, some reviving familial language to save their "twin" from perishing.[47] Pushback against anti-Haitian or anti-Black ideas exists.[48]

The permeability of racial categories did not somehow end abruptly after three centuries of Spanish colonization. Rather than racial solidarity taking precedence in political organization, multiple social identifiers offer Dominicans flexible identifiers, sometimes to preempt discrimination. Alongside anti-Haitianism and the inheritance of the Spanish racial spectrum, these factors have subdued Blackness within Dominican identities. In the early twentieth century, some ideologues, including Emilio Rodríguez Demorizi, Manuel Arturo Peña Batlle, Manuel de Jesús Troncoso, and Joaquín Balaguer, depicted Dominican society as a Spanish civilization safeguarded by white and indigenous descendants against alleged African savagery in Haiti, ideas that bolstered *trujillismo*. Illustrating this complexity, Dominicans have had more heads of state with known African ancestry than any other country in the Americas. However, this group includes Trujillo.[49]

Balaguer, a top adviser to Trujillo, who continued this influential nationalist ideation as an authoritarian head of state, portrayed Haitians as animistic Africans of ill repute against whom Dominicans struggled to maintain their Spanish and Catholic culture. The 1937 massacre was a response, he said, to

decades of supposed pillage by Haitians, and corresponded to Spanish massacres by Ovando at Jaragua four centuries prior, supposedly both having
been good governance necessary for progress.[50] Indeed, some contemporary
Dominican commentators have proposed a false equivalence between the
1937 massacre and unification in 1822, suggesting that they involved similar
levels of Haitian aggression. This is willful distortion.[51]

Balaguer insisted that Dominicans were the "most Spanish" people of the
Americas and that Haitians were backward, diseased, uneducated, immoral,
and violent toward Dominicans.[52] He continued to elevate hispanismo
with the lighting of the Faro de Colón (the Columbus Lighthouse, which
contains a tomb that supposedly holds the remains of Columbus) to mark
the five-hundredth anniversary of Santo Domingo as a prominent example
of early white Spanish colonization. However, Columbus was unclear about
where he was when he arrived, and so it is similarly unclear whether the
bones contained in the tomb are his. This tomb and questions about its
contents serve as one symbol of the displays, debates, and doubts about
Spanish heritage in Dominican history and culture.[53]

During a speech in Spain in 1992, Balaguer heralded the arrival of
Columbus, which he said started the fusion of two cultures—Spanish and
Indigenous. In this he was imagining Dominicans without much African
heritage. Balaguer also scorned Haitians as a rapidly breeding race that
could pose a threat to civilized Dominicans by simply outnumbering them.
He insisted that Dominican culture had no African influences and that it
was incumbent upon the nation to deter Haiti, which he said had African
and negative traits.[54] These anti-Haitian comments, and likely voter fraud,
marred two very narrow presidential losses, in 1994 and 1996, for Balaguer
rival José Francisco Peña Gómez, who had been born to Haitian parents
who had perished in the 1937 massacre and was raised by a Dominican
family.[55]

Similar fearmongering is still all too common.[56] It is not just deceased
authoritarians who have reinforced this kind of dubiously historicized
hispanismo in recent decades.[57] A coterie of nationalist ideologues have
constructed disparate, emotive memories of Haitian aggression and racial
anxiety as part of an ideology and statecraft that persists to the present day.[58]
Though perhaps 85 percent or more of the Dominican populace has some
African ancestry, the incidence of anti-Black racism, including the association of Blackness with Haitianness or foreignness, is still prevalent. Today,
these ideas are mostly directed at immigration, whereas in the past it was
applied to culture, politics, religion, or revolution.[59]

Contradictorily, Haitians have long been tolerated or even invited as workers in sugar production, or, more recently, to work in the construction booms in the capital and in resort areas. However, when the winds of economic contraction or political exigency shift, they quickly become "invaders" and scapegoats for Dominican malaise.[60] Public polling has shown that anti-Haitianism is a key component of political opinion. Court decisions in the twenty-first century reversed legal rights for resident Haitians and even for Dominican citizens of Haitian descent. Hundreds of thousands of Dominicans have faced losing their citizenship. Many of these individuals are not eligible for Haitian citizenship and have never been to Haiti. They face statelessness because of the interpretations of their parents' legal statuses. International human rights courts and organizations have condemned these interpretations.

Echoing contentions of the past, the Constitutional Tribunal, the country's highest court, has argued that legal protections were not the only component to nationality, but rather, that the Dominican collective also involved historical, linguistic, racial, and geopolitical traits. In restrictive continuity, to gain and hold power, the recently dominant Partido de la Liberación Dominicana, in a dramatic shift from its more socially compassionate past, appointed the Balaguer protégé Carlos Manuel Troncoso, the grandson of Trujillo's puppet president, as secretary of state. He and similar advisers suggested policies toward Haiti and the international courts during protracted legal struggles through 2014.[61] Unfortunately, hemispheric hypocrisy has emboldened hardliners in their abdication of the duty to pursue humane policies.[62]

The media has rhetorically used labels such as "invaders" to mistakenly appropriate 1822 as the precedent for Haitian imposition.[63] Occasional fear-mongering also derives from the claim, without evidence, that international entities might force the Dominican Republic and Haiti to unify again.[64] So current is this issue that for the 2022 bicentenary of unification with Haiti some Dominican nationalists plan to publicly lament the "invasion" and urge vigilance from their compatriots against supposedly never-ending existential threats from Haiti.[65] Their rhetoric has revived nationalist emotions against a reunification that will almost certainly not happen.

Nevertheless, daily reciprocity remains for millions on the island. There are many important examples of proud Dominicans who do not diminish, denigrate, or distort a shared Haitian past. Tearing apart individual families cannot reverse the fact, affirmed generation after generation, that Dominicans and Haitians were, and are, siblings of soil.

Arguably, given the trajectory of historical and cultural forms, there is no being Dominican without Haitians. Dominican history, from the period of independence from Spain through the political strains of the present, carries hidden Haitian historical legacies that prevailing narratives elide.[66] Although a spectrum of anti-Haitian ideas prevails, certainly not all Dominicans espouse them. Quotidian family life, respect, collaboration, and labor solidarities between many Dominicans and Haitians endure. These ties survive, and, as in the revolutionary era, sometimes thrive.[67] Policy and discourse have selectively suppressed this popular agency, much as it has suppressed many of the memories of 1822.

Layers of antagonism and amicability, hostility and harmony, and conflict and cooperation have long entangled Dominicans and Haitians. However, selective memories of a supposedly hallowed Spanish past haunted by Haitian intrusions have justified the most pronounced moments of anti-Haitianism, such as the 1937 massacre, or, more recently, the revocations of citizenship. It is easy for Dominicans now to forget that in the late colonial era their elites coveted the wealth of the west, and that later, the popular classes coveted its liberties and civil society, given that now Dominicans hold themselves as uniquely developed on the island. Unlike what demagogues claim, Haitians will not destroy the Dominican Republic. Indeed, they have contributed much to the recent economic expansion. Fearmongering will not change the cohabitation of Hispaniola by Dominicans and Haitians. Rather, unavoidable commonalities—past, present, and future—abound to encourage peaceful coexistence.[68]

Dominican society was born into modernity as a fraternal twin to its Haitian neighbor. These societies have always been locked in cooperation and conflict, or admiration and admonishment. When in 1785 the priest and writer Antonio Sánchez Valverde hoped for a better future for the "*criollos* of Hayti,*" he could not have imagined that in 1791 revolution would convulse the island, nor that thirty years later Dominicans would demand independence by unification to become citizens of a very different Haiti than what he meant.[69] This choice of a shared trajectory with Haiti is a truth that dominant Dominican nationalism refuses to believe. Even imperfect acceptance of this fact could reform whitewashed memories and inform a compassionate policy.

Dominican identities formed in dialogue and in co-citizenship with revolutionary Haiti upon their inherited Taíno terrain. Many Dominicans have since accepted elitist scripts and litmus tests written from precedents in the Age of Revolutions and perpetuated through ongoing misrepresentations of that same era. These tropes obscure the fact that the Dominican and Haitian societies grew up together and have more in common today than simply old, generative frictions of *fraternité*. Two centuries ago, many Dominicans accepted that the island had "only one family." Perhaps a more empathetic and cooperative future requires recalling the origins of the supposed irreconcilable differences as well as the forgotten past of a kinship that defeated empires.[70]

ARCHIVES CONSULTED

LES ARCHIVES NATIONALES DE FRANCE (AN), PIERREFITTE-SUR-SEINE, PARIS

D/XXV/12, D/XXV/23

LES ARCHIVES NATIONALES D'HAÏTI, PORT-AU-PRINCE

Registre 6

ARCHIVO GENERAL DE INDIAS (AGI), SEVILLE, SPAIN

Estado (AGI-E): 1, 3, 4, 5A, 5B, 7, 11A, 11B, 12, 13, 14, 17, 61, 65, 86A, 89
Papeles de Cuba: 2014
Santo Domingo (AGI-SD): 925, 929, 956, 964, 966, 970, 998, 999, 1001, 1002, 1008, 1014, 1015, 1016, 1017, 1029, 1030, 1031, 1032, 1033, 1034, 1035, 1040, 1041, 1042, 1084, 1089, 1091, 1102, 1107, 1110, 1112
Ultramar (AGI-U): 94, 132, 163, 329

ARCHIVO GENERAL DE LA NACIÓN DOMINICANA (AGN), SANTO DOMINGO, DOMINICAN REPUBLIC

Archivo Real de Bayaguana (AGN-ARB): 1, 3, 4, 49
Archivo Real de Higüey (AGN-ARH): 2, 3, 4, 5, 10, 22, 37, 39
Archivo Real el Seibo: 1
Colección César Herrera (AGN-CCH): 5
Colección José Gabriel García (AGN-JGG): 4

ARCHIVO GENERAL DE SIMANCAS (AGS), SIMANCAS, SPAIN

Secretaría del Despacho de Guerra (AGS-SG): 6854, 6855, 6856, 6873, 7151, 7152, 7155, 7157, 7159, 7160, 7161, 7165, 7246

ARCHIVO GENERAL MILITAR DE MADRID (AGMM), MADRID

Colección General (AGMM-CG): Rollo 65 (5-4-10-5, 5-4-11-1, 5-4-11-2)
Ultramar (Santo Domingo) (AGMM-U): 5636, 5647, 5650, 5665

ARCHIVO HISTÓRICO DEL ARZOBISPADO DE SANTO DOMINGO (AHASD), SANTO DOMINGO, DOMINICAN REPUBLIC

Cabildo Eclesiástico (AHASD-CE)
Cartas Pastorales (AHASD-CP)

ARCHIVO HISTÓRICO NACIONAL DE ESPAÑA (AHN), MADRID

Consejos (AHN-C): 20762
Estado (AHN-E): 111, 130, 1626, 3373, 3391, 3394, 3395, 3407, 3566, 3906, 3918, 4239, 4247, 4829, 5240, 5245, 5620, 8030

ARCHIVO NACIONAL DE CUBA (ANC), HAVANA

Asuntos Políticos (ANC-AP): legajos 17, 18

ARCHIVUM APOSTOLICUM VATICANUM / ARCHIVUM SECRETUM VATICANUM (ASV), VATICAN CITY, HOLY SEE

Nunziatura di Madrid (ASV-NM): 196, 200, 202, 270

BIBLIOTECA NACIONAL DE ESPAÑA (BNE), MADRID

MSS/13983, MSS/20144

BIBLIOTHÈQUE HAÏTIENNE DES FRÈRES DE L'INSTRUCTION CHRÉTIENNE (BHFIC), PORT-AU-PRINCE, HAÏTI

B-1a23, B-2a40, B-2a44, B-2a44e, B-2b2a, H-5a7i

BIBLIOTHÈQUE NATIONALE DE FRANCE (BNF), PARIS

Département de la Réserve des Livres Rares (BNF-DRLR)

BRITISH LIBRARY (BL), LONDON

General Reference Collection (BL-GRC): 936.f.6.(27), f.686.(4)
Western Manuscripts (BL-WM): Add. Ms. 13976, Add. Ms. 38074, Add. Ms. 38376, Add. Ms. 39824, Add. Ms. 41266, Egerton 1793, Egerton 1794 vol. 1, Egerton 1794 vol. 2

DERBYSHIRE RECORDS OFFICE (DRO), MATLOCK, UNITED KINGDOM

D239

DEVON HERITAGE CENTRE (DHC), EXETER, UNITED KINGDOM

Henry Addington Papers: 152M
John Simcoe Papers: 1038M

JOHN CARTER BROWN LIBRARY, PROVIDENCE, RHODE ISLAND

Archive of Early American Images

LIBRARY OF CONGRESS, WASHINGTON, DC

Geography and Map Division: 1/80

LOUISIANA STATE UNIVERSITY, SPECIAL COLLECTIONS, BATON ROUGE

Jean-Baptiste Drouillard Papers: Mss. 2590

THE NATIONAL ARCHIVES (TNA), KEW, LONDON

Colonial Office (TNA-CO): 28/91, 28/92, 28/93, 37/49, 137/50, 137/93, 137/116, 137/117, 137/119, 137/126, 137/127, 137/128, 245/2, 245/3
War Office (TNA-WO): 1/58, 1/59, 1/61, 1/63, 1/65, 1/66, 1/75, 1/78, 1/80, 1/81, 1/92, 6/5

NATIONAL RECORDS OF SCOTLAND (NRS), EDINBURGH

Gifts and Deposits (NRS-GD): 193/2, 216/202, 216/203

NEWBERRY LIBRARY (NL), CHICAGO

Edward E. Ayer Manuscript Collection (NL-A): 1885, 1897

SCHOMBURG CENTER FOR RESEARCH IN BLACK CULTURE (SCRBC), NEW YORK

Haiti Miscellanea: MG 119
Kurt Fisher Collection: MG 23

SERVICE HISTORIQUE DE LA DÉFENSE (SHD), VINCENNES, PARIS

Guerre et Armée de Terre (SHD-GR)

TULANE UNIVERSITY, SPECIAL COLLECTIONS (TUSC), NEW ORLEANS, LOUISIANA

Rosemonde E. and Emile Kuntz Collection (TUSC-KC): Box 4, Folder 103, and Box 5, Folder 2

UNIVERSITY OF MELBOURNE ARCHIVES (UMA), SPECIAL COLLECTIONS, MELBOURNE, AUSTRALIA

Bright Family Jamaica Papers (UMA-BFP): B1/F1, B5/F1

UNIVERSITY OF TORONTO LIBRARIES, TORONTO, CANADA

E. J. Pratt Library Special Collections: Blake no. 996T
Thomas Fisher Rare Book Library, Special Collections: Mss. 09290

NOTES

INTRODUCTION

1. Damien Herrera, José Herrera, Camilo Suero, Francisco de los Santos, Manuel del Castillo, Luis de los Santos, Remigio Alcanter, and Andrés Herrera, to Jean-Pierre Boyer, San Juan de la Maguana, 10 January 1822 (G), José Román Hernández and Francisco López to Jean-Pierre Boyer, Neiba, 13 January 1822 (H), "Proclamation du Citoyen Manuel Machado au peuple de Samaná," 10 February 1822 (L3), Diego Polanco to General Magny, Monte Cristi, 15 November 1821 (B), in *Réunion de la partie de l'est a la république* (Port-au-Prince: L'Imprimerie du Gouvernement, 1830), 10, 18–19, 28–30. Thanks to Antony Keane-Dawes for alerting me to the *Réunion* pamphlet in the Papeles de Cuba *legajo* 2014 at the Archivo General de Indias (AGI). "Gazeta del Gobierno de Hayti Francés," Port-au-Prince, 23 December 1821, AGI, Santo Domingo (SD) 970, no. 33.

2. "1.a Parte, Expediente sobre la reclamación de la parte española . . . Santo Domingo," Felipe Castro to Primer Sec. del Despacho de Estado, 6 July 1824, Archivo Histórico Nacional de España (AHN), Estado (E) 3395, exp. 4. For the prerevolutionary familial context, see Robert D. Taber, "The Issue of Their Union: Family, Law, and Politics in Western Saint-Domingue, 1777 to 1789" (PhD diss., University of Florida, 2015); Doris Garraway, *The Libertine Colony: Creolization in the Early French Caribbean* (Durham, NC: Duke University Press, 2005).

3. Michel-Rolph Trouillot, *Silencing the Past: Power and the Production of History* (Boston: Beacon, 1995).

4. Jennifer L. Shoaff, "The Right to a Haitian Name and a Dominican Nationality: 'La Sentencia' (TC 168–13) and the Politics of Recognition and Belonging," *Journal of Haitian Studies* 22, no. 2 (Fall 2016): 58–82; Richard Lee Turits, "A World Destroyed, A Nation Imposed: The 1937 Haitian Massacre in the Dominican Republic," *Hispanic American Historical Review* 82, no. 3 (2002): 589–635.

5. Carlos Esteban Deive, *Vodú y magia* (Santo Domingo: Fundación Cultural Dominicana, 1979); Martha Ellen Davis, "Vodú of the Dominican Republic," *Afro-Hispanic Review* 26, no. 1 (Spring 2007): 75–90.

6. Marlene Daut, *Tropics of Haiti: Race and the Literary History of the Haitian Revolution in the Atlantic World, 1789–1865* (Liverpool: Liverpool University Press, 2015), 200–206.

7. Pedro L. San Miguel, *La isla imaginada: Historia, identidad y utopia en La Española* (Santo Domingo: La Trinitaria, 1997), chapters 1 and 2; Sibylle Fischer, *Modernity Disavowed: Haiti and the Cultures of Slavery in the Age of Revolution* (Durham, NC: Duke University Press, 2004), part 2; Jean-Marie Theodat, *Haïti République Dominicaine—Une Île pour deux, 1804–1916* (Paris: Éditions Karthala, 2003); April Mayes and Kiran Jayaram, eds., *Transnational Hispaniola: New Directions in Haitian and Dominican Studies* (Gainesville: University Press of Florida, 2018).

8. Trouillot, *Silencing the Past*, xix, 2–4, 13, 26–27, 48–60, 73, 96–107, 150–153. See also David Scott, *Conscripts of Modernity: The Tragedy of Colonial Enlightenment* (Durham, NC: Duke University Press, 2004).

9. Daut, *Tropics*, 1–5.

10. Gonzalo Fernández de Oviedo, *Historia general y natural de las Indias, Tercera Parte*, vol. 4 (Madrid: Real Academia de la Historia, 1855), 96.

11. Juan Bosch, *Composición social dominicana: Historia e interpretación* (Santo Domingo: Alfa and Omega, 1970), chapters 1–8; Frank Moya Pons, *The Dominican Republic: A National History* (Princeton, NJ: Markus Wiener, 1998), chapters 1–4. Juan José Ponce-Vázquez, *Islanders and Empire: Smuggling and Political Defiance in Hispaniola, 1580–1690* (New York: Cambridge University Press, 2020); Tzevetan Todorov, *The Conquest of America: The Question of the Other* (Norman: University of Oklahoma Press, 1999), 14–21, 105–107, 185–202.

12. Peter van der Veer, "Nationalism and Religion," in *Oxford Handbook of the History of Nationalism*, ed. John Breuilly (New York: Oxford University Press, 2013); Benedict Anderson, *Imagined Communities* (New York: Verso, 2006), 148.

13. Suzanne Desan, *The Family on Trial in Revolutionary France* (Berkeley: University of California Press, 2004), 1–3, 60–67; Sarah Pearsall, *Atlantic Families: Lives and Letters in the Later Eighteenth Century* (New York: Oxford University Press, 2008), 11–17, 56–69; Lynn Hunt, *The Family Romance of the French Revolution* (Berkeley: University of California Press, 1992); Julie Hardwick, Sarah Pearsall, and Karin Wulf, "Centering Families in Atlantic History," *William and Mary Quarterly* 70 (April 2013): 205–224; Jennifer L. Palmer, *Intimate Bonds: Family and Slavery in the French Atlantic* (Philadelphia: University of Pennsylvania Press, 2016); Scott Eastman, *Preaching Spanish Nationalism Across the Hispanic Atlantic, 1759–1823* (Baton Rouge: Louisiana State University Press, 2012), 3, 25–40, 63, 90–91, 122–147, 153, 160; Jean Casimir, *The Haitians: A Decolonial History* (Chapel Hill: University of North Carolina Press, 2020).

14. Catherine Bell, *Ritual Theory, Ritual Practice* (New York: Oxford University Press, 1992); Ara Norenzayan, *Big Gods: How Religion Transformed Cooperation and Conflict* (Princeton, NJ: Princeton University Press, 2013), chapters 4, 7, 8, 10; Michael Stausberg and Steven Engler, "Theories of Religion," and Jason C. Bivins, "Belief," in *Oxford Handbook on the Study of Religion*, ed. Michael Stausberg and Steven Engler (New York: Oxford University Press, 2016), 62–64, 495–509; Dominic Johnson, *God Is Watching You:*

How the Fear of God Makes Us Human (New York: Oxford University Press, 2015), 13–97, 177; Anne Stensvold, ed., *Blasphemies Compared* (New York: Routledge, 2020); Clifford Geertz, "Religion as a Cultural System," in *Interpretations of Culture* (New York: Basic Books, 1973), 87–125. For other compelling views on these themes, see Slavoj Žižek, *On Belief* (New York: Routledge, 2001); Sheldon Solomon, Jeff Greenberg, and Thomas A. Pyszczynski, *The Worm at the Core: On the Role of Death in Life* (New York: Random House, 2015), vii–14, 63–126; Randall Studstill, "Eliade, Phenomenology, and the Sacred," *Religious Studies* 36, no. 2 (June 2000): 177–194; Albert Camus, *Le Mythe de Sisyphe* (Paris: Éditions Gallimard, 1941).

15. Antonio Sánchez Valverde, *Idea del valor de la isla Española* (Madrid: Pedro Marín, 1785), vi, 89, 138, 145–146; "Relación . . . Antonio Sánchez Valverde," 8 March 1763, AGI-SD 1107; "Antonio Sánchez Valverde . . . ," 1785, AGI-SD 1002. See also Oviedo, *Historia general*, 4:96; Roberto Cassá, *Antonio Sánchez Valverde: intelectual del criollismo* (Santo Domingo: Tobogan, 2000); David Howard, *Coloring the Nation: Race and Ethnicity in the Dominican Republic* (Boulder: Lynne Rienner, 2001), 46.

16. Sánchez Valverde, *Idea*, 9, 72, 109, 123–152. For comparisons in Saint-Domingue, see John Garrigus, *Before Haiti: Race and Citizenship in French Saint-Domingue* (New York: Palgrave, 2006), 8–11, 108, 144–151.

17. Spanish sources often inaccurately use *ingleses* and *británicos* interchangeably. Here "British" appears as the broader demonym.

18. Ashli White, *Encountering Revolution: Haiti and the Making of the Early Republic* (Baltimore: Johns Hopkins University Press, 2010).

19. Bianca Premo, *Children of the Father King: Youth, Authority, and Legal Minority in Colonial Lima* (Chapel Hill: University of North Carolina Press, 2006), 4, 79–87, 108, 137.

20. Julia Gaffield, "Race and the Haitian Constitution of 1805," Kislak Center for Special Collections, Rare Books, and Manuscripts, University of Pennsylvania (December 2015).

21. Colonel Ysnardi (aide to the president of Haiti) to Pablo Alí, San Juan de la Maguana, 9 November 1820, AGI-SD 970, no. 25.

22. New findings on Alí appear throughout. For context, see Michael A. Gomez, *Black Crescent: The Experience and Legacy of African Muslims in the Americas* (New York: Cambridge University Press, 2005), chapter 2; James Sweet, "Mistaken Identities? Olaudah Equiano, Domingos Álvares, and the Methodological Challenges of Studying the African Diaspora," *American Historical Review* 114, no. 2 (April 2009): 279–306; Maria del Mar Logroño Narbona, Paulo G. Pinto, and John Tofik Karam, eds., *Crescent over Another Horizon: Islam in Latin America, the Caribbean, and Latino USA* (Austin: University of Texas Press, 2015).

23. Stephen Jay Gould, *The Panda's Thumb* (New York: Norton, 1980), 151.

24. Howard, *Coloring the Nation*; Andrés L. Mateo, *Mito y cultura en la era de Trujillo* (Santo Domingo: La Trinitaria, 1993), 12, 25, 141; Moya Pons, *Dominican Republic*, 120–124; James Sidbury, *Becoming African in America: Race and Nation in the Early Black Atlantic* (New York: Oxford University Press, 2007).

25. Gustavo Mejía Ricart, *El Estado Independiente del Haiti Español* (Santiago: Editorial El Diario, 1938); Manuel Jesús Troncoso, *La ocupación de Santo Domingo por Haiti* (Santo Domingo: La Nación, 1942); Emilio Rodríguez Demorizi, *Santo Domingo y la Gran Colombia: Bolívar y Núñez de Cáceres* (Santo Domingo: Editora del Caribe, 1971); Victor Garrido, *Antecedentes de la Invasión Haitiana de 1822* (Santo Domingo: Impresora Arte y Cine, 1972).

26. Lara Putnam, "To Study the Fragments/Whole: Microhistory and the Atlantic World," *Journal of Social History* 39, no. 3 (Spring 2006): 615–630; João José Reis, Flávio dos Santos Gomes, and Marcus Joaquim de Carvalho, *O alufá Rufino: Tráfico, escravidão e liberdade no Atlântico negro (1822–1853)* (São Paulo: Companhia das Letras, 2010).

27. Ada Ferrer, *Freedom's Mirror: Cuba and Haiti in the Age of Revolution* (New York: Cambridge University Press, 2014); Aline Helg, *Liberty and Equality in Caribbean Colombia, 1770–1835* (Chapel Hill: University of North Carolina Press, 2005); Matt D. Childs, *The 1812 Aponte Rebellion in Cuba and the Struggle Against Atlantic Slavery* (Chapel Hill: University of North Carolina Press, 2006); Marixa Lasso, *Myths of Harmony: Race and Republicanism During the Age of Revolution, Colombia, 1795–1831* (Pittsburgh: University of Pittsburgh Press, 2007); Ernesto Bassi, *An Aqueous Territory: Sailor Geographies and New Granada's Transimperial Greater Caribbean World* (Durham, NC: Duke University Press, 2016); Marcela Echeverri, *Indian and Slave Royalists in the Age of Revolution: Reform, Revolution, and Royalism in the Northern Andes* (New York: Cambridge University Press, 2016), 5–6, 172–173; Cristina Soriano, *Tides of Revolution: Information, Insurgencies, and the Crisis of Colonial Rule in Venezuela* (Albuquerque: University of New Mexico Press, 2018); Alejandro E. Gómez, *Le spectre de la Révolution Noire: L'impact de la Révolution Haïtienne dans le monde atlantique* (Rennes, France: Presses Universitaires de Rennes, 2013).

28. Eric Van Young, *The Other Rebellion: Popular Violence, Ideology, and the Mexican Struggle for Independence, 1810–1821* (Stanford, CA: Stanford University Press, 2001), chapter 1.

29. Eastman, *Preaching*. For work on this promising direction, see Kate Ramsey, *The Spirits and the Law: Vodou and Power in Haiti* (Chicago: University of Chicago Press, 2012); Terry Rey, *The Priest and the Prophetess: Abbé Ouvière, Romaine Rivière, and the Revolutionary Atlantic World* (New York: Oxford University Press, 2017); Erica R. Johnson, *Philanthropy and Race in the Haitian Revolution* (New York: Palgrave, 2018).

30. C. L. R. James, *The Black Jacobins: Toussaint L'Ouverture and the San Domingo Revolution* (London: Secker and Warburg, 1938); David Geggus, *Slavery, War, and Revolution: The British Occupation of Saint Domingue, 1793–1798* (Oxford: Clarendon Press, 1982); David Geggus, *Haitian Revolutionary Studies* (Bloomington: Indiana University Press, 2002); David Geggus, ed., *The Impact of the Haitian Revolution in the Atlantic World* (Columbia: University of South Carolina Press, 2001); David Geggus and Norman Fiering, eds., *The World of the Haitian Revolution* (Bloomington: Indiana University Press, 2009); Carolyn Fick, *The Making of Haiti: The Saint Domingue Revolution from Below* (Knoxville: University of Tennessee Press, 1990); Garrigus, *Before Haiti*; Jane Landers, *Atlantic Creoles in the Age of Revolutions* (Cambridge, MA: Harvard University Press, 2010), chapter 2; John K. Thornton, "'I Am the Subject of the King of Congo': African

Political Ideology and the Haitian Revolution," *Journal of World History* 4, no. 2 (1993): 181–214; Laurent Dubois, *A Colony of Citizens: Revolution and Slave Emancipation in the French Caribbean, 1787–1804* (Chapel Hill: University of North Carolina Press, 2004); Jeremy Popkin, *You Are All Free: The Haitian Revolution and the Abolition of Slavery* (New York: Cambridge University Press, 2010).

31. Julia Gaffield, *Haitian Connections in the Atlantic World: Recognition After Revolution* (Chapel Hill: University of North Carolina Press, 2015); Julia Gaffield, "The Racialization of International Law After the Haitian Revolution: The Holy See and National Sovereignty," *American Historical Review* 125, no. 3 (June 2020): 841–868; Johnhenry Gonzalez, *Maroon Nation: A History of Revolutionary Haiti* (New Haven, CT: Yale University Press, 2019); Paul Cheney, *Cul de Sac: Patrimony, Capitalism, and Slavery in French Saint-Domingue* (Chicago: University of Chicago Press, 2017); Philippe Girard, *Toussaint Louverture: A Revolutionary Life* (New York: Basic Books, 2016); Sudhir Hazareesingh, *Black Spartacus: The Epic Life of Toussaint Louverture* (New York: Farrar, Straus, and Giroux, 2020); Philippe Girard, *The Slaves Who Defeated Napoléon: Toussaint Louverture and the Haitian War of Independence, 1801–1804* (Tuscaloosa: University of Alabama Press, 2011); Benjamin Hebblethwaite, *A Transatlantic History of Haitian Vodou* (Jackson: University Press of Mississippi, 2021), 3–44; Patrick Bellegarde-Smith and Claudine Michel, *Haitian Vodou: Spirit, Myth, and Reality* (Bloomington: Indiana University Press, 2006).

32. Christina Mobley, "The Kongolese Atlantic: Central African Slavery and Culture from Mayombe to Haiti" (PhD diss., Duke University, 2015); Crystal Eddins, "African Diaspora Collective Action: Rituals, Runaways, and the Haitian Revolution" (PhD diss., Michigan State University, 2017); Jesús Ruiz, "Subjects of the King: Royalism and the Origins of the Haitian Revolution, 1763–1806" (PhD diss., Tulane University, 2020); Erin Zavitz, "Revolutionary Memories: Celebrating and Commemorating the Haitian Revolution" (PhD diss., University of Florida, 2015); Winter Schneider, "'Free of Everything Save Independence': Property, Personhood and the Archive in Nineteenth-Century Haiti" (PhD diss., University of California–Los Angeles, 2018); Taber, "Issue of Their Union."

33. Among others cited throughout, see Emilio Cordero Michel, *La Revolución Haitiana y Santo Domingo* (Santo Domingo: Editorial Nacional, 1968); Frank Moya Pons, *La dominación haitiana, 1822–1844* (Santiago: UCMM, 1978). For recent scholarship, see Maria Cecilia Ulrickson, "Cultivators, Domestics, and Slaves: Slavery in Santo Domingo," *The Americas* 76 (April 2019): 241–266; José Luis Belmonte Postigo, "Las dos caras de una misma moneda: Reformismo y esclavitud en Santo Domingo a fines del periodo colonial," *Revista de Indias* 74, no. 261 (2014): 453–482; Antonio Pinto Tortosa, "Una colonia en la encrucijada: Santo Domingo, entre la Revolución Haitiana y la Reconquista Española, 1791–1809" (PhD diss., Universidad Complutense de Madrid, 2011); Graham Nessler, *An Islandwide Struggle for Freedom: Revolution, Emancipation, and Reenslavement on Hispaniola, 1789–1809* (Chapel Hill: University of North Carolina Press, 2016); César A. Cuevas Pérez and Guillermo A. Díaz Bidó, *Presencia francesa en Santo Domingo: 1802–1809* (Santo Domingo: Editora Nacional, 2008); Fernando Picó, *One Frenchman, Four Revolutions: General Ferrand and the Peoples of the Caribbean* (Princeton, NJ: Markus Wiener,

2011); Anne Eller, "'All Would Be Equal in the Effort': Santo Domingo's 'Italian Revolution,' Independence, and Haiti, 1809–1822," *Journal of Early American History* 1 (2011): 105–141; Quisqueya Lora, "El sonido de la libertad: 30 años de agitaciones y conspiraciones en Santo Domingo, 1791–1821," *Clío* 80, no. 182 (July–December 2011): 109–140; Sara Johnson, "The Integration of Hispaniola: A Reappraisal of Haitian-Dominican Relations in the Nineteenth and Twentieth Centuries," *Journal of Haitian Studies* 8, no. 2 (Fall 2002): 4–29; Antony Keane-Dawes, "A Divisive Community: Race, Nation, and Loyalty in Santo Domingo, 1822–1844" (PhD diss., University of South Carolina, 2018); Andrew Walker, "Strains of Unity: Emancipation, Property, and the Post-Revolutionary State in Haitian Santo Domingo, 1822–1844" (PhD diss., University of Michigan, 2018); Fidel J. Tavárez, "The Contested State: Political Discourse During the Independence of the Dominican Republic, 1844," in Mayes and Jayaram, *Transnational Hispaniola*.

34. José Alcántara Almánzar, *Estudios de poesía dominicana* (Santo Domingo: Editora Alfa y Omega, 1979); Anne Eller, *We Dream Together: Dominican Independence, Haiti, and the Fight for Caribbean Freedom* (Durham, NC: Duke University Press, 2016), epilogue; Lorgia García Peña, *The Borders of Dominicanidad: Race, Nation, and Archives of Contradiction* (Durham, NC: Duke University Press, 2016), 156–160; Alaí Reyes Santos, *Our Caribbean Kin: Race and Nation in the Neoliberal Antilles* (New Brunswick, NJ: Rutgers University Press, 2015), 105–144. For other appearances of familial analysis, see Eugenio Matibag, *Haitian-Dominican Counterpoint: Nation, State, and Race on Hispaniola* (New York: Palgrave, 2003), 1, 179; Gustavo de Peña, "The Siblings of Hispaniola: Political Union and Separation of Haiti and Santo Domingo, 1822–1844" (master's thesis, Vanderbilt University, 2011); Maria Cristina Fumagalli, *On the Edge: Writing the Border Between Haiti and the Dominican Republic* (Liverpool: Liverpool University Press, 2015), 272, 318–320; Bruce J. Calder, *Impact of Intervention: The Dominican Republic During the U.S. Occupation of 1916–1924* (Austin: University of Texas Press, 1984).

35. García Peña, *Borders*, 2–10, 163, 191; Ada Ferrer, *Insurgent Cuba: Race, Nation, and Revolution, 1868–1898* (Chapel Hill: University of North Carolina Press, 1999), 10–12; Silvio Torres-Saillant, *Introduction to Dominican Blackness* (New York: Dominican Studies Institute, City College of New York, 1999); Ernesto Ságas, *Race and Politics in the Dominican Republic* (Gainesville: University Press of Florida, 2000); Raj Chetty and Amaury Rodríguez, "Introduction," *The Black Scholar* 45, no. 2 (2015): 1–9; Maria Cecilia Ulrickson, "'Esclavos que fueron' in Santo Domingo, 1768–1844" (PhD diss., University of Notre Dame, 2018), 14–16; Ann Twinam, *Purchasing Whiteness: Pardos, Mulattos, and the Quest for Social Mobility in the Spanish Indies* (Stanford, CA: Stanford University Press, 2015), 42–55; Milagros Ricourt, *The Dominican Racial Imaginary: Surveying the Landscape of Race and Nation in Hispaniola* (New Brunswick, NJ: Rutgers University Press, 2016), 15–16, 135–154; April Mayes, *Mulatto Republic: Class, Race, and Dominican National Identity* (Gainesville: University Press of Florida).

36. Jeremy Adelman, *Sovereignty and Revolution in the Iberian Atlantic* (Princeton, NJ: Princeton University Press, 2009); Brian R. Hamnett, "Process and Pattern: A Re-Examination of the Ibero-American Independence Movements, 1808–1826," *Journal of Latin American Studies* 29, no. 2 (1997): 279–328; Victor Uribe-Uran, "Enigma of Latin

American Independence: Analyses of the Last Ten Years," *Latin American Research Review* 32, no. 1 (1997): 236–255.

37. John P. Walsh, *Free and French in the Caribbean: Toussaint Louverture, Aimé Césaire, and Narratives of Loyal Opposition* (Bloomington: Indiana University Press, 2013); Philip Kaisary, *The Haitian Revolution in the Literary Imagination: Radical Horizons, Conservative Constraints* (Charlottesville: University of Virginia Press, 2014).

38. Gabriel Paquette, "The Dissolution of the Spanish Atlantic Monarchy," *Historical Journal* 52, no. 1 (2009): 175–212; José Carlos Chiaramonte, "The Principle of Consent in Latin and Anglo-American Independence," *Journal of Latin American Studies* 36, no. 3 (August 2004): 563–586.

CHAPTER 1: RACE AND PLACE IN EIGHTEENTH-CENTURY HISPANIOLA

1. Antonio Sánchez Valverde, *Idea del valor de la isla Española* (Madrid: Pedro Marín, 1785), ii–iii, 51–55, 115–117, 138–154. See also Neal D. Polhemus, "A Culture of Commodification: Hemispheric and Intercolonial Migrations in the Trans-Atlantic Slave Trade, 1660–1807" (PhD diss., University of South Carolina, 2016), 159–160, 189, and chapter 4.

2. Massimo Livi-Bacci, "Return to Hispaniola: Reassessing a Demographic Catastrophe," *Hispanic American Historical Review* 83, no. 1 (February 2003): 1–50; Lawrence A. Clayton, *Bartolomé de las Casas* (New York: Cambridge University Press, 2012); Frank Moya Pons, *The Dominican Republic: A National History* (Princeton, NJ: Markus Wiener, 1998), 29–37; Donald R. Hopkins, *The Greatest Killer: Smallpox in History* (Chicago: University of Chicago Press, 2002), 204–206.

3. Genaro Rodríguez Morel, "The Sugar Economy of Española in the Sixteenth Century," in *Tropical Babylons: Sugar and the Making of the Atlantic World, 1450–1680*, ed. Stuart Schwartz (Chapel Hill: University of North Carolina Press, 2004), 85–114. For regional contexts of race and space, see Angela Sutton and Charlton W. Yingling, "Projections of Desire and Design in Early Modern Caribbean Maps," *Historical Journal* 63, no. 4 (2020): 789–810.

4. Médéric Louis Elie Moreau de Saint-Méry, *Description topographique et politique de la partie espagnole de l'isle Saint-Domingue*, vols. 1–2 (Philadelphia: author, 1796–1798); Sánchez Valverde, *Idea*. Both authors drew heavily from the sixteenth-century chronicler Oviedo.

5. Juan José Ponce-Vázquez, *Islanders and Empire: Smuggling and Political Defiance in Hispaniola, 1580–1690* (New York: Cambridge University Press, 2020).

6. Marc Eagle, "Restoring Spanish Hispaniola, the First of the Indies: Local Advocacy and Transatlantic Arbitrismo in the Late Seventeenth Century," *Colonial Latin American Review* 23, no. 3 (2014): 384–412; Trevor Burnard and John Garrigus, *The Plantation Machine: Atlantic Capitalism in French Saint-Domingue and British Jamaica* (Philadelphia: University of Pennsylvania Press, 2016), chapters 1–2, 7, 9–10; Raymundo González,

"Campesinos y sociedad colonial en el siglo XVIII dominicano," *Estudios Sociales* 25, no. 87 (1992): 15–28.

7. About 6,900 cattle went to Cap-Français alone. In 29 November 1787, AHN, Consejos (C) 20762; Moya Pons, *Dominican Republic*, 73–89. See also John Garrigus, "'Like an Epidemic One Could Only Stop with the Most Violent Remedies': African Poisons Versus Livestock Disease in Saint Domingue, 1750–88," *William and Mary Quarterly* 78, no. 4 (October 2021): 617–652; Nathaniel Millett, "Borderlands in the Atlantic World," *Atlantic Studies* 10, no. 2 (April 2013): 268–295.

8. Francisco Arango to Marqués de Someruelos, Havana, 17 June 1803, AHN-E 3395, exp. 1. Arango said that in 1788 Saint-Domingue had 38,000 to 40,000 white people, 28,000 free people of color, and 452,000 enslaved people. He reported plantation numbers as follows: 793 sugar, 3,107 coffee, 3,150 indigo, and 799 cotton. See also John Garrigus, *Before Haiti: Race and Citizenship in French Saint-Domingue* (New York: Palgrave, 2006), 172–174; Trans-Atlantic Slave Trade Database, www.slavevoyages.org /voyage/database, accessed 16 February 2014.

9. Sánchez Valverde, *Idea*, 117–150; David Geggus, *Haitian Revolutionary Studies* (Bloomington: Indiana University Press, 2002), 5, 69–74; Moya Pons, *Dominican Republic*, 89.

10. David Geggus, "The Slaves and Free People of Color of Cap-Français," in *The Black Urban Atlantic in the Age of the Slave Trade*, ed. Jorge Cañizares Esguerra, Matt D. Childs, and James Sidbury (Philadelphia: University of Pennsylvania Press, 2013), 101–121; Geggus, *Haitian Revolutionary Studies*, 5–11; James E. McClellan III, *Colonialism and Science: Saint-Domingue in the Old Regime* (Chicago: University of Chicago Press, 2010), 63–65; Alan Dye, *Cuban Sugar in the Age of Mass Production: Technology and the Economics of the Sugar Central, 1899–1929* (Stanford, CA: Stanford University Press, 1998), 25–27; Laurent Dubois, *Avengers of the New World: The Story of the Haitian Revolution* (Cambridge, MA: Belknap Press of Harvard University Press, 2004), 20–22; Gelabert, "Documentos referentes a la isla de Cuba," Biblioteca Nacional de España (BNE), MSS/20144.

11. "Testimonio de los informes pedidos . . . a los hacendados, y demas sugeros de inspeccion de la ciudad de Santo Domingo para la formacion del Carolino Código Negro, con arreglo al extraordinario celebrado por los señores . . . ," José de Gálvez to the Governor of Santo Domingo, Madrid, 23 December 1783, 7 February and 7 March 1784, AGI-SD 1034, 1–2v.

12. Malick Ghachem, *The Old Regime and the Haitian Revolution* (New York: Cambridge University Press, 2012), 7–19, 29–31, 55–67, 221, 280; Erica R. Johnson, *Philanthropy and Race in the Haitian Revolution* (New York: Palgrave, 2018), 24–27; Carolyn Fick, *The Making of Haiti: The Saint Domingue Revolution from Below* (Knoxville: University of Tennessee Press, 1990), 32–39. For contemporary conversations regarding land usage and provisions for the enslaved, see David Duncomb to Lowbridge Bright, Kingston, Jamaica, 28 December 1786, BF5/F1, 80/75, Box 20, Unit 35, Bright Family Jamaica Papers (BFP), University of Melbourne Archives (UMA).

13. Javier Malagón Barceló, *Código negro carolino (1784)* (Santo Domingo: Editora Taller, 1974); Reyes Fernández Durán, *La corona española y el tráfico de negros: Del monopo-*

lio al libre comercio (Madrid: Ecobook/Editorial del Economista, 2011), 342–343; José F. Buscaglia-Salgado, *Undoing Empire: Race and Nation in the Mulatto Caribbean* (Minneapolis: University of Minnesota Press, 2003), 185–186.

14. "Testimonio . . . ," Audiencia de Santo Domingo, 6–7 March 1784, AGI-SD 1034, 1v–4v.

15. "Testimonio . . . ," Antonio Dávila Coca, 10 March 1784, AGI-SD 1034, 6–8; "Testimonio . . . ," Antonio Mañon, 11 March 1784, AGI-SD 1034, 8–10; Joaquín García to Secretaría del Despacho de Guerra, Santo Domingo, 20 January 1790, Archivo General de Simancas (AGS), Secretaría del Despacho de Guerra (SG), 7155; "Testimonio . . . ," Andrés Heredia, 20 March 1784, AGI-SD 1034, 50–55v; "Testimonio . . . ," Ignacio Caro, 12 March 1784, AGI-SD 1034, 10–16v; "Testimonio . . . ," Francisco Cabral, 19 March 1784, AGI-SD 1034, 43v–47; "Testimonio . . . ," Francisco de Tapia, 16 March 1784, AGI-SD 1034, 33–35v; "Testimonio . . . ," José Núñez, 18 March 1784, AGI-SD 1034, 41–43. Some suggest this was the José Núñez de Cáceres who later became famous as a writer and politician. The writer, however, was born in 1772, and it is unlikely that he testified at around the age of twelve.

16. "Testimonio . . . ," Ignacio Caro, 12 March 1784, AGI-SD 1034, 10–16v.

17. "Testimonio . . . ," Antonio Dávila Coca, 10 March 1784, AGI-SD 1034, 6–8; "Testimonio . . . ," Antonio Mañon, 11 March 1784, AGI-SD 1034, 8–10. For regional comparisons, see Lisa Voigt, *Spectacular Wealth: The Festivals of Colonial South American Mining Towns* (Austin: University of Texas Press, 2016), chapters 3 and 4.

18. "Testimonio . . . ," José Núñez and Francisco Cabral, 19 March 1784, AGI-SD 1034, 41–47.

19. Carlos Esteban Deive, *La esclavitud del negro en Santo Domingo, 1492–1844*, vol. 2 (Santo Domingo: Museo del Hombre Dominicano, 1980), 391–393; Charles Gilpin, *The Gospel in Central America: Containing a Sketch of the Country* (London: Gilpin, 1850), 296–297; David Turnbull, *Travels in the West: Cuba, with Notices of Porto Rico, and the Slave Trade* (London: Longman, Orme, Brown, Green, and Longman, 1840), 25.

20. "Testimonio . . . ," Ignacio Caro, 12 March 1784, AGI-SD 1034, 10–16v.

21. Sue Peabody, "A Dangerous Zeal: Catholic Missions to Slaves in the French Antilles, 1635–1800," *French Historical Studies* 25, no. 1 (Winter 2002): 53–90; Johnson, *Philanthropy*, 26–37; Sue Peabody and Keila Grinberg, *Slavery, Freedom, and the Law in the Atlantic World: A Brief History with Documents* (New York: Bedford, 2007), 23–26; Garrigus, *Before Haiti*, 10–13; Leslie Desmangles, *Face of the Gods: Vodou and Roman Catholicism in Haiti* (Chapel Hill: University of North Carolina Press, 1992), 23–38.

22. Carlos Esteban Deive, *Vodú y magia* (Santo Domingo: Fundación Cultural Dominicana, 1979).

23. Alan Watson, *Slave Law in the Americas* (Athens: University of Georgia Press, 1989), 52–60; Matt D. Childs and Manuel Barcia, "Cuba," in *Oxford Handbook of Slavery in the Americas*, ed. Robert L. Paquette and Mark M. Smith (New York: Oxford University Press, 2010), 94–96. Self-purchase was common in Santo Domingo, though perhaps not as formalized as in Cuba. See also Deive, *Esclavitud*, 2:409–410. For other processes in Saint-Domingue, see Robert D. Taber, "The Issue of Their Union: Family, Law, and

Politics in Western Saint-Domingue, 1777 to 1789" (PhD diss., University of Florida, 2015), 116–132.

24. "Testimonio . . . ," Antonio Mañon, 11 March 1784, AGI-SD 1034, 8–10.

25. "Testimonio . . . ," Andrés Heredia, 20 March 1784, AGI-SD 1034, 50–55v.

26. "Testimonio . . . ," Ignacio Caro, 12 March 1784, AGI-SD 1034, 10–16v.

27. Sánchez Valverde, *Idea*, 152–153.

28. José Luis Cortes López, *Los orígenes de la esclavitud negra en España* (Salamanca: Ediciones Universidad de Salamanca, 1986); Alejandro de la Fuente, "Slave Law and Claims-Making in Cuba: The Tannenbaum Debate Revisited," *Law and History Review* 22, no. 2 (Summer 2004): 339–369; Matt D. Childs, *The 1812 Aponte Rebellion in Cuba and the Struggle Against Atlantic Slavery* (Chapel Hill: University of North Carolina Press, 2006), 64–66.

29. "Testimonio . . . ," Andrés Heredia, 20 March 1784, AGI-SD 1034, 50–55v; Ana Hontanilla, "Sentiment and the Law: Inventing the Category of the Wretched Slave in the Real Audiencia of Santo Domingo, 1783–1812," *Eighteenth-Century Studies* 48, no. 2 (2015): 181–200.

30. "Testimonio . . . ," Antonio Dávila Coca, 10 March 1784, AGI-SD 1034, 6–8; "Testimonio . . . ," Francisco Cabral, 19 March 1784, AGI-SD 1034, 43v–47; "Testimonio . . . ," Ignacio Caro, 12 March 1784, AGI-SD 1034, 10–16v; "Testimonio . . . ," Francisco de Tapia, 16 March 1784, AGI-SD 1034, 33–35v; "Testimonio . . . ," Andrés Heredia, 20 March 1784, AGI-SD 1034, 50–55v; "Testimonio . . . ," Antonio Mañon, 11 March 1784, AGI-SD 1034, 8–10. See also Richard Lee Turits, *Foundations of Despotism: Peasants, the Trujillo Regime, and Modernity in the Dominican Republic* (Stanford, CA: Stanford University Press, 2003), 25–51; Johnhenry Gonzalez, *Maroon Nation: A History of Revolutionary Haiti* (New Haven, CT: Yale University Press, 2019); Karol K. Weaver, *Medical Revolutionaries: The Enslaved Healers of Eighteenth-Century Saint-Domingue* (Urbana: University of Illinois Press, 2006).

31. "Testimonio . . . ," Joaquín García, 16 March 1784, AGI-SD 1034, 17–32v; Joaquín García, 16 March 1784, British Library (BL), Western Manuscripts (WM), Add. Ms. 13976, ff. 8–14. See also Fernando Carrera Montero, *Las complejas relaciones de España con La Española: El Caribe hispano frente a Santo Domingo y Saint Domingue, 1789–1803* (Santo Domingo: Fundación García Arévalo, 2004), 24–26.

32. "Extracto del Código Negro Carolino," Audiencia de Santo Domingo, Santo Domingo, 14 March 1785, AGI-E 7, no. 3; Lluís Sala Molins, "Slavery in Law Codes," in *From Chains to Bonds: The Slave Trade Revisited* (New York: Berghahn, 2001), 209–215; Watson, *Slave Law*, 57–61.

33. Consejo de Indias to Joaquín García, Aranjuez, 29 May 1788, AGI-SD 1102, no. 24; Marqués de Bajamar to Consejo de Indias, San Lorenzo, 27 September 1791, AGI-SD 1102; Arzobispo Isidoro, Primer Quaderno, Santo Domingo, 20 September 1787; Fernando Portillo to José Urízar, Neiba, 6 June 1794, AGI-SD 1014; Fernando Portillo to Eugenio Llaguno y Amirola, Santo Domingo, 20 October 1794, AGI-SD 1031. See also Christine Rivas, "The Spanish Colonial Military: Santo Domingo, 1701–1779," *The Americas* 60, no. 2 (October 2003): 249–272; Carlos Larrazábal Blanco, *Los negros*

y la esclavitud en Santo Domingo (Santo Domingo: Postigo, 1975), 135–139; Richard L. Kagan, *Urban Images of the Hispanic World, 1493–1793* (New Haven, CT: Yale University Press, 2000), 19–44; J. H. Elliott, *Empires of the Atlantic World: Britain and Spain in America, 1492–1830* (New Haven, CT: Yale University Press, 2006), 73–75; David J. Weber, *Bárbaros: Spaniards and Their Savages in the Age of Enlightenment* (New Haven, CT: Yale University Press, 2005).

34. Deive, *Esclavitud*, 2:532–543; Manuel Barcia, *Seeds of Insurrection: Domination and Resistance on Western Cuban Plantations, 1808–1848* (Baton Rouge: Louisiana State University Press, 2008), 129–130; Robin Law, "Ethnicities of Enslaved Africans in the Diaspora: On the Meanings of 'Mina' (Again)," *History in Africa* 32 (2005): 247–268; Kwasi Konadu, *The Akan Diaspora in the Americas* (New York: Oxford University Press, 2010), 3–26.

35. "Ordenanzas del Cabildo," Cabildo de Santo Domingo, 5 April 1786, Santo Domingo, Archivo General de la Nación Dominicana (AGN), Archivo Real de Higüey (ARH), 2, leg. 10R, exp. 89, ff. 1–19v.

36. Carlos Andújar, *The African Presence in Santo Domingo*, trans. Rosa María Andújar (East Lansing: Michigan State University Press, 2012); Marc Eagle, "Chasing the Avença: An Investigation of Illicit Slave Trading in Santo Domingo at the End of the Portuguese Asiento Period," *Slavery and Abolition* 35, no. 1 (2014): 99–120; Fick, *Making of Haiti*, 49–57; Carlos Esteban Deive, *Los guerrilleros negros: Esclavos fugitivos y cimarrones en Santo Domingo* (Santo Domingo: Fundación Cultural Dominicana, 1997), 7–75; Trans-Atlantic Slave Trade Database, www.slavevoyages.org/voyage/database.

37. Andrés Álvarez Calderón, 24 December 1791, AGI-SD 1014. For the Caribbean context, see William Van Norman, "The Process of Cultural Change Among Cuban Bozales During the Nineteenth Century," *The Americas* 62, no. 2 (October 2005): 177–207.

38. Vicente Tudela to Manuel González, 26 August 1787, AGI-SD 1102; Joaquín García to Fernando Portillo, 30 October 1789, AGI-SD 1102, no. 2; *Affiches Américaines* 21, 12 March 1791, 131; Consejo de Indias to Joaquín García, 29 May 1788, AGI-SD 1102, no. 24.

39. Charlton W. Yingling, "The Maroons of Santo Domingo in the Age of Revolutions: Adaptation and Evasion, 1783–1800," *History Workshop Journal* 79 (2015): 25–51.

40. Isidoro Rodríguez to Consejo de Indias, 23 October 1784, AGI-SD leg. 1102, no. 1.

41. Jane Landers, *Black Society in Spanish Florida* (Urbana: University of Illinois Press, 1999); N. A. T. Hall, "Maritime Maroons: 'Grand Marronage' from the Danish West Indies," *William and Mary Quarterly* 42, no. 4 (October 1985): 476–498; Linda M. Rupert, *Creolization and Contraband: Curaçao in the Early Modern Atlantic* (Athens: University of Georgia Press, 2012), 95–97, 163–211; Crystal Eddins, "Runaways, Repertoires, and Repression: Marronnage and the Haitian Revolution, 1766–1791," *Journal of Haitian Studies* 25, no. 1 (Spring 2019): 4–38.

42. Joaquín García to Fernando Portillo, 30 October 1789, AGI-SD 1102, no. 2; Marqués de Bajamar to Consejo de Indias, 27 September 1791, AGI-SD 1102, no. 32; "Convención . . . de Maniel . . . ," 12 July 1778, AHN-E 3373, exp. 6; 29 November 1787,

AHN-C 20762; Embajador de Francia to Conde Floridablanca, 5 September 1786, AGI-SD 1102, sub no. 13; Embajador de Francia to Conde Floridablanca, 7 August 1786, AGI-SD 1102; Deive, *Guerrilleros negros*, 69–90. See also "Defense interieure de St. Domingue," 1769, Mss. 09290, Thomas Fisher Rare Book Library, University of Toronto; Carlos Esteban Deive, *Los cimarrones del Maniel de Neiba* (Santo Domingo: Banco Central de la República Dominicana, 1985), 5–16; Ida Altman, "The Revolt of Enriquillo and the Historiography of Early Spanish America," *The Americas* 63, no. 4 (April 2007): 587–614.

43. Sánchez Valverde, *Idea*, 55–57; Médéric Louis Élie Moreau de Saint-Méry, *Description topographique, physique, civile, politique et historique de la partie française de l'isle Saint-Domingue*, vol. 2 (Philadelphia: author, 1798), 497–500; *Moreau, Partie espagnole*, 1:79–88; Martin Lienhard, *Disidentes, rebeldes, insurgentes: Resistencia indígena y negra en América Latina, ensayos de historia testimonial* (Madrid: Iberoamericana, 2008), 83–85; Manuel Arturo Peña Batlle, *La rebelión del Bahoruco* (Santo Domingo: Editora Taller, 1948).

44. Felipe Frómesta to Isidoro Peralta, 17 May 1783, AGI-SD 1102; 'Testimonio . . . Para la formación del Carolino Código Negro . . . ,' 7 February 1784 to 25 March 1785, AGI-SD 1034, ff. 1–55; Audiencia de Santo Domingo to Cabildo de Santo Domingo, 4 May 1786, AGN-ARH 10, exp. 89; Isidoro Peralta to José Gálvez, 24 July 1783, AGI-SD 1102; "Extracto del Código Negro Carolino . . . Capitulo 34, Negros Cimarrones," Audiencia de Santo Domingo, 14 March 1785, AGI-E 7, no. 3, ff. 77–80; *Moreau, Partie française*, 2:500–503; Deive, *Cimarrones*, 17–20; Lienhard, *Disidentes*, 109–111.

45. Joaquín García and Jean Formati to Audiencia de Santo Domingo, 18 July 1785, AGI-SD 1102, no. 20; Isidoro Rodríguez to Consejo de Indias, 25 November 1787, AGI-SD 1102; *Moreau, Partie française*, 2:497–503.

46. John K. Thornton, "'I Am the Subject of the King of Kongo': African Political Ideology and the Haitian Revolution," *Journal of World History* 4, no. 2 (1993): 181–214; Fick, *Making of Haiti*, 57–59; Jane Landers, "The Central African Presence in Spanish Maroon Communities," in *Central Africans and Cultural Transformations in the American Diaspora*, ed. Linda M. Heywood (New York: Cambridge University Press, 2002), 235–239.

47. Thanks to John Thornton for sharing his perspective. Joaquín García and Jean Formati to Audiencia de Santo Domingo, Neiba, 18 July 1785, AGI-SD 1102, no. 20; James Sweet, *Recreating Africa: Culture, Kinship, and Religion in the African-Portuguese World, 1441–1770* (Chapel Hill: University of North Carolina Press, 2004), 148–151; Konadu, *Akan Diaspora*; Deive, *Cimarrones*, 19–29, 45, 86; Lienhard, *Disidentes*, 93. On the freeborn, see Crystal Eddins, "'Rejoice! Your Wombs Will Not Beget Slaves!' Marronnage as Reproductive Justice in Colonial Haiti," *Gender and History* (October 2020): 1–19.

48. For sources on politics, culture, religion, and enslavement across Atlantic Africa, yet often with a racist bias, see Liévin Proyart, *Histoire de Loango, Kakongo, et autres royaumes d'Afrique* (Lyon, France: Bruyset-Ponthus, 1776); Giovanni Antonio Cavazzi da Montecuccolo, *Istorica descrizione de tre regni Conco, Matamba et Angola nel presente stile* (Bologna, Italy: Giacomo Monti, 1687); Antonio Zucchelli, *Relazioni del viaggio e mis-*

sione di Congo (Venice, Italy: Bartolomeo Giavarina, 1712); Willem Bosman, *A New and Accurate Description of the Coast of Guinea* (London: Knapton, Bell, Smith, Midwinter, Haws, Davis, Strahan, Lintott, Round, and Wale, 1705); John Duncan, *Travels in Western Africa in 1845 and 1846* (London: Richard Bentley, 1847); Gaspard Théodore Comte de Mollien, *Travels in Africa, to the Sources of the Senegal and Gambia* (London: Phillips, 1820); Jean-Baptiste-Léonard Durand, *A Voyage to Senegal* (London: Richard Phillips, 1806); Frederick Forbes, *Dahomey and the Dahomans* (London: Longman, Brown, Green, and Longmans, 1851); Richard Lander and John Lander, *Journal of an Expedition to Explore the Course and Termination of the Niger* (New York: Harper, 1833); John Adams, *Remarks on the Country Extending from Cape Palmas to the River Congo* (London: Whittaker, 1823); Henry Meredith, *An Account of the Gold Coast of Africa* (London: Longman, Hurst, Rees, Orme, and Brown, 1812); G. A. Robertson, *Notes on Africa: Particularly Those Parts Which Are Situated Between Cape Verd and the River Congo* (London: Sherwood, Neely and Jones, 1819); Alexander Falconbridge, *An Account of the Slave Trade on the Coast of Africa* (London: Phillips, 1788); Sylvain Meinrad Xavier de Golbéry, *Travels in Africa* (London: Jones, 1803); William Gray and the Late Staff Surgeon Dochard, *Travels in Western Africa* (London: Murray, 1825).

49. Luis Cháves y Mendoza to Isidoro Peralta, 7 April 1785, AGI-SD 1102; Embajador de Francia to Conde Floridablanca, 7 August 1786, AGI-SD 1102; Ignacio Caro to Isidoro Peralta, 28 August 1785, AGI-SD 1102; Joaquín García to Fernando Portillo, 30 October 1789, AGI-SD 1102, no. 2; Consejo de Indias to Joaquín García, 29 May 1788, AGI-SD 1102, no. 24.

50. Lienhard, *Disidentes*; Deive, *Cimarrones*; Weber, *Bárbaros*, 1–118, 247–248, 303n14.

51. Isidoro Rodríguez to Consejo de Indias, 25 October 1787, AGI-SD 1102, no. 18; Real Cédula, 23 May 1787, AGI-SD 1102.

52. Sasha Turner, *Contested Bodies: Pregnancy, Childrearing, and Slavery in Jamaica* (Philadelphia: University of Pennsylvania Press, 2017), 4–10, 19–43, 103, 185–186, 211–243; Ondina E. González and Bianca Premo, eds., *Raising an Empire: Children in Early Modern Iberia and Colonial Latin America* (Albuquerque: University of New Mexico Press, 2007).

53. Isidoro Rodríguez, "Testimonio de . . . la reduccion a vida sociable de los negros del Maniel de Neiva," Primer Quaderno, 20 September 1787 and 9 October 1787, AGI-SD 1102, no. 18.

54. Ignacio Caro to Joaquín García, 6 January 1785, AGI-SD 1102; Consejo de Indias, 9 July 1798, AGI-SD 925; José Gabriel García, *Compendio de la historia de Santo Domingo*, vol. 1 (Santo Domingo: Imprenta García Hermanos, 1893), 234; Spanish references to maroons as *salvaje* (savage) paralleled colonialist lexicons on the indigenous. See Weber, *Bárbaros*, 15, 286n56; Deive, *Cimarrones*, 25–43; *Mercurio de España: Abril de 1790*, 316.

55. Consejo de Indias to Joaquín García, 29 May 1788, AGI-SD 1102, no. 24.

56. Joaquín García to Fernando Portillo, 30 October 1789, AGI-SD 1102, no. 2; Marqués de Bajamar to Consejo de Indias, 27 September 1791, AGI-SD 1102, no. 32; Deive, *Guerrilleros*, 69–90.

57. Juan Bobadilla to Antonio Porlier, 25 January 1790, AGI-SD 1102, no. 26.

58. Isidoro Rodríguez to Consejo de Indias, 25 January 1788, AGI-SD 1102, no. 21; Isidoro Rodríguez, Primer Quaderno, 10 and 15 October 1787, AGI-SD 1102, no. 18; Fernando Portillo to Joaquín García, 13 September 1789, AGI-SD 1110.

59. Isidoro Rodríguez, Primer Quaderno, 16 and 20 October 1787, AGI-SD 1102, no. 18; Deive, *Cimarrones*, 57–61.

60. Consejo de Indias, 15 April 1791, AGI-SD 1102, no. 28; Fernando Portillo to Antonio Porlier, 24 January and 26 December 1790, AGI-SD 1110.

61. Lorenzo Nuñéz to Joaquín García, 29 August 1791, AGI-SD 1102; Marqués de Bajamar to Consejo de Indias, 27 September 1791, AGI-SD 1102, no. 32; Juan Bobadilla to Joaquín García, 8 August 1791, AGI-SD 1102; Dubois, *Avengers*, 52–55, 99–102; Robert D. Taber, "Navigating Haiti's History: Saint-Domingue and the Haitian Revolution," *History Compass* 13, no. 5 (May 2015): 235–250.

62. Joaquín García to Antonio Porlier, 25 April 1791, AGI-SD 1102, no. 34.

63. Juan Bobadilla to Joaquín García, 25 February 1791, AGI-SD 1102; Lorenzo Núñez to Joaquín García, 9 November 1790, AGI-SD 1102; Deive, *Cimarrones*, 62–65.

64. Embajador de Francia to Conde Floridablanca, 7 August 1786, AGI-SD 1102.

65. "Real Cédula de Carlos IV . . . ," Aranjuez, 31 May 1789, in José Luis Saez, *La iglesia y el negro esclavo en Santo Domingo: Una historia de tres siglos* (Santo Domingo: Patronato de la Ciudad Colonial de Santo Domingo, 1994). On the *asiento*, see Polhemus, "Culture of Commodification."

66. Abad, Urízar, Catani, and Bravo, Santo Domingo, 17 May 1791, AGI-SD 1029.

CHAPTER 2: FOLLOWING A REVOLUTIONARY FUSE, 1789–1791

1. "N.1, Daxabon . . . ," Santo Domingo, 3 September 1791, AGI-SD 1029.

2. Joaquín García, Santo Domingo, 25 October 1791, AGI-SD 1030.

3. Arata to Joaquín García, Las Cahobas, 6 March 1791, AGI-SD 1029.

4. Consejo de Indias to José Urízar, Aranjuez, AGI-SD 1029; John D. Garrigus, "Vincent Ogé *Jeune* (1757–1791), Social Class and Free Colored Mobilization on the Eve of the Haitian Revolution," *The Americas* 68, no. 1 (July 2011): 33–62; Melania Rivers Rodríguez, "Los colonos americanos en la sociedad prerrevolucionaria de Saint Domingue: La rebelión de Vicente Ogé y su apresamiento en Santo Domingo (1789–1791)," *Memorias* 2, no. 2 (2005): 1–22; Stewart R. King, *Blue Coat or Powdered Wig: Free People of Color in Pre-Revolutionary Saint-Domingue* (Athens: University of Georgia Press, 2001), 20, 30–40, 58–64; Christine Levecq, *Black Cosmopolitans: Race, Religion, and Republicanism in an Age of Revolution* (Charlottesville: University of Virginia Press, 2019).

5. Joaquín García to Conde de Serena, Santo Domingo, 25 March 1791, AGI-SD 1029, no. 259.

6. Joaquín García to Antonio Porlier, Santo Domingo, 16 March 1791, AGI-SD 1029, no. 29.

7. Philibert-François Rouxel Blanchelande to Joaquín García, Las Cahobas, 6 March 1791, AGI-SD 1029. Printed just before his Parisian guillotining in 1793, Blanchelande's

self-defense omitted his Dominican retreat. See *Discours justificatif de Philibert-François Rouxel Blanchelande* (Paris: N. H. Nyon, 1793). For more context, see Jeremy Popkin, "The French Revolution's Royal Governor: General Blanchelande and Saint-Domingue, 1790–92," *William and Mary Quarterly* 71, no. 2 (April 2014): 203–228.

8. Joaquín García to Antonio Porlier, Santo Domingo, 16 March 1791, AGI-SD 1029, no. 29.

9. Joaquín García to Philibert-François Rouxel Blanchelande, Santo Domingo, 11 March 1791, AGI-SD 1029.

10. Anne Eller, *We Dream Together: Dominican Independence, Haiti, and the Fight for Caribbean Freedom* (Durham, NC: Duke University Press, 2016), 3–6. For context on French racial ideas, see Jennifer L. Palmer, *Intimate Bonds: Family and Slavery in the French Atlantic* (Philadelphia: University of Pennsylvania Press, 2016); Guillaume Aubert, "'The Blood of France': Race and Purity of Blood in the French Atlantic World," *William and Mary Quarterly* 61, no. 3 (2004): 439–478; Manuel Covo, "Race, Slavery, and Colonies in the French Revolution," in *Oxford Handbook of the French Revolution*, ed. David Andress (New York: Oxford University Press, 2015), 290–307.

11. John Garrigus, *Before Haiti: Race and Citizenship in French Saint-Domingue* (New York: Palgrave, 2006), 242–252; David Geggus, *Haitian Revolutionary Studies* (Bloomington: Indiana University Press, 2002), 9–13, 159–164; Laurent Dubois, *Avengers of the New World: The Story of the Haitian Revolution* (Cambridge, MA: Belknap Press of Harvard University Press, 2004), 73–87; Carolyn Fick, *The Making of Haiti: The Saint Domingue Revolution from Below* (Knoxville: University of Tennessee Press, 1990), 78–82; Alyssa Goldstein Sepinwall, *The Abbé Grégoire and the French Revolution: The Making of Modern Universalism* (Berkeley: University of California Press, 2005); Bryan Banks and Erica Johnson, eds., *The French Revolution and Religion in Global Perspective* (New York: Palgrave, 2017).

12. "Nouvelles de Saint-Domingue, paroisses Ouanaminthe, Dondon, Fort-Dauphin, Trou, et Limonade," 8–30 August 1790, Bibliothèque Haïtienne des Frères de l'Instruction Chrétienne (BHFIC), B-2a44. For parish politics, see Chris Bongie, "A Flexible Quill: Abbé De Lahaye's Role in Late Colonial Saint-Domingue, 1787–1791—The Legend and the Life," *Atlantic Studies* 15, no. 4 (2018): 476–503.

13. Abbé de Cournand, 1790, "Requête présentée a nosseigneurs de l'Assemblée nationale, en faveur des gens de couleur de l'ile de Saint-Domingue," BHFIC, B-2b2a.

14. Consejo de Indias, Madrid, 15 July 1791, AGI-SD 1029; Lorenzo Núñez to Joaquín García, 9 November 1790, AGI-SD 1102; Thomas Madiou, *Histoire d'Haïti*, vol. 1 (Port-au-Prince: Courtois, 1847), 53–66; Garrigus, "Vincent Ogé *Jeune*"; Fick, *Making of Haiti*, 130–131; Geggus, *Haitian Revolutionary Studies*, 8; Dubois, *Avengers*, 60–88. For regional context, see Robert D. Taber and Charlton W. Yingling, "Networks, Tastes, and Labor in Free Communities of Color: Transforming the Revolutionary Caribbean," *Atlantic Studies* 14 (Fall 2017): 263–274; John Garrison Marks, *Black Freedom in the Age of Slavery: Race, Status, and Identity in the Urban Americas* (Columbia: University of South Carolina Press, 2020); Andrew N. Wegmann, *An American Color: Race and Identity in New Orleans and the Atlantic World* (Athens: University of Georgia Press, 2022); Richard Graham,

Feeding the City: From Street Market to Liberal Reform in Salvador, Brazil, 1780–1860 (Austin: University of Texas Press, 2010).

15. Joaquín García to Antonio Porlier, Santo Domingo, 20 January 1791, AGI-SD 1029, no. 27; Consejo to José Urízar, Aranjuez, 6 April 1791, AGI-SD 1029.

16. Consejo de Indias, Madrid, 15 July 1791, AGI-SD 1029.

17. Joaquín García to Conde de Serena, Santo Domingo, 25 February 1791, AGI-SD 1029; *Affiches Américaines* 21, 12 March 1791, 129.

18. Consejo de Indias, Madrid, 15 July 1791, AGI-SD 1029.

19. José Urízar to Antonio Porlier, Santo Domingo, 26 January 1791, AGI-SD 1029.

20. *Courrier Politique et Litteraire du Cap-Français, par M. Gatrau,* 6 January 1791.

21. Fernando Portillo to Antonio Porlier, 24 January 1790, AGI-SD 1110.

22. Fick, *Making of Haiti,* 79–85.

23. Consejo de Indias, 15 April 1791, AGI-SD 1102, no. 28. See also Garrigus, "Vincent Ogé *Jeune*"; Fick, *Making of Haiti,* 79–85.

24. "Noticias de Neiba," 8 March 1791, AGI-SD 1029; Joaquín García to Antonio Porlier, Santo Domingo, 16 March 1791, AGI-SD 1029, no. 29; Herbert Elmer Mills, "The Early Years of the French Revolution in San Domingo" (PhD diss., Cornell University, 1889, 65–94). The ships flew a white flag with purple and black stripes in the top-left corner.

25. José Arata to Joaquín García, Las Cahobas, 6 March 1791, AGI-SD 1029; Joaquín García to Conde de Serena, Santo Domingo, 25 March 1791, AGI-SD 1029, no. 250; Joaquín García to Antonio Porlier, Santo Domingo, 16 March 1791, AGI-SD 1029, no. 30.

26. "Capitaine general du district de Port-au-Prince: Preuves de la faussete de la relation impr. De M. Mauduit, colonel du regiment du Port-au-Prince," 1790, Port-au-Prince, BHFIC, B-2a44e.

27. Joaquín García to Marqués de Bajamar, Santo Domingo, 18 June 1791, AGI-SD 1029, no. 35.

28. Joaquín García, Santo Domingo, 24 July 1791, AGI-SD 1029, no. 36.

29. Joaquín García to Conde de Serena, Santo Domingo, 24 July 1791, AGI-SD 1030, no. 262. See also Sepinwall, *Abbé Grégoire,* 89–136.

30. Joaquín García to Conde de Serena, Santo Domingo, 18 June 1791, AGI-SD 1030, no. 256; Joaquín García to Conde del Campo de Alange, Santo Domingo, 18 June 1791, AGI-SD 1030, no. 90.

31. José Urízar to Diego de Gardoqui, Santo Domingo, 17 June 1794, AGI-SD 1031, no. 25; Joaquín García to Diego de Gardoqui, Santo Domingo, 25 October 1793, AGI-SD 1031, no. 418; José Urízar to Diego de Gardoqui, Santo Domingo, 12 June and 20 July 1794, AGI-SD 1032.

32. Joaquín García to Conde de Serena, Santo Domingo, 24 August 1791, AGI-SD 1030, no. 267.

33. Joaquín García to Conde de Serena, Santo Domingo, 25 August 1791, AGI-SD 1030, no. 268.

34. Geggus, *Haitian Revolutionary Studies*, 81–92; Kate Ramsey, *The Spirits and the Law: Vodou and Power in Haiti* (Chicago: University of Chicago Press, 2012), 41–45; "The Bois-Caïman Ceremony," in *Haitian Revolution: A Documentary History*, ed. David Geggus (Indianapolis: Hackett, 2014), 78–79; Dubois, *Avengers*, 93–95.

35. "Mons. Cadush . . . 27 Sept. 1791," The National Archives (TNA), War Office (WO), 1/58, 1–4. For more context, see Erica R. Johnson, *Philanthropy and Race in the Haitian Revolution* (New York: Palgrave, 2018).

36. "N.1, Daxabon . . . ," Santo Domingo, 29 August 1791, AGI-SD 1029.

37. "N.1, Daxabon . . . ," Santo Domingo, 6 September 1791, AGI-SD 1029.

38. "N.1, Daxabon . . . ," Santo Domingo, 7 September 1791, AGI-SD 1029.

39. "N.1, Daxabon . . . ," Santo Domingo, 8 September 1791, AGI-SD 1029.

40. Cap-Français, 15 September 1791, AGI-SD 1029 (L).

41. Marquis de Rouvray, September 1791, AGI-SD 1029 (E).

42. "N.1, Daxabon . . . ," Santo Domingo, 30 August 1791, AGI-SD 1029; Latour Maire and Coussac to Commander of San Rafael, Dondon, 24 August 1791, AGI-SD 1029, no. 1; Jacques de la Ville, n.d., AGI-SD 1029. On royalist emancipation rumors, see Wim Klooster, "Slave Revolts, Royal Justice, and a Ubiquitous Rumor in the Age of Revolutions," *William and Mary Quarterly* 71, no. 3 (July 2014): 401–424; Geggus, *Haitian Revolutionary Studies*, 12.

43. "N.1, Daxabon . . . ," Santo Domingo, 24 August 1791, AGI-SD 1029.

44. Joaquín García, Santo Domingo, 25 September 1791, AGI-SD 1030.

45. Philibert-François Rouxel Blanchelande to Pepin, Cap-Français, 24 August 1791, AGI-SD 1029 (A); Philibert-François Rouxel Blanchelande to Francisco Núñez, Cap-Français, 24 August 1791, AGI-SD 1029, no. 2; Philibert-François Rouxel Blanchelande to Andrés Heredia, Cap-Français, 26 August 1791, AGI-SD 1029 (B).

46. Joaquín García, Santo Domingo, 25 September 1791, AGI-SD 1030. The Spanish called Fort Dauphin "Bayajá."

47. Alexandre Petitbois to Marcellis Mercader, Mirebalais, 13 September 1791, AGI-SD 1029; Monsieur Coustard, 8 September 1791, AGI-SD 1029, no. 5; Alexandre Petitbois to Marcellis Mercader, Mirebalais, 13 September 1791, AGI-SD 1029; Joaquín García to Marqués de Bajamar, Santo Domingo, 25 September 1791, AGI-SD 1029, no. 40; Geggus, *Haitian Revolutionary Studies*, 102–104; Coustard to Joaquín García, 20 September 1791, AGI-SD 1029; Audiencia de Santo Domingo, Santo Domingo, September 1791, AGI-SD 1029.

48. Monsieur Coustard, 8 September 1791, AGI-SD 1029, no. 5.

49. Marquis de Rouvray to Andrés Heredia, 31 August 1791, AGI-SD 1029 (D).

50. Marquis de Rouvray, Jaquezy, 6 September 1791, AGI-SD 1029 (C).

51. Marquis de Rouvray to Andrés Heredia, Caracoles, 28 August 1791, AGI-SD 1029 (C).

52. Marquis de Rouvray, September 1791, AGI-SD 1029 (E).

53. "N.1, Daxabon . . . ," Santo Domingo, 1 September 1791, AGI-SD 1029.

54. Joaquín García to Marqués de Bajamar, September 1791, AGI-SD 1029, no. 39.

55. Jean-Marie Jan, *Les congrégations religieuses à Saint-Domingue, 1681–1793* (Port-au-Prince: H. Deschamps, 1951), 225–229. Details on Améthyste are murky; surviving accounts about her appear to be summarized from primary sources that no longer exist. See also Ramsey, *Spirits and the Law*, 275n83; Fick, *Making of Haiti*, 104–105; Geggus, *Haitian Revolutionary Studies*, 90.

56. "N.1, Daxabon . . . ," Santo Domingo, 13 September 1791, AGI-SD 1029.

57. "N.1, Daxabon . . . ," Santo Domingo, 8 September 1791, AGI-SD 1029.

58. "N.1, Daxabon . . . ," Santo Domingo, 24 August to 25 September 1791, AGI-SD 1029.

59. Audiencia de Santo Domingo, Santo Domingo, September 1791, AGI-SD 1029.

60. General Assembly of Saint-Domingue to the National Assembly of France, Cap-Français, 13 September 1791, AGI-SD 1029 (F).

61. Philibert-François Rouxel Blanchelande to Joaquín García, Cap-Français, 8 September 1791, AGI-SD 1029.

62. Alexandre Petitbois to Marcellis Mercader, Mirebalais, 13 September 1791, AGI-SD 1029; Joaquín García to Conde de Serena, Santo Domingo, 15 November 1791, AGI-SD 1030, no. 279.

63. Joaquín García to Philibert-François Rouxel Blanchelande, Santo Domingo, 23 September 1791, AGI-SD 1029.

64. Joaquín García to Andrés Heredia, Santo Domingo, 7 September 1791, AGI-SD 1029 (D).

65. "N.1, Daxabon . . . ," Santo Domingo, 7 and 8 September 1791, AGI-SD 1029.

66. Joaquín García, Santo Domingo, 25 October 1791, AGI-SD 1030; "Lettre de M. de Blanchelande, au minister de la marine," Cap-Français, 14 and 29 September 1791, in *Archives parlementaires de 1787 à 1860: Recueil complet des débats législatifs et politiques des chambres françaises,* ser. 1, vol. 37 (Paris: Paul Dupont, 1891), 261–263.

67. Pablo derived from the French "Paul." In 1796, Spanish officials recorded him as a "natural" of the Sainte-Rose parish (Nord), the name of Grande-Rivière's church. He later "confessed his origins from Africa" in 1821. "Testimonio . . . ," Santo Domingo, 19 December 1796 and 20 April 1797, AGI-E 1, no. 27, 42–48, 316–318; "Pablo Aly," 2 January 1821, AGI-SD 1017. See also Céligni Ardouin, *Essais sur l'histoire d'Haïti* (Port-au-Prince: Bouchereau, 1865), 16–18, 146.

68. José Urízar to Marqués de Bajamar, Santo Domingo, 25 September 1791, AGI-SD 1029. See also Geggus, *Haitian Revolutionary Studies*, 9–14; Jeremy Popkin, *You Are All Free: The Haitian Revolution and the Abolition of Slavery* (New York: Cambridge University Press, 2010), 23–52.

69. Bellair, Santo Domingo, n.d., AGI-SD 1031. This was almost certainly Gabriel Belair.

70. Joaquín García to Marqués de Bajamar, Santo Domingo, 25 September 1791, AGI-SD 1029.

71. Joaquín García to Conde de Serena, Santo Domingo, 18 September 1791, AGI-SD 1030, no. 273.

72. "Lettre d'un nègre, signée Fayette, du Dondon, le 22 octobre 1791," Dondon, 22 October 1791, and "Lettre signée Bouce et Jean-François," n.d., in *Archives parlementaires*, vol. 37, 312. See also Popkin, *You Are All Free*, 129–130; Yves Benot, "The Insurgents of 1791, Their Leaders, and the Concept of Independence," in *World of the Haitian Revolution*, ed. David Geggus and Norman Fiering (Bloomington: Indiana University Press, 2009), 107.

73. Joaquín Cabrera to Joaquín García, San Rafael, 13 October 1791, AGI-SD 1030.

74. José Urízar to Marqués de Bajamar, Santo Domingo, 25 September 1791, AGI-SD 1029.

75. James Sweet, "New Perspectives on Kongo in Revolutionary Haiti," *The Americas* 74, no. 1 (January 2017): 83–97; Terry Rey, *The Priest and the Prophetess: Abbé Ouvière, Romaine Rivière, and the Revolutionary Atlantic World* (New York: Oxford University Press, 2017), 7–9; John K. Thornton, "'I Am the Subject of the King of Kongo': African Political Ideology and the Haitian Revolution," *Journal of World History* 4, no. 2 (1993): 181–214; Jane Landers, *Atlantic Creoles in the Age of Revolutions* (Cambridge, MA: Harvard University Press, 2010), chapter 2; Geggus, *Haitian Revolutionary Studies*; Ada Ferrer, *Freedom's Mirror: Cuba and Haiti in the Age of Revolution* (New York: Cambridge University Press, 2014), 90–93, 120–124, 136–138; Catherine Bell, *Ritual Theory, Ritual Practice* (New York: Oxford University Press, 1992), 181, 206, 218. For a newer read on Jean-François's well-known Catholic professions, see Miriam Franchina, "From Slave to Royal Vassal: Jean-François's Negotiation Strategies in the Haitian Revolution," *Slavery and Abolition* (forthcoming 2021). On evangelization, see Johnson, *Philanthropy*, chapter 1; Sue Peabody, "A Dangerous Zeal: Catholic Missions to Slaves in the French Antilles, 1635–1800," *French Historical Studies* 25, no. 1 (Winter 2002): 53–90; Rey, *Priest*, chapter 5. On ethnicities, see Christina Mobley, "The Kongolese Atlantic: Central African Slavery and Culture from Mayombe to Haiti" (PhD diss., Duke University, 2015), chapter 6.

76. "Lettre de M. de Blanchelande, au minister de la marine," Cap-Français, 14 and 29 September 1791, in *Archives parlementaires*, vol. 37, 261–263.

77. Audiencia de Santo Domingo, Santo Domingo, September 1791, AGI-SD 1029.

78. Joaquín García, Santo Domingo, 25 October 1791, AGI-SD 1030. See also Hénock Trouillot, "La condition de la femme de couleur à Saint-Domingue," *Revue de la Société Haïtienne d'Histoire* 20, no. 103 (1957): 21–80.

79. "Lettre signée Médecin, général, datée de Grande-Rivière, ce 4 octobre 1791," in *Archives parlementaires*, vol. 37, 311. See also Geggus, *Haitian Revolutionary Studies*, 78–81; Fick, *Making of Haiti*, 92.

80. "Lettre signée Médecin, général, datée de Grande-Rivière, ce 15 octobre 1791," in *Archives parlementaires*, vol. 37, 311–312.

81. "Lettre d'un nègre, signée Fayette, du Dondon, le 22 octobre 1791," Dondon, 22 October 1791, and "Lettre signée Bouce et Jean-François," n.d., in *Archives parlementaires*, vol. 37, 312.

82. Laurent Dubois, "Avenging America: The Politics of Violence in the Haitian Revolution," in Geggus and Fiering, *World of the Haitian Revolution*, 114–116. For similar

examples of Jeannot's violence, see, among others, Landers, *Atlantic Creoles*, 62; Dubois, *Avengers*, 123.

83. Jan, *Les congrégations religieuses*, 228–229; Madiou, *Histoire*, 1:73–75. Evidence is limited that "Nanett allé n'en fontaine, Cherché d'l'eau, Cruche à li cases," or some variant, was this shibboleth. See also Hénock Trouillot, *Les origines sociales de la littérature haïtienne* (Port-au-Prince:Théodore, 1962), 21–25. For an earlier, racist French recounting that includes Dessalines using this phrase, see "Les Mœurs et la littérature nègres," *Revue des deux mondes* 90 (1852): 776–778.

84. Benot, "Insurgents of 1791," in Geggus and Fiering, *World of the Haitian Revolution*, 108; Landers, *Atlantic Creoles*, 64–65; Fick, *Making of Haiti*, 112–114.

85. Madiou, *Histoire*, 1:73–76.

86. Joaquín García, Santo Domingo, 25 October 1791, AGI-SD 1030. See also Rey, *Priest*, 116–121; "The First Days of the Slave Insurrection," in *Facing Racial Revolution: Eyewitness Accounts of the Haitian Insurrection*, ed. Jeremy D. Popkin (Chicago: University of Chicago Press, 2007), 49–58; Geggus, *Haitian Revolution: A Documentary History*, esp. 16, 35.

87. Médéric Louis Élie Moreau de Saint-Méry, *Description topographique, physique, civile, politique et historique de la partie française de l'isle Saint-Domingue*, vol. 1 (Philadelphia: author, 1797), 68–70; Pierre Pluchon, *Vaudou, sorciers, empoissoneurs: De Saint-Domingue à Haïti* (Paris: Éditions Karthala, 1987), 67–71; Doris Garraway, *The Libertine Colony: Creolization in the Early French Caribbean* (Durham, NC: Duke University Press, 2005), 253–255; Ramsey, *Spirits and the Law*, 40–41; Elizabeth W. Kiddy, "Who Is the King of Congo? A New Look at African and Afro-Brazilian Kings in Brazil," in *Central Africans and Cultural Transformations in the American Diaspora*, ed. Linda M. Heywood (New York: Cambridge University Press, 2002), 153–182; Rey, *Priest*, 67–70.

88. Cabildo of Santo Domingo, 27 September 1791, AGI-SD 1029; Joaquín García to Conde de Serena, Santo Domingo, 17 October 1791, AGI-SD 1030, no. 278; Joaquín García, Santo Domingo, 25 October 1791, AGI-SD 1030.

89. Letter from Ouanaminthe, 3 November 1791, AGI-SD 1030.

90. "Testimonio . . . Gérard . . . 4.a Pieza," Dajabón, 20 November 1791, AGI-SD 1030, no. 9, 410.

91. Joaquín García, Santo Domingo, 25 November 1791, AGI-SD 1030.

92. Ouanaminthe, 3 November 1791, AGI-SD 1030.

93. Joaquín García, Santo Domingo, 25 November 1791, AGI-SD 1030. See also Fick, *Making of Haiti*, 114–117; Dubois, *Avengers*, 125–127.

94. "Testimonio de la causa criminal seguida contra el francés Carlos César Agustín Gérard por sospechoso, 1.a Pieza," Santo Domingo, 27 January 1792, AGI-SD 1030, no. 9, 325–328; "Testimonio . . . Gérard . . . 1.a P.," Santo Domingo, 23 March 1792, AGI-SD 1030, no. 9, 359–367.

95. "Testimonio . . . Gérard . . . 1.a P.," Santo Domingo, 26 January 1792, AGI-SD 1030, no. 9, 321–325.

96. "Testimonio ... Gérard ... 1.a P.," Santo Domingo, 27 January 1792, AGI-SD 1030, no. 9, 328–334; "Testimonio del oficio de remision del francés Mr. Gérard con varios documentos del mismo, 2.a Pieza," n.d., AGI-SD 1030, no. 9, 372–376.

97. "Testimonio de varias cartas relativas a los execsos y apprehension de Mr. Gérard, 4.a Pieza," Dajabón, 4 June 1789, AGI-SD 1030, no. 9, 396–397; Emilio Rodríguez Demorizi, ed., *Papeles de Espaillat* (Santo Domingo: Editora del Caribe), 474.

98. "Testimonio ... Gérard ... 1.a P.," Santo Domingo, 27 January 1792, AGI-SD 1030, no. 9, 330–334.

99. "Testimonio ... Gérard ... 1.a P.," Santo Domingo, 28 January 1792, AGI-SD 1030, no. 9, 334–337.

100. "Testimonio ... Gérard ... 1.a P.," Santo Domingo, 28 January 1792, AGI-SD 1030, no. 9, 345–347.

101. "Testimonio de los documentos aprehendidos y exhividos por Monsieur Gérard, 3.a Pieza," Ouanaminthe, 24 December 1791, AGI-SD 1030, no. 9, 378–382; "Testimonio ... Gérard ... 3.a P.," Ouanaminthe, 14 January 1792, AGI-SD 1030, no. 9, 382–383; *Affiches Americaines de Saint-Domingue*, 19 Floréal an XI / 9 May 1803, no. 37.

102. "Testimonio ... Gérard ... 2.a P.," 9 and 15 November 1791, AGI-SD 1030, no. 9, 369–372.

103. "Testimonio ... Gérard ... 1.a P.," Santo Domingo, 28 January 1792, AGI-SD 1030, no. 9, 336–345; "Testimonio ... Gérard ... 4.a P.," Dajabón, 20 November 1792, AGI-SD 1030, no. 9, 410.

104. "Testimonio ... Gérard ... 2.a P.," Versailles, 1 February 1789, AGI-SD 1030, no. 9, 372; "Testimonio ... Gérard ... 1.a P.," Santo Domingo, 28 January 1792, AGI-SD 1030, no. 9, 337–339.

105. Fick, *Making of Haiti*, 111–112, 304n105.

106. "Testimonio ... Gérard ... 1.a P.," 2 March 1792, Dajabón, AGI-SD 1030, no. 9, 347–349; "Lettre de M. Hurvoy, commandant pour le roi, à Ouanaminthe, du 4 novembre, à l'assemble générale," in *Archives parlementaires*, vol. 37, 309.

107. "Testimonio ... Gérard ... 1.a P.," Santo Domingo, 28 January 1792, AGI-SD 1030, no. 9, 337–341.

108. "Testimonio ... Gérard ... 4.a P.," Dajabón, 9 November 1791, AGI-SD 1030, no. 9, 404–410; Fick, *Making of Haiti*, 111–113.

109. M. Gros, *Précis historique, qui expose dans le plus grand jour les manœuvres contre-révolutionnaires employées contre St Domingue* (Paris: n.p., 1793), 25–27, BL, General Reference Collection (GRC), 936.f.6.(27).

110. "Testimonio ... Gérard ... 1.a P.," Dajabón, 3 March 1792, AGI-SD 1030, no. 9, 349–358. "Rapport fait à M. Hurvoy, commandant des troupes patriotiques de Ouanaminthe, par M. De Fondeviolle ...," Ouanaminthe, 2 October 1791, in *Archives parlementaires*, vol. 37, 308–309. "Testimonio ... Gérard ... 1.a P.," Dajabón, 7 March 1792, AGI-SD 1030, no. 9, 358–359; "Testimonio ... Gérard ... 1.a P.," Santo Domingo, 23 March 1792, AGI-SD 1030, no. 9, 359–367; "Testimonio ... Gérard ... 3.a P.," 23 November 1791, AGI-SD 1030, no. 9, 389–394.

III. Fick, *Making of Haiti*, 114–117; Dubois, *Avengers*, 125–127.

112. "Testimonio . . . Gérard . . . 1.a P.," Santo Domingo, 27 January 1792, AGI-SD 1030, no. 9, 325–331. See also Marlene Daut, *Tropics of Haiti: Race and the Literary History of the Haitian Revolution in the Atlantic World, 1789–1865* (Liverpool: Liverpool University Press, 2015), 230–233.

113. "Testimonio . . . Gérard . . . 1.a P.," Santo Domingo, 26 January 1792, AGI-SD 1030, no. 9, 323–324; "Testimonio . . . Gérard . . . 3.a P.," n.d., AGI-SD 1030, no. 9, 383–384.

114. Joaquín García to Conde de Serena, Santo Domingo, 25 December 1791, AGI-SD 1030, no. 287.

115. Joaquín García to Conde de Serena, Santo Domingo, 25 January 1792, AGI-SD 1030, no. 291; "Testimonio . . . Gérard . . . 4.a P.," 1 October 1791, AGI-SD 1030, no. 9, 399–400.

CHAPTER 3: BELIEF, BLASPHEMY, AND THE BLACK AUXILIARIES, 1792–1794

1. Joaquín García to Diego de Gardoqui, Santo Domingo, 3 July 1793, AGI-SD 1030, no. 390.

2. Jeremy Popkin, *You Are All Free: The Haitian Revolution and the Abolition of Slavery* (New York: Cambridge University Press, 2010).

3. Ada Ferrer, *Freedom's Mirror: Cuba and Haiti in the Age of Revolution* (New York: Cambridge University Press, 2014), 90–92; Popkin, *You Are All Free*, 209–211, 250–260; Laurent Dubois, *Avengers of the New World: The Story of the Haitian Revolution* (Cambridge, MA: Belknap Press of Harvard University Press, 2004), 157–164; Jacques de Cauna, "Polverel et Sonthonax: Deux voices pour l'abolition de l'esclavage," *Outre-mers* 84, no. 319 (1997): 47–53.

4. Carolyn Fick, *The Making of Haiti: The Saint Domingue Revolution from Below* (Knoxville: University of Tennessee Press, 1990); Jane Landers, *Atlantic Creoles in the Age of Revolutions* (Cambridge, MA: Harvard University Press, 2010).

5. Bellair, Santo Domingo, n.d., AGI-SD 1031. Belair, the spelling he typically used, most likely wrote this letter in January 1794.

6. For context on belief and blasphemy, see Catherine Bell, *Ritual Theory, Ritual Practice* (New York: Oxford University Press, 1992), 140–141, 181, 206–218; Scott Eastman, *Preaching Spanish Nationalism Across the Hispanic Atlantic, 1759–1823* (Baton Rouge: Louisiana State University Press, 2012), 1–44; Terry Rey, *The Priest and the Prophetess: Abbé Ouvière, Romaine Rivière, and the Revolutionary Atlantic World* (New York: Oxford University Press, 2017), 6–10; Kate Ramsey, *The Spirits and the Law: Vodou and Power in Haiti* (Chicago: University of Chicago Press, 2012), 36–42; Anne Stensvold, ed., *Blasphemies Compared* (New York: Routledge, 2020).

7. Fernando Portillo to Eugenio Llaguno, Bánica, 14 September 1794, AGI-SD 1031; 14 December 1793, AGS-SG 6850, f. 655; Henry Dundas to Adam Williamson,

6 November 1794, TNA-WO 6/5, 15–18; David Geggus, *Haitian Revolutionary Studies* (Bloomington: Indiana University Press, 2002), 130–135, 179–180; Landers, *Atlantic Creoles*, chapter 2; John K. Thornton, "'I Am the Subject of the King of Kongo': African Political Ideology and the Haitian Revolution," *Journal of World History* 4, no. 2 (1993): 181–214.

8. Joaquín García to Diego de Gardoqui, Santo Domingo, 3 July 1793, AGI-SD 1030, no. 390.

9. Joaquín García to Conde de Serena, Santo Domingo, 25 February 1792, AGI-SD 1030, no. 298.

10. See the multiple references to when Pablo Alí's career with Spain began in the "Testimonio," AGI-E 1, no. 27.

11. José Urízar to Marqués de Bajamar, Santo Domingo, 25 June 1792, AGI-SD 1030.

12. Joaquín García to Marqués de Bajamar, Santo Domingo, 21 March 1792, BL-WM, Egerton 1794, ff. 293–300; Philippe Roume to Heredia, 20 February 1792, BL-WM, Egerton 1794, ff. 303–305; Jean-François, n.d. and 5 March 1792, BL-WM, Egerton 1794, ff. 313, 314.

13. Rey, *Priest*, 45–70; Robert D. Taber, "The Issue of Their Union: Family, Law, and Politics in Western Saint-Domingue, 1777 to 1789" (PhD diss., University of Florida, 2015), 138–144. A French officer who fought in this area identified Romaine as a *griffe* (three-quarters African descent) of Spanish origins. Pamphile Lacroix, *Mémoires pour servir à l'histoire de la révolution de Saint-Domingue*, vol. 1 (Paris: Chez Pillet, 1819), 142.

14. Dubois, *Avengers*, 136–137.

15. Joaquín García to Marqués de Bajamar, Santo Domingo, 11 June 1792, AGI-SD 1030, no. 59.

16. Joaquín García, 22 July 1793, AGI-SD 1031, no. 129; Fick, *Making of Haiti*, 139–140.

17. Joaquín García to Diego de Gardoqui, Santo Domingo, 25 June 1792, AGI-SD 1030, no. 314.

18. Urízar, Catani, Bravo, and Toncerrada to Marqués de Bajamar, Santo Domingo, 25 June 1792, AGI-SD 1030; Joaquín García to Diego de Gardoqui, Santo Domingo, 25 June 1792, AGI-SD 1030, no. 311.

19. Joaquín García to Marqués de Bajamar, Santo Domingo, 11 June 1792, AGI-SD 1030, no. 59.

20. Fernando Portillo to Marqués de Bajamar, Santo Domingo, 24 June 1792, AGI-SD 1030.

21. José Urízar to Marqués de Bajamar, Santo Domingo, 25 June 1792, AGI-SD 1030.

22. Joaquín García to Marqués de Bajamar, Santo Domingo, 25 June 1792, AGI-SD 1030, no. 62.

23. Joaquín García to Diego de Gardoqui, Santo Domingo, 23 September 1792, AGI-SD 1030, no. 326.

24. Joaquín García to Diego de Gardoqui, Santo Domingo, 25 October 1792, AGI-SD 1030, no. 330.

25. Fick, *Making of Haiti*, 315n3; Graham Nessler, *An Islandwide Struggle for Freedom: Revolution, Emancipation, and Reenslavement on Hispaniola, 1789–1809* (Chapel Hill: University of North Carolina Press, 2016), 46–51; Popkin, *You Are All Free*, 85–92.

26. Joaquín García to Diego de Gardoqui, Santo Domingo, 18 November 1792, AGI-SD 1030, no. 336.

27. Joaquín García to Diego de Gardoqui, Santo Domingo, 25 November 1792, AGI-SD 1030, no. 338.

28. José Urízar to Pedro Acuña, 30 October 1792, AGS-SG 7157, exp. 23, no. 256; Fernando Portillo, Santo Domingo, 23 October 1793, AGS-SG 7157, exp. 22.

29. *Lettre de Biassou, de Jean-François, et de Belair, chefs des insurgés nègres de St. Domingue, aux commissaires nationaux civils dans cette colonie, 13 Décembre 1792* (Paris: l'Imprimerie Patriotique et Republicaine, 1793), BL-GRC, f. 686.(4). Though more widely printed than Popkin thought, this is the same text (with minor distinctions) from that said to be from July 1792. For the debate, see Popkin, *You Are All Free*, 50–52.

30. Joaquín García to Diego de Gardoqui, Santo Domingo, 25 December 1792, AGI-SD 1030, no. 346.

31. Joaquín García to Diego de Gardoqui, Santo Domingo, 25 January 1793, AGI-SD 1030, no. 352. Rochambeau had explained this development to García.

32. Joaquín García to Diego de Gardoqui, Santo Domingo, 25 February 1793, AGI-SD 1030, no. 359. Rochambeau departed for Martinique in mid-January, a strategic benefit for Jean-François.

33. Pedro Acuña to Conde del Campo de Alange, Aranjuez, 27 February 1793, AGS-SG 7161; Pedro Acuña to Joaquín García, Aranjuez, 26 March 1793, AGS-SG 7161; Popkin, *You Are All Free*, 250–260; Ferrer, *Freedom's Mirror*, 90–92.

34. Matt D. Childs, *The 1812 Aponte Rebellion in Cuba and the Struggle Against Atlantic Slavery* (Chapel Hill: University of North Carolina Press, 2006), chapter 3; Jane Landers, *Black Society in Spanish Florida* (Urbana: University of Illinois Press, 1999), chapter 9; Elena A. Schneider, *The Occupation of Havana: War, Trade, and Slavery in the Atlantic World* (Chapel Hill: University of North Carolina Press, 2018), part 3.

35. Joaquín García to Diego de Gardoqui, Santo Domingo, 25 March 1793, AGI-SD 1030, no. 365; Fick, *Making of Haiti*, 157–158.

36. Joaquín García to Diego de Gardoqui, Santo Domingo, 25 April 1793, AGI-SD 1030, no. 372.

37. Fernando Portillo to Pedro Acuña, Santo Domingo, 24 April 1793, BL-WM, Egerton 1794, vol. 2, 317–324.

38. Linda M. Heywood and John K. Thornton, *Central Africans, Atlantic Creoles, and the Foundation of the Americas, 1585–1660* (New York: Cambridge University Press, 2007); Terry Rey, "Kongolese Catholic Influences on Haitian Popular Catholicism," in *Central Africans and Cultural Transformations in the American Diaspora*, ed. Linda M. Heywood (New York: Cambridge University Press, 2002), 271; Childs, *Aponte*, 78–119.

39. Thornton, "'I Am the Subject of the King of Kongo'"; John Thornton, "African

Soldiers in the Haitian Revolution," *Journal of Caribbean History* 25 (1993): 58–80; Terry Rey, *Our Lady of Class Struggle: The Cult of the Virgin Mary in Haiti* (Trenton, NJ: Africa World Press, 1999), 32, 189, 209–222; Adrian Hastings, *The Church in Africa, 1450–1950* (New York: Oxford University Press, 1994), 71–126; Landers, *Atlantic Creoles*, 72, 147, 233; Heywood and Thornton, *Central Africans*; James Sweet, *Recreating Africa: Culture, Kinship, and Religion in the African-Portuguese World, 1441–1770* (Chapel Hill: University of North Carolina Press, 2004), 103–148.

40. Georges Biassou and Gabriel Bellair to Joaquín García, San Miguel, 15 July 1793, AGS-SG 7157, no. 7. Biassou clearly calls himself *jefe* ("chief") and not the usurping title of "king." Also see Landers, *Atlantic Creoles*, 55; Nessler, *Islandwide*, 25.

41. Thomas Madiou, *Histoire d'Haïti*, vol. 1 (Port-au-Prince: Courtois, 1847), 72–74. See also Ramsey, *Spirits and the Law*, 44–46; Landers, *Atlantic Creoles*, 61–64, 276n28.

42. Joaquín García to Manuel Godoy, 19 June 1793, AHN-E 3407, exp. 2. For later religious pluralism, see R. Andrew Chesnut, *Competitive Spirits: Latin America's New Religious Economy* (New York: Oxford University Press, 2003).

43. Joaquín García to Diego de Gardoqui, Santo Domingo, 25 March 1793, AGI-SD 1030, no. 365; Madiou, *Histoire*, 1:100–101; Also see Geggus, *Haitian Revolutionary Studies*, 49, 78, 117; Fick, *Making of Haiti*, 157–158; Popkin, *You Are All Free*, 43; David Geggus, *Slavery, War, and Revolution: The British Occupation of Saint Domingue, 1793–1798* (Oxford: Clarendon Press, 1982), 58.

44. Fernando Portillo to Pedro Acuña, Santo Domingo, 2 June 1793, BL-WM, Egerton 1794, vol. 2, 325–328.

45. Joaquín García, 20 July 1793, AGI-SD 1031, no. 127.

46. Joaquín García to Diego de Gardoqui, Santo Domingo, 3 July 1793, AGI-SD 1030, no. 390.

47. Jean-François, 9 July 1793, Tannerie, Les Archives Nationales de France (AN), D/XXV/12. Special thanks to Julia Gaffield for sharing select sources from the AN. José Vázquez, Dajabón, 1 October 1793, AGS-SG 7157, exp. 22, no. 459.

48. Joaquín García, 14 July 1793, AGI-SD 1031, no. 124.

49. Geggus, *Haitian Revolutionary Studies*, 15–16; Philippe Girard, *Toussaint Louverture: A Revolutionary Life* (New York: Basic Books, 2016), 17–18, 137.

50. "Révolution de St. Domingue, par M. Périès, trésorier . . . ," BL-WM, Add. Ms. 38074, 12.

51. See a similar conclusion from a later source with somewhat different details in Sudhir Hazareesingh, *Black Spartacus: The Epic Life of Toussaint Louverture* (New York: Farrar, Straus, and Giroux, 2020), 42–43, 377n5.

52. Antonio Barba, "Diario . . . diciembre de 1793," Archivo General Militar de Madrid (AGMM), Colección General (CG) rollo 65, 5-4-10-5.

53. Fernando Portillo, 1 July 1793, AGI-SD 1031.

54. Fernando Portillo, 25 August 1793, AGI-SD 1031.

55. Joaquín García to Diego de Gardoqui, Santo Domingo, 7 July 1793, AGI-SD 1030, no. 393; Joaquín García, 19 July 1793, AGI-SD 1031, no. 126. Jean-François considered permanently separating émigrés and Black Auxiliaries.

56. Joaquín García, 23 August 1793, AGI-SD 1031, no. 132.

57. Bramante Lazzary to Toussaint Louverture, La Tannerie, 1 September 1793, AN D/XXV/23.

58. Jean-François to José Vázquez, 17 October 1793, AGS-SG 7157, exp. 22, no. 454.

59. Joaquín García, 22 July 1793, AGI-SD 1031, no. 129; Diego de Gardoqui to Conde del Camp de Alange, 7 January 1794, AGS-SG 7159, exp. 7.

60. Antonio Barba, "Continuación de las noticias . . . hasta 25 de marzo de 1794," AGMM-CG rollo 65, 5-4-11-1.

61. Joaquín García to Diego de Gardoqui, Santo Domingo, 7 July 1793, AGI-SD 1030, no. 393.

62. Michele Reid-Vazquez, *The Year of the Lash: Free People of Color in Cuba and the Nineteenth-Century Atlantic World* (Athens: University of Georgia Press, 2011), 35–38. Also see chapters by Jane Landers and David Geggus in Christopher Leslie Brown and Philip D. Morgan, eds., *Arming Slaves: From Classical Times to the Modern Age* (New Haven, CT: Yale University Press, 2006).

63. Joaquín García to Diego de Gardoqui, Santo Domingo, June 1793, AGI-SD 1030, no. 387.

64. For additional context, see Sara Johnson, *Fear of French Negroes: Transcolonial Collaboration in the Revolutionary Americas* (Berkeley: University of California Press, 2012), chapter 2.

65. Joaquín García, 4 June 1793, AGN-ARH 22, exp. 50. The underscoring is in the original.

66. Joaquín García to Diego de Gardoqui, Santo Domingo, 23 July 1793, no. 398; Fernando Portillo, 24 August 1793, AGI-SD 1031.

67. Joaquín García to Diego de Gardoqui, Santo Domingo, 3–4 July 1793, AGI-SD 1030, nos. 390–391; Joaquín García to Manuel Godoy, 19 June 1793, AHN-E 3407, exp. 2. Before sale, Spanish officials recorded their "signs" or brandings, stature, age, residence in Saint-Domingue, skills, and "creole of Guinea."

68. Martin Mueses to Joaquín García, Santo Domingo, 21 August 1793, AGI-SD 1031, no. 410.

69. Joaquín García to Diego de Gardoqui, 23 August 1793, AGI-SD 1031, no. 408.

70. Juan Creagh to Diego de Gardoqui, Puerto Rico, 16 September 1793, AGI-SD 1031, no. 49.

71. Antonio Barba, "Continuación de las noticias ocurridas," 1793, AGMM-CG rollo 65, 5-4-10-5. See also Geggus, *Haitian Revolutionary Studies*, 267n50.

72. Joaquín García, 25 August 1793, AGI-SD 1031, no. 133; Juan Creagh to Diego de Gardoqui, Puerto Rico, 6 August 1793, AGI-SD 1031, no. 35. For prisoners in nearby Spanish colonies, see Cristina Soriano, *Tides of Revolution: Information, Insurgencies, and the Crisis of Colonial Rule in Venezuela* (Albuquerque: University of New Mexico Press, 2018), 106–109.

73. José Urízar to Eugenio Llaguno, Santo Domingo, 25 August 1794, AGI-SD 1032.

74. Joaquín García, 12 August 1793, AGI-SD 1031, no. 131. Jean-François then commanded over 6,600 troops himself.

75. 6 September 1793, AGI-SD 1031, no. 135. See also Popkin, *You Are All Free*, 236, 251–255.

76. Joaquín García, 4 and 25 September 1793, AGI-SD 1031, nos. 134, 143.

77. Étienne Polverel, "Sure les evenements qui ont eu lieu dans cette isle, depuis le commencement de la Revolution, jusqu'a la proclamation de la Liberté general," BHFIC, B-2a40; Joaquín García to Pedro Acuña, Santo Domingo, 23 November 1793, AGI-SD 956.

78. 13 and 25 September 1793, AGI-SD 1031, nos. 136, 142.

79. Lacroix, *Mémoires*, 159–160, 300; "Mon Odyssée," and "Inside the Insurgency," in *Facing Racial Revolution: Eyewitness Accounts of the Haitian Insurrection*, ed. Jeremy D. Popkin (Chicago: University of Chicago Press, 2007), 90, 136.

80. 13 and 25 September 1793, AGI-SD 1031, nos. 136, 142.

81. Lacroix, *Mémoires*, 160; "Mon Odyssée," and "Inside the Insurgency," in Popkin, *Facing Racial Revolution*, 91–92, 144–146.

82. 13 September 1793, AGI-SD 1031, no. 137.

83. Ferrer, *Freedom's Mirror*, 90–93; Fick, *Making of Haiti*, 139–140, 157–158, 185–187; Geggus, *Haitian Revolutionary Studies*, 49, 78, 117, 248n69.

84. 13 and 25 September 1793, AGI-SD 1031, nos. 136, 141, and 142. See also Geggus, *Haitian Revolutionary Studies*, 264n14.

85. 17 September 1793, AGI-SD 1031, no. 138.

86. Pedro Catani to Eugenio Llaguno, 25 May 1793, AGI-SD 929; Eugenio Llaguno to Consejo de Indias, 31 December 1793, AGI-SD 929. Additionally, a few *expedientes* appear in AGI-SD 956. For other context, see Johnson, *Fear*, 83–88.

87. "Listas de las causas . . . ," Audiencia de Santo Domingo, 25 January 1793, AGI-SD 998.

88. José Urízar to Pedro Acuña, Santo Domingo, 25 March 1793, AGI-SD 929; "Testimonio de auto," Real Audiencia de Santo Domingo, Santo Domingo, 27 February 1793, AGN-ARH 22, exp. 46.

89. Antonio Vent. a de Taranco to Eugenio de Llaguno, 20 May 1794, AGI-SD 929.

90. José Urízar to Pedro Acuña, Santo Domingo, 21 September 1793, AGI-SD 1014.

91. 23 September 1793, AGI-SD 1031, no. 140. See also Antonio Valdez to Manuel Godoy, Aranjuez, 17 June 1794, AHN-E 4829; Gabriel Aristizabal to Antonio Valdez, Bayajá, 19 March 1794, AHN-E 4829.

92. José Urízar to Manuel Godoy, Santo Domingo, 8 December 1793, AGI-SD 1030; 25 September 1793, AGI-SD 1031, no. 142.

93. Juan Bobadilla to Fernando Portillo, Neiba, 5 and 9 January 1794, AGI-SD 1031; Juan Bobadilla to Fernando Portillo, Neiba, 10 January 1794, AGI-SD 1031; Fick, *Making of Haiti*, 120–245; Geggus, *Haitian Revolutionary Studies*, 8, 14, 104–106.

94. Juan Quiñones to Fernando Portillo, Monte Cristi, 30 November 1793, AGI-SD 1031; Luis de las Casas to Manuel Godoy, Havana, 7 March 1794, AGI-E 14, no. 71.

Spain thought France might subvert Louisiana in retribution for campaigns in Saint-Domingue.

95. Joaquín García to Diego de Gardoqui, Santo Domingo, 17 December 1793, AGI-SD 1031, no. 431; 15 September 1794, AGI-E 13, no. 11.

96. 25 September 1793, AGI-SD 1031, no. 142.

97. José Urízar to Pedro Acuña, Santo Domingo, 25 September 1793, AGI-SD 1031.

98. Juan Bobadilla to Fernando Portillo, 12 January 1794, AGI-SD 1031.

99. Fernando Portillo to Eugenio Llaguno, Santo Domingo, 20 December 1793, AGI-SD 1031.

100. José Vázquez to Fernando Portillo, Dajabón, 18 December 1793, AGI-SD 1031.

101. Joaquín García to Conde del Campo de Alange, Santo Domingo, 17 September 1793, AGS-SG 7151, no. 353.

102. José Vázquez to Fernando Portillo, Dajabón, 18 December 1793, AGI-SD 1031; Cardinal Archbishop of Toledo to Eugenio Llaguno, 17 May 1794, AGI-SD 1031; Consejo de Estado, Aranjuez, 12 May 1793, AGI-SD 1031.

103. José Vázquez to Fernando Portillo, Dajabón, 23 December 1793, AGI-SD 1031.

104. José Urízar to Manuel Godoy, Santo Domingo, 8 December 1793, AGI-SD 1030.

105. Fernando Portillo to Joaquín García, Santo Domingo, 9 January 1794, AGI-SD 1031.

106. Fernando Portillo to Manuel Godoy, Santo Domingo, 29 January 1794, AGI-SD 1031.

107. Consejo de Estado, Aranjuez, 14 and 20 February 1794, AGI-SD 1031.

108. Antonio Barba, "Continuación de lo ocurrido en este mes de Nov.re . . . ," AGMM-CG rollo 65, 5-4-10-5.

109. Fernando Portillo to Manuel Godoy, Santo Domingo, 29 January 1794, AGI-SD 1031.

110. Joaquín García to Diego de Gardoqui, 22 January 1794, AGI-SD 1031, no. 434.

111. Joaquín García to Pedro Acuña, Bayajá, 5 February 1794, AGI-SD 1031; Joaquín García to Conde del Campo de Alange, Bayajá, 5 February 1794, AGS-SG 7159, exp. 32.

112. Fernando Portillo to Manuel Godoy, Santo Domingo, 29 January 1794, AGI-SD 1031.

113. Bellair, Santo Domingo, n.d., AGI-SD 1031. He most likely wrote this letter in January 1794.

114. Ferrer, *Freedom's Mirror*, 1–6; Geggus, *Haitian Revolutionary Studies*, 81–98, 179; Ramsey, *Spirits and the Law*, 42–45; David P. Geggus, "Saint-Domingue on the Eve of the Haitian Revolution," in *World of the Haitian Revolution*, ed. David Geggus and Norman Fiering (Bloomington: Indiana University Press, 2009), 6–7.

115. Bellair, Santo Domingo, n.d., AGI-SD 1031.

116. José Vázquez to Fernando Portillo, Dajabón, 8 and 9 January 1794, AGI-SD 1031.

117. "Proposiciones de la Guarnicion, y vecinos del Fuerte Delfin," Gabriel Aristizabal, Bahia de Manzanillo, 28 January 1794, AGI-SD 1031, no. 2.

118. Joaquín García to Diego de Gardoqui, Bayajá, 5 February 1794, AGI-SD 1031, nos. 436, 437; Joaquín García to Diego de Gardoqui, Bayajá, 6 February 1794, AGI-SD 1031, nos. 438, 444; Conde del Campo de Alange to Diego de Gardoqui, Aranjuez, 14 May 1794, AGI-SD 1031; Joaquín García to Diego de Gardoqui, Bayajá, 19 and 21 February 1794, AGI-SD 1031, nos. 441–442.

119. Joaquín García, 19 February 1794, Bayajá, AGS-SG 7159, exp. 35; José Vázquez to Fernando Portillo, Dajabón, 1 January 1794, AGI-SD 1031.

120. Joaquín García to Manuel Godoy, Bayajá, 24 February 1794, AGI-SD 1031, no. 66.

121. Fick, *Making of Haiti*, 159.

122. José Urízar to Manuel Godoy, 25 March 1794, AGI-E 13, no. 9.

123. Manuel Godoy to Eugenio Llaguno, Aranjuez, 2 March 1794, AGI-SD 1031; Joaquín García to Consejo de Indias, Bayajá, 10 April 1794, AGI-SD 1031, no. 446; Juan Creagh to Diego de Gardoqui, Puerto Rico, 28 April 1794, AGI-SD 1031, no. 112; José Urízar to Consejo de Indias, Santo Domingo, 25 February 1794, AGI-SD 1031; José Urízar to Conde del Campo de Alange, 25 February 1794, AGS-SG 7159, exp. 65; Joaquín García to Conde del Campo de Alange, Bayajá, 26 April 1794, AGS-SG 7159, exp. 36.

124. Fernando Portillo to Eugenio Llaguno, 6 August 1794, AGI-SD 1031; Pierre-Victor Malouet, 12 March 1795, TNA-WO 1/61, 123–130.

125. José Urízar to Manuel Godoy, 24 March 1794, AGI-E 13, no. 8.

126. Joaquín García to Conde del Campo de Alange, Bayajá, 13 April 1794, AGS-SG 7159, exp. 61.

127. Antonio Barba, "Continuación de las noticias . . . mes de Abril de 1794," AGMM-CG rollo 65, 5-4-11-1. On multiple partners, see Tyler D. Parry, "Love and Marriage: Domestic Relations and Matrimonial Strategies Among the Enslaved in the Atlantic World" (PhD diss., University of South Carolina, 2014), chapter 1.

128. Ferrer, *Freedom's Mirror*, 116.

129. Juan López Cancelada Dubroca, *Vida de J. J. Dessalines: Gefe de los negros de Santo Domingo* (México: Zúñiga y Ontiveros, 1806), 11–14. This source requires the caveat in the text.

130. Antonio Barba, "Novedades . . . correo anterior . . . ," April to 11 May 1794, AGMM-CG rollo 65, 5-4-11-1.

131. Geggus, *Haitian Revolutionary Studies*, 120–122.

132. Toussaint Louverture to Citoyen Rallier, 26 Germinal an VII / 15 April 1799, TNA-CO 245/2.

133. Louis-Antoine-Esprit Rallier, *Nouvelles observations sur Saint-Domingue* (Paris: Baudoin, 1796), 15n1, 42–43. See also Malick Ghachem, "The Colonial Vendée," in Geggus and Fiering, *World of the Haitian Revolution*, 156–176.

134. Landers, *Atlantic Creoles*, 55–76; Jacques de Cauna, "Dessalines esclave de Toussaint?," *Outre-mers* 99, nos. 374–375 (2012): 319–322; Girard, *Toussaint Louverture*; Dubois,

Avengers, 171–176; Geggus, *Haitian Revolutionary Studies,* 122–136; Fick, *Making of Haiti,* 183–185.

135. José Urízar to Eugenio Llaguno, Santo Domingo, 21 July 1794, AGI-SD 1031, no. 21. For mosquito-borne disease, see J. R. McNeill, *Mosquito Empires: Ecology and War in the Greater Caribbean, 1620–1914* (New York: Cambridge University Press, 2010), 235–295.

136. Pedro Cabellos to Fernando Portillo, San Rafael, 10 May 1794, AGI-SD 1031; Santo Domingo, 20 May 1794, AGS-SG 7159, exp. 67; Geggus, *Haitian Revolutionary Studies,* 120–123.

137. Cardinal Archbishop of Toledo to Eugenio Llaguno, 17 May 1795, AGI-SD 1031; Consejo de Estado, Aranjuez, 12 May 1793, AGI-SD 1031; Diego de Gardoqui to Eugenio Llaguno, Aranjuez, 20 June 1794, AGI-SD 1031; Cardinal Archbishop of Toledo to Eugenio Llaguno, Toledo, 4 June 1794, AGI-SD 1031.

138. José Nicolas de Azara to Eugenio Llaguno, Rome, 30 July 1794, AGI-SD 1031.

139. Fernando Portillo to José Nicolas de Azara, Santo Domingo, 12 May 1794, AGI-SD 1031.

140. Fernando Portillo to Eugenio Llaguno, San Juan de la Maguana, 12 July 1794, AGI-SD 1014; Geggus, *Slavery,* 165.

141. Fernando Portillo to Fray Gaspar Arcanio, n.d., AGI-SD 1031; Cardinal Casoni to Cardinal Zelada, 16 January 1796, Archivum Apostolicum Vaticanum / Archivum Secretum Vaticanum (ASV), Nunziatura di Madrid (NM), 196, 355–359. Portillo referenced Pope Pius VI's breve of 13 April 1791 that encouraged clergy to resist French secularization.

142. To Cardinal Casoni, Madrid, January 1795, ASV-NM 196, 34–36. This encompassed all Spanish forces fighting France. See also Diego Gardoqui to Cardinal Casoni, 17 August 1794, ASV-NM 196, 29–30.

143. Fernando Portillo to Eugenio Llaguno, 20 October 1794, AGI-SD 1031. See also Médéric Louis Élie Moreau de Saint-Méry, *Description topographique, physique, civile, politique et historique de la partie française de l'isle Saint-Domingue,* vol. 1 (Philadelphia: author, 1797), 497–502; Madiou, *Histoire,* 1:243; Geggus, *Haitian Revolutionary Studies,* 125–129, 267n50; Carlos Esteban Deive, *Vodú y magia* (Santo Domingo: Fundación Cultural Dominicana, 1979), 113–117.

144. Fernando Portillo to José Urízar, 6 June 1794, AGI-SD 1014; Fernando Portillo to Eugenio Llaguno, 6 August and 20 October 1794, AGI-SD 1031; Juan Bobadilla to Fernando Portillo, 8 January 1794, AGI-SD 1031; Fernando Portillo to Real Fiscal, 20 June 1794, AGI-SD 1102, no. 35; José Urízar to Eugenio Llaguno, Santo Domingo, 25 July 1794, AGI-SD 1014; Antonio Ventura de Faranaco to Audiencia de Santo Domingo, 23 March 1795, AGI-SD 1102, no. 39; Fernando Portillo to Juan Bobadilla, 5 June 1795, AGI-SD 1102; Antonio Sánchez Valverde, *Idea del valor de la isla Española* (Madrid: Pedro Marín, 1785), xvi and 87; Carlos Esteban Deive, *Los guerrilleros negros: Esclavos fugitivos y cimarrones en Santo Domingo* (Santo Domingo: Fundación Cultural Dominicana, 1997), 71–72, 230–231. For Spaniards praising affiliated maroons' efficient return of uninvited

runaways, see Antonio Barba, Santo Domingo, 8 December 1793, AGMM-CG rollo 65, 5-4-10-5.

145. Fernando Portillo to José Urízar, 30 June 1794, AGI-SD 1014.

146. Antonio Barba to Francisco Sabatini, Santo Domingo, 8 February 1797, AGMM-CG rollo 65, 5-4-11-2.

147. "Complément aux mémoire d'un vieux officeur française sur la guerre dans l'isle de St. Domingue," 14 October 1797, TNA-WO 1/66, 577–588; September 1796, TNA-WO 1/65, 267–322; Consejo de Indias, 12 June 1798, AGI-SD 1008.

148. José Urízar to Eugenio Llaguno, Santo Domingo, 25 July 1794, AGI-SD 1031, no. 7.

149. Dubois, *Avengers*, 180; James Alexander Dun, *Dangerous Neighbors: Making the Haitian Revolution in Early America* (Philadelphia: University of Pennsylvania Press, 2016), 13–16; Geggus, *Haitian Revolutionary Studies*, 19; Landers, *Atlantic Creoles*, 76–78.

150. Fermín Montaño, "Con el mayor . . . ," Bayajá, 12 July 1794, AGMM-CG rollo 65, 5-4-11-1.

151. "Before the Council of Cape Nicholas Mole," 15 July 1794, TNA, Colonial Office (CO), 137/93, 236–238; "An Account of the Massacre," *Philadelphia Gazette*, 15 August 1794, 3; "From Fort Dauphin," *Weekly Museum* (New York), 23 August 1794, 3; "Capt. Baker," *Farmer's Library* (Rutland, VT), 9 September 1794, 3; "Tuesday Arrived," *Virginia Chronicle* (Norfolk), 21 August 1794, 3.

152. Popkin, *Facing Racial Revolution*, 256–257; Landers, *Atlantic Creoles*, 76–77; Dun, *Dangerous Neighbors*, 1–6; Ferrer, *Freedom's Mirror*, 110–128.

153. "Relación de Juan Fran.co de los echos . . . Lunes 7 del presente," 11 July 1794, AGMM-CG rollo 65, 5-4-11-1.

154. "Before the Council of Cape Nicholas Mole," 15 July 1794, TNA-CO 137/93, 236–238.

155. Joaquín García to Conde del Campo de Alange, Santiago, 1 August 1794, AGI-SD 1089, no. 494.

156. Ferrer, *Freedom's Mirror*, 120–124.

157. "Before the Council of Cape Nicholas Môle," 15 July 1794, TNA-CO 137/93, 236–238; José Urízar to Eugenio Llaguno, Santo Domingo, 21 July 1794, AGI-SD 1031, no. 21.

158. José Urízar to Eugenio Llaguno, Santo Domingo, 25 August 1794, AGI-SD 1032.

159. "N.15," Gaspar Casasola, et al., Bayajá, 14 July 1794, AGI-SD 1089, no. 504.

160. Joaquín García to Conde del Campo de Alange, Santiago, 11 August 1794, AGI-SD 1089, no. 503; Pedro Cabellos to Fernando Portillo, San Rafael, 11 August 1794, AGI-SD 1031; Esteban Palomares, Santiago, 11 August 1794, AGS-SG 7160, exp. 3. See also Fick, *Making of Haiti*, 74, 304n105.

161. José Urízar to Eugenio Llaguno, Santo Domingo, 25 August 1794, AGI-SD 1032; Antonio Boville to Conde del Campo de Alange, Santo Domingo, 25 August 1795, AGS-SG 7165.

162. Fernando Portillo to Eugenio Llaguno, Bánica, 14 September 1794, AGI-SD 1031.

163. Pierre François Venault de Charmilly, "Letter on the State of St. Domingo," 24 August 1794, TNA-WO 1/59, 497–520.

164. Francisco Cubillan to Fernando Portillo, Las Cahobas, 10 September 1794, AGI-SD 1031; Eugenio Llaguno to Manuel Godoy, San Yldefonso, 22 and 25 July 1794, AGI-SD 1031.

165. José Urízar to Eugenio Llaguno, Santo Domingo, 24 September 1794 and 25 October 1794, AGI-SD 1032; Antonio Segovia, 25 November 1794, AGI-SD 1035, no. 2. Most of *legajo* 1035 deals with this theft audit.

166. Fernando Portillo to Francisco Xavier de Herrera, Santo Domingo, 20 November 1794, AGI-SD 1031; Fernando Portillo to Eugenio Llaguno, Santo Domingo, 24 November 1794, AGI-SD 1031.

167. Toussaint Louverture to Juan Lleonart, " . . . 15 octubre estilo viejo . . . copia de la traducción . . . ," AGMM-CG rollo 65, 5-4-11-1; Juan Lleonart and Matias Armona, "Relacion ocurrido en la frontera del oeste el 16 del pasado," AGMM-CG rollo 65, 5-4-11-1. See also Ferrer, *Freedom's Mirror*, 140–142.

168. José Urízar to Eugenio Llaguno, Santo Domingo, 25 November 1794, AGI-SD 1032. See also AGS-SG 6856, exp. 39; AGS-SG 6855, exps. 51–54.

169. Ygnacio Batista, Juan Ximenes, Francisco Gomes, Manuel Ortis, Bartholome Vasallo, 3 November 1794, AGI-SD 1032.

170. Urízar, Toncerrada, Bravo, 5 November 1794, AGI-SD 1032.

171. Urízar, Bravo, and Toncerrada, Santo Domingo, 25 November 1794, AGI-SD 1032.

172. "Jacobin Club, 19th Thermidor," *Gazette of the United States*, 4 November 1794, 2.

173. Juan Sánchez Valverde to José Nolasco Mañon, Bánica, 1 September 1794, AGI-SD 1031. Romana was from "Cartie Morien" (Quartier-Morin) a few miles southeast of Cap-Français.

174. Fernando Portillo to Eugenio Llaguno, Bánica, 14 September 1794, AGI-SD 1031.

175. Urízar, Catani, Bravo, and Toncerrada, Santo Domingo, 25 August 1795, AGI-SD 999.

176. Antonio Barba, "Noticias . . . hasta 25 Junio de 1795," AGMM-CG rollo 65, 5-4-11-1.

CHAPTER 4: MANY ENEMIES WITHIN, 1795–1798

1. Fernando Portillo to Eugenio Llaguno, Santo Domingo, 24 October 1795, AGI-SD 1033. For the Hispanic Atlantic context, see Scott Eastman, *Preaching Spanish Nationalism Across the Hispanic Atlantic, 1759–1823* (Baton Rouge: Louisiana State University Press, 2012), chapter 4.

2. Committee of Public Safety Secretary of Colonial Administration to Citizens, Governor, and Administrators of Saint-Domingue, Paris, 4 Fructidor an III / 21 August 1795, AHN-E 3407, exp. 2.

3. Cambacérès, Sieyès, Révellière-Lépeaux, Daunou, Louvet, Henry-Larivière, Merlin, and Boissy, "Instrucción que debe servir de regla al Agente Interino del Gov.no Francés . . . de Santo Domingo," Paris, an IV / 1795, AHN-E 3407, exp. 1.

4. Fernando Portillo to Eugenio Llaguno, Santo Domingo, 24 August 1795, AGI-SD 1033.

5. Étienne Laveaux to Joaquín García, Port-de-Paix, 4 Frimaire an IV / 25 November 1795, AHN-E 3407, exp. 2.

6. Cardinal Casoni, 28 July 1795, ASV-NM 196, 143–152; Cardinal Casoni, 1 September 1795, ASV-NM 196, 222–224.

7. Fernando Portillo to José Urízar, Neiba, 6 June 1794, AGI-SD 1014.

8. Joaquín García to Manuel Godoy, Santo Domingo, 4 January 1796, AHN-E 3407, exp. 2, no. 38; Joaquín García to Diego de Gardoqui, Santo Domingo, 7 December 1796, AGI-SD 1033; Fernando Portillo to Manuel Godoy, Santo Domingo, 25 April 1796, AGI-E 11A, no. 10.

9. Pedro L. San Miguel, *La Isla imaginada: Historia, identidad y utopia en La Española* (Santo Domingo: La Trinitaria, 1997), chapters 1 and 2; Lester D. Langley, *The Americas in the Age of Revolution, 1750–1850* (New Haven, CT: Yale University Press, 1996), 1–12.

10. Fernando Portillo to Manuel Godoy, Santo Domingo, 25 April 1796, AGI-E 11A, no. 10.

11. Fernando Portillo to Manuel Godoy, 4 August 1796, AGI-E 11A, no. 2.

12. Joaquín García to Conde del Campo de Alange, 7 January 1796, AGI-SD 1091, no. 796.

13. José Urízar to Manuel Godoy, 29 April 1797, AGI-E 13, no. 42.

14. On Spanish management of continued Dominican slavery, see AGN, Archivo Real de Bayaguana (ARB), leg. 1, exp. 58; leg. 3, exp. 38; leg. 4, exp. 54; and leg. 49, exp. 25, and AGN-ARH, leg. 37, exps. 77, 85, and 95, and leg. 39R, exps. 28, 36, 64–65, 69, and 73. No invisible emancipation transpired for Dominican slaves. Graham Nessler, *An Islandwide Struggle for Freedom: Revolution, Emancipation, and Reenslavement on Hispaniola, 1789–1809* (Chapel Hill: University of North Carolina Press, 2016), 63; Laurent Dubois, *Avengers of the New World: The Story of the Haitian Revolution* (Cambridge, MA: Belknap Press of Harvard University Press, 2004), 217.

15. Joaquín García to Conde del Campo de Alange, Santo Domingo, 17 May 1795, AGS-SG 7165, exp. 25, no. 624; Jenny Marsh, *Penguin Book of Classical Myths* (New York: Penguin, 2008), chapter 5.

16. Joaquín García to Conde del Campo de Alange, Santo Domingo, 17 May 1795, AGS-SG 7160, exp. 18, f. 126.

17. Fernando Portillo to Conde del Campo de Alange, Santo Domingo, 24 August 1795, AGMM, Ultramar (U), Santo Domingo (SD) 5647, exp. 1; Fernando Portillo to Eugenio Llaguno, Santo Domingo, 25 June 1795, AGI-SD 1032.

18. Urízar, Toncerrada, Bravo, 5 November 1794, AGI-SD 1032.

19. Fernando Portillo to Eugenio Llaguno, Santo Domingo, 24 August 1795, AGI-SD 1033; Antonio Barba to Francisco Sabatini, 24 August 1795, AGMM-CG rollo 65, 5-4-11-1.

20. Antonio Barba, 11–15 August and 24 September 1795, AGMM-CG rollo 65, 5-4-11-1.

21. Fernando Portillo to Eugenio Llaguno, Santo Domingo, 25 January 1795 (2), AGI-SD 1031; Manuel Godoy to José Urízar, 21 March 1795, AGI-SD 1032.

22. José Urízar to Eugenio Llaguno, Santo Domingo, 25 June 1795, AGI-SD 1033; José Urízar to Eugenio Llaguno, Santo Domingo, 25 February 1795, AGI-SD 1032; Batista, Ximenes, Gomes, Ortis, and Vasallo, 3 November 1794, AGI-SD 1032.

23. José Urízar to Eugenio Llaguno, Santo Domingo, 25 June 1795, AGI-SD 1032.

24. Antonio López Quintana, 25 April 1795, AGI-SD 1032, no. 22; José Reyna, Joaquín Sonodo, La Guira, 1 May 1795, AGI-SD 1032, no. 16.

25. Roberto Cassá, "Les effets du Traité de Bâle," in *Saint-Domingue espagnol et la révolution nègre d'Haïti, 1790–1822*, ed. Alain Yacou (Paris: Éditions Karthala, 2007), 203–210.

26. Joaquín García to Eugenio Llaguno, Bayajá, 23 May 1794, AGI-SD 1031, no. 69.

27. Carlos Lesec to Joaquín García, Santa Susana, 9 April 1794, AGS-SG 7159, exp. 33, ff. 152–153; Joaquín García to Eugenio Llaguno Amirola, Bayajá, 12 April 1794, AGS-SG 7159, exp. 33, ff. 150–151; 22 September 1794, AGS-SG leg. 7159, exp. 60, ff. 301–302.

28. Joaquín García to Conde del Campo de Alange, Santo Domingo, 20 June 1795, AGI-SD 1089, no. 658.

29. David Geggus, *Haitian Revolutionary Studies* (Bloomington: Indiana University Press, 2002), 119–135.

30. Manuel Godoy to Joaquín García, San Ildefonso, 23 September 1794, AGS-SG leg. 7159, exp. 60, f. 305.

31. J. C. Dorsainvil, *Manuel d'histoire d'Haïti* (Port-au-Prince: Henri Deschamps, 1924), 84.

32. Joaquín García to Conde del Campo de Alange, 23 April 1795, AGS-SG leg. 7151, exp. 97, no. 619. For comparable regional cases of racialized inscription, see Ada Ferrer, *Insurgent Cuba: Race, Nation, and Revolution, 1868–1898* (Chapel Hill: University of North Carolina Press, 1999), 48–52, 127–129, 148, 180–182.

33. Aware of geopolitical shifts, Portillo angled for a vacant archbishopric in Andalucía. Fernando Portillo to Eugenio Llaguno, Santo Domingo, 24 August 1795, AGI-SD 1033. See also Jonathan Smyth, *Robespierre and the Festival of the Supreme Being: The Search for a Republican Morality* (Manchester, UK: Manchester University Press, 2016).

34. José Urízar to Eugenio Llaguno, Santo Domingo, 25 August 1795, AGI-SD 1033.

35. Gordon Forbes to Ralph Abercrombie, Port-au-Prince, 25 August 1796, BL-WM, Add. Ms. 39824.

36. José Urízar to Eugenio Llaguno, Santo Domingo, 25 August and 25 September 1795, AGI-SD 1033.

37. José Urízar to Eugenio Llaguno, Santo Domingo, 25 September 1795, AGI-SD 1033; Anonymous to "Tabares," Môle Saint-Nicolas, 28 July 1796, AHN-E 3407, exp. 2.

38. Committee of Public Safety Office of the Navy to Étienne Laveaux, Paris, 1 Fructidor an III / 18 August 1795, AHN-E 3407, exp. 2.

39. Committee of Public Safety Secretary of Colonial Administration to Citizens, Governor, and Administrators of Saint-Domingue, Paris, 4 Fructidor an III / 21 August 1795, AHN-E 3407, exp. 2; Marquis Bute to Manuel Godoy, 12 July 1795, AHN-E 3407, exp. 2.

40. Cardinal Casoni to Cardinal Zelada, 29 March 1796, ASV-NM 196, 405–406.

41. Joaquín García to Manuel Godoy, Santo Domingo, 25 October 1795, AHN-E 3407, exp. 2, no. 17; José Urízar to Eugenio Llaguno, Santo Domingo, 22 December 1795, AGI-SD 1033.

42. José Urízar to Eugenio Llaguno, Santo Domingo, 3 November 1795, AGI-SD 1033; Manuel Godoy to Joaquín García, Sevilla, 24 February 1796, AHN-E 3407, exp. 2.

43. José Urízar to Eugenio Llaguno, Santo Domingo, 22 December 1795, AGI-SD 1033; David Geggus, *Slavery, War, and Revolution: The British Occupation of Saint Domingue, 1793–1798* (Oxford: Clarendon Press, 1982), 178–182.

44. Joaquín García to Marqués de Casa Calvo, Santo Domingo, 9 November 1795, AHN-E 3407, exp. 2; Manuel Godoy to José Chacon, 24 February 1796, AHN-E 3407, exp. 2; Manuel Godoy to Marqués de Casa Calvo, Sevilla, 24 February 1796, AHN-E 3407, exp. 2.

45. Joaquín García to Manuel Godoy, Santo Domingo, 17 December 1795, AHN-E 3407, exp. 2, no. 32.

46. José Urízar to Eugenio Llaguno, Santo Domingo, 8 January 1796, AGI-SD 1033; José Urízar to Eugenio Llaguno, Santo Domingo, 23 January 1796, AGI-SD 1033; Manuel Godoy to Joaquín García, 27 January 1796, AHN-E 3407, exp. 1.

47. José Pablo Valiente to Diego de Gardoqui, Havana, 13 January 1796, AGI-SD 1033, no. 522. For Black Auxiliaries in Florida, see Jane Landers, *Black Society in Spanish Florida* (Urbana: University of Illinois Press, 1999), 91–97, 128–133, 209–220. For their dispersal elsewhere in the Americas, and specifically Central America, see Miriam Martin Erickson, "The Black Auxiliary Troops of King Carlos IV: African Diaspora in the Entangled Spanish Atlantic World" (PhD diss., Vanderbilt University, 2015).

48. François Chappotin to Joaquín García, Neiba, 7 December 1795, AGI-E 5B, no. 90.

49. Consejo de Indias, 12 December 1815, AGI, Ultramar (U), 329, no. 11.

50. Fernando Portillo to Eugenio Llaguno, Santo Domingo, 24 October 1795, AGI-SD 1033.

51. Fernando Portillo, 20 October 1795, AGI-SD 1033.

52. Joaquín García to Manuel Godoy, Santo Domingo, 19 November 1795, AHN-E 3407, exp. 2, no. 23.

53. Laveaux, Manlau, Grandet, Baubert, Pierre-Paul, Noel Leveitte, and Laratett, Cap-Français, 30 Vendémiaire an IV / 22 October 1795, AHN-E 3407, exp. 1; Joaquín García to Manuel Godoy, Santo Domingo, 22 December 1795, AHN-E 3407, exp. 2, no. 36; Antonioa Barba to Francisco Sabatini, Santo Domingo, 24 August 1795, AGMM-CG rollo 65, 5-4-11-1.

54. José Urízar to Eugenio Llaguno, Santo Domingo, 23 November 1795, AGI-SD 1033; Gabriel Aristizabal to Joaquín García, Ocoa, 15 November 1795, AHN-E 3407, exp. 2; Joaquín García to Manuel Godoy, Santo Domingo, 19 November 1795, AHN-E 3407, exp. 2, no. 23.

55. Fernando Portillo to Manuel Godoy, Santo Domingo, 24 January 1796, AGI-E 11B, no. 44.

56. José del Orbe to Joaquín García, La Vega, 8 November 1795, AGI-E 5A, no. 50; Joaquín García to Manuel Godoy, Santo Domingo, 21 November 1795, AGI-E 5A, no. 50. See also Carlos Esteban Deive, *Los guerrilleros negros: Esclavos fugitivos y cimarrones en Santo Domingo* (Santo Domingo: Fundación Cultural Dominicana, 1997), 191–201, 235–245; Carolyn Fick, *The Making of Haiti: The Saint Domingue Revolution from Below* (Knoxville: University of Tennessee Press, 1990), 51–52.

57. Joaquín García to Manuel Godoy, Santo Domingo, 7 December 1795, AHN-E 3407, exp. 2, no. 30.

58. Adam Williamson to Henry Dundas, Port-au-Prince, January 1796, TNA-WO 1/65, 9.

59. José Urízar to Eugenio Llaguno Amirola, Santo Domingo, 8 January 1796, AGI-E 13, no. 19.

60. Joaquín García to Léger-Félicité Sonthonax, Santo Domingo, 19 December 1795, AHN-E 3407, exp. 2; Joaquín García to Étienne Laveaux, Santo Domingo, 19 December 1795, AGI-SD 1033.

61. Étienne Laveaux to Joaquín García, Port-de-Paix, 4 Frimaire an IV / 25 November 1795, AHN-E 3407, exp. 2.

62. Étienne Laveaux to Joaquín García, Port-de-Paix, 4 Frimaire an IV / 25 November 1795, AHN-E 3407, exp. 2.

63. M. d'Hermand to Manuel Godoy, Madrid, 2 Pluviôse an IV / 22 January 1796, AHN-E 3407, exp. 1.

64. M. d'Hermand to Manuel Godoy, Escorial, 7 Frimaire an IV / 28 November 1795, AHN-E 3407, exp. 1.

65. *L'Impartial de Saint-Domingue*, 29 Pluviôse an IV / 17 February 1796, AHN-E 3407, exp. 1; Emilio La Parra López, *La alianza de Manuel Godoy con los revolucionarios: España y Francia a fines del siglo XVIII* (Madrid: Editorial CSIC, 1992), 111–116.

66. Manuel Godoy to M. d'Hermand, San Lorenzo, 10 December 1795, AHN-E 3407, exp. 1.

67. Philippe Roume to Vice Admiral Laurent Jean François Truguet, Madrid, 30 Frimaire an IV / 21 December 1795, Tulane University Special Collections (TUSC), Rosemonde E. and Emile Kuntz Collection (KC), Box 4, Folder 103; Manuel Godoy, *Memoirs of Don Manuel de Manuel Godoy, Prince of the Peace, Duke del Alcudia,* ed. J. B. D'Esmenard (London: Richard Bentley, 1826), 178–179, 393, 411–412, 426, 466.

68. Godoy, *Memoirs*, 412.

69. "Instrucción que debe servir de regla al Agente Interino . . . ," Cambacérès, Sieyès, Révellière-Lépeaux, Daunou, Louvet, Henry-Larivière, Merlin, and Boissy, Paris, an

IV / 1795, AHN-E 3407, exp. 1. For the Vendée, see Hugh Gough, "Genocide and the Bicentenary: The French Revolution and the Revenge of the Vendée," *Historical Journal* 30 (1987): 977–988.

70. Cardinal Casoni, 24 November and 12 December 1795, and 12 and 19 January and 15 March 1796, ASV-NM 196, 295–296, 312–315, 342–343, 349–351, 394–395.

71. Philippe Roume to Manuel Godoy, Madrid, 3 Nivôse an IV / 24 December 1795, AHN-E 3407, exp. 1.

72. Cardinal Casoni, 12 April 1796, ASV-NM 196, 416–417.

73. Manuel Godoy, 26 February 1796, AHN-E 3407, exp. 1; Marqués del Socorro to Manuel Godoy, Bay of Cádiz, 12 March 1796, AHN-E 3407, exp. 1; Marqués del Socorro to Manuel Godoy, 7 June 1796, AHN-E 3407, exp. 1; Joaquín García to Manuel Godoy, Santo Domingo, 12 April 1796, AHN-E 3407, exp. 2, no. 59.

74. Manuel Godoy, February 1796, AHN-E 3395, exp. 2; Manuel Candido Moreno to Manuel Godoy, Sevilla, 26 February 1796, AHN-E 3395, exp. 2; Juan Ignacio de Bejarano y Frias to Manuel Godoy, Madrid, 16 January 1796, AHN-E 3395; "Relativo a los procedimientos judiciales hechos en Sevilla . . . ," AHN-E 3918, exp. 22; Felix Fabre, Sevilla, 26 August 1795, ASV-NM 196, 228–229. Several exiled French priests in Sevilla asked the papacy for an assignment on Hispaniola.

75. José Urízar to Manuel Godoy, Santo Domingo, 16 April 1796, AHN-E 3407, exp. 2. By mid-1796, Spain had transferred a few strategic positions to France. For example, see José Urízar to Eugenio Llaguno, Santo Domingo, 25 May 1796, AGI-SD 1033; Esteban Fernández de León to Diego de Gardoqui, Caracas, 8 June 1796, AGI-SD 1033; Joaquín García to Manuel Godoy, Santo Domingo, 13 July 1796, AHN-E 3407, exp. 2, no. 73.

76. Antonio Barba to Francisco Sabatini, Santo Domingo, 4 August 1796, AGMM-CG rollo 65, 5-4-11-2.

77. Fernando Portillo to Manuel Godoy, Santo Domingo, 4 August 1796, AGI-E 11A, no. 2.

78. Philippe Roume to Joaquín García, Santo Domingo, 26 July 1796, AGI-E 11A, no. 2.

79. For earlier, comparable cases nearby, see Martin Nesvig, *Promiscuous Power: An Unorthodox History of New Spain* (Austin: University of Texas Press, 2018).

80. Philippe Roume to Fernando Portillo, Santo Domingo, 16 Brumaire an V / 6 November 1796, AHN-E 3395, exp. 2.

81. "Révolution de St. Domingue, par M. Périès, trésorier . . . ," BL-WM, Add. Ms. 38074, 222. See also Marlene Daut, *Tropics of Haiti: Race and the Literary History of the Haitian Revolution in the Atlantic World, 1789–1865* (Liverpool: Liverpool University Press, 2015), 215–223; Doris Garraway, *The Libertine Colony: Creolization in the Early French Caribbean* (Durham, NC: Duke University Press, 2005); Philippe Girard, *The Slaves Who Defeated Napoléon: Toussaint Louverture and the Haitian War of Independence, 1801–1804* (Tuscaloosa: University of Alabama Press, 2011), 31.

82. Philippe Roume to Fernando Portillo, Santo Domingo, 22 May 1796, AGI-E 11A, no. 2. Roume's mention of adopting the name of Ayti for the entire island came in

May 1796. For another early reference, seemingly from July 1796 and only referring to Saint-Domingue, see Geggus, *Haitian Revolutionary Studies*, 212–216.

83. Philippe Roume to Fernando Portillo, Santo Domingo, 22 May 1796, AGI-E 11A, no. 2.

84. Fernando Portillo to Manuel Godoy, Santo Domingo, 24 January 1796, AGI-E 11B, no. 44; Fray Gregorio Ramos to Fernando Portillo, Santiago, 11 January 1796, AGI-E 11B, no. 44.

85. Juan Caballero to Fernando Portillo, Santiago, 8 January 1796, AGI-E 11B, no. 44; Fernando Portillo to Conde del Campo de Alange, Santo Domingo, 24 January 1796, AGI-E 11B, no. 44.

86. Fernando Portillo to Manuel Godoy, Santo Domingo, 8 June 1796, AGI-E 11A, no. 11.

87. Fernando Portillo to Manuel Godoy, Santo Domingo, 4 August 1796, AGI-E 11A, no. 2.

88. Fernando Portillo to Manuel Godoy, Santo Domingo, 25 April 1796, AGI-E 11A, no. 10.

89. José Urízar to Manuel Godoy, Santo Domingo, 22 July 1796, AGI-E 13, no. 26.

90. José Urízar to Eugenio Llaguno, Santo Domingo, 22 December 1795, AGI-SD 1033; José Urízar to Eugenio Llaguno, Santo Domingo, 8 January 1796, AGI-SD 1033.

91. See also Michel-Rolph Trouillot, *Silencing the Past: Power and the Production of History* (Boston: Beacon, 1995), chapter 4; Ada Ferrer, *Freedom's Mirror: Cuba and Haiti in the Age of Revolution* (New York: Cambridge University Press, 2014), 137, 322; Maria Cecilia Ulrickson, "'Esclavos que fueron' in Santo Domingo, 1768–1844" (PhD diss., University of Notre Dame, 2018), 17.

92. Ministerio de la Gobernación de España, "Continúa la venta de las fincas," *Gaceta de Madrid* 1, no. 18 (February 11, 1817): 172; Ministerio de la Gobernación de España, "Continúa la venta de las fincas," *Gaceta de Madrid* 1, no. 29 (March 8, 1817): 272; Médéric Louis Elie Moreau de Saint-Méry, *Description topographique et politique de la partie espagnole de l'isle Saint-Domingue*, vol. 1 (Philadelphia: author, 1796), 105; Antonio Sánchez Valverde, *Idea del valor de la isla Española* (Madrid: Pedro Marín, 1785), 22–24, 121; Kathleen Ann Myers, *Fernández de Oviedo's Chronicle of America: A New History for a New World* (Austin: University of Texas Press, 2007), 18–22.

93. Joaquín García to Conde de Santa Clara, Santo Domingo, 20 November 1796, AGS-SG 6858, exp. 5, f. 16.

94. David P. Geggus, "Slave Resistance in the Spanish Caribbean in the Mid-1790s," in *A Turbulent Time: The French Revolution and the Greater Caribbean*, ed. David Barry Gaspar and David Patrick Geggus (Bloomington: Indiana University Press, 1997), 139–149; Antonio Pinto Tortosa, "Santo Domingo's Slaves in the Context of the Peace of Basel: Boca Nigua's Black Insurrection, 1796," *Journal of Early American History* 3 (2013): 131–153.

95. Joaquín García to Manuel Godoy, Santo Domingo, 1 November 1796, AHN-E 3407, exp. 2, no. 89. See also Manuel Bravo to Joaquín García, Santo Domingo, 14 December 1796, AGI-SD 1033. Officials called them enslaved because they were still

legally so under Spanish law. See also Nessler, *Islandwide*, 120–124. French republicans sometimes referred to the enslaved in Santo Domingo as *cultivateurs*, a reflection of their nomenclature for free Black laborers in Saint-Domingue. For example, see Comité de Salut Public, Paris, 4 Fructidor an III / 21 August 1795, AHN-E 3407, exp. 2; Philippe Roume to Joaquín García, Cap-Français, 7 Floréal an VIII / 27 April 1800, AHN-E 3395, exp. 2.

96. Antonio Barba, "Relación . . . ," n.d., AGMM-CG rollo 65, 5-4-11-2. For more on Barba, one of the longest-serving Spanish officers on Hispaniola, see Antonio Barba, 8 February 1771, BL-WM, Egerton 1793.

97. Manuel Bravo to Joaquín García, Santo Domingo, 14 December 1796, AGI-SD 1033.

98. Robin Law, "West Africa's Discovery of the Atlantic," *International Journal of African Historical Studies* 44, no. 1 (2011): 9–24. For "Congo" slaves known to commit suicide to fly home, though not as often as those from the Bights of Benin or Biafra, see Louis A. Pérez, *To Die in Cuba: Suicide and Society* (Chapel Hill: University of North Carolina Press, 2005), 35–36; William D. Piersen, "White Cannibals, Black Martyrs: Fear, Depression, and Religious Faith as Causes of Suicide Among New Slaves," *Journal of Negro History* 62, no. 2 (April 1977): 147–159.

99. Manuel Barcia, *West African Warfare in Bahia and Cuba: Soldier Slaves in the Atlantic World, 1807–1844* (New York: Oxford University Press, 2014).

100. Manuel Bravo to Joaquín García, Santo Domingo, 14 December 1796, AGI-SD 1033.

101. Aisha K. Finch, *Rethinking Slave Rebellion in Cuba: La Escalera and the Insurgencies of 1841–1844* (Chapel Hill: University of North Carolina Press, 2015), 157–165; David Barry Gaspar, *Bondmen and Rebels: A Study of Master-Slave Relations in Antigua, with Implications for Colonial British America* (Baltimore: Johns Hopkins University Press, 1985), 171–254.

102. Manuel Bravo to Joaquín García, Santo Domingo, 14 December 1796, AGI-SD 1033.

103. "Testimonio de la sentencia pronunciada contra los negros de la hacienda de Boca Nigua . . . ," José Urízar, Pedro Catani, Manuel Bravo, and José Francisco Hidalgo, Santo Domingo, 28 November 1796, AGI-SD 1033; African Origins Database, african -origins.org; Trans-Atlantic Slave Trade Database, www.slavevoyages.org/voyage/ database; Walter Henry Stapleton, *Comparative Handbook of Congo Languages* (Yakusu Stanley Falls, Congo Independent State: Hannah Wade Printing, 1903), 268–271. On François Espaillat's family purchasing captives from Charles Gérard, see Emilio Rodríguez Demorizi, ed., *Papeles de Espaillat* (Santo Domingo: Editora del Caribe), 474.

104. "Testimonio . . . ," Urízar et al., Santo Domingo, 28 November 1796, AGI-SD 1033. The archbishop used the word *amartelado*, meaning infatuated, enamored, or in love. See *Nuevo diccionario portátil español e inglés: Compuesto según los mejores diccionarios que hasta ahora han salido a luz en ambas nacional* (Paris: Bossange, Masson, Besson, 1803), 30; *A New Dictionary of the Spanish and English Languages in Four Volumes*, vol. 1 (Madrid: Cámara de Su Majestad, 1798), 127.

105. Fernando Portillo to Pedro Acuña, Santo Domingo, 25 October 1793, AGI-SD 1110; Marqués del Campo to Manuel Godoy, London, 3 July 1795, AHN-E 4247; Marqués del Campo to Manuel Godoy, London, 23 January 1795, AHN-E 4247; Vicente Matos to Joaquín García, Monte Cristi, 16 August 1795, AHN-E 3407; 8 March 1796, ASV-NM 196, 386; Marqués del Campo to Manuel Godoy, London, 10 July 1795, AHN-E 4247; Manuel Godoy to José Chacon, Sevilla, 24 February 1796, AHN-E 3407; Joaquín García to Manuel Godoy, Santo Domingo, 17 December 1795, AHN-E 3407, no. 32; Gordon Forbes to Henry Dundas, Isabella Bay, 9 February 1796, TNA-WO 1/65, 45–46; Luis de las Casas to Manuel Godoy, Havana, 25 January 1796, AGI-E 5A, no. 28.

106. Gordon Forbes to Henry Dundas, Isabella Bay, 7 January 1796, BL-WM, Add. Ms. 39824.

107. Gordon Forbes and Parker, "Copy of an Answer . . . ," Isabella Bay, 25 January 1796, BL-WM, Add. Ms. 39824.

108. Gordon Forbes to Henry Dundas, Isabella Bay, 9 February 1796, TNA-WO 1/65, 45–46; Henry Dundas, 23 December 1794 and 30 September 1795, TNA-WO 6/5, 114–116, 165–167.

109. Étienne Laveaux to Marqués de Casa Calvo, 20 February 1796, AHN-E 3407, nos. 2–3; Gordon Forbes to Henry Dundas, Isabella Bay, February 1796, BL-WM, Add. Ms. 39824; Francisco, Rio Masacre, 18 February 1796, AHN-E 3407, exp. 2; Joaquín García to Manuel Godoy, Santo Domingo, 23 February 1796, AHN-E 3407, exp. 2; Gordon Forbes to Henry Dundas, Isabella Bay, 9 February 1796, TNA-WO 1/65, 47–48; Gordon Forbes to Henry Dundas, Môle Saint-Nicolas, 2 March 1796, BL-WM, Add. Ms. 39824.

110. Gordon Forbes to Henry Dundas, 28 January 1796, BL-WM, Add. Ms. 39824; Gordon Forbes to Henry Dundas, Môle Saint-Nicolas, 28 February 1796, TNA-WO 1/65, 97–105; "Declaration," Jac. Decamps, 18 February 1796, AHN-E 3407, exp. 2; 7 and 27 September and 25 October 1795, and 11 and 30 January 1796, Derbyshire Record Office (DRO), D239/M/E/17175–17176, 17178, 17183–17184, 17189–17190, and 17191–17192; Gordon Forbes to Henry Dundas, Port-au-Prince, 11 March 1796, TNA-WO 1/65, 127–133; Étienne Laveaux to Marqués de Casa Calvo, 20 February 1796, AHN-E 3407, no. 3; Marqués de Casa Calvo to Joaquín García, Santo Domingo, 23 February 1796, AHN-E 3407, exp. 2, no. 8; Joaquín García to Manuel Godoy, Santo Domingo, 3 March 1796, AHN-E 3407, exp. 2, no. 48; Beaubrun Ardouin, *Études sur l'histoire d'Haïti*, vol. 3 (Paris: Dezobry, 1853), 107–109; Adam Williamson to Henry Dundas, Port-au-Prince, 15 January 1796, TNA-WO 1/65, 21–24; "Instructions," Gordon Forbes, Port-au-Prince, 29 September 1796, National Records of Scotland (NRS), Gifts and Deposits (GD), 216/202/1; Esteban Palomares to Joaquín García, Punta de Cañas, 3 August 1796, AHN-E 3407, exp. 1; Joaquín García to Manuel Godoy, Santo Domingo, 12 September 1796, AHN-E 3407, exp. 2, no. 84. For more on British attacks on Jamaican maroons, see January–February 1796, TNA-WO 1/92, 239–245, 247–248, 217–277, 279–282, 285–287; Tyler D. Parry and Charlton W. Yingling, "Slave Hounds and Abolitionism in the Americas," *Past and Present* 246 (February 2020): 69–108.

111. Governor Balcarres, Jamaica, 4 July 1798, NRS-GD 193/2/3/2–3; "Jérémie," 15 June 1797, Devon Heritage Centre (DHC), 1038M/0/1/42; Pierre François Venault de Charmilly, "To the Earl of Liverpool," 1810, TNA-WO 1/75, 239–247.

112. Marqués del Campo to Manuel Godoy, London, 18 September 1795, AHN-E 4247; Geggus, *Slavery*, chapter 8.

113. José Urízar to Manuel Godoy, 16 April 1796, AHN-E 3407; Anonymous to Charles Rousselot, Môle Saint-Nicolas, 24 and 26 July 1796, AHN-E 3407, exp. 2; Joaquín García to Manuel Godoy, Santo Domingo, 26 February 1796, AHN-E 3407, exp. 2; Joaquín García to Manuel Godoy, Santo Domingo, 3 March 1796, AHN-E 3407, exp. 2, no. 48.

114. Anonymous French officer, "Note concernant les Antilles . . . la partie espagnole . . . ," 8 Ventôse an IV / 27 February 1796, TUSC-KC, Box 5, Folder 2.

115. "Proclamación," Gordon Forbes, 12 July 1796, AHN-E 3407; Gordon Forbes to Henry Dundas, Port-au-Prince, 18 July 1796, BL-WM, Add. Ms. 39824; "Our Affairs in St. Domingo," *The Times* (London), 12 September 1796, 2–3.

116. Joaquín García to Manuel Godoy, Santo Domingo, 8 August 1796, AHN-E 3407, exp. 2, no. 76; Gregorio Ugarte to Joaquín García, Cahobas, 22 July 1796, AHN-E 3407, exp. 1.

117. José Urízar to Manuel Godoy, Santo Domingo, 9 August 1796, AHN-E 3407, exp. 2.

118. "Décret," Giraud, Le Blanc, Sonthonax, and Raymond, 17 Messidor an IV / 5 July 1796, AHN-E 3407, exp. 1; Léger-Félicité Sonthonax to Étienne Laveaux, 27 Messidor an IV / 15 July 1796, AHN-E 3407, exp. 1; Léger-Félicité Sonthonax to Étienne Laveaux, 28 Messidor an IV / 16 July 1796, AHN-E 3407, exp. 1; Étienne Laveaux to Toussaint Louverture, 29 Messidor an IV / 17 July 1796, AHN-E 3407, exp. 1; Toussaint Louverture, 13 Thermidor an IV / 31 July 1796, AHN-E 3407, exp. 1; "Entrega," Esteban Palomares and Toussaint Louverture, Bánica, 31 July 1796, AHN-E 3407, exp. 1; Esteban Palomares to Joaquín García, 31 July 1796, AHN-E 3407, exp. 1; Anonymous to Count de Ogorman, 6 August 1796, AHN-E 3407, exp. 1; "Registre contenant les proclamations, les ordonnances, et les addresses du Général Toussaint Louverture . . . ," 18 Germinal an IV / 28 March 1796, Schomburg Center for Research in Black Culture (SCRBC), MG 119.

119. LeBlanc to Joaquín García, 7 Fructidor an IV / 24 August 1796, AHN-E 3407, exp. 2.

120. "Réflexions sur Banique," 1796, DHC, 1038M/0/1/66.

121. Geggus, *Slavery*, 202.

122. "Instructions," Gordon Forbes, Port-au-Prince, 29 September 1796, NRS-GD, 216/202/1.

123. Pascal to Philippe Roume, Cap-Français, 9 Fructidor an IV / 26 August 1796, AHN-E 3407, exp. 2, no. 6.

124. Joaquín García to Esteban Palomares, Santo Domingo, 5 August 1796, AHN-E 3407, exp. 1; Joaquín de Zubillaga to Manuel Godoy, Caracas, 23 August 1796, AGI-E 65, no. 54.

125. Toussaint Louverture to Esteban Palomares, Bánica, 13 Thermidor an IV / 31 July 1796, AHN-E 3407, exp. 2; José Urízar to Manuel Godoy, Santo Domingo, 29 August 1796, AHN-E 3407, exp. 1; Joaquín García to Manuel Godoy, Santo Domingo, n.d., AHN-E 3407, exp. 2, no. 79; Joaquín García to Manuel Godoy, Santo Domingo, 26 September 1796, AHN-E 3407, exp. 2, no. 86; Joaquín García to French Colonial Directorate, 6 August 1796, AHN-E 3407, exp. 1; "Aux Habitans de la partie de Saint-Domingue, cédée à la France par le Traité de Paix," LeBlanc, 6 Fructidor an IV / 23 August 1796, AHN-E 3407, exp. 2.

126. Anonymous to Monsieur Duranton, Môle Saint-Nicolas, 28 July 1796, AHN-E 3407, exp. 2.

127. Anonymous to "Tabares," Môle Saint-Nicolas, 28 July 1796, AHN-E 3407, exp. 2.

128. Antonio Chinchilla to Joaquín García, Neiba, 14 August 1796, AHN-E 3407, exp. 2.

129. Grandet to Citizen Commission Delegates of Santo Domingo, Fort Liberte, 21 Fructidor an IV / 7 September 1796, AHN-E 3407, exp. 2; LeBlanc to Joaquín García, 7 Fructidor an IV / 24 August 1796, AHN-E 3407, exp. 2; Vicente Matos to Joaquín García, Monte Cristi, 16 August 1796, AHN-E 3407, exp. 2; José María de la Torre to Étienne Laveaux, Monte Cristi, 9 August 1796, AHN-E 3407, exp. 2; LeBlanc to Joaquín García, 7 Fructidor an IV / 24 August 1796, AHN-E 3407, exp. 2; Fernando Portillo to Joaquín García, Santo Domingo, 14 September 1796, AHN-E 3407, exp. 2; José Urízar to Manuel Godoy, Santo Domingo, 9 August 1796, AHN-E 3407; "No. 1," John Simcoe to Henry Dundas, 1796, DHC, 1038M/o/1/41; Antonio Chinchilla to Joaquín García, Neiba, 14 August 1796, AHN-E 3407; "Confidential letter from St. Jago," 21 December 1795, TNA-WO 1/65, 61–63; Parker and Gordon Forbes, Isabella Bay, 25 January 1796, TNA-WO 1/65, 53.

130. Raimond, LeBlanc, Sonthonax, and Pascal, "Proclamation," 7 Brumaire an V / 28 October 1796, AHN-E 3407, exp. 2; Augustin Lasala to Jean-Pierre Levellies, Dajabón, 4 November 1796, AHN-E 3407, exp. 2.

131. Philippe Roume to Joaquín García, Santo Domingo, 16 Fructidor an IV / 2 September 1796, AHN-E 3407, exp. 1.

132. "Our Affairs in St. Domingo," *The Times* (London), 12 September 1796, 2–3.

133. Fernando Portillo to Eugenio Llaguno, Santo Domingo, 15 October 1796, AGI-SD 1110 and AGI-SD 1015.

134. José Nolasco Mañon, "Discours en l'honneur du roi d'Angleterre . . . 27 Novembre 1796," NRS-GD, 216/203/1.

135. José Urízar to Manuel Godoy, Santo Domingo, 29 August 1796, AHN-E 3407, exp. 1.

136. Joaquín García to Manuel Godoy, Santo Domingo, 29 September 1796, AHN-E 3407, exp. 2, no. 87.

137. LeBlanc to Joaquín García, 7 Fructidor an IV / 24 August 1796, AHN-E 3407, exp. 2; José María de la Torre to Étienne Laveaux, Monte Cristi, 9 August 1796,

AHN-E 3407; Roberto Cassá, "Les effets du Traité de Bâle," in *Saint-Domingue espagnol et la révolution nègre d'Haïti, 1790–1822*, ed. Alain Yacou (Paris: n.p., 2007), 203–210.

138. Esteban Palomares to Joaquín García, Punta de Cañas, 3 August 1796, AHN-E 3407; Joaquín García to Esteban Palomares, Santo Domingo, 5 August 1796, AHN-E 3407; José Urízar to Manuel Godoy, Santo Domingo, 29 August 1796, AHN-E 3407; Joaquín García to Manuel Godoy, Santo Domingo, 12 September 1796, AHN-E 3407, no. 84; "Evacuación de Santo Domingo," 1795/1796, AGS-SG 7152, exp. 37, ff. 128–159; "Evacuación de la isla: Peticiones," 1795/1796, AGS-SG 7152, exp. 59, ff. 332–357.

139. Joaquín García to Philippe Roume, Santo Domingo, 15 August 1796, AHN-E 3407, exp. 2; Fernando Portillo to Manuel Godoy, Santo Domingo, 4 May 1796, AGI-E 11A; Joaquín García to Manuel Godoy, Santo Domingo, 28 August 1796, AGI-E 5A. See also AGI-SD 1069; Francisco Gascue to Philippe Roume, Santo Domingo, 6 April 1796, AGI-E 5A, no. 2; Francisco Gascue, "Testimonio . . . ," Santo Domingo, 20 August 1796, AGI-E 5A, exp. 74; José Urízar to Manuel Godoy, Santo Domingo, 29 August 1796, AGI-E 13 and AHN-E 3407, exp. 1; Joaquín García to Manuel Godoy, Santo Domingo, 28 August 1796, AGI-E 5A; Joaquín García to Manuel Godoy, Santo Domingo, 30 August 1796, AHN-E 3407, exp. 2, no. 81.

140. "Proclamación," Gordon Forbes, 21 December 1796, AHN-E 3407.

141. Cardinal Zelada to Cardinal Casoni, Rome, 10 February 1796, ASV-NM 200, ff. 123–124; Cardinal Zelada to Cardinal Casoni, Rome, 21 October 1795, ASV-NM 200, ff. 85–88; Duke of Portland to Adam Williamson, 4 October 1794, TNA-CO 245/3; José Nicolas de Azara to Manuel Godoy, Rome, 24 September 1794, AHN-E 3906; King George III to Duke of Portland, Weymouth, 30 August 1794, in *The Later Correspondence of George III*, vol. 2, ed. Arthur Aspinall (Cambridge: Cambridge University Press, 1963), 236; Duke of Portland to King George III, Burlington House, 28 August 1794, in Aspinall, *Later Correspondence of George III*, 235.

142. Manuel Godoy to Joaquín García, San Lorenzo, 24 December 1796, AHN-E 3407, exp. 1; Marqués del Campo to Manuel Godoy, London, 18 August 1795, AHN-E 4247; Joaquín García to Manuel Godoy, Santo Domingo, 31 December 1796, AHN-E 3407, exp. 2, no. 92.

143. "Testimonio de la Causa Criminal Seguida de oficio contra Dn Juan Antonio Angulo y los morenos Pablo Aly y Agustín por seductores a favor de la nacion ynglesa," Santo Domingo, 8 and 17 December 1796, 20 January 1797, and 28 October 1797, AGI-E 1, nos. 27, 1–31, 232–235, and 357; 29 September 1795, San Yldefonso, AGS-SG, 6854, exp. 49; "Pasaporte para regresarse a la Havana," San Lorenzo, 29 December 1795, AGS-SG 6854, exp. 82. For his time in Louisiana, see Gilbert C. Din, "Domingo de Assereto: An Adventurer in Carondelet's Louisiana," *Louisiana History* 34, no. 1 (Winter 1993): 69–85.

144. "Testimonio . . . ," Santo Domingo, 19 December 1796 and 20 April 1797, AGI-E 1, nos. 27, 31–54, 316–318, and 326–327; William Grenville to Marquis Bute, Downing Street, 16 June 1796, AHN-E 4239, no. 21.

145. "Testimonio . . . ," Santo Domingo, 20 and 22 December 1796 and 6 February 1797, AGI-E 1, no. 27, 54–66, 187–191.

146. "Testimonio . . . ," Santo Domingo, 19 January 1797, AGI-E 1, no. 27, 169–171.

147. "Testimonio . . . ," Santo Domingo, 27, 28, and 30 December 1796, 13, 17, and January 1797, 3 February 1797, AGI-E 1, nos. 27, 67–68, 71–83, 111–117, 139–143, 153–154, and 183–187.

148. Antonio Chinchilla to Joaquín García, Neiba, 14 August 1796, AHN-E 3407, exp. 2.

149. "Testimonio . . . ," Santo Domingo, 31 December 1796, 3 and 23 January 1797, AGI-E 1, no. 27, 117–128, 156–158.

150. "Testimonio . . . ," Santo Domingo, 21 December 1796, AGI-E 1, no. 27, 109–110.

151. "Testimonio . . . ," Santo Domingo, 28 December 1796, AGI-E 1, no. 27, 71–83.

152. "Testimonio . . . ," Santo Domingo, 23 January 1797, AGI-E 1, no. 27, 156–166.

153. Marisa Fuentes, *Dispossessed Lives: Enslaved Women, Violence, and the Archive* (Philadelphia: University of Pennsylvania Press, 2016), 48–58; Kit Candlin and Cassandra Pybus, *Enterprising Women: Gender, Race, and Power in the Revolutionary Atlantic* (Athens: University of Georgia Press, 2015); Sandra Lauderdale Graham, *House and Street: The Domestic World of Servants and Masters in Nineteenth-Century Rio de Janeiro* (Austin: University of Texas Press, 1992).

154. "Testimonio . . . ," Santo Domingo, 31 December 1796, 25 January, and 6 and 7 February 1797, AGI-E 1, nos. 27, 124–127, 173–174, and 194–232.

155. "Testimonio . . . ," Santo Domingo, 21 and 30 December 1796, 4, 12, 13, 17, and 23 January, and 6 February 1797, AGI-E 1, nos. 27, 109, 128–136, 143–149, 162–164, 191–192, and 235–237.

156. "Testimonio . . . ," Santo Domingo, 7–11 February 1797, AGI-E 1, nos. 27, 230–284.

157. "Testimonio . . . ," Santo Domingo, 25–28 January 1797, AGI-E 1, nos. 27, 154–156, 171–180.

158. "Testimonio . . . ," Santo Domingo, 22 and 25 February and 4, 15, and 21 March 1797, AGI-E 1, nos. 27, 284–287, 291–298, and 302–316.

159. "Testimonio . . . ," Santo Domingo, 20 April 1797, AGI-E 1, nos. 27, 316–333.

160. "Testimonio . . . ," Santo Domingo, 28 April 1797, AGI-E 1, nos. 27, 356.

161. "Testimonio . . . ," Santo Domingo, 7, 9–12, and 14 June 1797, AGI-E 1, nos. 27, 407–466, 470–489.

162. "Testimonio . . . ," Santo Domingo, 15 July 1797, AGI-E 1, nos. 27, 505. For the Black Auxiliaries in Florida, see AGS-SG 7246, exp. 14.

163. Pablo Aly, Santo Domingo, 29 August 1800, AGI-SD 1091.

164. "Testimonio . . . ," Santo Domingo, 22, 24, and 25 April and 31 May 1797, AGI-E 1, nos. 27, 333–356, 385–388.

165. "Testimonio . . . ," Santo Domingo, 10 June and 15 July 1797, AGI-E 1, nos. 27, 400–401, 505. See also Fuentes, *Dispossessed*, 87–89.

166. "Testimonio . . . ," Santo Domingo, 12 June 1797, AGI-E 1, nos. 27, 401–402.

167. Sasha Turner, *Contested Bodies: Pregnancy, Childrearing, and Slavery in Jamaica* (Philadelphia: University of Pennsylvania Press, 2017), 78, 118; Jennifer L. Morgan, *Laboring Women: Reproduction and Gender in New World Slavery* (Philadelphia: University of Pennsylvania Press, 2004), chapter 1.

168. Abraham Nasatir and Gary Elwyn Monell, eds., *French Consuls in the United States: A Calendar of Their Correspondence in the Archives Nationales* (Washington, DC: Library of Congress, 1967), 398–399.

169. Charles-François Delacroix to del Campo, Paris, 24 Pluviôse an V / 12 February 1797, AHN-E 3407; Joaquín García to Manuel Godoy, Santo Domingo, 26 January 1797, AHN-E 3407, no. 95; del Campo to Manuel Godoy, Paris, 17 January 1797, AHN-E 3407, exp. 2; Joaquín García to Manuel Godoy, Santo Domingo, 25 April 1797, AHN-E 3394, no. 100; Joaquín García to Manuel Godoy, Santo Domingo, 30 April 1797, AHN-E 3407; Joaquín García to Manuel Godoy, Santo Domingo, 3 March 1797, AHN-E 3407, no. 96; Antonio Barba to Francisco Sabatini, Santo Domingo, 8 February 1797, AGMM-CG rollo 65, 5-4-11-2; Ramón Castro to Joaquín García, Puerto Rico, 23 April 1797, AHN-E 3394, exp. 1; Joaquín García to Commission Delegated of the French Government in Guarico, Santo Domingo, 4 July 1797, AHN-E 3394.

170. Manuel Godoy to Joaquín García, Aranjuez, 22 February 1797, AHN-E 3407, exp. 2.

171. Joaquín García to José Pablo Valiente, Santo Domingo, 24 March 1797, AHN-E 3394, exp. 1; Joaquín García to Manuel Godoy, Santo Domingo, 3 March 1797, AHN-E 3407, exp. 2, no. 96.

172. Joaquín García to Manuel Godoy, Santo Domingo, 24 March 1797, AHN-E 3394, exp. 1, no. 97.

173. Joaquín García to Manuel Godoy, Santo Domingo, 25 April 1797, AHN-E 3394, exp. 1, no. 100; Joaquín García to the Commission Delegated of the French Government in Guarico, Santo Domingo, 4 July 1797, AHN-E 3394, exp. 1; Joaquín García to Manuel Godoy, Santo Domingo, 10 July 1797, AHN-E 3394, exp. 1, no. 103; John Simcoe to Henry Dundas, Port-au-Prince, 8 May 1797, DHC, 1038M/0/1/84. See also Geggus, *Slavery*, 373–391; J. R. McNeill, *Mosquito Empires: Ecology and War in the Greater Caribbean, 1620–1914* (New York: Cambridge University Press, 2010).

174. Joaquín García to Manuel Godoy, Santo Domingo, 11 September 1797, AHN-E 3394, exp. 1, no. 109; Joaquín García to Manuel Godoy, Santo Domingo, 14 July 1797, AHN-E 3394, exp. 1, no. 104; Joaquín García to Consejo de Castilla, Santo Domingo, 31 October 1797, AHN-E 3407, exp. 2; "Testimonio sobre la reclamación que hace . . . Roume . . . ," AHN-E 3407, exp. 2; "Testimonio de las diligencias obradas . . . Agente de la Republica Francesa . . . ," AHN-E 3407, exp. 2; "Libro . . . Reales Cédulas . . . Audiencia de Santo Domingo," 1794–1797, BNE, MSS/13983.

175. Philippe Roume to Joaquín García, Santo Domingo, 22 Nivôse an VI / 11 January 1798, AHN-E 3394, exp. 1.

176. Dubois, *Avengers*, 67, 196, 204, 232, 242.

177. Toussaint Louverture and Thomas Maitland et al., 15 Fructidor an 5 / 31 August 1798, TNA-WO 6/5, 383–385; Henry Dundas, 11 January 1799, TNA-WO 6/5, 376–383;

John Simcoe to William Pitt, 22 December 1796, DHC, 1038M/0/1/41. The British sheltered allies "connected with the soil of St. Domingo." See Governor Balcarres, Jamaica, 31 July 1798, NRS-GD, 193/2/3/8; Governor Balcarres, Jamaica, 19 August 1798, NRS-GD, 193/2/3/13. For more context, see George Dunbar, n.d., Blake no. 996T, Box 18, E. J. Pratt Library, University of Toronto; Geggus, *Slavery*, 380–382.

178. Joaquín García to Manuel Godoy, Santo Domingo, 15 April 1798, AHN-E 3407, exp. 2, no. 129; 10 and 17 May 1798, ASV-NM 196, 452–456.

179. Governor Balcarres, Spanish Town, 8 June 1798, AHN-E 3407, exp. 2; Philippe Roume to Joaquín García, Santo Domingo, 25 Fructidor an VI / 11 September 1798, AHN-E 3407, exp. 2; Duke of Portland, St. James Palace, 20 November 1797, AHN-E 3407; Duke of Portland, St. James Palace, 27 November 1797, AHN-E 3407, exp. 2; Joaquín García to Manuel Godoy, Santo Domingo, 20 June 1798, AHN-E 3394, exp. 1, no. 132; Joaquín García to Sec. de Estado, 25 September 1798, AHN-E 3407, no. 134; Joaquín García to Philippe Roume, Santo Domingo, 14 September 1798, AHN-E 3407.

180. Joaquín García to Philippe Roume, Santo Domingo, 14 September 1798, AHN-E 3407, exp. 2; John Simcoe to Henry Addington, Môle Saint-Nicolas, 23 February 1797, DHC 152M/C/1797/OM1. See also Jesse Cromwell, *The Smugglers' World: Illicit Trade and Atlantic Communities in Eighteenth-Century Venezuela* (Chapel Hill: University of North Carolina Press, 2018); Rory Miller, *Britain and Latin America* (London: Longmans, 1993), 1–93; James Stephen, *The Opportunity* (London: Hatchard, 1804), 53–69; Nathalie Frédéric Pierre, "'The Vessel of Independence . . . Must Save Itself': Haitian Statecraft, 1789–1815" (PhD diss., New York University, 2018), chapter 3.

181. Toussaint Louverture to Ministre de la Marine et des Colonies, 4 Germinal an VII / 24 March 1799, TNA-CO 245/2; Toussaint Louverture to Citoyen Pascal, 26 Germinal an VII / 15 April 1799, TNA-CO 245/2.

CHAPTER 5: FRENCH FAILURES, 1799–1807

1. Philippe Roume, "Discours . . . a la célébration des fêtes reunites de la jeunesse et des époux," 10 Floréal an VII / 29 April 1799, AHN-E 3394, exp. 1.

2. Antonio Barba to José de Urrutia, Santo Domingo, 9 February 1799, AGMM-CG rollo 65, 5-4-11-2.

3. Joaquín García to Philippe Roume, Santo Domingo, 12 May 1800, AHN-E 3395, exp. 2, no. 3; Cambacérès, Sieyès, Révellière-Lépeaux, Daunou, Louvet, Henry-Larivière, Merlin, and Boissy, "Instrucción que debe servir de regla al Agente Interino del Gov.no Francés destinado a parte Española de la Isla de Santo Domingo," Paris, an IV / 1795, AHN-E 3407, exp. 1. For more context, see also Philippe Girard, *The Slaves Who Defeated Napoléon: Toussaint Louverture and the Haitian War of Independence, 1801–1804* (Tuscaloosa: University of Alabama Press, 2011), 329–342; Diana Walsh Pasulka, *Heaven Can Wait: Purgatory in Catholic Devotional and Popular Culture* (New York: Oxford University Press, 2015), chapter 3.

4. José de Limontas, Cádiz, 31 March 1813, AGI-SD 1041.

5. André Rigaud, "A ses concitoyens du département du Sud," 22 Nivôse an V / 11 January 1797, SCRBC, MG 23, Boxes 1a-1b.

6. Joaquín García to Manuel Godoy, Santo Domingo, 2 April 1798, AHN-E 3394, exp. 1, no. 128; Gabriel-Marie-Théodore-Joseph d'Hédouville to Joaquín García, Santo Domingo, 24 Germinal an VI / 13 April 1798, AHN-E 3394, exp. 1; Joaquín García to Gabriel-Marie-Théodore-Joseph d'Hédouville, Santo Domingo, 1 May 1798, AHN-E 3394, exp. 1; Joaquín García to Manuel Godoy, Santo Domingo, 18 January 1798, AHN-E 3394, exp. 1, no. 114; Joaquín García to Manuel Godoy, Santo Domingo, 20 June 1798, AHN-E 3394, exp. 1, no. 132.

7. Joaquín García to Francisco Saavedra, Santo Domingo, 7 November 1798, AHN-E 3394, no. 135; Letter from Cap-Français, 25 October 1798, AHN-E 3394, exp. 1.

8. 8 December 1798, NRS-GD, 193/2/3/17.

9. Christophe Huin, Port Republicain, 14 August 1798, NRS-GD, 193/2/12/2. See also Erica R. Johnson, *Philanthropy and Race in the Haitian Revolution* (New York: Palgrave, 2018), 157–158, 218–219.

10. Joaquín García to Francisco Saavedra, Santo Domingo, 29 November 1798, AHN-E 3394, no. 136.

11. "Précis du voyage . . . S.to Domingo . . . commencement du mois de Brumaire de l'an 7 . . . ," October 1798–January 1799, Newberry Library (NL), Edward E. Ayer Manuscript Collection (A), MS 1897.

12. André Rigaud to Philippe Roume, Prairal an VII / June 1799, SCRBC, MG 23, Boxes 1a-1b.

13. Toussaint Louverture, *Mémoires du général Toussaint L'Ouverture, écrits par lui-même*, ed. Joseph Saint-Rémy (Paris: Pagnerre, 1853); Carolyn Fick, *The Making of Haiti: The Saint Domingue Revolution from Below* (Knoxville: University of Tennessee Press, 1990), 198–229; David Geggus, *Haitian Revolutionary Studies* (Bloomington: Indiana University Press, 2002), 21–22; Philippe Girard, *Toussaint Louverture: A Revolutionary Life* (New York: Basic Books, 2016), chapters 15 and 17; Carlos Esteban Deive, *Las emigraciones dominicanas a Cuba (1795–1808)* (Santo Domingo: Fundación Cultural Dominicana, 1989); Laurent Dubois, *Avengers of the New World: The Story of the Haitian Revolution* (Cambridge, MA: Belknap Press of Harvard University Press, 2004), 197–236, 287–294.

14. Edward Stevens to Thomas Pickering, L'Arcahaye, 24 June 1799, *American Historical Review* 16, no. 1 (October 1910): 82–85 (AHR 1910).

15. Roume, "Discurso . . . en la Fiesta de la Declaración de la Libertad General," Port-Republicaine, 16 Pluviôse an VII / 4 February 1799, AHN-E 3394, exp. 1.

16. Toussaint Louverture, "Respuesta del General en Gefe al discurso pronunciado en el Puerto Republicano por el Agente del Gobierno el 16 Pluviôse del an 7," Pluviôse an VII / February 1799, AHN-E 3394, exp. 1; Joaquín García to Francisco Saavedra, Santo Domingo, 15 March 1799, AHN-E 3394, no. 139.

17. Roume, "Discours . . . a la celebration des fêtes reunites de la jeunesse et des époux," 10 Floréal an VII / 29 April 1799, AHN-E 3394, exp. 1.

18. Antonio Barba to Francisco Sabatini, Santo Domingo, 4 August 1796, AGMM-CG rollo 65, 5-4-11-2.

19. Margaret C. Jacob, *Living the Enlightenment: Freemasonry and Politics in Eighteenth-Century Europe* (New York: Oxford University Press, 1991), 203–224; Dubois, *Avengers*, 142–143. During the 1793 British blockade of Port-au-Prince, two officers swam into the harbor under fire, swords in teeth, to request a French surrender. French troops arrested and took them before Sonthonax, who threatened execution. Noticing Sonthonax with a Freemasonry emblem, one of the prisoners used a secret handshake to show he was a Mason. Sonthonax changed his tune, feasted with the British officers, and released them. Robert Rollo Gillespie, *A Memoir of Major-General Sir R. R. Gillespie* (London: T. Egerton, 1816), 24–30.

20. Jonathan Smyth, *Robespierre and the Festival of the Supreme Being: The Search for a Republican Morality* (Manchester, UK: Manchester University Press, 2016).

21. Kate Ramsey, *The Spirits and the Law: Vodou and Power in Haiti* (Chicago: University of Chicago Press, 2012), 47–49.

22. Roume, "Discours . . . a la celebration des fêtes reunites de la jeunesse et des époux," 10 Floréal an VII / 29 April 1799, AHN-E 3394, exp. 1.

23. Fick, *Making of Haiti*, 105, 264.

24. Toussaint Louverture, *The Memoir of Toussaint Louverture*, ed. and trans. Philippe Girard (New York: Oxford University Press, 2014), 31; Girard, *Toussaint Louverture*, 138, 154; Dubois, *Avengers*, 203. See also Terry Rey, *The Priest and the Prophetess: Abbé Ouvière, Romaine Rivière, and the Revolutionary Atlantic World* (New York: Oxford University Press, 2017), 194–200.

25. Ramsey, *Spirits and the Law*, 46–51.

26. Joaquín García to Mariano Luis Urquijo, Santo Domingo, 21 May 1799, AHN-E 3394, exp. 1, no. 140; Joaquín García to Mariano Luis Urquijo, Santo Domingo, 8 August 1799, AHN-E 3394, exp. 1, no. 144.

27. Pierre François Venault de Charmilly to Thomas Maitland, Jérémie, 17 July 1798, NRS-GD, 193/2/11/3; Joaquín García to Mariano Luis Urquijo, Santo Domingo, 21 August 1799, AHN-E 3394, exp. 1, no. 145.

28. Joaquín García to Mariano Luis Urquijo, Santo Domingo, 19 July 1799, AHN-E 3394, exp. 1, no. 142; Fick, *Making of Haiti*, 202.

29. Gregorio Ugarte, "Estado que manifiesta la fuerza efectiva . . . ," Santo Domingo, 4 July 1799, AHN-E 3394, exp. 1.

30. Johann Rudolph Lauffer to Joaquín García, Curaçao, 23 September 1799, AHN-E 3394, exp. 1; José de Liano y Bustamante, "Declaración," Santo Domingo, 18 September 1799, AHN-E 3394, exp. 1; Joaquín García to Mariano Luis Urquijo, Santo Domingo, 28 September 1799, AHN-E 3394, exp. 1, no. 147.

31. "Copia de una carta escrita en Santiago de los Caballeros . . . ," Santiago, 27 December 1799, AHN-E 3394, exp. 1; Edward Stevens to Timothy Pickering, Cap-Français, 30 September 1799, AHR 1910; Joaquín García to Mariano Luis Urquijo, Santo Domingo, 6 November 1800, AHN-E 3394, exp. 1, no. 166; Joaquín García to Mariano Luis Urquijo, Santo Domingo, 10 January 1800, AHN-E 3394, exp. 1, no. 153; Georges-Henri-Victor Collot, *Mémoire sur la réorganisation de la colonie de Saint Domingue* (Paris:

n.p., 1800), 18–20; 23 December 1799, DRO, D239/M/E/17310. See also David Geggus, "Slave Rebellion During the Age of Revolution," Ramón Aizpurua, "Revolution and Politics in Venezuela and Curaçao, 1795–1800," and Han Jordan, "Patriots, Privateers and International Politics: The Myth of the Conspiracy of Jean-Baptiste Tierce Cadet," in *Curaçao in the Age of Revolutions, 1795–1800*, ed. Wim Klooster and Gert Oostindie (Leiden: KITLV Press, 2011), 31–33, 109–110, 141–170; Ronald Angelo Johnson, *Diplomacy in Black and White: John Adams, Toussaint Louverture, and Their Atlantic World Alliance* (Athens: University of Georgia Press, 2014), 43, 68–86, 109–111, 119, 161; Julia Gaffield, *Haitian Connections in the Atlantic World: Recognition After Revolution* (Chapel Hill: University of North Carolina Press, 2015), 66, 107.

32. Joaquín García to Mariano Luis Urquijo, Santo Domingo, 30 September 1799, AHN-E 3394, exp. 1. For context on perceptions, see Andrew Kettler, *The Smell of Slavery: Olfactory Racism and the Atlantic World* (New York: Cambridge University Press, 2020), 40–41, 173–193.

33. Pierre François Venault de Charmilly to Thomas Maitland, Jérémie, 17 July 1798, NRS-GD, 193/2/11/3. On Charmilly, see Marlene Daut, *Tropics of Haiti: Race and the Literary History of the Haitian Revolution in the Atlantic World, 1789–1865* (Liverpool: Liverpool University Press, 2015), 14, 96, 438, 535.

34. Joaquín García to Mariano Luis Urquijo, Santo Domingo, 30 September 1799, AHN-E 3394, exp. 1; Dubois, *Avengers*, 235–236. Bellegarde remained loyal to France, but later returned to Hispaniola under unified Haitian rule as a commander on the Dominican side. See, for example, Charles Mackenzie, *Notes on Haiti: Made During a Residence in that Republic*, vol. 1 (London: Colburn and Bentley, 1830), 300–306.

35. Philippe Roume, "Extrait du registre des délibérations . . . ," Cap-Français, 12 Vendémiaire an VIII / 4 October 1799, AHN-E 3394, exp. 1 (A). For more context, see François-Marie Kerversau, *Rapport fait au gouvernement, sur Saint-Domingue* (Paris: Pain, 1797), 70–71.

36. Philippe Roume to Chanlatte, Cap-Français, 12 Vendémiaire an VIII / 4 October 1799, AHN-E 3394, exp. 1 (B) and (C).

37. Edward Stevens to Timothy Pickering, Cap-Français, 26 October 1799, AHR 1910. See also Edward Stevens to Timothy Pickering, Cap-Français, 3 December 1799, AHR 1910.

38. Joaquín García to Mariano Luis Urquijo, Santo Domingo, 26 October 1799, AHN-E 3394, exp. 1, no. 150. The Audiencia increasingly withdrew to Cuba but continued to manage Santo Domingo. Joaquín García to Mariano Luis Urquijo, Santo Domingo, 10 November 1799, AHN-E 3394, exp. 1, no. 151; Joaquín García to Mariano Luis Urquijo, Santo Domingo, 12 November 1799, AHN-E 3394, exp. 1, no. 152; Joaquín García to Philippe Roume, Santo Domingo, 23 October 1799, AHN-E 3394, exp. 1 (D).

39. "Traducción literal de una carta francesa . . . a un vecino de Santo Domingo español," Cap-Français, 13 December 1799, AHN-E 3394, exp. 1.

40. William Sutherland to William Perrin, 18 January 1800, DRO, D239/M/E/17880.

41. "Copia de una carta . . . ," Santiago, 27 December 1799, AHN-E 3394, exp. 1; Toussaint Louverture to Ministre de la Marine et des Colonies, 25 Germinal an VII / 14 April 1799, TNA-CO 245/2; Joaquín García to Mariano Luis Urquijo, Santo Domingo, 10 January 1800, AHN-E 3394, exp. 1, no. 153; Joaquín García to Mariano Luis Urquijo, Santo Domingo, 6 November 1800, AHN-E 3394, exp. 1, no. 166.

42. Philippe Roume to Joaquín García, Cap-Français, 7 Floréal an VIII / 27 April 1800, AHN-E 3395, exp. 2; Deive, *Emigraciones*.

43. Edward Stevens to Timothy Pickering, Cap-Français, 27 April 1800, AHR 1910, 97–98.

44. Antoine Chanlatte to Joaquín García, Santo Domingo, 30 Floréal an VIII / 20 May 1800, AHN-E 3395, exp. 2, no. 13; Joaquín García to Antoine Chanlatte, Santo Domingo, 20 May 1800, AHN-E 3395, exp. 2, no. 12.

45. Toussaint Louverture to Joaquín García, 7 Floréal an VIII / 27 April 1800, AHN-E 3395, exp. 2, no. 4; Edward Stevens to Timothy Pickering, Cap-Français, 27 April 1800, AHR 1910, 97–98.

46. Joaquín García to Philippe Roume, Santo Domingo, 12 May 1800, AHN-E 3395, exp. 2, no. 3.

47. Sulaure, Ferbos, Quilleron, Diace, and Barthélemy, Cap-Français, 7 Floréal an VIII / 27 April 1800, AHN-E 3395, exp. 2; Joaquín García to Antoine Chanlatte, Santo Domingo, 20 May 1800, AHN-E 3395, exp. 2, no. 12.

48. Joaquín García to Toussaint Louverture, Santo Domingo, 14 May 1800, AHN-E 3395, no. 5.

49. Vecinos de Santo Domingo to Cabildo de Santo Domingo, Santo Domingo, 16 May 1800, AHN-E 3395. Intriguingly, the letter used his original Corsican surname.

50. Ysidro Mota, Vicente Pérez, Juan Díaz, Fernando Abreu, Pablo Pérez, and Antonio Abad de Mena to Cabildo de Santo Domingo, San Carlos, 18 May 1800, AHN-E 3395, no. 8; Pedro Francisco de Prado, Francisco Vicente González, and Francisco Xavier de Herrera, Santo Domingo, 19 May 1800, AHN-E 3395, exp. 2, no. 9; Vecinos de Santo Domingo to Ayuntamiento de Santo Domingo, Santo Domingo, 24 May 1800, AHN-E 3395, exp. 2, no. 15.

51. Antonio Dávila Coca, Manuel de Miedes, and Francisco Labastida to Joaquín García, 19 May 1800, AHN-E 3395, exp. 2, no. 10.

52. Toussaint Louverture to Joaquín García, 7 Floréal an VIII / 27 April 1800, AHN-E 3395, exp. 2, no. 4; Edward Stevens to Timothy Pickering, Cap-Français, 27 April 1800, AHR 1910, 97–98; "Citoyen Premier Consul," 1 Fructidor an VIII / 19 August 1800, TNA-CO 37/49, 218–229.

53. Antoine Chanlatte to Joaquín García, Santo Domingo, 30 Floréal an VIII / 20 May 1800, AHN-E 3395, exp. 2, no. 13.

54. Joaquín García to Philippe Roume, Antoine Chanlatte, and Agé, Santo Domingo, 21 May 1800, AHN-E 3395, exp. 2, no. 14; Joaquín García to Mariano Luis Urquijo, Santo Domingo, 28 May 1800, AHN-E 3394, exp. 1, no. 155.

55. Antonio Dávila Coca, Manuel de Miedes, and Francisco Labastida to Joaquín García, Santo Domingo, 25 May 1800, AHN-E 3395, exp. 2, no. 16.

56. Joaquín García to Mariano Luis Urquijo, Santo Domingo, 13 June 1800, AHN-E 3394, exp. 1, no. 159; Joaquín García to Mariano Luis Urquijo, Santo Domingo, 8 June 1800, AHN-E 3394, exp. 1, no. 157; Girard, *Defeated Napoléon*, 39.

57. Isidoro de los Santos et al., San Juan de la Maguana, 22 July 1800, AHN-E 3394, exp. 1.

58. André Rigaud to Joaquín García, Les Cayes, 17 Prairial an VIII / 6 June 1800, AHN-E 3394, exp. 1.

59. Joaquín García to Mariano Luis Urquijo, Santo Domingo, 14 June 1800, AHN-E 3394, exp. 1, no. 160.

60. Joaquín García to Mariano Luis Urquijo, Santo Domingo, 8 August 1800, AHN-E 3394, exp. 1, no. 164.

61. Dubois, *Avengers*, 235–238.

62. Joaquín García to André Rigaud, Santo Domingo, 22 August 1800, AHN-E 3394, exp. 1.

63. Joaquín García to Mariano Luis Urquijo, Santo Domingo, 20 June 1800, AHN-E 3394, exp. 1; Dubois, *Avengers*, 236–238.

64. Joaquín García to Mariano Luis Urquijo, Santo Domingo, 22 August 1800, AHN-E 3394, exp. 1, no. 165; Julien Raimond, "Memoire sur la colonie de saint-domingue . . . ," 1799, BHFIC, H-5a7i; Charlton W. Yingling, "The Maroons of Santo Domingo in the Age of Revolutions: Adaptation and Evasion, 1783–1800," *History Workshop Journal* 79 (2015): 25–51. For more on LaFortune, see Girard, *Defeated Napoléon*, 84, 124, 196; Geggus, *Haitian Revolutionary Studies*, 117.

65. Joaquín García to Mariano Luis Urquijo, Santo Domingo, 20 November 1800, AHN-E 3394, exp. 1, no. 167.

66. Joaquín García to Philippe Roume, Santo Domingo, 22 and 24 November 1800, AHN-E 3394, exp. 1.

67. Joaquín García to Mariano Luis Urquijo, 9 December 1800, AHN-E 3394, exp. 1, nos. 168–169. See also Dubois, *Avengers*, 162–165, 185–186.

68. Girard, *Defeated Napoléon*, 5–6, 37–39, 57–60, 145–147.

69. Toussaint Louverture, "A todos los habitantes de la partida antes española," San Juan de la Maguana, 14 Nivôse an IX / 4 January 1801, AGMM-U, SD 5650, exp. 2, and, AHN-E 3394, exp. 1.

70. Joaquín García to Toussaint Louverture, Santo Domingo, 6 January 1801, AHN-E 3394, exp. 1.

71. Agustín Franco to Commander of Baní, 8 January 1801, AHN-E 3394, exp. 1; "Memorandum," 1799, DHC, 152M/C/1799/OC/6.

72. Toussaint Louverture to the Cabildo de Santo Domingo, Azua, 20 Nivôse an IX / 10 January 1801, AHN-E 3394, exp. 1.

73. Adrian Campuzano, Rodrigo de la Rocha, and Francisco Labastida to Joaquín García, 15 January 1801, AHN-E 3394, exp. 1; Adrian Campuzano, Andrés de Angulo, Rodrigo de la Rocha, Francisco de Tapia y Castro, Luis Franco, Manuel de Heredia, Manuel de Miedes, Pedro Fernández de Castro to Toussaint Louverture, 17 January 1801, AHN-E 3394, exp. 1.

74. Toussaint Louverture, "A los habitantes de Baní," Azua, 21 Nivôse an IX / 11 January 1801, AHN-E 3394, exp. 1; Aillard, "Permiso . . . ," 24 Nivôse an IX / 14 January 1801, AGMM-U, SD 5650, exp. 2; Agustín Franco to Francisco Pérez, Baní, 13 January 1801, AHN-E 3394, exp. 1; Agustín Franco to Pedro Garrico, Baní, 13 January 1801, AHN-E 3394, exp. 1.

75. Joaquín García to Mariano Luis Urquijo, Santo Domingo, 4 February 1801, AHN-E 3394, exp. 1, no. 171. Chanlatte, Kerversau, and others fled to Caracas, where they issued a decree condemning Louverture's actions. Manuel Vasconcelos to Mariano Urquijo, Caracas, 25 February 1801, AGI-E 61; Manuel Vasconcelos, Caracas, May 1801, AGI-E 61; Antoine Chanlatte and François-Marie Kerversau, Caracas, 20 Pluviôse an IX / 8 February 1801, AGI-E 61, no. 12, f. 1.

76. Toussaint Louverture, 21 Nivôse an IX / 11 January 1801; 7, 13, 16, 18, 19, and 22 Pluviôse an IX / 27 January 1801, 2, 5, 7, 8, and 11 February 1801; and 10 Ventôse an IX / 1 March 1801, AGMM-U, SD 5650, exp. 2.

77. Toussaint Louverture, "A todos los habitantes de la partida antes española," San Juan de la Maguana, 14 Nivôse an IX / 4 January 1801, AHN-E 3394, exp. 1.

78. "Périès, revolution de St Domingue, 1799–1804," BL-WM, Add. Ms. 38074, f. 42; Thomas Madiou, Histoire d'Haiti, vol. 2 (Port-au-Prince: Courtois, 1847), 85–86; Beaubrun Ardouin, Études sur l'histoire d'Haïti, vol. 3 (Paris: Dezobry, 1853), 299–300. See also Erin Zavitz, "Revolutionary Narrations: Early Haitian Historiography and the Challenge of Writing Counter-History," Atlantic Studies 14 (2017): 336–353.

79. Joaquín García to José Antonio Caballero, Madrid, 22 October 1803, AGMM-U, SD 5650, exp. 4, f. 7; Pedro Prado, 6 July 1801, Archivo Histórico del Arzobispado de Santo Domingo (AHASD), Cartas Pastorales (CP), 61/3. Citations of the AHASD here follow the most publicly available catalog, which their longtime archivist published. On the Cartas Pastorales, for example, see José Luis Sáez, Inventario del Archivo Histórico del Arzobispado de Santo Domingo (Santo Domingo: Amigo del Hogar, 2012), 153–156.

80. Miguel Marmion to José de Urrutia, Puerto Cabello, 26 January 1801, AGMM-CG rollo 65.

81. Joaquín García to Mariano Luis Urquijo, Santo Domingo, 4 February 1801, AHN-E 3394, exp. 1, no. 171. For a regional context on enslaved child-care providers, see Sarah L. Franklin, Women and Slavery in Nineteenth-century Colonial Cuba (Rochester, NY: University of Rochester Press, 2012), chapter 5.

82. Joaquín García to Mariano Luis Urquijo, Maracaibo, 4 March 1801, AHN-E 3394, exp. 1; W. L. Whitfield to Edward Corbet, Port Republicain, 13 June 1801, TNA-CO 137/50, 14–15; Beaubrun Ardouin, Études sur l'histoire d'Haïti, vol. 3 (Paris: Dezobry, 1853), 406–413; Geggus, Haitian Revolutionary Studies, 20–28.

83. Maria Cecilia Ulrickson, "Cultivators, Domestics, and Slaves: Slavery in Santo Domingo," The Americas 76 (April 2019): 241–266; Antonio Pinto Tortosa, "'No habrá de sufrirse que los negros abandonen las plantaciones': Toussaint Louverture ante la esclavitud," Boletín del Archivo General de La Nación 132 (2012): 63–89; Antonio Pinto Tortosa, "Una colonia en la encrucijada: Santo Domingo, entre la Revolución Hai-

tiana y la Reconquista Española, 1791–1809" (PhD diss., Universidad Complutense de Madrid, 2011); Girard, *Defeated Napoléon*, 39. The Dominican historian José Luis Saez said only that Toussaint "supposedly" called for emancipation. See Saez, *La iglesia y el negro esclavo en Santo Domingo: Una historia de tres siglos* (Santo Domingo: Patronato de la Ciudad Colonial de Santo Domingo, 1994), 66. For a different interpretation, see Graham Nessler, *An Islandwide Struggle for Freedom: Revolution, Emancipation, and Reenslavement on Hispaniola, 1789–1809* (Chapel Hill: University of North Carolina Press, 2016), 130–131. Other scholars have cited Saez and rhetoric regarding extensions of extant French policies, which had never ceased since 1795, as "clear evidence" of emancipation in 1801, and that fifteen thousand were freed the day Louverture arrived in Santo Domingo. See Sudhir Hazareesingh, *Black Spartacus: The Epic Life of Toussaint Louverture* (New York: Farrar, Straus, and Giroux, 2020), 232–233.

84. Toussaint Louverture to Joaquín García, Santo Domingo, 8 Pluviôse an IX / 28 January 1801, AHN-E 3394, exp. 1. See also Antonio Barba to José de Urrutia, Santo Domingo, 20 August 1800, AGMM-CG rollo 65, 5-4-11-3.

85. Joaquín García to Toussaint Louverture, Santo Domingo, 28 January 1801, AHN-E 3394, exp. 1.

86. Manuel Bravo to Joaquín García, Santo Domingo, 14 December 1796, AGI-SD 1033. Abadía took a few captives to Puerto Rico, including one person from Ouanaminthe and one who was Kongolese. Abadía settled near Moca, where he died owning over fifty slaves in 1828. See Antonio Nieves Méndez, *Historia de un pueblo: Moca, 1772–2000* (Aguada: Editorial Aymaco, 2008), 119, 144, 359–362.

87. Joaquín García to Toussaint Louverture, Santo Domingo, 28 January 1801, AHN-E 3394, exp. 1; Toussaint Louverture to Joaquín García, Santo Domingo, 13 Pluviôse an IX / 2 February 1801, AHN-E 3394, exp. 1; Joaquín García to Toussaint Louverture, Santo Domingo, 2 February 1801, AHN-E 3394, exp. 1.

88. Marqués de Someruelos to Sec. de Estado y del Despacho, Havana, 25 June 1809, AGI-SD 1040. Luis Robledo to Domingo Márquez, Puerto Príncipe (Cuba), 18 February 1811, AGI-SD 1040; José Bernal to Oidores Ramos and Hidalgo, Puerto Príncipe (Cuba), 21 April 1804, AGI-SD 1040. See also Deive, *Emigraciones*.

89. Juan Bosch, *Composición social dominicana: Historia e interpretación* (Santo Domingo: Alfa and Omega, 1970), 189–204; Frank Moya Pons, *The Dominican Republic: A National History* (Princeton, NJ: Markus Wiener, 1998), 116; Antonio Sánchez Valverde, *Idea del valor de la isla Española* (Madrid: Pedro Marín, 1785), 149–151.

90. Joaquín García to Mariano Luis Urquijo, Maracaibo, 4 March 1801, AHN-E 3394, exp. 1; "El cuerpo de abogados . . . ," Santo Domingo, 27 August 1800, AGI-SD 1015; Martin de Mueses to Manuel Godoy, Santiago de Cuba, 15 August 1802, AGI-SD 1015.

91. Joaquín García to Pedro Ceballos, Havana, 1 October 1801, AHN-E 3394, exp. 1; Manuel Godoy to Joaquín García, Aranjuez, 20 March 1801, AHN-E 3391, exp. 8.

92. Pedro Ceballos to Joaquín García, San Ildefonso, 16 September 1801, AHN-E 3395, exp. 1; Marqués de Someruelos to Joaquín García, Havana, 10 May 1802,

AHN-E 3394, exp. 1; Pedro Ceballos to Marqués de Someruelos, Aranjuez, 20 May 1802, AHN-E 3395, exp. 1; Pedro Ceballos to Joaquín García, Aranjuez, 23 June 1802, AHN-E 3395, exp. 1; Godoy, Azara, Ceballos, and Urquijo to Joaquín García, Madrid, July 1802, AHN-E 3394, exp. 1; Joaquín García to Mariano Luis Urquijo, Maracaibo, 8 March 1801, AHN-E 3394, exp. 1, no. 175.

93. Joaquín García to José Antonio Caballero, Madrid, 22 October 1803, AGMM-U, SD 5650, exp. 4; José Antonio Caballero to Miguel Cayetano Soler, Aranjuez, 3 June 1804, AGI-SD 1084; José Antonio Caballero, Aranjuez, 19 June 1804, AGI-SD 1084.

94. Andrés Boggiero to Antonio Guevara, Coro, 28 January 1801, AGMM-U, SD 5650, exp. 3.

95. "Constitution républicaine des colonies française de Saint-Domaingue," 1801, Bibliothèque Nationale de France (BNF)-Département de la Réserve des Livres Rares (DRLR), 8-LK12-554; Lucien Bonaparte to Pedro Ceballos, Madrid, 6 Vendémiaire an X / 28 September 1801, AHN-E 3391, exp. 8.

96. Lucien Bonaparte to Pedro Ceballos, Aranjuez, 6 Germinal an IX / 27 March 1801, AHN-E 3391, exp. 8.

97. "Révolution de St. Domingue, par M. Périès, trésorier . . . ," BL-WM, Add. Ms. 38074, 6; Girard, *Defeated Napoléon*, 27–32; Fick, *Making of Haiti*, 206–207. Representations of Louverture have been numerous and complex. See Grégory Pierrot, *The Black Avenger in Atlantic Culture* (Athens: University of Georgia Press, 2019), chapter 3.

98. Joaquín García to José Antonio Caballero, Madrid, 22 October 1803, AGMM-U, SD 5650, exp. 4, ff. 8–13; Auguste Matinée, *Anecdotes de la révolution de Saint-Domingue racontées par Guillaume Mauviel, évêque de la colonie (1799–1804)* (Saint-Lo, France: D'Elie Fils, 1885), 81–84; Emilio Cordero Michel, *La revolución haitiana y Santo Domingo* (Santo Domingo: Editora Nacional, 1968), 56–72.

99. "Profesión de fe . . . dirijida al General en Gefe Todos Santos Louverture," 1801, AHASD-CP, 61/3.

100. Cardinal Consalvi, Rome, 10 October 1802, ASV-NM 202, 915.

101. "Guillermo Mauviel," 20 Brumaire an 11 / 11 November 1802, AHASD-CP, 61/3; Matinée, *Anecdotes*, 3, 30–46; Abate Berault-Bercastel, *Historia general de la iglesia*, vol. 8 (Barcelona: Pons, 1855), 537–538; Gabriel Debien, *Guillaume Mauviel, évêque constitutionnel de Saint-Domingue, 1801–1805* (Basse-Terre, Guadeloupe: Société d'histoire de la Guadeloupe, 1981).

102. Charles Leclerc, "Le général en chef . . . ," *Journal de Paris*, Mercredi 6 Prairial an X / 26 May 1802, 1; Girard, *Defeated Napoléon*, 1–5, 224; Geggus, *Haitian Revolutionary Studies*, 25–27.

103. Charles Maurice de Talleyrand to Pedro Ceballos, Paris, 9 Brumaire an X / 9 November 1801, AHN-E 3391, exp. 8.

104. Lucien Bonaparte to Pedro Ceballos, Madrid, 6 Vendémiaire an X / 28 September 1801, AHN-E 3391, exp. 8; Manuel Godoy to Pedro Ceballos, Aranjuez, 9 May 1802, AHN-E 3391, exp. 8; Lucien Bonaparte to Pedro Ceballos, Aranjuez, 6 Germinal an IX / 27 March 1801, AHN-E 3391, exp. 8.

105. Manuel Godoy to Pedro Ceballos, Aranjuez, 9 May 1802, AHN-E 3391, exp. 8.

106. Charles Maurice de Talleyrand, "Le ministre de relation extérieure," Paris, 9 Brumaire an 10 / 31 October 1801, AHN-E 3391, exp. 8; José Nicolas de Azara to Charles Maurice de Talleyrand, 9 November 1801, AHN-E 3391, exp. 8; Charles Maurice de Talleyrand to Charles Leclerc, 9 Germinal an X / 30 March 1802, SCRBC, MG 23, Boxes 1a-1b.

107. François-Marie Kerversau, "Arrête," Santo Domingo, 30 Ventôse an X / 21 March 1802; 13 and 14 Pluviôse an X / 2 and 3 February 1802, SCRBC, MG 23, Boxes 1a-1b; Bosch, *Composición*, 173–188; Girard, *Defeated Napoléon*, 92–98.

108. Berault-Bercastel, *Historia general de la iglesia*, 8:537–538; Moya Pons, *Dominican Republic*, 108–109.

109. Cardinal Consalvi, Rome, 15 November 1802, ASV-NM 202, 1018; Matinée, *Anecdotes*, 139–144.

110. Pedro Xavier de Vera to Consejo de Estado, Madrid, 24 February 1803, AGI-SD 1035, no. 21.

111. Tomás de Monla to Miguel Cayatano Soler, Cádiz, 16 January 1801, AGI-SD 1035, no. 16. For the Black Auxiliaries' migration to Cádiz, see AGS-SG 6973, exp. 43; AGS-SG 7161, exps. 32–33; AGI-E 3, exp. 10; AGS-SG 7161, exp. 24; AGI-E 5B, exp. 176; AHN-E 3391, exp. 10.

112. Jane Landers, *Black Society in Spanish Florida* (Urbana: University of Illinois Press, 1999), 133; Geggus, *Haitian Revolutionary Studies*, 196–199.

113. Jean-François to Tomás de Monla, Cádiz, 16 January 1801, AGI-SD 1035. Jean-François rejected responsiblity for the 1794 theft at the Spanish treasury in Fort Dauphin (Bayajá).

114. José Vázquez to Sec. de Gracia y Justicia, 28 July 1802, AGI-SD 1015.

115. "José Vázquez," 1803, AGI-U 163, no. 17; "En América," *Gazeta de Madrid*, 19 August 1803, no. 66, p. 719.

116. José Vázquez to Sec. de Gracia y Justicia, 22 July 1802, AGI-SD 1015.

117. J. R. McNeill, *Mosquito Empires: Ecology and War in the Greater Caribbean, 1620–1914* (New York: Cambridge University Press, 2010), 251–266.

118. Napoléon Bonaparte and Charles Maurice de Talleyrand to King Carlos IV, Paris, 23 Pluviôse an XI / 12 February 1803, AHN-E 1626, exp. 33.

119. Marqués de Someruelos to Pedro Ceballos, "... comisión con que tiene determinado pase al Guarico el oidor honorario D. Francisco de Arango," Havana, 23 February 1803, AHN-E 3395, exp. 1.

120. Marqués de Someruelos to Pedro Ceballos, Havana, 17 March 1803, AHN-E 3395, exp. 1.

121. Jean-Baptiste Drouillard, Port-au-Prince, 13 May 1803, Mss. 2590, Jean-Baptiste Drouillard Papers, Louisiana State University, Special Collections.

122. Marqués de Someruelos to Francisco Arango, Havana, 5 March 1803, AHN-E 3395, exp. 1.

123. Marqués de Someruelos to Pedro Ceballos, Havana, 2 June 1803, AHN-E 3395, exp. 1; Matt D. Childs, *The 1812 Aponte Rebellion in Cuba and the Struggle Against Atlantic Slavery* (Chapel Hill: University of North Carolina Press, 2006), 28–91; Ada Ferrer, *Free-*

dom's Mirror: Cuba and Haiti in the Age of Revolution (New York: Cambridge University Press, 2014), 63–74, 160–164.

124. Marqués de Someruelos to Pedro Ceballos, Havana, 26 May 1803, AHN-E 3395, exp. 1.

125. Marqués de Someruelos to Pedro Ceballos, Havana, 2 June 1803, AHN-E 3395, exp. 1.

126. Francisco Arango to Marqués de Someruelos, Havana, 17 June 1803, AHN-E 3395, exp. 1.

127. Francisco Arango to Marqués de Someruelos, Havana, 17 June 1803, AHN-E 3395, exp. 1.

128. Girard, *Defeated Napoléon*, 203–266, 291–348.

129. Francisco Arango to Marqués de Someruelos, Havana, 17 June 1803, AHN-E 3395, exp. 1; Marqués de Someruelos, n.d., AHN-E 3395, exp. 1. See also Tyler D. Parry and Charlton W. Yingling, "Slave Hounds and Abolitionism in the Americas," *Past and Present* 246 (February 2020): 69–108; John Jaques to William Philp Perrin, 5 January 1796, DRO, D239/M/E/17178. See also Bryan Banks, "Real and Imaginary Friends in Revolutionary France: Quakers, Political Culture, and the Atlantic World," *Eighteenth-Century Studies* 50, no. 4 (2017): 361–379; Julie L. Holcomb, *Moral Commerce: Quakers and the Transatlantic Boycott of the Slave Labor Economy* (Ithaca, NY: Cornell University Press, 2016).

130. Julia Gaffield, ed., *The Haitian Declaration of Independence: Creation, Context, and Legacy* (Charlottesville: University of Virginia Press, 2016).

131. Geggus, *Haitian Revolutionary Studies*, 207–220; Marlene Daut, "Wrongful Death of Toussaint Louverture," *History Today* 70, no. 6 (6 June 2020), www.historytoday.com /archive/feature/wrongful-death-toussaint-louverture; Dubois, *Avengers*, 296–297; Girard, *Toussaint Louverture*, 253–264.

132. Tomás de Monla to Pedro Ceballos, Cádiz, 6 September 1803, AHN-E 5240, exp. 69; LeRoy to Tomás de Monla, 19 Fructidor an XI / 6 September 1803, AHN-E 5240, exp. 69.

133. Matinée, *Anecdotes*, 47–57, 99–118; Edward Stevens to Thomas Pickering, L'Arcahaye, 24 June 1799, AHR 1910, 76–81; Marcus Rainford, *An Historical Account of the Black Empire of Hayti* (London: Albion, 1805), 288–305.

134. Fick, *Making of Haiti*, 211–216; Dubois, *Avengers*, 269; Girard, *Defeated Napoléon*, 150–151, 251.

135. Tomás de Monla to Pedro Ceballos, Cádiz, 6 September 1803, AHN-E 5240, exp. 69; LeRoy to Tomás de Monla, 19 Fructidor an XI / 6 September 1803, AHN-E 5240, exp. 69.

136. Capitan General de Andalucía, 27 March 1809, AGI-SD 1041. In the Napoleonic invasion of Iberia state papers supporting the ex–Black Auxiliaries disappeared. "En el tiempo de nuestra anterior guerra con la Francia," 27 March 1809, Cádiz, AGI-SD 1041. For additional context, see Geggus, *Haitian Revolutionary Studies*, 199–200, 294n103; Gaffield, *Haitian Connections*, 93–152.

137. "Révolution de St. Domingue, par M. Périès, trésorier . . . ," BL-WM, Add. Ms. 38074, 196–200.

138. 3 September 1806, AGI-E 86A, n. 21.

139. Matinée, *Anecdotes*, 111–131; Pedro Prado to Jean-Louis Ferrand, 5 November 1805, AHASD-CP, 61/3; G. Hallam, 1 July 1804, TNA-WO 1/75, 33–36; "L. Ferrand . . . A Los Vecinos del Cibao . . . ," 7 Vendémiaire an XIII / 19 September 1804, Service Historique de la Défense (SHD), Guerre et Armée de Terre (GR) 7, B 11. It is not absolutely clear that this was the same priest who was famous for his association with the Black Auxiliaries, but given the individual's reputation, the distance that correspondence had to travel, and the fact that the news from the update merited a printed decree, evidence suggests that it probably was. See also Pinto Tortosa, "Una colonia," 246–259; Fernando Picó, *One Frenchman, Four Revolutions: General Ferrand and the Peoples of the Caribbean* (Princeton, NJ: Markus Wiener, 2011), 33–47; Maria Cecilia Ulrickson, "'*Esclavos que fueron*' in Santo Domingo, 1768–1844" (PhD diss., University of Notre Dame, 2018), 83–106, 128–138; Moya Pons, *Dominican Republic*, 108–116; Nessler, *Islandwide*, 160–165; Anne Eller, "'All Would Be Equal in the Effort': Santo Domingo's 'Italian Revolution,' Independence, and Haiti, 1809–1822," *Journal of Early American History* 1 (2011): 111.

140. Deborah Jenson, *Beyond the Slave Narrative: Politics, Sex, and Manuscripts in the Haitian Revolution* (Liverpool: Liverpool University Press, 2011), 99–101, 152–154; Eugenio Matibag, *Haitian-Dominican Counterpoint: Nation, State, and Race on Hispaniola* (New York: Palgrave, 2003), 81–88.

141. Jean-Louis Ferrand, "Proclamación . . . ," 25 Prairal an XII / 14 June 1804, SHD-GR 7, B 11. Special thanks to Julia Gaffield for sharing select sources from the SHD.

142. Eyre Coote to William Windham, Jamaica, 2 November 1806, TNA-CO 137/117, 12–13; *Constitution d'Haïti*, 20 May 1805; Gaffield, *Haitian Connections*, 19, 103–104, 153–181; Geggus, *Haitian Revolutionary Studies*, 199–200; Childs, *Aponte*, 163–168.

143. Robert Sutherland to George Shee, 12 October 1806, TNA-WO 1/75, 66–77.

144. Laurent Férou to Eyre Coote, Jérémie, 20 October 1806, TNA-CO 137/117, 14–20; Henri Christophe, "Liberté ou la Mort," 7 January 1807, TNA-CO 137/119, 9–10; Étienne Élie Gérin, "Liberté, égalité, République d'Hayti," 25 March 1807, TNA-CO 137/119, 11–12; "Le Général de division Pétion à Mme Dessalines," 19 October 1806, BNF-DRLR, 4-PU-14. See also Colin [Joan] Dayan, *Haiti, History, and the Gods* (Berkeley: University of California Press, 1995), 16–53; "Forum: Jean-Jacques Dessalines and the Haitian Revolution," *William and Mary Quarterly* 69, no. 3 (July 2012): 541–638; Chelsea Stieber, *Haiti's Paper War: Post-Independence Writing, Civil War, and the Making of the Republic, 1804–1954* (New York: NYU Press, 2020); Celucien L. Joseph and Nixon S. Cleophat, eds., *Vodou in the Haitian Experience: A Black Atlantic Perspective* (Lanham, MD: Lexington, 2016).

145. Juan Sánchez Ramírez, *Diario de la Reconquista* (Santo Domingo: Editora Montalvo, 1957); Moya Pons, *Dominican Republic*, 110–116. For detailed work on slavery during French rule, see Nessler, *Islandwide*, chapters 5 and 6.

CHAPTER 6: CROSS-ISLAND COLLABORATION
AND CONSPIRACIES, 1808–1818

1. Prince Saunders, *Haytian Papers: A Collection of the Very Interesting Proclamations and Other Official Documents* (London: Reed, 1816), 77–78.

2. For context, see Scott Eastman and Natalia Sobrevilla Perea, *The Rise of Constitutional Government in the Iberian Atlantic World: The Impact of the Cádiz Constitution of 1812* (Tuscaloosa: University of Alabama Press, 2015).

3. "Espero a ver si el Gobierno Ingles . . . ," 29 March 1811, AHN-E 5620, caja 2. Sánchez Ramírez collected twenty-eight notebooks of diaries and correspondence about the Reconquista. See Juan Sánchez Ramírez, Santo Domingo, 16 July 1810, AHN-E 5620, caja 2, no. 17.

4. Cabildo de Cartagena, "Edicto," 19 June 1810, TNA-CO 137/128, 161–162; Marqués de Someruelos, "Fidelisimos habitantes de la isla de Cuba," Havana, 30 April 1810, TNA-CO 137/128, 103–112; Gilbert de Guillermin, *Précis historique des derniers événemens de la partie de l'est de Saint-Domingue* (Paris: A. Bertrand, 1811), 27–28, 230–235.

5. Juan Sánchez Ramírez, *Diario de la Reconquista* (Santo Domingo: Editora Montalvo, 1957), 37–39. For a time, Cap-Haïtien was also called Cap-Henry for Henry Christophe.

6. Toribio Montes to Jean-Louis Ferrand, San Juan, 2 August 1808, in Guillermin, *Précis*, 28–29.

7. "Proclamation du général Ferrand," in Guillermin, *Précis*, 35–40.

8. Jean-Louis Ferrand, Santo Domingo, 1808, in Guillermin, *Précis*, 29–31.

9. Toribio Montes to Sec. de Estado, Puerto Rico, 6 April 1809, AGMM-U, SD 5636, exp. 5, no. 473; Guillermin, *Précis*, 41–56, 430–431; Sánchez Ramírez, *Diario*, 23–25, 79, 155, 279.

10. "Aux Habitans de la Partie de l'Est," *Bulletien-Officiel de Santo-Domingo*, 12 October 1808, p. 1, SHD-GR 7, B 11.

11. "Manifiesto . . . ," 29 October 1808, SHD-GR 7, B 11.

12. *Bulletin-Officiel de Santo-Domingo*, 15 February 1809, SHD-GR 7, B 11.

13. Guillermin, *Précis*, 66–79; Toribio Montes to Sec. de Estado, Puerto Rico, 30 May 1809, AGMM-U, SD 5636, exp. 5, no. 502.

14. *Carte de l'entrée de la rade et Port Napoléon dans la Baye de Samaná, Isle St. Domingue* (1807), *Plan de projet pour l'etablissement de la ville du Port Napoléon dans l'Isle Saint Domingue* (1807), and *Plan des environs du Port Napoléon dans la Baye de Samaná* (1807), Library of Congress, Geography and Map Division; "Marine et Colonie," Samaná, 21 Thermidor an XIII / 9 August 1805, TNA-WO 1/80, 329.

15. Guillermin, *Précis*, 80–110, 449–450.

16. Sánchez Ramírez, *Diario*, 176; Guillermin, *Précis*, 165–234; Frank Moya Pons, *The Dominican Republic: A National History* (Princeton, NJ: Markus Wiener, 1998), 110–116.

17. Toribio Montes to Juan Sánchez Ramírez, Puerto Rico, 5 February 1809, AGI-SD 1042.

18. "Correspondencia de . . . Toribio Montes . . . ," 12 February 1809, AGI-SD 1042. Sánchez Ramírez also seems to have sold "fifteen Black slaves" of unclear origin in Havana to fund the Reconquista. See Juan Villavicencio to Juan Sánchez Ramírez, Havana, 29 March 1809, AGI-SD 1042.

19. William Price Cumby, "Monsieur . . . ," 16 May 1809, in Guillermin, *Précis*, 291.

20. "Convencion concluida . . . ," Santo Domingo, 6 July 1809, AGI-U 94; Guillermin, *Précis*, 325–354; "Articles of Capitulation," Santo Domingo, 6 July 1809, TNA-CO 137/126, 160–163; Myers, 1 July 1809, TNA-CO 137/126, 178–179.

21. "Almanach colonial de Santo Domingo, pour l'année 1809," BHFIC, B-1a23.

22. Juan Sánchez Ramírez to Intendente General de Cuba, Santo Domingo, 28 July 1809, AGI-SD 1040, no. 1.

23. Aguilar to Francisco Saavedra, Havana, 6 October 1809, AGI-SD 1040; Juan Sánchez Ramírez, Santo Domingo, 28 July 1809, AGI-SD 1042.

24. "Espero a ver si el Gobierno Ingles . . . ," 29 March 1811, AHN-E 5620, caja 2; Hugh Lyle Carmichael and Juan Sánchez Ramírez, "Duplicado del pacto celebrado con el Gral. Yngles Carmichael . . . ," Santo Domingo, 9 August 1809, AGI-SD 1042; Hugh Lyle Carmichael to Lord Castlereagh, 9 July 1809, TNA-CO 137/127, 3–4; "St. Domingo," 1803, DHC, 152M/C/1803/OL/23. See also Julia Gaffield, *Haitian Connections in the Atlantic World: Recognition After Revolution* (Chapel Hill: University of North Carolina Press, 2015), 153–181.

25. Juan Sánchez Ramírez, Santo Domingo, 16 July 1810, AGMM-U, SD 5636, exp. 9.

26. Juan Sánchez Ramírez to Toribio Montes, Santo Domingo, 22 November 1809, AGI-SD 1042.

27. Sánchez Ramírez, *Diario*, 176–177, 192–198.

28. Juan Sánchez Ramírez, 17 July 1810, AGI-SD 1041, no. 18.

29. Juan Sánchez Ramírez, Santo Domingo, 23 May 1810, AGI-SD 1112.

30. "Deseando la Junta Central Suprema Gubernativa . . . ," Sevilla, 12 January 1810, AHN-E 5620, caja 2.

31. Consejo de Indias, Cádiz, 26 March 1810, AGI-SD 1041. Soon the Cortes would entertain returning Columbus's remains to Santo Domingo. See "Representación de D. Fran.co Mosquera y Cabrera, diputado . . . ," 17 April 1811, AGI-SD 1041. The return of the archdiocese to Santo Domingo caused a dispute over primacy with Cuba. See Luis Chávez, Luis Robleado, and Ramón José de Mendiola, Puerto Príncipe, Cuba, 4 December 1811, AGI-SD 1041.

32. Antonio Coronel, Sevilla, 20 January 1810, AGI-SD 1041; Pedro de Rivero, Sevilla, 12 January 1810, AGMM-U, SD 5665, exp. 2; Ministerio de Guerra, "Deseando el Rey . . . ," Madrid, 1 June 1817, AGMM-U, SD 5665, exp. 3; Juan Sánchez Ramírez to Pedro Ceballos, Santo Domingo, 24 January 1810, AGI-SD 1042, 1; Gregorio Moriel de Santa Cruz, Santiago, 14 March 1811, AGI-SD 1017; Martín Gil to Franciso Caro, Bogotá, 19 November 1809, AHN-E 3566, exp. 60; "Exposición hecha . . . ," 1821, AHN-E 111, exp. 31.

33. Juan Sánchez Ramírez, Santo Domingo, 2 July 1810, AGI-SD 1042.

34. Juan Sánchez Ramírez, Santo Domingo, 24 July 1810, AGI-SD 1040, no. 23.

35. Juan Sánchez Ramírez to Pedro Ceballos, Santo Domingo, 24 January 1810, AGI-SD 1042, 2; Juan Sánchez Ramírez to Hugh Lyle Carmichael, 4 July 1809, TNA-CO 137/127, 7–8; William Walton, London, 16 January 1813, TNA-WO 1/78, 411–413; "Statement . . . of William Walton," TNA-WO 1/78, 418; William Walton, London, 27 April 1810, TNA-WO 1/81, 5–8; William Walton, *Present State of the Spanish Colonies* (London: Longmans, 1810), 224–228; BL-WM, Add. Ms. 38376.

36. Juan Ruiz de Apodaca to Eusebio de Bardaxi y Azara, London, 25 June 1811, AHN-E 5620, caja 2; Juan Ruiz de Apodaca, London, 29 March 1811, AHN-E 5620, caja 2.

37. Luis Chávez, Luis Robledo, and José Torrez de Zelaya, Puerto Príncipe, Cuba, 28 April 1810, AGI-U 94; Juan Sánchez Ramírez, Santo Domingo, 13 March 1810, AGI-SD 1042.

38. "El Consejo pleno en consulta," 3 April 1810, AGI-SD 1041. For the regional agricultural context, see Stuart George McCook, *States of Nature Science: Agriculture, and Environment in the Spanish Caribbean, 1760–1940* (Austin: University of Texas Press, 2002).

39. "Etat d'Haity," Le Secretaire d'Etat to Monsieur Peltier, Le Cap, 29 March 1810, AGI-SD 1041. For more on Philadelphia, see James Alexander Dun, *Dangerous Neighbors: Making the Haitian Revolution in Early America* (Philadelphia: University of Pennsylvania Press, 2016), 6–25, 90–97, 105–118, 125–133, 209–220; Terry Rey, *The Priest and the Prophetess: Abbé Ouvière, Romaine Rivière, and the Revolutionary Atlantic World* (New York: Oxford University Press, 2017), 171–187.

40. "Copie d'une dépêche de M. Peltier agent d'Haity à Lord Liverpool," 27 June 1810, AGI-SD 1041; Juan Sánchez Ramírez to Ministerio de Estado, Santo Domingo, 2 July 1810, AGI-SD 1042. For recognition in Jamaica of Bonapartist threats and anti-French sentiments across the Spanish Americas, see Lowbridge Bright to David Duncombe, Bristol, 6 July 1808, B1/F1, 80/75, Box 20, Unit 35, UMA-BFP.

41. "Estrait d'un autre lettre," 23 April 1810, AGI-SD 1041; Juan Sánchez Ramírez, Santo Domingo, 12 July 1810, AGI-SD 1017, exp. 10. On the citadel, also see Michel-Rolph Trouillot, *Silencing the Past: Power and the Production of History* (Boston: Beacon, 1995), chapter 2.

42. Juan Sánchez Ramírez, Santo Domingo, 16 July 1810, AGMM-U, SD 5636, exp. 9.

43. Juan Sánchez Ramírez, Santo Domingo, 17 October 1810, AGI-SD 1016; Consejo de Regencia to Gobernador Capital General de Santo Domingo, Cádiz, April 1811, AGI-SD 1016, f. 574; José Núñez de Cáceres to Sec. de Gracia y Justicia, Santo Domingo, 31 July 1811, AGI-SD 1016, no. 576.

44. Toribio Montes to Juan Sánchez Ramírez, Puerto Rico, 5 February 1809, AGI-SD 1042.

45. Pedro Mir, *La noción de período en la historia dominicana*, vol. 2 (Santo Domingo: Universidad Autónoma de Santo Domingo, 1983), 349–352.

46. Anne Eller, "'All would be equal in the effort': Santo Domingo's 'Italian Revolution,' Independence, and Haiti, 1809–1822," *Journal of Early American History* 1 (2011): 105–141. Although likely not participants in this plot, the Maniel maroons continually reemerged in Santo Domingo. After Juan Sánchez Ramírez suggested it, in 1813 officials again considered relocating the hundreds scattered from Naranjo during the French cession, who returned to the Baoruco Mountains under the leaders Juan Musundi, Manuel de Rosario, and Figareau. For this, see Juan Sánchez Ramírez, Santo Domingo, 9 January 1811, AGI-SD 1041; Cádiz, 2 February 1813, AGI-SD 1041; "Al Capt. Gen.l de la Isla de Santo Domingo," Cádiz, 31 March 1813, AGI-SD 1041.

47. "Santo Domingo 1811," Cádiz, 11 May 1811, AGI-SD 1042.

48. 8 March 1816, Archivo Nacional de Cuba (ANC), Asuntos Políticos (AP), leg. 15, exp. 44. Special thanks to Anne Eller for sharing these sources from the ANC.

49. Juan Manuel Francisco Caballero to Ministerio de Estado, Santo Domingo, 19 February 1811, AGI-SD 1042.

50. Juan Sánchez Ramírez to Juan Antonio Aybar, Santo Domingo, 19 September 1810, AGN, Colección José Gabriel García (JGG) 4, 1, C14, exp. 4, no. 27.

51. Juan Manuel Francisco Caballero to Sec. de Estado, Santo Domingo, 30 July 1811, AGI-SD 1042; Juan Manuel Francisco Caballero to Sec. de Estado, Santo Domingo, 2 December 1811, AGI-SD 1042.

52. Juan Manuel Francisco Caballero to Sec. de Estado, Santo Domingo, 31 July 1811, AGI-SD 1042.

53. Francisco Xavier Caro, Santo Domingo, 29 November 1810, AGI-SD 1017. His father, Ignacio, had been a prominent officer in Santo Domingo. Pedro Valera, Santo Domingo, 26 September 1815, NL-A, MS 1885.

54. Francisco Xavier Caro to Nicolas Sierra, Santo Domingo, 18 December 1810, AGI-SD 1041, nos. 8–9.

55. José de Limontado to Sec. del Despacho de Estado, Cádiz, 22 December 1812, AHN-E 5620, caja 2; January to October 1811, AGI-SD 1016, exp. 25.

56. Francisco Martínez Marina, Teoría de las Cortes o grandes Juntas Nacionales, vol. 1 (Madrid: Villalpando, 1813), 83; María Isabel Paredes Vera, "Francisco Javier Caro de Torquemada, diputado dominicano en las Cortes Ordinarias de Cádiz (1813–1814)," *Boletín del Arhivo General de la Nación* 129 (2011): 91–120; *Córtes: Actas de las Sesiones de la Legislatura Orginaria de 1813* (Madrid: García, 1876), 17, 47, 61, 72, 417; Jaime E. Rodríguez O., *The Independence of Spanish America* (New York: Cambridge University Press, 1998), 82–102.

57. "Actos y ceremonias con que fue proclamada y jurada en Bayaguana la Constitución de Cádiz," AGN-ARB 3, 24, exp. 14; "Isla española de Santo Domingo . . . objeto de fomentar la prosperidad . . . ," Cádiz, 4 March 1813, AGI-SD 1017; Rodríguez O., *Independence of Spanish America*, 90–93.

58. José Núñez de Cáceres to Sec. de Gracia y Justicia, Santo Domingo, 28 August 1811, AGI-SD 1017, exp. 9.

59. José Núñez de Cáceres, 24 July 1812, AHASD-CP, 61/4.

60. José Núñez de Cáceres to Sec. de Gracia y Justicia, Santo Domingo, 27 August 1811, AGI-SD 1041, no. 3. Cádiz allowed British commerce and reduced taxes. See Consejo de Indias, 14 June 1811, AGI-SD 1041.

61. José Núñez de Cáceres, Santo Domingo, 11 December 1811, AGI-SD 1017, exp. 8.

62. Juan Manuel Francisco Caballero, Santo Domingo, 28 December 1811, AGI-SD 1041.

63. Ramón Posada et al., Cádiz, 14 June 1811, AGI-SD 1017; "Año de 1809 a 1811," AHN-E 130, exp. 6.

64. Fray Pedro Zamora, 24 September 1808, AGI-SD 1112; Consejo de Indias, Sevilla, 3 April 1810, AGI-SD 1041.

65. Scott Eastman, *Preaching Spanish Nationalism Across the Hispanic Atlantic, 1759–1823* (Baton Rouge: Louisiana State University Press, 2012), chapter 3.

66. Arzobispo Pedro to Sec. de la Gobernación de Ultramar, Santo Domingo, 23 December 1813, AGI-SD 929; Arzobispo Pedro to Sec. de Estado y del Despacho de Yndias, Santo Domingo, 29 September 1815, AGI-SD 929; "Testimonio del expediente promovieo por los religiosos . . . ," Santo Domingo, 1815, AGI-SD 964, no. 71; "El fiscal . . . restableciendo la silla Arzobispal . . . ," 12 May 1817, NL-A, MS 1885.

67. "Instrucción publica . . . ," 23 December 1812, AGN, Colección César Herrera (CCH), 5, 2, 77, exp. 3, no. 1.

68. September 1817, AGI-U 132, no. 23.

69. Agustín Tabares, Santo Domingo, 2 September 1813, AGI-SD 1112; Agustín Tabares to Carlos de Urrutia, 16 May 1817, AGI-SD 1112; Joaquín de Sedano y Caballero, Cádiz, 13 April 1811, AGI-SD 1112.

70. Carlos de Urrutia to Sec. de Estado y del Despacho Universal, Santo Domingo, 9 October 1815, AGI-SD 964; 14 November 1817, 19 June 1818, and 6 June 1820, AHASD, Cabildo Eclesiástico (CE) 24/4; "Aunque en varias provincias . . . ," 11 September 1818, NL-A, MS 1885.

71. Manuel Gonzales and Manuel de Mena, Santo Domingo, 25 January 1815, AGI-SD 929.

72. Fernando VII, 4 May 1814, AHASD-CP, 61/5. See also Rodríguez, *Independence of Spanish America*, 103–108.

73. Francisco Caballero to Sec. de Estado, 28 December 1811, AGI-SD 1042, exp. 7.

74. Carlos de Urrutia to Juan Antonio Ariban, 30 January 1817, AGN-JGG, 4, 12, c. 42, exp. 6, f. 18.

75. José Núñez de Cáceres, 5 December 1811, AGN-ARH 3, 11A, exp. 195.

76. José Núñez de Cáceres to Consejo de Indias, 11 December 1811, AGI-SD 1017, exp. 8.

77. José Núñez de Cáceres to Juan Narciso de Torres, 22 August 1811, in *Boletín del Archivo General de la Nación* 4, no. 48–49 (1946): 285–286. See also Ernesto Bassi, *An Aqueous Territory: Sailor Geographies and New Granada's Transimperial Greater Caribbean World* (Durham, NC: Duke University Press, 2016), 148.

78. José Gabriel García, *Compendio*, vol. 2 (Santo Domingo: García Hermanos, 1894), 36–39; Antonio del Monte y Tejada, *Historia de Santo Domingo*, vol. 3 (Santo Domingo: García Hermanos, 1894), 277. These authors sometimes had access to primary sources that today are missing.

79. Matt D. Childs, *The 1812 Aponte Rebellion in Cuba and the Struggle Against Atlantic Slavery* (Chapel Hill: University of North Carolina Press, 2006), 149–167.

80. Carlos de Urrutia to Sec. del Estado, 8 April 1815, AGI-SD 964, no. 54; "A ruego de Rosa Berné . . . ," Santo Domingo, 31 March 1815, AGI-SD 964; "Habiendo resuelto el Rey . . . ," Madrid, 6 January 1816, AGI-SD 1084; Carlos de Urrutia to Sec. de Estado del Despacho y Hacienda, Santo Domingo, 2 May 1816, AGI-SD 1084, no. 10; Marqués Campo Sagrado to Governor of Santo Domingo, Palacio, 7 February 1817, AGI-SD 1084; "Indice de los oficios y representaciones . . . ," 12 July 1815, AGI-SD 964.

81. "Los oficiales del batallón de morenos . . . ," Santo Domingo, 14 December 1814, AGI-SD 964.

82. "Yndice de las representaciones y oficios . . . ," Santo Domingo, 22 April 1815, AGI-SD 964.

83. Carlos de Urrutia to Sec. de Estado y Despacho Universal de Indias, Santo Domingo, 8 April 1815, AGI-SD 964, no. 58.

84. Gregorio Morel de Portes, "Orden de Aprehension," 20 November 1812, AGN-ARH 4, 26R, exp. 7.

85. "Testigos," 13 and 23 February and 8 and 29 March 1813, AGN-ARH 3, 11A, exp. 297; Édouard Montulé, *A Voyage to North America and the West Indies in 1817* (London: Phillips, 1821), 19–22. Elsewhere, the informant was called a *negro francés esclavo*. For example, see José Núñez de Cáceres, 15 February 1815, in *Boletín del Archivo General de la Nación* 4, nos. 48–49 (1946): 285–286; Bartolo Rijo, "Orden del Alcalde," 9 February 1813, AGN-ARH 4, 26R, exp. 8. See the epilogue for more on Montas and his prominent family. It is possible that Estudillo, burdened with an expensive lawsuit, was also making himself indispensable to officials. For this, see "Sentencia por cobro de deuda," 17 February 1813, AGN-ARH 5, 26R, exp. 10.

86. José Núñez de Cáceres, "Auto," 14 February 1813, AGN-ARH 3, 11A, exp. 297; "S.res del Cabildo . . . ," 12 December 1810, AGN-ARH 3, 5A, exp. 62.

87. Francisco de Miranda, "Proclamación," March 1806, TNA-CO 137/116, 263; Karen Racine, *Francisco de Miranda: A Transatlantic Life in the Age of Revolution* (Wilmington, DE: Scholarly Resources, 2003), esp. 159–161; Michael P. Costeloe, *Response to Revolution: Imperial Spain and the Spanish American Revolutions, 1810–1840* (New York: Cambridge University Press, 2009).

88. Cabildo, Justicia, y Regimiento de las Capitales, Ministerio Universal de Indias, 27 October 1815, AGI-SD 964.

89. Pedro Celestino Duhart to Juan Ruiz de Apodaca, Cuba, 9 May 1815, AHN-E 5245, exp. 1; Juan Ruiz de Apodaca to Miguel de Lardizábal y Uribe, Havana, 30 June 1815, AHN-E 5245, exp. 1, no. 80; Sec. del Despacho del Estado, 24 October 1815 and 6 November 1815, AHN-E 5245, exp. 1.

90. Conde de Peralva to Pedro Ceballos, Paris, 23 November 1815, AHN-E 5245, exp. 1, no. 85.

91. Fernán Núñez to José Pizarro, Paris, 24 May 1817, AHN-E 5245, exp. 1; R.W. Bampfield to Henry Addington, 4 October 1814, DHC, 152M/C/1814/OF28; "Royaume d'Haiti: Déclaration du Roi" and "Pièces Justificatives," 1816, DHC, 152M/C/1816/OF13; "Registre de distributions journalières de rations faites dans la Grand'Anse ... provisions fournies aux navires partant en mission ... frais quotidiens de certains militaires blessés et aussi de certains postes militaires ... contre Goman," Département de l'intérieur, 1815, Les Archives Nationales d'Haïti, registre 6, 3772; "No. 3," Consul-General Charles Mackenzie to Secretary Canning, Port-au-Prince, 9 September 1826, *British and Foreign State Papers* (London: Ridgway, 1832), 662–667.

92. Bassi, *Aqueous*, chapter 5; Moya Pons, *Dominican Republic*, 16–22; Gaffield, *Haitian Connections*, 188–190.

93. Marqués Campo Sagrado to José García de León y Pizarro, 24 February 1817, AGI-E 17, no. 46; Sec. del Despacho del Estado, 8 March 1817, AGI-E 17.

94. Fernán Núñez to José Pizarro, Paris, 4 July 1817, AHN-E 5245, exp. 1.

95. Fernán Núñez, "Muy reservado," Paris, 15 June 1817, AHN-E 5245, exp. 1; Francisco Eguia to Sec. del Despacho de Estado, Palacio, 19 February 1818, AGI-E 17, no. 45.

96. José Vargas Figueroa, 25 August 1816, AGI-E 12, no. 87; Manuel González Salmón to José Pizarro, Paris, 13 March 1817, AHN-E 5245, exp. 1, no. 154; Manuel González Salmón to José Pizarro, Paris, 22 February 1817, AHN-E 5245, exp. 1, no. 110; 27 September 1819, ANC-AP, leg. 17, exp. 20.

97. "List of Vessels of War ... Southern States of Hayti ...," TNA-WO 1/75, 261; "List of Vessels of War ... Northern States of Hayti ...," TNA-WO 1/75, 265.

98. J. Nicholl to Lord Castlereagh, 19 January 1809, TNA-WO 1/75, 179–182; Rowley, Jamaica, 8 November 1808, TNA-WO 1/75, 199–202; Samuel Warsom, London, 22 November 1816, TNA-WO 1/78, 265–280.

99. "Testimonio de la causa seguida contra Fermín Núñez por el delito de sublevación," 1817, AGI-SD 1001; "Yncidente relative a la causa criminal ... Fermín Núñez sobre insurrección," 1817, AGI-SD 1001; "Testimonio de la causa criminal ... en Puerto de Plata contra Fermín Núñez ...," 1817, AGI-SD 1001; Consejo de Indias, May–June 1818, AGI-SD 1001. For a different take on this plot and more detail on Ceri, see Maria Cecilia Ulrickson, "'Esclavos que fueron' in Santo Domingo, 1768–1844" (PhD diss., University of Notre Dame, 2018), chapter 4. For more on Fantaisie, see David Geggus, *Haitian Revolutionary Studies* (Bloomington: Indiana University Press, 2002), 186, 201; Childs, *Aponte*, 167.

100. Martín Garay to Sec. del Estado, 11 October 1817, AGI-E 4, no. 8.

101. Carlos de Urrutia to Sec. de Estado y del Despacho Universal de Indias, Santo Domingo, 18 January 1815, AGI-SD 964, no. 17.

102. "State of the Political World," 1803, DHC, 152M/C/1803/OL/8.

103. Duque de Fernán Núñez to José Pizarro, 27 September 1818, AHN-E 5245, exp. 1.

104. Sebastian Kindelán to Sec. de Estado y del Despacho de Hacienda, 13 January 1819, AGI-SD 966.

105. Sebastian Kindelán to Sec. de Estado, 26 March 1820, AGI-E 12, no. 94; Pedro Arzobispo to Sec. del Despacho de Gracia y Justicia, Santo Domingo, 29 April 1820, AGI-SD 966.

106. "Real cedula de su majestad y señores del consejo," Madrid, 1818, AHN-E 8030, exp. 1.

107. "Papeles interceptados . . . ," March–April 1817, AGI-E 4, no. 13.

108. Michel-Rolph Trouillot, *Haiti: State Against Nation* (New York: Monthly Review Press, 1990), 43–76.

109. "A la plus grande gloire d'Alexandre Pétion," 1818, BHFIC (manuscript copy).

CHAPTER 7: THE "SPANISH PART OF HAITI" AND UNIFICATION, 1819–1822

1. Andrés Amarante, José Dominguez Arias, and Joaquín Oliva Adhenet, "Au très-honorable Général Magny, commandant de l'Arrondissement du Cap-Haïtien," Dajabón, 15 November 1821 (C), in *Réunion de la partie de l'est a la république* (Port-au-Prince: L'Imprimerie du Gouvernement, 1830), 11.

2. Diego Polanco to General Magny, Monte Cristi, 15 November 1821 (B), in *Réunion*, 10.

3. ". . . Gazeta del Gobierno de Hayti Francés," Port-au-Prince, 23 December 1821, AGI-SD 970, no. 33.

4. Provisional Government of Santo Domingo, "Acta Constitutiva del Gobierno Provisional del Estado Independiente de la Parte Española de Hayti," 1 December 1821, AGI-SD 970.

5. Colonel Ysnardi (aide to the president of Haiti) to Pablo Alí, San Juan de la Maguana, 9 November 1820, AGI-SD 970, no. 25.

6. *Declaratoria de independencia* (Santo Domingo: Imprenta de la Presidencia del Estado independiente de la parte española de Hayti, 1821). See also Rudolf Widmer, "Los negros, los franceses y la invención de la nación hispana," *Estudios Sociales* 39, no. 145 (2008): 11–37.

7. Sebastian Kindelán to Sec. de Estado y del Despacho de Hacienda, 13 January 1819, AGI-SD 966.

8. Joseph Balthazar Inginac, *Mémoires de Joseph Balthazar Inginac, ex-secrétaire-général près S. E. l'ex-président d'Haïti* (Kingston, Jamaica: Cordova, 1843), 44–48.

9. *Réunion*, 1–3.

10. Prince Saunders to Thomas Clarkson, Philadelphia, 22 May 1823, BL-WM, Add. Ms. 41266, ff. 235–236.

11. Michel-Rolph Trouillot, *Haiti: State against Nation* (New York: Monthly Review Press, 1990), 47–49, 73; Michel-Rolph Trouillot, *Silencing the Past: Power and the Production of History* (Boston: Beacon, 1995), 59–60; Chelsea Stieber, *Haiti's Paper War: Post-*

Independence Writing, Civil War, and the Making of the Republic, 1804–1954 (New York: NYU Press, 2020), 71–73, 85–87, and chapter 4.

12. Sebastian Kindelán to Prophète Daniel, Ichar, and Monpoint, Santo Domingo, 4 November 1820, AGI-SD 970, no. 2.

13. Colonel Ysnardi (aide to the president of Haiti) to Pablo Báez, San Juan de la Maguana, 9 November 1820, AGI-SD 970, no. 24. Agents also operated in Puerto Plata. See Alejandro Infante to Sebastian Kindelán, Santiago, 16 December 1820, AGI-SD 970, no. 16; Sebastian Kindelán to Alejandro Infante, Santo Domingo, 24 December 1820, AGI-SD 970, no. 17; Inginac, *Mémoires*, 45–58; Thomas Madiou, *Histoire d'Haïti: 1819–1826* (Port-au-Prince: Deschamps, 1988), 162–176; Felipe Dávila Cruz de Castro to Estado Universal de Hacienda, 11 December 1820, AGI-SD 966.

14. Colonel Ysnardi (aide to the president of Haiti) to Pablo Alí, San Juan de la Maguana, 9 November 1820, AGI-SD 970, no. 25.

15. Jean Price-Mars, *République d'Haïti et la République dominicaine*, vol. 1 (Port-au-Prince: Éditions Fardin, 1953), 78; Thalès Jean-Jacques, *Histoire du droit haïtien*, vol. 1 (Port-au-Prince: Imprimerie N. Telhomme, 1933), 255.

16. José Lasala to Sebastian Kindelán, Las Matas de Farfán, 5 December 1820, AGI-SD 970, no. 5; Sebastian Kindelán to José Lasala, Santo Domingo, 10 December 1820, AGI-SD 970, no. 6; Pablo Báez to Sebastian Kindelán, Azua, 8 December 1820, AGI-SD 970, no. 7; Domingo Pérez Guerra to Sebastian Kindelán, Neiba, 9 December 1820, AGI-SD 970, no. 11; Gobernación de Ultramar, 4 July 1821, AGI-SD 970, no. 4.

17. "Manifiesto . . . Dezir Dalmassi," 10 January 1821, AGI-SD 970; Sebastián Kindelán to Cabildo de Higuey, 10 January 1821, AGN-ARH 3, 14A.

18. Pedro Valera to Sebastian Kindelán, Santo Domingo, 8 December 1820, AGI-SD 970, no. 3; Sebastian Kindelán to Pedro Valera, Santo Domingo, 9 December 1820, AGI-SD 970, no. 4. For examples of race war discourses, see Marixa Lasso, *Myths of Harmony: Race and Republicanism During the Age of Revolution, Colombia, 1795–1831* (Pittsburgh: University of Pittsburgh Press, 2007), 11–13, 129–150; Ana Sabau, *Riot and Rebellion in Mexico: The Making of a Race War Paradigm* (Austin: University of Texas Press, 2022).

19. Felipe Dávila Cruz de Castro to Estado Universal de Hacienda, 13 December 1820, AGI-SD 966, no. 21.

20. Title 4, sec. 48 of the 1816 revision to the 1806 Constitution d'Haïti.

21. Pedro Valera, "Apologia," Santo Domingo, 1821, AGI-SD 970.

22. 22 September 1820, AHASD-CE, 24/4; Emilio Rodríguez Demorizi, *La imprenta y los primeros periódicos de Santo Domingo* (Santo Domingo: Taller, 1973), 116–127.

23. Madiou, *Histoire, 1819–1826*, 200–206; *El Duende*, 24 June 1821, AGI-SD 970; Thomas Clarkson to Jean-Pierre Boyer, 25 May 1821, in *Henry Christophe and Thomas Clarkson: A Correspondence*, ed. Earl Griggs and Clifford Prator (Berkeley: University of California Press, 1952), 224–226. On the concordat, see Julia Gaffield, "The Racialization of International Law after the Haitian Revolution: The Holy See and National Sovereignty," *American Historical Review* 125, no. 3 (June 2020): 841–868.

24. Inginac, *Mémoires*, 45–49; Madiou, *Histoire, 1819–1826*, 162–176.

25. Ramón Gil de la Cuadra, 27 February 1821, AGI-E 89, n. 101; An Officer, *Present State of Colombia* (London: Murray, 1827), 102–103; 4 October 1820, Madrid, ANC-AP, leg. 18, exp. 40.

26. Domingo Pérez Guerra to Sebastian Kindelán, Neiba, 1 January 1821, AGI-SD 970, no. 22.

27. Sebastian Kindelán to Carabajal, Santo Domingo, n.d., AGI-SD 970, no. 19; Sebastian Kindelán to Carabajal, Santo Domingo, 18 December 1820, AGI-SD 970, no. 18.

28. Sebastian Kindelán to Ayuntamiento de Neiba, Santo Domingo, 17 December 1820, AGI-SD 970, no. 14.

29. Jean-Pierre Boyer to Sebastian Kindelán, n.d., in Madiou, *Histoire, 1819–1826,* 167–168.

30. Sebastian Kindelán, Felipe Dávila, José Basera, Juan Uri, Antonio Pineda, Antonio Martinez de Valdes, and Francisco Brenes to Ultramar, Santo Domingo, 16 January 1821, AGI-SD 970, no. 794; Gobernación de Ultramar to Jefe Politico de Santo Domingo, Madrid, 25 January 1821, AGI-SD 970.

31. Gobernación de Ultramar, 6 November 1821, AGI-SD 970.

32. "Prospecto," *Telegrafo Constitucional de Santo Domingo,* 4 March 1821.

33. Sebastian Kindelán to Ultramar, Santo Domingo, 27 June 1820, AGI-SD 970, no. 20.

34. Sebastian Kindelán to Fidelisimos Naturales y Habitantes de La Española, Santo Domingo, 10 June 1820, AGI-SD 970.

35. Sebastian Kindelán to Ayuntamiento de Neiba, Santo Domingo, 17 December 1820, AGI-SD 970, no. 14.

36. Sebastian Kindelán, "Manifiesto de la correspondencia entre el gobierno de esta parte Española y el de la vecina de la Republica de Hayti sobre la verdadera o falsa mission del teniente coronel Dezir Dalmassi," 10 January 1821, AGI-SD 970.

37. Gobernación de Ultramar, 6 November 1821, AGI-SD 970.

38. Inginac, *Mémoires,* 55–58.

39. *Réunion,* 3–4.

40. José Justo de Sylva to Jean-Pierre Boyer, Santo Domingo, 8 January 1821 (A), in *Réunion,* 9–10. For examples of Haitian legal constraints and foreign relations, see Julia Gaffield, *Haitian Connections in the Atlantic World: Recognition After Revolution* (Chapel Hill: University of North Carolina Press, 2015).

41. Gobernación de Ultramar, 4 July 1821, AGI-SD 970, no. 4; Palacio to Ultramar, Santo Domingo, 31 August 1821, AGI-SD 970; Ministerio de la Guerra to Gobernación de Ultramar, Madrid, 21 October 1821, AGI-SD 970; Gobernación de Ultramar to Ministerio de la Guerra, Madrid, 7 July 1821, AGI-SD 970; "Estado de la poblacion de la parte española de Santo Domingo . . . ," Santo Domingo, 29 June 1820, AGI-SD 970; Prophète Daniel, Ichar, and Monpoint to Sebastian Kindelán, 12 October 1820, AGI-SD 970, no. 1.

42. Diego Polanco to General Magny, Monte Cristi, 15 November 1821 (B), in *Réunion,* 10.

43. Andrés Amarante, José Dominguez Arias, and Joaquín Oliva Adhenet, "Au très-honorable Général Magny, commandant de l'Arrondissement du Cap-Haïtien," Dajabón, 15 November 1821 (C), in *Réunion*, 11.

44. "... Gazeta del Gobierno de Hayti Francés," Port-au-Prince, 23 December 1821, AGI-SD 970, no. 33.

45. *Réunion*, 2–5.

46. Pascual Real, Gobernación de Ultramar, Liverpool, 24 January 1822, AGI-SD 970, no. 8; Pascual Real to Governacion de Ultramar, Santo Domingo, 23 November 1821, AGI-SD 970.

47. Pascual Real to Ultramar, Santo Domingo, 15 November 1821, AGI-SD 970, no. 4.

48. "Carta de un caraqueño a sus compatriotas de Santo Domingo," Puerto Rico, 19 April 1821, AGI-SD 970. For more on Dessalines, see David Geggus, *Haitian Revolutionary Studies* (Bloomington: Indiana University Press, 2002), 27, 213–215. For more on Christophe, see Griggs and Prator, *Henry Christophe and Thomas Clarkson*.

49. "Num. del Sec. 1003, el ministerio de gracia y justicia ...," Santo Domingo, 1821, AGI-SD 970.

50. Provisional Government of Santo Domingo, "Acta Constitutiva del Gobierno Provisional del Estado Independiente de la Parte Española de Hayti," 1 December 1821, AGI-SD 970; Pedro Valera, Santo Domingo, 18 December 1821, AGI-SD 970.

51. Pascual Real, Gobernación de Ultramar, Liverpool, 24 January 1821, AGI-SD 970, no. 8; "2.a Parte, Expediente ... ," Felipe Castro to Primer Secratario del Despacho de Estado, 9 July 1824, AHN-E 3394, exp. 4; Sebastian Kindelán, Santo Domingo, 31 January and 20 February 1821, AGI-SD 1017, exp. 72–73; Carlos Esteban Deive, *La esclavitud del negro en Santo Domingo, 1492–1844*, vols. 1–2 (Santo Domingo: Museo del Hombre Dominicano, 1980); José Gabriel García, *Compendio de la historia de Santo Domingo*, vol. 2 (Santo Domingo: Imprenta García Hermanos, 1894); Geggus, *Haitian Revolutionary Studies*, 202.

52. Pascual Real, Gobernación de Ultramar, Liverpool, 24 January 1821, AGI-SD 970, no. 8.

53. José Núñez de Cáceres to Joaquín Morell, Santo Domingo, 6 December 1821, AGI-SD 970.

54. *Réunion*, 5–6.

55. Inginac, *Mémoires*, 59–62.

56. Tomás Pérez Guerra to Captain General of Puerto Rico, Puerto Rico, 31 June 1822, AGI-SD 970.

57. "2.a Parte, Expediente ... ," Felipe Castro to Primer Secratario del Despacho de Estado, 9 July 1824, AHN-E 3394, exp. 4; Manuel Marqués to Francisco Dionisio Vives, Havana, 4 March 1826, AHN-E 3395, exp. 4, no. 1.

58. Nicolas Malos to Ultramar, Havana, 5 March 1822, AGI-SD 970, nos. 268–269.

59. Junta Central Provisorio de Santiago, "Très-Excellent Seigneur," 29 December 1821 (D), in *Réunion*, 11–13.

60. Joaquín Bidos, Luis Rodríguez Pilantes, and Francisco Antonio del Campo to Jean-Pierre Boyer and General Magny, Puerto Plata, 13 December 1821 (E), in *Réunion*, 13–14.

61. Antonio López de Villanueva to Junta Central de Santiago, Puerto Plata, 31 December 1821 (E3), in *Réunion*, 16–17.

62. "Au citoyen Antonio López de Villanueva, commandant militaire de Porte-Plate," 29 December 1821 (E2), in *Réunion*, 15.

63. Damien Herrera, José Herrera, Camilo Suero, Francisco de los Santos, Manuel del Castillo, Luis de los Santos, Remigio Alcanter, and Andrés Herrera to Jean-Pierre Boyer, San Juan de la Maguana, 10 January 1822 (G), in *Réunion*, 18.

64. José Román Hernández and Francisco López to Jean-Pierre Boyer, Neiba, 13 January 1822 (H), in *Réunion*, 18–19.

65. Juan Zerano and Julio Borja, "Les vrais citoyens de la ville de Neybe, a Son Excellence J.-P. Boyer, président d'Haiti," Neiba, 19 January 1822 (H2), in *Réunion*, 19–20.

66. Juan Ramón to Jean-Pierre Boyer, La Vega, 4 January 1822 (F), in *Réunion*, 17.

67. "Les citoyens . . . ," Azua, 21 January 1822 (I3), in *Réunion*, 22–23; Pablo Báez, José Díaz, Manuel Feliz, Angel de Noboa, Ramón Pichardo, Raphael, García Cazuela, José Joaquín Jirpo, Ramón Martinez, Juan de la Cruz, and José Maria Belanez, Azua, 16 January 1822 (I), in *Réunion*, 20; José Díaz, Manuel Reyes, Manuel Feliz, Agustin de Castro, Juan Clemente Obando, and Jacinto Ortiz, Azua, 22 January 1822 (I2), in *Réunion*, 21–22.

68. Juan Núñez Blanco, Santiago, 14 January 1822 (J), in *Réunion*, 25–26; Manuel Machado to José Núñez de Cáceres, Samaná, 6 February 1822 (L), in *Réunion*, 27; Manuel Machado to Jean-Pierre Boyer, Samaná, February 1822 (L2), in *Réunion*, 27.

69. "Proclamation du Citoyen Manuel Machado au peuple de Samaná," 10 February 1822 (L3), in *Réunion*, 28–30.

70. ". . . Gazeta del Gobierno de Hayti Francés," Port-au-Prince, 23 December 1821, AGI-SD 970, no. 33.

71. Toussaint Louverture, "A todos los habitantes de la partida antes española," San Juan de la Maguana, 14 Nivôse an IX / 4 January 1801, AGMM-U, SD 5650, exp. 2; AHN-E 3394, exp. 1; "Révolution de St. Domingue, par M. Périès, trésorier," BL-WM, Add. Ms. 38074, 196–200; Madiou, *Histoire, 1819–1826*, 271–273; *Constitution d'Haïti*, 20 May 1805. See Title II, sec. 40 of the 1816 revision of the 1806 Constitution d'Haïti. For more on the constitutional debate, see Antony Keane-Dawes, "The Benefits of French Recognition: Haitian and Dominican Challenges to Slavery and Empire in the Atlantic World," *Atlantic Studies* (April 2020): 1–25.

72. Jean-Pierre Boyer to José Núñez de Cáceres, Port-au-Prince, 11 January 1822, AHN-E 3395, exp. 4.

73. José Núñez de Cáceres to Jean-Pierre Boyer, Santo Domingo, 19 January 1822 (K), in *Réunion*, 26–27.

74. José Núñez de Cáceres to Loyal Dominicans and Beloved Compatriots, Santo Domingo, 19 January 1822, AHN-E 3395, exp. 4.

75. Nicolas Matos to Sec. de Estado y la Gobernación de Ultramar, Havana, 18 January 1822, AGI-SD 970, no. 262.

76. *Réunion*, 5–8. For details on the aftermath of unification in the Caribbean, see Andrew Walker, "All Spirits Are Roused: The 1822 Antislavery Revolution in Haitian Santo Domingo," *Slavery and Abolition* 40, no. 3 (2019): 583–605. For broader context, see Frank Moya Pons, *The Dominican Republic: A National History* (Princeton, NJ: Markus Wiener, 1998), 118–126.

77. Jean-Pierre Boyer, José Núñez de Cáceres, et al., "Procès-verbal de l'entrée du président d'Haïti a Santo-Domingo" (M), in *Réunion*, 30–32.

78. Agustín Sánchez Andrés, "La búsqueda de un nuevo modelo de relaciones con los territorios ultramarinos durante el Trienio Liberal (1820–1823)," *Revista de Indias* 57, no. 210 (1997): 451–474; Scott Eastman, *Preaching Spanish Nationalism Across the Hispanic Atlantic, 1759–1823* (Baton Rouge: Louisiana State University Press, 2012), chapter 6.

79. "1.a Parte, Expediente . . . ," Felipe Castro to Primer Secretario del Despacho de Estado, 6 July 1824, AHN-E 3395, exp. 4. This quotation came from a conversation with Jean-Pierre Boyer that Castro recounted. Manuel Marqués to Francisco Dionisio Vives, Havana, 4 March 1826, AHN-E 3395, exp. 4, no. 1; Juan Nepomuceno de Cardenas to Nicolas Mahi, Puerto Rico, 4 March 1822, AHN-E 3395, exp. 4.

EPILOGUE

1. David Scott, *Conscripts of Modernity: The Tragedy of Colonial Enlightenment* (Durham, NC: Duke University Press, 2004), 71–97.

2. Tomás Pérez Guerra to Captain General of Puerto Rico, Puerto Rico, 31 June 1822, AGI-SD 970.

3. David Geggus, *Haitian Revolutionary Studies* (Bloomington: Indiana University Press, 2002), 201.

4. Joseph Balthazar Inginac, *Mémoires de Joseph Balthazar Inginac, ex-secrétaire-général près S. E. l'ex-président d'Haïti* (Kingston, Jamaica: Cordova, 1843), 61–63.

5. Francisco Brenes to Gefe Politico de Puerto Rico, Puerto Rico, 16 September 1822, AGI-SD 970, no. 88; Ultramar, Madrid, 3 October 1822, AGI-SD 970.

6. "1.a Parte, Expediente . . . ," Felipe Castro to Primer Secretario del Despacho de Estado, 6 July 1824, AHN-E 3395, exp. 4; Manuel Marqués to Francisco Dionisio Vives, Havana, 4 March 1826, AHN-E 3395, exp. 4, no. 1; Juan Nepomuceno de Cardenas to Nicolas Mahi, Puerto Rico, 4 March 1822, AHN-E 3395, exp. 4.

7. Segretario di Stato, Rome, 24 June and 15 September 1822, and 25 September 1825, ASV-NM 270, 214–219, 291, 329.

8. Ministerio de Guerra, 22 January 1823, AGI-SD 970; Juan Nepomuceno de Cardenas to Nicolas Mahi, Puerto Rico, 4 March 1822, AHN-E 3395, exp. 4; Inginac, *Mémoires*, 46–48.

9. "Mon bien cher papa," Samaná, 4 March 1822, SCRBC, MG 23, Boxes 1a–1b. See

also Gregory Pierrot, "The Samaná Affair," *Haiti and the Atlantic World*, https://haitidoi .com/2013/10/09/the-samana-affair-2.

10. Inginac, *Mémoires*, 64–68.

11. "1.a Parte, Expediente . . . ," Felipe Castro to Primer Secratario del Despacho de Estado, 6 July 1824, AHN-E 3395, exp. 4; Manuel Marqués to Francisco Dionisio Vives, Havana, 4 March 1826, AHN-E 3395, exp. 4, no. 1; Juan Nepomuceno de Cardenas to Nicolas Mahi, Puerto Rico, 4 March 1822, AHN-E 3395, exp. 4.

12. Manuel Márquez, Havana, 27 February 1826, AHN-E 3395, exp. 4; Luis Salazar to Sec. de Despacho de Gracia y Justicia, Palacio, 16 July 1824, AGI-SD 1017.

13. Miguel de la Torre to Henry Warde, Puerto Rico, 14 October 1822, TNA-CO 28/91, 120–123; Miguel de la Torre to Henry Warde, Puerto Rico, 12 September 1823, TNA-CO 28/92, 241–242; François-Xavier Donzelot to Henry Warde, Martinique, 10 January 1824, TNA-CO 28/93, 25.

14. Anne Eller, "Rumors of Slavery: Defending Emancipation in a Hostile Caribbean," *American Historical Review* 122, no. 3 (June 2017): 653–679.

15. *Réunion de la partie de l'est a la république* (Port-au-Prince: L'Imprimerie du Gouvernement, 1830), 6–7.

16. Ernesto Bassi, *An Aqueous Territory: Sailor Geographies and New Granada's Transimperial Greater Caribbean World* (Durham, NC: Duke University Press, 2016), 168–169; Marixa Lasso, *Myths of Harmony: Race and Republicanism During the Age of Revolution, Colombia, 1795–1831* (Pittsburgh: University of Pittsburgh Press, 2007); Michel-Rolph Trouillot, *Haiti: State Against Nation* (New York: Monthly Review Press, 1990), 51–53; Germán A. de la Reza, "El intento de integración de Santo Domingo a la Gran Colombia (1821–1822)," *Secuencia* (September–December 2015): 65–82; Daniel Florencio O'Leary, *Bolívar and the War of Independence* (Austin: University of Texas Press, 1970), 91–107. For more regional context, see James E. Sanders, *The Vanguard of the Atlantic World: Creating Modernity, Nation, and Democracy in Nineteenth-Century Latin America* (Durham, NC: Duke University Press, 2014); Don H. Doyle, ed., *American Civil Wars: The United States, Latin America, Europe, and the Crisis of the 1860s* (Chapel Hill: University of North Carolina Press, 2017).

17. Charles R. Venator Santiago, "Race, the East, and the Haitian Revolutionary Ideology: Rethinking the Role of Race in the 1844 Separation of the Eastern Part of Haiti," *Journal of Haitian Studies* 10, no. 1 (Spring 2004): 103–119.

18. Julia Gaffield, *Haitian Connections in the Atlantic World: Recognition After Revolution* (Chapel Hill: University of North Carolina Press, 2015), 182–196.

19. Frank Moya Pons, *Dominación haitiana 1822–1844* (Santiago: UCMM, 1978).

20. Antony Keane-Dawes, "A Divisive Community: Race, Nation, and Loyalty in Santo Domingo, 1822–1844" (PhD diss., University of South Carolina, 2018); Antony Keane-Dawes, "The Benefits of French Recognition: Haitian and Dominican Challenges to Slavery and Empire in the Atlantic World," *Atlantic Studies* (April 2020): 1–25; Alex Dupuy, *Rethinking the Haitian Revolution: Slavery, Independence, and the Struggle for Recognition* (Lanham, MD: Rowman and Littlefield, 2019), chapter 4.

21. Quisqueya Lora, *Transición de la esclavitud al trabajo libre en Santo Domingo: El caso de Higüey, 1822–1827* (Santo Domingo: Academia Dominicana de la Historia, 2012).

22. Maria Cecilia Ulrickson, "'Esclavos que fueron' in Santo Domingo, 1768–1844" (PhD diss., University of Notre Dame, 2018); Andrew Walker, "Strains of Unity: Emancipation, Property, and the Post-Revolutionary State in Haitian Santo Domingo, 1822–1844" (PhD diss., University of Michigan, 2018).

23. Quisqueya Lora, "¿Llamamientos o invasión? El debate en torno a los llamamientos de 1821 y 1822," *Clío* 85, no. 192 (July–December 2016): 98–151.

24. Sara Johnson, "The Integration of Hispaniola: A Reappraisal of Haitian-Dominican Relations in the Nineteenth and Twentieth Centuries," *Journal of Haitian Studies* 8, no. 2 (Fall 2002): 4–29.

25. Lorgia García Peña, *The Borders of Dominicanidad: Race, Nation, and Archives of Contradiction* (Durham, NC: Duke University Press, 2016), 1–15, 202, 211.

26. Jean Price-Mars, *République d'Haïti et la République dominicaine*, vol. 1 (Port-au-Prince: Éditions Fardin, 1953), 202–207; Marlene Daut, *Tropics of Haiti: Race and the Literary History of the Haitian Revolution in the Atlantic World, 1789–1865* (Liverpool: Liverpool University Press, 2015), 465–466, 539, 577–578; Vanessa Mongey, "A Tale of Two Brothers: Haiti's Other Revolutions," *The Americas* 69, no. 1 (2012): 37–60; Silvio Torres-Saillant, "The Tribulations of Blackness: Stages in Dominican Racial Identity," *Callaloo* 23, no. 3 (Summer 2000), esp. 1096–1099.

27. Venator Santiago, "Race, the East, and the Haitian Revolutionary Ideology."

28. Pedro L. San Miguel, *La Isla imaginada: Historia, identidad y utopia en La Española* (Santo Domingo: La Trinitaria, 1997), chapter 2; Peter van der Veer, "Nationalism and Religion," in *Oxford Handbook of the History of Nationalism*, ed. John Breuilly (New York: Oxford University Press, 2013).

29. "Transacción de litis," 30 March 1806, AGN-ARH 1, 27R, exp. 142; "Venta de Terrenos," 16 July 1806, AGN-ARH 1, 24R, exp. 53A; "Otorgamiento de poder," 2 May 1808, AGN, Archivo Real el Seibo, 1, 32, exp. 55; "Venta de terrenos," 3 May 1810, AGN-ARH 1, 24R, exp. 53; Bartolo Rijo, "Orden del Alcalde," 9 February 1813, AGN-ARH 4, 26R, exp. 8; "Otorgamiento de poder," 14 March 1817, AGN-ARB 1, 30.

30. Emilio Rodríguez y Demorizi, *San Cristóbal de Antaño* (Santo Domingo: Archivo General de la Nación, 1946), 57–63. Bartolina del Maniel's *apellido* was Mansebi or Mancebo. James Franklin, *The Present State of Hayti* (London: Murray, 1828), 297–298.

31. Eugenio Matibag, *Haitian-Dominican Counterpoint: Nation, State, and Race on Hispaniola* (New York: Palgrave, 2003), 113–115; Gerald Horne, *Confronting Black Jacobins: The U.S., the Haitian Revolution, and the Origins of the Dominican Republic* (New York: Monthly Review Press, 2015), 195–198; Silvio Torres-Saillant, "The Tribulations of Blackness: Stages in Dominican Racial Identity," *Callaloo* 23, no. 3 (Summer 2000): 1086–1111; Venator Santiago, "Race, the East, and the Haitian Revolutionary Ideology"; Orlando Inoa, *Biografía de Juan Pablo Duarte* (Santo Domingo: Gráfica, 2008), 81; Laurent Dubois, *Avengers of the New World: The Story of the Haitian Revolution* (Cambridge, MA: Belknap Press of Harvard University Press, 2004), 293.

32. Thomas Madiou, *Histoire d'Haïti: 1843–1846* (Port-au-Prince: Verrollot, 1904), 115; Thomas Madiou, *Histoire d'Haïti*, vol. 3 (Port-au-Prince: Courtois, 1848), 507.

33. Beaubrun Ardouin, *Études sur l'histoire d'Haïti*, vol. 3 (Paris: Dezobry, 1853), 104–106.

34. Madiou, *Histoire*, 3:325.

35. Vetilio Alfau Durán, *Mujeres de la Independencia* (Santo Domingo: Trinitaria, 1999), 46–48; "Resolución 2751 de 1889," *Colección de leyes, decretos y resoluciones . . . de la Republica Dominicana*, vol. 9 (Santo Domingo: Hermanos García, 1895), 109–110.

36. Joaquín Balaguer, *El centinela de la frontera: Vida y hazañas de Antonio Duvergé* (Santo Domingo: Chiesino, 1962), esp. 19–21; Vetilio Alfau Durán, "La Romana: Evaluación histórica," *Boletín del Archivo General de la Nación* 30, no. 111 (2005): 82. Even if his grandfather was related to the Rochejaquelein family of lesser French nobility, as some hagiographies posit, that does not exclude his probable African descent. Jean Price-Mars, *La République d'Haïti et la République dominicaine*, vol. 2 (Port-au-Prince: Trieinquantenaire, 1953), 200; Orlando Inoa, *Azúcar: árabes, cocolos, y haitianos* (Santo Domingo: Editora Cole, 1999), 145.

37. "Develizan retrato heroina Rosa Montás de Duvergé, Madame Bois," *Diario Dominicano*, 23 March 2008; "Un día como hoy muere Antonio Duvergé," *El Nacional*, 11 April 2019; "Las mujeres también lucharon por la Independencia," *El Día*, 27 February 2014. For an exception, see "Familias haitianas al servicio de nuestra independencia," *Hoy*, 9 December 2005.

38. Lauren H. Derby, *The Dictator's Seduction: Politics and the Popular Imagination in the Era of Trujillo* (Durham, NC: Duke University Press, 2009), 199, 218; Valentina Peguero, *The Militarization of Culture in the Dominican Republic, from the Captains General to General Trujillo* (Lincoln: University of Nebraska Press, 2004), 44–46; Edward Paulino, *Dividing Hispaniola: The Dominican Republic's Border Campaign Against Haiti, 1930–1961* (Pittsburgh: University of Pittsburgh Press, 2016), chapter 2.

39. Geggus, *Haitian Revolutionary Studies*, 82, 201; Walker, "Strains," 51, 67, 133–136.

40. Anne Eller, *We Dream Together: Dominican Independence, Haiti, and the Fight for Caribbean Freedom* (Durham, NC: Duke University Press, 2016), 1, 31–34, 53–235 (esp. 229); Eric Roorda, Lauren Derby, and Raymundo González, eds., *The Dominican Republic Reader: History, Culture, Politics* (Durham, NC: Duke University Press, 2016), 141–148; Eller, "Rumors of Slavery."

41. Lorgia García Peña, "Translating Blackness," *The Black Scholar* 45, no. 2 (2015): 10–20; Silvio Torres-Saillant, *Introduction to Dominican Blackness* (New York: Dominican Studies Institute, City College of New York, 1999).

42. Dixa Ramírez, *Colonial Phantoms: Belonging and Refusal in the Dominican Americas, from the 19th Century to the Present* (New York: New York University Press, 2018), 1–31, 41–42; Ginetta Candelario, *Black Behind the Ears: Dominican Racial Identity from Museums to Beauty Shops* (Durham, NC: Duke University Press, 2007), 1–128; April Mayes, *Mulatto Republic: Class, Race, and Dominican National Identity* (Gainesville: University Press of Florida); Jorge Duany, "Transnational Migration from the Dominican

Republic: The Cultural Redefinition of Racial Identity," *Caribbean Studies* 29, no. 2 (1996): 253–282; Kimberly Eison Simmons, *Reconstructing Racial Identity and the African Past in the Dominican Republic* (Gainesville: University Press of Florida, 2009). On *indigenismo*, see Rebecca Earle, *Return of the Native: Indians and Myth-Making in Spanish America, 1810–1930* (Durham, NC: Duke University Press, 2007), chapter 7. On challenges for Dominican immigrants, see Inés M. Miyares, "Changing Latinization of New York City," in *Hispanic Spaces, Latino Places: Community and Cultural Diversity in Contemporary America*, ed. Daniel D. Arreola (Austin: University of Texas Press, 2004), 145–165; Frank Graziano, *Undocumented Dominican Migration* (Austin: University of Texas Press, 2013).

43. Michiel Baud, "'Constitutionally White,'" in *Ethnicity in the Caribbean: Essays in Honor of Harry Hoetink*, ed. Gert Oostindie (London: Macmillan, 1996), 121–151; Derby, *Dictator's Seduction*, 24, 57, 275n130; Richard Lee Turits, *Foundations of Despotism: Peasants, the Trujillo Regime, and Modernity in the Dominican Republic* (Stanford, CA: Stanford University Press, 2003), 171–180, 309n3; Sibylle Fischer, *Modernity Disavowed: Haiti and the Cultures of Slavery in the Age of Revolution* (Durham, NC: Duke University Press, 2004), 156–160.

44. Légation de la République d'Haïti, Santo Domingo, 5 May 1937, SCRBC, MG 119. For more on diplomacy toward Trujillo, see Eric Roorda, *Dictator Next Door: The Good Neighbor Policy and the Trujillo Regime in the Dominican Republic, 1930–1945* (Durham, NC: Duke University Press, 1998).

45. Maria Cristina Fumagalli, *On the Edge: Writing the Border Between Haiti and the Dominican Republic* (Liverpool: Liverpool University Press, 2015), 2, 99–100, 350.

46. Teresita Martínez-Vergne, *Nation and Citizen in the Dominican Republic, 1880–1916* (Chapel Hill: University of North Carolina Press, 2006), 100–104; Milagros Ricourt, *The Dominican Racial Imaginary: Surveying the Landscape of Race and Nation in Hispaniola* (New Brunswick, NJ: Rutgers University Press, 2016).

47. Myrna Pichardo, "¡Se nos muere el hermano siamés!," *Listín Diario*, 16 January 2010; Matías Bosch, "República Dominicana y Haití: Entre la fraternidad y la doctrina del conflicto," *El País*, 30 November 2015; Roberto Valenzuela, "Se crea estructura militar y civil para unificar RD y Haití," *El Nuevo Diario*, 29 June 2020; Martha Ellen Davis, "Vodú of the Dominican Republic," *Afro-Hispanic Review* 26, no. 1 (Spring 2007): 75–90.

48. Raj Chetty and Amaury Rodríguez, "Introduction," *The Black Scholar* 45, no. 2 (2015): 1–9. The icon of democracy Juan Bosch implied that Haiti had impeded Dominican development, yet he was racially inclusive in politics, nuanced to Haitians, and initially promoted the Haitian-descended politician José Francisco Peña Gómez. See Juan Bosch, *Trujillo, causas de una tiranía sin ejemplo* (Santo Domingo: Editora Alfa and Omega, 1991); Charlton W. Yingling, "'To the Reconciliation of All Dominicans': The Transnational Trials of Dominican Exiles in the Trujillo Era," in *Crossing Boundaries: Ethnicity, Race, and National Belonging in a Transnational World*, ed. Brian Behnken and Simon Wendt (Lanham, MD: Lexington, 2013), 39–61.

49. David Howard, *Coloring the Nation: Race and Ethnicity in the Dominican Republic* (Boulder: Lynne Rienner, 2001), 58–60; Emilio Rodríguez Demorizi, "La revolución de 1843, Apuntes y documentos," *Boletín del Archivo General de la Nación* 6, nos. 26–27 (1943): 28–109; Manuel Jesús Troncoso, *La ocupación de Santo Domingo por Haiti* (Santo Domingo: La Nación, 1942); Jacinto Gimbernard, *Historia de Santo Domingo* (Santo Domingo: Sardá, 1971). Rodríguez Demorizi accepted Trujillo's anti-Haitianism and attacked scholars who detailed this shared past.

50. Médar Serrata, "Anti-Haitian Rhetoric and the Monumentalizing of Violence in Joaquín Balaguer's *Guía emocional de la ciudad romántica*," *Hispanic Review* 81, no. 3 (Summer 2013): 263–284. See also Megan Jeanneatte Myers and Edward Paulino, eds., *The Border of Lights Reader: Bearing Witness to Genocide in the Dominican Republic* (Amherst, MA: Amherst College Press, 2021); Richard Lee Turits, "A World Destroyed, A Nation Imposed: The 1937 Haitian Massacre in the Dominican Republic," *Hispanic American Historical Review* 82, no. 3 (2002): 589–635.

51. Ramón Benito de la Rosa y Carpio, "Invasión y matanza haitiana," *Listín Diario*, 7 February 2017; Silvio Herasme Peña, "El informe de la infamia," *Listín Diario*, 26 October 2014.

52. Joaquín Balaguer, *La isla al revés: Haiti y el destino dominicano* (Santo Domingo: Fundación Caro, 1983), 62–66.

53. Edgardo Rodríguez Juliá, "Faro del mundo, luz de América," *Inti: Revista de literatura hispánica* 39 (1994): 177–186; Natalia Junquera, "Colón sí es Colón," *El País*, 1 August 2006; Michel-Rolph Trouillot, *Silencing the Past: Power and the Production of History* (Boston: Beacon, 1995), 113–115; Lyman L. Johnson, *Death, Dismemberment, and Memory: Body Politics in Latin America* (Albuquerque: University of New Mexico Press, 2004), 6–8.

54. Howard, *Coloring the Nation*, 46–47; Fischer, *Modernity Disavowed*, 146–148; San Miguel, *Isla imaginada*, chapter 2.

55. Danilo Antonio Contreras, "Exit over Voice in Dominican Ethnoracial Politics," *Latin American Research Review* 51, no. 3 (2016): 202–226.

56. Adriana Peguero, "Por respeto a haitianos no leerán Biblia en aulas," *Listín Diario*, 13 June 2019; Juan F. Puello Herrera, "Biblia y vudú," *Listín Diario*, 28 June 2019; Homero Luis Lajara Solá, "El mito de la isla indivisible," *Listín Diario*, 15 July 2017; Vinicio Castillo Semán, "Se reanuda la invasión haitiana," *Listín Diario*, 27 July 2015.

57. Carlos Cornielle, *Proceso histórico dominico-haitiano: Una advertencia a la juventud dominicana* (Santo Domingo: Publicaciones América, 1980); Luis Julián Pérez, *Santo Domingo frente al destino* (Santo Domingo: Taller, 1990).

58. For analysis, see Ernesto Ságas, *Race and Politics in the Dominican Republic* (Gainesville: University Press of Florida, 2000), 44–47; Maja Horn, "Dictates of Dominican Democracy: Conceptualizing Caribbean Political Modernity," *Small Axe* 44 (July 2014): 18–35; April Yoder, *Pitching Democracy: Baseball and Politics in the Dominican Republic* (Austin: University of Texas Press, forthcoming).

59. Luisa América Mateo Dicló, "La afrodescendencia en la sociedad dominicana: Entre la blancofilia y la negrofobia" (PhD diss., Universidad Complutense de Madrid,

2018); João Solano Carneiro da Cunha, "La republica dominicana y los afrodescendientes," *Archipelago* 94 (October–December 2016).

60. Eugenio Matibag and Teresa Downing-Matibag, "Sovereignty and Social Justice: The 'Haitian Problem' in the Dominican Republic," *Caribbean Quarterly* 57, no. 2 (June 2011): 92–117; David Simmons, "Structural Violence as Social Practice: Haitian Agricultural Workers, Anti-Haitianism, and Health in the Dominican Republic," *Human Organization* 69, no. 1 (Spring 2010): 10–18.

61. Trenita Brookshire Childers, *In Someone Else's Country: Anti-Haitian Racism and Citizenship in the Dominican Republic* (Lanham, MD: Rowman and Littlefield, 2021); Leiv Marsteinredet, "Mobilisation Against International Human Rights: Re-Domesticating the Dominican Citizenship Regime," *Iberoamericana* 44 (2014): 73–98; Zach Hindin and Mario Ariza, "When Nativism Becomes Normal," *The Atlantic*, 23 May 2016; Rachel Nolan, "Displaced in the D. R.," *Harper's Magazine*, May 2015.

62. Manuel Fermín, "Trump no es Danilo," *Listín Diario*, 8 December 2017; "Gobierno de Trump separó más de 900 niños de sus padres desde junio pasado," *Listín Diario*, 30 July 2019.

63. For examples linking 1822 with ongoing debates, see Jaime Fernández Lazala, "Siete invasiones haitianas," *Listín Diario*, 6 September 2015; José Guerrero, "Los haitianos del 1822,1844 y 2018," *El Nuevo Diario*, 28 December 2018; Cristal Acevedo, "Desde la ocupación haitiana hasta la veda a pollos y huevos," *Hoy*, 2 July 2013; Ramón Antonio Veras, "Invasión pacífica," *Hoy*, 9 January 2007; Fabio Herrera Miniño, "La explosiva invasión haitiana y pasividad dominicana," *Hoy*, 25 March 2017. For the Trujillo era, see Edward Paulino, *Dividing Hispaniola: The Dominican Republic's Border Campaign Against Haiti, 1930–1961* (Pittsburgh: University of Pittsburgh Press, 2016), chapter 4; Megan Jeanette Myers, *Mapping Hispaniola: Third Space in Dominican and Haitian Literature* (Charlottesville: University of Virginia Press, 2019), chapter 1. See also Amelia Hintzen, "The Origins of Anti-Haitian Sentiment," North American Congress on Latin America, 14 July 2015, https://nacla.org/news/2015/07/14/origins-anti-haitian-sentiment-dominican-republic; Amelia Hintzen, "Historical Forgetting and the Dominican Constitutional Tribunal," *Journal of Haitian Studies* 20, no. 1 (Spring 2014): 108–116.

64. "Rechazan campaña unificar RD-Haití," *El Nacional*, 31 August 2014.

65. Luis Villaverde, "Piden recordar 200 años de la invasión haitiana," *El Caribe*, 17 January 2019.

66. Diógenes Abréu, *Sin haitianidad no hay dominicanidad: Cartografía de una identidad que se bifurca* (Santo Domingo: Editora Nacional, 2014).

67. Samuel Martínez, "Not a Cockfight: Rethinking Haitian-Dominican Relations," *Latin American Perspectives* 30, no. 3 (May 2003): 80–101; April Mayes and Kiran Jayaram, eds., *Transnational Hispaniola: New Directions in Haitian and Dominican Studies* (Gainesville: University Press of Florida, 2018); Fumagalli, *On the Edge*, chapters 6 and 10; Tirso Mejía Ricart, "Xenofobia, racismo e interés nacional: A propósito de la decisión infortunada del TC," *Hoy*, 3 November 2013; Tirso Mejía Ricart, "Migraciones, nacionalismo patriotero y otros demonios," *Hoy*, 28 December 2018; Diógenes Céspedes, "Paradojas de la

separación de 1844," *Hoy*, 6 November 2010; Santiago Castro Ventura, "¿La independencia de Núñez de Cáceres?," *Hoy*, 22 December 2010.

68. Santiago Benjamín de la Cruz, "Denuncian hay invasión haitiana descontrolada," *Listín Diario*, 23 April 2018; Homero Luis Lajara Solá, "Haití ¿Víctima de quién?," *Listín Diario*, 5 September 2017; Orlando Gil, "Hay que echar nueva ojeada a historia respecto a Haití," *Listín Diario*, 13 July 2015.

69. Antonio Sánchez Valverde, *Idea del valor de la isla Española* (Madrid: Pedro Marín, 1785), vi, 9, 59, 72.

70. Damien Herrera, José Herrera, Camilo Suero, Francisco de los Santos, Manuel del Castillo, Luis de los Santos, Remigio Alcanter, and Andrés Herrera to Jean-Pierre Boyer, San Juan de la Maguana, 10 January 1822 (G), in *Réunion*, 18.

INDEX

Page numbers followed by f denote illustrations.

Jean-Louis Ferrand, 159–160; finances of, 95; founding of, 6, 25–26; and French expedition, 156; French influence in, 13–14; and French Revolution, 71; and Joaquín García, 30; and *gens de couleur* insurgents, 41; and Charles Gérard, 58; and Gran Colombia, 197; and Haitian agents, 178–180, 183; and Haitian independence, 162; and Haitian revolutionaries, 11–12; and *hispanismo*, 215; and Jean-François, 59–61, 73; and Junta officials, 171–172, 174; and Sebastian Kindelán, 185, 190; and Toussaint Louverture, 89, 103–104, 136–139, 140–151, 153–154; and maroons, 33–35, 79, 285n46; and Francisco de Miranda, 182; and Rosa Montas de Duvergé, 210–211; and Alexandre Pétion, 186; and Reconquista, 15, 166–169; and religion, 98, 134; and revolutionary conspiracies, 101; and Philippe Roume, 109–112; and Marquis de Rouvray, 47; and Saint-Domingue, 24, 27; and Juan Sánchez Ramírez, 165; scholarship on, 19–21; and self-purchase, 233–234n23; and slavery, 36, 262–263n95; and Spanish Empire, 44; and Treaty of Basel, 100, 106–108; and unification of Hispaniola, 1, 200–203, 205–207; white evacuees to, 46, 69

Saunders, Prince, 191
secularism: analysis of, 10; and Blackness, 65; challenging Iberian colonialism, 4; and Dominican elites, 9, 135; and French Republic, 12; public role of, 6; and re-evangelization, 177
Seda, Pedro de, 179
self-purchase, 29, 32, 233–234n23
Senegui, Lorenso, 117
Sengui, Basilio, 117
Siete Partidas, 29
Silva, José Justo de, 192, 196

Simón (Boca Nigua rebel), 114
slavery: abolition of, 45, 201; and Age of Revolutions, 2–3, 6; and Pablo Alí, 17, 49; in annexed Saint-Domingue, 65, 79; and anti-Haitianism, 213; and Boca Nigua revolt, 114; and Napoleón Bonaparte, 154; British debates on, 158; and Catholicism, 29; and Códigos Negros, 28; and cosmology, 9; and Dominican elites, 36, 187, 207; and Dominican identity, 22; and Dominican separation, 210; and Fort Dauphin massacre, 93; French commitment to, 69; French intent to revive, 14, 156; and French Republic, 12; and French Revolution, 50, 62; and French rule of Santo Domingo, 281n145; and Joaquín García, 31, 61, 76, 107; and Bartolomé de las Casas, 25; and Étienne Laveaux, 108; and Toussaint Louverture, 88, 148, 150; and José Núñez de Cáceres, 188, 190, 199; and Alexandre Pétion, 186; and Reconquista, 15; and Saint-Domingue, 7, 26; and Juan Sánchez Ramírez, 173; and Antonio Sánchez Valverde, 10, 24; and Spanish officials, 102–103; Spanish views on, 82; trade in, 32; and Treaty of Basel, 13; and unification of Hispaniola, 194, 203; western expansion of, 18. *See also* emancipation
Société des Amis des Noirs (Society of the Friends of the Blacks), 40
Sonthonax, Léger-Félicité: and abolition, 77; and Black Auxiliaries, 64, 71, 74, 75; and Black soldiers, 76; and Dominicans of color, 147; and Freemasonry, 140, 272n19; and Jean-François, 69; and kidnapping plot, 81; and Toussaint Louverture, 88; recruitment efforts of, 63; removal of, 96, 131–132, 138; and Vodou, 141
Sopó, Francisco, 115–116, 117